He had his weaknesses — women, for one thing, and a flair for the spectacular. - **J. Edgar Hoover**

When all of the known facts about Dillinger are dragged into publicity, it will be found that no desperado in America can approach this bad man's record.... There are enough angles on his tribe and its history to write a great big book.
Captain Matt Leach, Indiana State Police, 1933

We do not expect any trouble with our newest prisoner. Of course, I warned the first thing that we would stand for no monkey business.
Indiana Sheriff Lillian Holley --- from whose jail Dillinger escaped with a wooden pistol

Johnnie's an ordinary fellow. Of course, he goes out and holds up banks and things, but he's really just like any other fellow, aside from that.
Mary Kinder

I don't smoke much and I drink very little. I guess my only bad habit is robbing banks.
John Dillinger

Dead Men Do Tell Tales

One Night at the Biograph

Murder, Mayhem & the Mysterious
Afterlife of John Dillinger

Troy Taylor

© Copyright 2016 by Troy Taylor & American Hauntings Ink

All Rights Reserved, including the right to copy or reproduce this book, or portions thereof, in any form, without express permission from the author and publisher.

Original Cover Artwork Designed by
© Copyright 2016 by April Slaughter & Troy Taylor

This Book is Published By:
Whitechapel Press
American Hauntings Ink
Jacksonville, Illinois | 217.791.7859
Visit us on the Internet at http://www.whitechapelpress.com

First Edition – April 2016
ISBN: 978-1-892523-77-8

Printed in the United States of America

One Night at the Biograph

Chicago's North Lincoln Avenue was stifling in the summer heat. Earlier that day, the temperature at the city's municipal airport had topped out at 108 degrees and nightfall had brought little relief. In spite of the temperatures, the street was busy. Diners and shoppers filled the sidewalks, strolling to nearby restaurants and stores. A crowd had earlier packed into the Biograph Theater, which offered air-conditioned comfort to its patrons. It was a benefit that was well worth the price of the ticket.

Outside of the theater, two men were seated in an automobile. They were parked on the street, just to the left of the Biograph's entrance. One of the men, Melvin J. Purvis, the head of the Chicago office of the Department of Justice's Bureau of Investigation, was neatly attired in a single-breasted blue jacket, white trousers, white shoes, and a straw hat. He was seated next to one of his agents, Ralph Brown. The two men had watched the theater fill up for more than an hour, fearing that they had arrived too late, or that their quarry had gone to the Marbro Theater instead. Just as they were about to give up, their contact, Ana Sage, and a couple walked past the car. The girl, Polly Hamilton, hung onto the man's arm. The dapper-looking man wore gray trousers, a white-striped shirt, gray-flecked tie, a straw hat, and dark glasses.

Ana and Polly waited while the man bought tickets. Under the lights of the theater's marquee, Ana's orange skirt appeared to be vividly red. For a moment, it was the color of blood.

As soon as the three of them entered the theater, Brown telephoned Assistant Director Sam Cowley and Purvis purchased his own ticket and went into the air-conditioned auditorium. As the cool air washed over him, Purvis impulsively started to walk down the aisle. Nearly blind in the darkened auditorium, since his eyes had not adjusted to the dim light, he hurried back to the foyer, pausing near the doors. After a moment, he could see and he anxiously looked out over the seats. The theater was packed. Almost every seat was filled. It was impossible to find the man he was looking for. Not daring to venture down the aisle again and potentially spook his target, Purvis returned to the ticket office and learned that the film, *Manhattan Melodrama*, had just started. The newsreel, shorts, and serials were over, but the feature still had another 94 minutes to go.

Purvis went back to the car and told Brown what was going on. Anxious, pacing, he went back to the cashier and checked the times once more. Impatiently, she gave him the same information again. Purvis then went to speak to the ticket taker, looked past him at the flickering light in the theater, and returned to the car.

At the Bankers Building, Sam Cowley, who Director J. Edgar Hoover had placed in charge of the operation, was busy telephoning Hoover with the latest developments. Hoover, who was restlessly waiting in his library at home in

Washington, D.C., had demanded to be kept abreast of everything that was taking place in the Windy City. The two men discussed the possibility of capturing their target inside of the Biograph, but vetoed it because of the chance of gunplay in the crowded auditorium. He would be taken, as originally planned, when he walked out of the theater.

Cowley ordered his men to take up their positions at the Biograph. One agent, along with a police detective from East Chicago, Indiana, were at the Marbro Theater and were instructed at once to report to the Biograph. By the time that Cowley arrived there, Purvis had questioned the cashier a third time and again nervously checked inside of the auditorium. Since Purvis had never identified himself as a federal agent, the cashier was getting worried. There had been hold-ups at the theater in the past. Was another one about to take place?

Cowley was calm and curt when he arrived. He told Purvis to stand in the doorway just left of the theater's front entrance. When the target and the two women came out, they would likely walk in that direction to return to Ana's apartment. As they passed by him, Purvis was to light a cigar as a signal that he recognized them. About a dozen feet away, Agent H.E. Hollis would be chatting with Brown, who sat in the parked government car. A few yards past, in another doorway, another agent would be stationed. About 100 feet beyond was an alley, a short cut to Ana Sage's apartment, which also led to the back of the theater. At the mouth of this alley, two more agents were to head toward the theater as soon as they saw Purvis light his cigar. This would trap their quarry from both directions.

Two East Chicago policemen, along with two agents, were stationed to the right of the entrance in the unlikely event that the man and two women turned in that direction after leaving the theater.

Across the street from the theater were Cowley, five agents, and a detective and a captain from the East Chicago police force. They were to go into action in case the target somehow escaped from the two converging forces. Despite the fact that the theater was in the middle of their jurisdiction, no Chicago police officers were used in the operation. In fact, they had no idea that it was taking place.

As the men waited on the street, it became clear that no one knew exactly when the man would leave the Biograph. It could be a few minutes; or an hour. Would he turn right or left, or slip out through a fire exit? Purvis was visibly nervous. His hands shook. He bit off the end of his cigar and began to chew it.

About this same time, the theater engineer in charge of the air conditioning unit went outside to take temperature readings. When he saw men loitering in the alley, along with one standing ominously on the catwalk about the boiler room, he hurried to the office of the theater manager, Charles Shapiro. Concerned that another hold-up was about to take place, the engineer told him that he was frightened. Shapiro escorted the man to the boiler room and told him to get inside and lock the door. He would be safe in there.

The manager wasn't worried about a robbery. He knew that thieves wouldn't wait in the alley. They would be after the ticket window if they wanted cash. As he was walking toward the lobby, the cashier came hurrying toward him. She was as nervous as the engineer. She pointed across the street to a man sitting on the bakery steps. Several others were lurking nearby and she told Shapiro that a jumpy man had asked her three times about the running time of the show.

Shapiro spoke with the ticket taker. As soon as he learned that Purvis had gone into the foyer, returned, and peered back several times, he locked himself in the office and called the Sheffield Street police station. He told the desk sergeant: "I want you to send a plainclothes squad. It might be a hold-up."

At about 10:20 p.m., a patrol car with two detectives inside entered the other end of the alley and approached the two men standing at the mouth of it, along Lincoln Avenue. A detective jumped out of the car and aimed a shotgun at Agent Ray Suran. Luckily for the agent, the detective decided to ask for identification before he pulled the trigger on the shotgun. Suran managed to convince the two Chicago officers that he was a federal agent on assignment, tracking down a fugitive. The police car backed up, and then disappeared.

Meanwhile, two more Chicago detectives were walking into Shapiro's office. The manager closed the door and told them about the "suspicious" characters that were loitering outside. He told the detectives how they had been placed, but said that he wasn't crazy enough to go to the door and point them out. The two plainclothes men went outside, turned right, walked up to an agent, and asked who he was and what he was doing.

In the auditorium, *Manhattan Melodrama* was approaching the end. William Powell, who played the prosecutor in the film, had convicted his friend, Clark Gable, of murder. He offered Gable life in prison, but Gable said that he would rather die than spend the rest of his life in prison. The picture ended with him walking to the electric chair.

At 10:30 p.m., some of the audience members, not wanting to see the added attractions, began leaving the theater. Ana Sage and her two companions were among the first to leave, and they came out just as one of the four men placed to the right of the entrance was showing his credentials to the Chicago plain-clothes officers. But the three turned left, toward Purvis, and didn't see what was happening.

Purvis had torn a match from a book as soon as the first customer walked out of the theater doors. The cigar in his mouth was shaking. He gazed intently at every man who passed by. Suddenly, he saw the target, flanked by two women, one of whom was Ana Sage in her dark orange skirt. As Purvis nervously tried to strike the match and light his cigar, the man gazed directly at him. Then, not recognizing the federal agent, he looked away. Although Purvis was never able to strike the match, the agents caught his signal.

As the trio passed the next doorway, the National Tea Company Store, the agent who had been stationed there saw Purvis' signal and walked across the sidewalk in front of them.

Ana lagged behind, but Polly Hamilton saw men with guns and shoved her elbow into her companion's ribs, alerting him to trouble. By then, Purvis and Hollis had moved in behind the three on the sidewalk, their guns drawn. According to the official report, Purvis called out to the gangster and ordered him to surrender; however, several witnesses said no warning was given.

The man jerked forward, running toward the nearby alley, allegedly reaching into his pocket for a gun. Three agents fired five shots at the fleeing man, striking him three times and also wounding two women standing nearby. One bullet struck the man in the left side, one grazed his face, and another went into his back as he doubled over, exiting below his right eye.

He fell to the street, just into the mouth of the alley. He was sprawled face down on the pavement, his feet still on the curb. The brim of his straw hat and the wire-framed dark glasses were crushed between his forehead and the dirty cobblestones of the alley. The sharp crack of the gunshots that brought him down – fired at point-blank range and so close together that onlookers claimed they only heard two shots – echoed in the humid night air. The dark stain of blood spread across the man's shirt where the bullet had ripped into his side, while a second, larger pool began to form across his head.

A number of startled onlookers, many of whom also emerged from the Biograph Theater, screamed, ducked for cover, or ran, unsure if they were witnessing a gang murder, or a hold-up, two things that the people of Chicago had experienced plenty of over the last decade.

Quickly, Purvis and the agents formed a tight circle around the bleeding figure. There were nearly two dozen of them on the street, only now flashing badges that identified them as government agents.

The time was 10:35 p.m. It was a Sunday night, July 22, 1934.

Word began to spread about the dead man and when it did, bystanders pushed forward to dip their handkerchiefs in his pooling blood. Government agents, several people on Lincoln Avenue cried out, had ended the life of America's most famous bank robber and favorite public enemy, John Herbert Dillinger.

But the question remains: Had they really?

1. Dust Bowl Days
FDR, the Great Depression & Hoover's "War on Crime"

When President Franklin D. Roosevelt took office in March 1933, he inherited an America that had become a surreal and nightmarish version of its former self. The country had become a wasteland of poverty, hunger, joblessness, and environmental disaster. After thirteen years of Prohibition, America was infected by unprecedented lawlessness, and it seemed the new president needed to rescue every town, city, and county in the 48 states.

Since the 1929 Stock Market Crash, almost 90 percent of the nation's value had been lost. Most of the upper class had been wiped out. The ripple effect of these losses decimated the working class, as well as the poor. Average household incomes were cut by a third. Thousands of banks shut down, while scores of others foreclosed on more than one million homes and farms. Business failures and the collapse of the real estate market deprived cities and states of tax revenue, which resulted in cuts in the few social services that existed. City workers, police officers, and teachers were laid off, or went unpaid. Thousands of schools were closed or reduced hours. Millions of students dropped out, either because their schools were gone or out of the necessity to help support their families.

The gross national product fell to half of its 1929 level. Industrial investment dropped by 90 percent. Automobile production was down by nearly 70 percent, as were iron and steel production and nearly every other industry that provided work for American men. In a few years, more than 16 million jobs had vanished and the per capita income was lower than it was in the early 1900s.

The national unemployment rate, which was as low as three percent before the stock market crash, pushed beyond 25 percent. For those who didn't work on farms, it was almost 40 percent, and in many cities, it was north of 80 percent. But even those grim numbers masked the reduced hours and trimmed wages of the workers who managed to hang onto their jobs. Those who couldn't began walking the city streets in despair, looking for work, food, and hope. But there was none to be found.

The men and women who populated America's cities – from the managers and office workers to the street cleaners and waitresses – stood in breadlines for hours. Occasionally, they formed into mobs and attacked the food trucks that passed by making their deliveries. At night, a desperate few raided local grocery stores, kicking in windows, and looting them before the police arrived. Parents were starving and their children went to bed night after night with empty stomachs.

Millions of Americans waited in bread lines, outside of soup kitchens, every day.

The misery was even greater on the farms of the Midwest and the Plains, where the Great Depression began years earlier. The droughts that started in the late 1920s continued without relief into the 1930s. During the years of the Great War, Europe's farmland had been destroyed and American farmers stepped up, increased production, expanded their fields, and fed the world. After the war ended and the fields of Europe returned, the bottom dropped out on everything produced in America.

Overproduction during the war years stripped much of the land of its fertility. The droughts dried it up and it began to blow away. It was slow at first, but eventually the winds created dust clouds so thick that they choked the cattle, covered the farms, and blackened the sky at noon. The American Plains became known as the "Dust Bowl," and the winds and drought destroyed farming for decades. The residents of the region fled to California, or remained behind to starve, sicken, and die on the land that was once the breadbasket of the entire world.

This was the nation that Roosevelt had been elected to rescue – it was starving, bankrupt, without hope, and growing more violent with each passing day.

A short time before he took office, Roosevelt himself had narrowly escaped being killed by an assassin. While attending a celebration rally in Miami, an assassin fired five shots at him, fatally wounding Anton Cermak, the mayor of Chicago, who was standing next to him. And while the violence that day was seen as a national disgrace, it was commonplace in the nation that Roosevelt was soon to govern. In major cities, particularly Chicago, large criminal organizations had been established to provide the residents with the very things that the government had outlawed: liquor, gambling, prostitution, and every other kind of

The Dust Bowl storms wreaked havoc on the Great Plains

vice imaginable. To protect their interests, the organized crime outfits created their own codes, laws, and accepted business practices. They bribed local policemen, government officials, and judges to either look the other way or to lend a hand for a price.

In the late 1920s and early 1930s, law enforcement was carried out almost exclusively on a local basis. Law officers were beholden to local politicians, many of whom were beholden to the local mob. The poorly trained and poorly financed collection of law enforcement units in 1933 consisted of about 4,000 county sheriffs, 11 state police forces, and a handful of big city operations – all with conflicting degrees of cooperation, political affiliations, and depths of corruption. It many towns, it was not too much to say that the local mob not only ran the criminal activities, but the local government and police department, as well.

The *New York Times* ran an editorial in 1931 that bemoaned the fact that America's criminal courts had become so mired in delays, appeals, paroles, pardons, and unscrupulous attorneys that they were now protecting criminals instead of prosecuting them. The editorial went on to say that since America had entered World War I in 1917, the number of murders associated with the current crime wave was three times greater than all of the American deaths during the war. To compare it with today, it can be noted that the murder rate of the 1930s was twice that of contemporary times, and the vast majority of them were never solved.

Into the midst of this violent nation where the outlaws who began plying their trade in the Midwest. These men, who operated in loosely organized small gangs, were viewed by the local populace as the descendants of the legendary Old West outlaws who robbed trains, banks, and wealthy ranchers in times gone by.

President Franklin D. Roosevelt had the daunting task of repairing America's finances, putting people back to work, and declaring war on the criminal element in the nation.

Bank robberies had been taking place almost since the time that the first Americans entrusted an establishment with their hard-earned money, but the bank robbers of the 1920s were different. They were no longer outlaws on horseback. The new breed of outlaws had the new novel advantage of motorized transportation. Never before in American crime had outlaws possessed the means to escape so easily from law enforcement officials. Motorcars sent them on a rampage through various states. The bank robbers operated with impunity and were well aware that fleeing across county and state lines left local law without the authority to give chase, and that handing off that authority was a nightmare of jumbled coordination and paperwork.

Many of them had gotten their start because of law enforcement's preoccupation with bootleggers, allowing the better-equipped bank robbers to work with little harassment. Many of the jobs made huge headlines because of the amount of loot that was stolen, but as author William Helmer has noted, identification methods were so primitive that newspapers could only report that a group of "unknown strangers" had pulled off a "daring daylight robbery" and had disappeared without a trace. Because of this, some criminals were able to plunder the Midwest with an anonymity that leaves them unknown today, while lesser outlaws became Depression-era celebrities after Al Capone went to prison on tax evasion charges.

The outlaws of the 1930s had fast cars and superior firepower but, most of all, they had the tacit support of the local populace. Not only did they earn their spots on the "Most Wanted" list, but they became folk heroes in the process. There were far too many Americans who felt a twinge of jealousy when they saw the freewheeling gangsters "get revenge" on the banks, the wealthy fat cats at the top of the food chain, and on the government itself. There were stories that spread that claimed that some of the outlaws stole from the rich and then gave back some of the money to those who really needed it. And in the grim America of the 1930s, there were a lot of folks who needed it.

Many of "folk hero" personas were created by the newspapers, which thanks to the competitiveness of the market in cities like Chicago, were always looking for a headline. The crime magazines and pulps of the day, many of which abandoned fiction for "fact" at a time when gangsters were making daily news, also had a hand in the making of modern legends. Many officials were well aware of the fact that the criminals were more recognizable – and better liked – by the general public than honest members of law enforcement were.

This dilemma was apparent to FDR, who was hatching plans to expand the federal government to combat the Depression. He recognized the need to create a national law enforcement branch that would combat the rampant criminality that was infesting the country.

What President Roosevelt wanted was a national police force that would be small, well-trained, and largely invisible to the public. But, most importantly, it would not be beholden to any state or local politician. It would be the law enforcement branch of the federal government. Prior to this, national police departments were perceived by many as the stuff of dictators and sinister European potentates. In the United States, with its aversion to concentrated federal power and big government, there had been no appetite for one.

But that was all changing. In the summer of 1933, as Roosevelt completed his ambitious first 100 days in office, those fears of a big government started to abate as a terrible criminal event put the need for a national police force on center stage.

The national police force would center around the leadership of a little-known government bureaucrat named J. Edgar Hoover, who, while FDR was being sworn into office in March 1933, was trying to figure out how to hang onto his job.

Today, it is difficult for us to remember a time when Hoover was not the ominous figure whose secret files threatened American presidents, who underwrote Senator Joseph McCarthy, and who hounded national figures like Martin Luther King, Jr. For four decades, Hoover dominated national law enforcement as no person before or since, singlehandedly creating America's first national police force. His accomplishments were as complex as Hoover himself. Before Hoover, law enforcement in the country was little more than county sheriff departments and urban police forces that were crippled by corruption. It was Hoover who brought the level of efficiency, professionalism, and centralized control that America knows today. But his legacy will always be sullied by the abuses of power – rampant illegal wiretaps, break-ins, and harassment of civil rights groups – during his later years.

Hoover's power did not come about gradually. It erupted in 1933 and 1934, an era of unprecedented crime in American history. He entered this period as an anonymous federal functionary with his bureau struggling to shake off past scandals. In less than two years, he became a national hero, a household name lauded in films, books, and comic strips. During that time, the modern FBI was born – but it would not be born without difficulty, scandal, and disaster.

John Edgar Hoover was born on New Year's Day 1895 in Washington, D.C. and grew up in the district's Capitol Hill neighborhood. He attended Central High, where he sang in the school choir, participated in the Reserve Officers' Training Corps program, and competed on the debate team. Hoover stuttered badly as a

J. Edgar Hoover as a young man in Washington. He spent years climbing political ladders to build the future FBI.

young boy, but his fierce determination overcame it. He taught himself to talk fast, eventually speaking with such ferocious speed that stenographers had a hard time taking notes and letters from him.

Hoover obtained his law degree from the George Washington University Law School, working his way through school as a clerk at the Library of Congress. In 1917, he joined the Justice Department, a job that had draft-exempt status, a designation Hoover appreciated because his father had recently suffered a nervous breakdown and lost his job. Hoover felt he could not afford to serve because he had become his family's sole breadwinner and his mother was desperately in need of support. In less than a year, he had been promoted twice and, at the age of 22, found himself in charge of the Justice Department's Enemy Alien Registration Section. During and immediately after World War I, the country was leery of all things German, foreign, or smacked of radicalism, socialism, or communism.

He found himself a busy man, helping to stage raids on organizations suspected of radical or socialist ideals and labor unions of any kind, all the while compiling a master list of suspected radicals, terrorists, and draft dodgers. His lists would expand to include hundreds of thousands of names.

After the war, with new Attorney General A. Mitchell Palmer, Hoover established the General Intelligence Division, which expanded his operation to include more general intelligence gathering at home and overseas, as well as work to prevent labor disputes and strikes. Hoover became an early proponent of communist hunts, and helped stage coordinated raids that resulted in as many as 10,000 arrests of suspected radical aliens and suspected communists in a single day – most of whom were not aliens, communists, or guilty of anything at all. Hoover managed to make himself the country's leading authority on communist activities and how to combat them.

When President Warren G. Harding took office in 1921, he appointed his campaign manager, Harry Daughtery, as Attorney General. Daughtery purged the department of pretty much anyone left from the last administration and filled it with a collection of political appointments and partisans who were eager to do the new administration's dirty work – as long as there was good money in it. Daughtery found Hoover's lists the perfect material for political blackmail, so Hoover managed to keep his job. Before long, the bureau had succumbed to the corrupting influences of the Harding administration, much to the chagrin of the moralistic Hoover, who nevertheless found himself wallowing in the nefarious practices that Daughtery allowed the division to engage in. His activities during the Harding administration nearly torpedoed his career when Roosevelt came into office.

On the day that Roosevelt was sworn in, Hoover was the director of the Justice Department's Bureau of Investigation – it would not become the Federal Bureau of Investigation (FBI) for another two years. He had been in that position for nine years, since 1924, but he had many enemies and Roosevelt's men had made it clear that he was going to be replaced. The final decision would be made by the new attorney general, a man who hated Hoover more than most, named Thomas Walsh. Walsh's history with Hoover was a bad one. When Walsh and fellow Montana Senator Burton Wheeler were investigating corruption in the Harding administration, Hoover organized a campaign to discredit them. His tactics included tapping their telephones, intercepting their mail, tailing their family members, and breaking into the offices. He tried to lure Wheeler into a hotel room with a prostitute, but the ploy failed because Wheeler had been forewarned. Walsh made no secret of the fact that one of his first acts as the new attorney general would be to fire Hoover.

Two days before Roosevelt's swearing-in, the 72-year-old Walsh, who had been a widower for 16 years, had boarded a train from Miami to Washington with his new bride, a Cuban debutante. Friday morning, Mrs. Walsh awakened aboard the train in North Carolina and found her husband dead. Whispers in the capital suggested that the elderly senator had expired after an athletic bout of sex.

For Hoover, the reprieve was temporary. After everything that he had achieved over the last nine years, he was infuriated by the fact that politicians held his fate. If not for him, the Bureau of Investigation would have been eliminated years before. It was an odd outfit that was responsible for investigating a strange collection of federal offenses, including sedition, interstate auto theft, escapes from federal prisons, and crimes on Indian reservations. Hoover's agents did not have the power to make arrests. If they wanted to mount a raid, they were obliged to bring along a local policeman. Nor did they carry firearms. This was a policy, not a law, though. Hoover had modeled the bureau on Britain's Scotland Yard. His men were investigators, not policemen.

The Bureau had a sordid history. Created in 1908 to investigate antitrust cases, it had devolved over the course of the next decade and a half into a cesspool of nepotism and corruption. By the early 1920s, its agents, scattered across 50 domestic offices, were hired mostly as favors to politicians. Its most notorious employee, a con man named Gaston Means, earned his money blackmailing congressmen, selling liquor licenses to bootleggers, and auctioning off presidential pardons.

But starting in 1924, Hoover began making every effort to clean up the bureau. The dour civil servant, who was then a 29-year-old government attorney who still lived with his mother, made transforming his force of field agents his first priority. He knew what he wanted: young, energetic white men between the ages of 29 and 35, with law degrees, clean, neat, well-spoken, bright, and from solid families – essentially men like he considered himself. And he got them. In a matter of weeks, Hoover cleared out the dead weight, stopped patronage hiring, and started screening applicants on "general intelligence," "conduct during interview," and "personal appearance," either "neat," "flashy," "poor," or "untidy."

Hoover ruled with an iron hand. His men lived and worked in fear of him. Inspection teams appeared at field offices with no notice, writing up agents who were even one minute tardy for work. Hoover tolerated no laziness, sloppiness, or deviation from the new set of rules that were posted in every field office, each commanded by a special agent in charge, known as a SAC. The smallest infraction would cost a man his job.

Those who survived, and those that Hoover hired, were almost an interchangeable lot. More than a few came from Hoover's alma mater, George Washington, especially the Kappa Alpha chapter that he belonged to. Harold "Pop" Nathan, an administrator at the Bureau since 1917 was a Kappa Alpha; for years he was also the Bureau's only Jew. Hugh Clegg was also a Kappa Alpha. The courtly Mississippi attorney, who would rise to become an FBI assistant director, rotated through a series of field offices in his first few months. It was in the field that many of the new hires, like Clegg, first encountered the hostility of local police departments, who regarded Hoover's men as unarmed, overeducated, inept dilettantes who were intent on taking over their cases.

The agents soon became objects of ridicule, and in the beginning, it was understandable. In Hoover's new bureau, appearance, loyalty, and hard work were prized above law enforcement experience. Few of the new hires had any, as Hoover was uncomfortably aware. Whispers suggested that Hoover liked his men "young and grateful." While publicly mandating that all agents have law degrees, Hoover quietly kept around some non-lawyers, too, mostly veteran lawmen from the Southwest. These men were a breed apart from the typical agents. They chewed tobacco and drank, infractions that Hoover ignored. They knew how to run investigations, and they did so very well. In violation of Bureau regulations, they all carried guns. John Keith wore twin Colt .45's; Charles Winstead in Dallas carried a .357 Magnum; in Chicago, former Texas Ranger James "Doc" White proudly wore a bone-handled Colt, along with a knife in his boot. The two agents assigned to run key cases in Hoover's early years were veteran lawmen: Gus Jones from San Antonio, and Doc White's older brother, another ex-Ranger named Thomas White, who ran the Oklahoma City office. These men became crucial to Hoover's initial success and, in the midst of a number of bungled efforts by the director's "college boys," managed to actually solve some cases.

Hoover's reorganization transformed the Bureau. Unproductive field offices were closed, bureaucracy was streamlined, paperwork was standardized, and a chain of command was created. After six months, the Bureau was on its way to becoming a model of a modern, efficient government organization. Once this was completed, the challenge became finding something for its agents to do. During Hoover's first years, his men spearheaded a corruption investigation at the federal prison in Atlanta and a probe of murders and oil-rights thievery on Indian lands in Oklahoma. They were minor cases, all run by Hoover's more seasoned agents with Tom White in the lead. When White was named as warden of Leavenworth in 1927, Hoover summoned Gus Jones to supervise what became a failed attempt to recapture some prison escapees.

On all of these cases, Hoover's men did the legwork, but stepped aside when it was time to make arrests. This situation was usually accompanied by snickers from the police officers involved. The agents had no guns and if they were along on a raid, they just had to hope that there was no gunplay involved.

Hoover's role was strictly administrative. He seldom left his Washington office. In the spring of 1933, while billing himself as the nation's leading law enforcement expert, Hoover himself had never made an arrest, much less fired a gun in the line of duty. His special agents in charge ran the investigations, with Hoover looking over their shoulders, sending memos about anything he disliked. He could be scathing in his appraisals, although he privately knew that he had few competent men. Pop Nathan wrote in a memo to Hoover in 1932: "I believe that the trouble with many of our offices is that our Agents in Charge are somewhat foggy mentally. Or at any rate they function slowly along mental lines."

Hoover always wanted the public to know how well he was doing. He gave speeches and occasional newspaper interviews, emphasizing the Bureau's integrity and its devotion to what he called "scientific policing," which was based on fingerprints and the analysis of evidence. Not all of the press was receptive, though. A *Collier's* magazine article first reported on Hoover's "personal and political machine" and hinted at his sexual orientation. It noted: "In appearance Mr. Hoover looks utterly unlike the story-book sleuth. He dresses fastidiously, with Eleanor blue as the favored color for the matched shades of his tie, handkerchief, and socks... He is short, fat, businesslike, and walks with a mincing step."

After eight years of pursuing a variety of more minor crimes, Hoover's first opportunity to step into the national spotlight came in June 1932, with the passage of the Lindbergh Law, three months after the kidnapping (and subsequent murder) of Charles Lindbergh's infant son in New Jersey. The new law made kidnapping a federal crime, but only when the kidnapper or his victim crossed state lines. The Lindbergh kidnapping spawned a rash of copycat crimes throughout 1932, but to Hoover's frustration, none of the kidnappings could be tackled by the Bureau.

As word spread in the underworld of the massive ransoms to be had, kidnappings flourished. The year 1933 brought 27 major cases, more than twice the number reported in any previous year. Beginning with the kidnapping of millionaire Charles Boetscher II in Denver in February, Bureau agents pushed their way into a half-dozen high profile cases, for the first time involved in solving crimes that the public actually cared about. But would it be enough to save Hoover's job in the new administration?

As Roosevelt took office that spring, kidnapping stories filled the front pages of newspapers around the country. Coming soon after the surge in crime during the 1920s, these reports added fuel to the debate over the need for a federal police force. On one side were the reformers who stated that local police departments were often corrupt or ineffective, and unable to deal with the new mobile criminals who easily crossed state lines. On the other side were powerful city governments, backed by congressmen who viewed federal policing as the first step toward an American dictatorship. Big government was seen with great disdain, especially in the South and Midwest, where Washington was viewed with deep distrust. It was in these areas where the majority of residents blamed politicians for the Depression. The debate intensified with Roosevelt's election. His advisers were pushing hard for a strong central government that would revive the economy by taking control of many areas managed by state and municipal governments, including law enforcement.

During the first 100 days of the Roosevelt administration, a period that famously saw dozens of pieces of New Deal legislation pass easily through Congress, the leading voice for a federal police force was a Roosevelt advisor named Louis Howe. The attorney general chosen to replace the late Thomas Walsh was Connecticut attorney Homer S. Cummings, a man of similar views. Cummings had big ideas for raising the profile of the Justice Department. His ideas fit well with Roosevelt's vision for his administration. He was going to war against the forces of the Depression. Cummings liked that positioning. He would start a "war on crime" to raise the profile of the department and make it a major player in the new administration's ambitious efforts to federalize the nation's government. He crafted a plan to merge the Prohibition Bureau's investigators, who would soon be out of work with the end of Prohibition in sight, with Hoover's Bureau of Investigation. With that as a start, he hoped to begin crafting the kind of national police force that the Roosevelt administration wanted. He also began to craft a major crime bill that would give that force greater powers and tough federal laws to enforce.

Once he had those things in place, he could start targeting the lawbreakers. And there were plenty of them in the Dust Bowl states of the west, where bootlegging, kidnapping, and bank robbing were almost commonplace. This was the enemy that Cummings wanted to confront. He was well aware of how entrenched and protected the criminal empires in Chicago and New York were, but with a few good men, he believed that he could tame the new "Wild West" of the 1930s.

Hoover was in the perfect position to play up his own role in the reorganization of the Bureau to Cummings. If he could persuade the new attorney general of his value, he believed that the Bureau could be the centerpiece of a federal police force. That spring, he launched a vigorous lobbying campaign to keep his job and put himself in a position for something even bigger. His Special Agents in Charger were ordered to arrange letters of support from prominent politicians. Hoover's old boss, Harlan Fiske Stone, now a Supreme Court justice, wrote Justice Felix Frankfurter, who contacted Roosevelt. But even through all of this, anti-Hoover sentiment remained widespread. One Roosevelt adviser later wrote there was "tremendous pressure on Roosevelt by various city politicians to replace Hoover with this or that police chief whom they believed would be more amendable to them for patronage."

Union Station in Kansas City, Missouri

Throughout the spring, Hoover's future hung in the balance. What Hoover needed to insure his position was a tangible achievement, something that would grab headlines, and a case that would put him on the national stage and show how the Bureau had been transformed. He was about to get just what he wanted – from a massacre that took place in Kansas City.

In June 1933, two of Hoover's agents – along with McAlester, Oklahoma Police Chief Otto Reed, a veteran cop who accompanied agents Joe Lackey and Frank Smith since they weren't authorized to make arrests – snatched up a bank robber and prison escapee named Frank "Jelly" Nash off the streets of the notorious underworld safe haven of Hot Springs, Arkansas. Nash was one of the old school bank robbers who had made a name for himself since the 1920s, robbing banks across the Midwest. Hoover wanted him back behind bars and sent his men to capture him and bring him to Leavenworth Federal Penitentiary. To get there, the agents and lawmen had to run a gauntlet of gangsters and corrupt cops to get him aboard a train that was headed for Kansas City. Not taking any chances, they decided to take Nash off the train at Kansas City and drive him the remaining distance to Leavenworth. Two Kansas City police officers, W.J. "Red" Grooms and Frank Hermanson, were assigned to meet them at the station and assist them.

When the officers arrived at the station to meet the 7:15 a.m. train, they parked, and went inside to meet up with Lackey, Smith, and Reed, as well as two other federal agents, Reed Vetterli and Ray Caffrey, who had just arrived from Nebraska.

Union Station was crowded that morning, with nearly a dozen trains arriving between 7:00 and 8:00 a.m. The sun was rising over the crowded parking lot and it was going to be another warm summer day. The lawmen flanked Nash as they led him quickly through the station. Officers Grooms and Hermanson had their .38-caliber handguns in plain view and, against Bureau policy, the federal agents were armed with automatic pistols and shotguns. They knew there was a real danger that some of Nash's friends might try and free him from custody. The group cut a path through the crowd, quickly arriving at their waiting vehicle.

Lackey and Chief Reed climbed into the backseat with Nash climbing in beside them. But then Lackey told Nash to get up front, where he could watch him. Smith then climbed into the back between Lackey and Reed. Nash got in the front seat and Caffrey closed the door and began walking around the front of the car to get into the driver's seat.

With the lawmen's firepower now bottled up inside of the car, several men stepped forward in the direction of their car. To this day, their identities remain officially unknown, but they were most likely led by bank robber Verne Miller, who was intent on freeing Nash. The identity of the other men remains open to date, but it's possible that they were Charles "Pretty Boy" Floyd and his friend, Adam Richetti. Both of them had recently arrived in town, fleeing from Oklahoma, and witness descriptions seem to match the two young men.

Whoever they were, it's likely that they planned to snatch Frank Nash without ever firing a shot. The leader placed his machine gun across the hood of the car he was using for cover and aimed directly at the lawmen as his partner moved closer. "Put 'em up! Up! Up!" he shouted at the lawmen's automobile.

The gunmen had the advantage of firepower and surprise and it should have been simple for them to convince the agents and police officers to surrender their captive. But, it was not to be. Tragically, though, the first shot was not fired by the gunmen – it came from inside the car.

In the back seat, Agent Lackey pulled up the riot gun that had been nestled between his seat and the car door and furiously began trying to cock the unfamiliar weapon without releasing its trigger mechanism. When he finally fumbled the release, the gun discharged unexpectedly, blowing off half of Frank Nash's head and killing him instantly. The blast shattered the car's windshield and hit Caffrey in the back of the head as he stood near the front of the car. Panicked, Lackey jerked the gun to the left as it discharged again, hitting Officer Hermanson in the head and shattering a window on the Plymouth parked in the adjacent space.

The gunmen immediately reacted and unleashed a hail of return gunfire. Two bullets hit Grooms in the chest as he tried to shoot back, killing him. Vetterli, who had ducked for cover after taking a bullet in the arm, sprang to his feet and ran for the station with machine gun bullets nipping at his heels and tearing chunks from the station's granite walls. Lackey was hit three times and Chief Reed, hit multiple times, fell to the ground.

The ferocious firefight was over in less than a minute and a half.

The gunmen cautiously approached the car and found Hermanson and Grooms lying in a spreading pool of blood on the passenger side of the automobile.

The aftermath of the Kansas City Massacre, the event that began Hoover's "War on Crime" in America.

Caffrey was sprawled out next to the driver's door with half of his head missing. Agent Frank Smith, unharmed, was on the floor of the car next to Lackey. He dared not move until the gunmen walked away. Frank Nash, who the killers had been trying to rescue, was slumped in the front seat. He was clearly dead, his head a mass of shattered bone and gore.

The gunmen retreated to their getaway car and sped off as the early morning crowds at Union Station looked on in horror. In the aftermath, few of the spectators could agree on anything about the massacre, from the description of the gunmen to just how many of them there were.

Police officers raced to the scene, their guns drawn. News photographers, who had been tipped off by a wire story about Nash's capture, went to work at the bloody scene. In no time, they were rearranging evidence, moving people, and handling the discarded weapons to get more graphic shots. Bedlam had broken out among the bystanders, some of whom fled screaming, while others picked up spent shells and casings or dipped their handkerchiefs in blood for gruesome souvenirs.

News of the shootout reached J. Edgar Hoover within minutes. A telegram had arrived from Kansas City, describing the massacre and the deaths of the police officers and Bureau agent and the wounding of several others. Hoover had set the events in motion with his kidnapping of Nash from the streets of Hot Springs, Arkansas. Attorney General Cummings wanted results and Hoover was determined to give them to him, and now Nash, three lawmen, and one of his own agents were dead in a Kansas City parking lot.

Hoover knew that if he allowed gangsters to get away with the murder of federal agents, none of his men would be safe. He put one of his saltiest men in charge of the investigation, a San Antonio agent named Gus "Buster" Jones, who, while not the model of Hoover's image of a modern agent, was a lawman who knew how to get things done.

In the end, the "Kansas City Massacre" was never officially solved, even though the hunt for the gunmen went on for years. However, it did provide the opening volley in Hoover's "War on Crime," cemented his job in the new administration, and created the urgency needed to make the hunt for America's desperadoes and bank robbers front page news.

Over the next year-and-a-half, the country's most famous bank robbers would be hunted down – and usually killed – one by one. It was a period of American history like no other, before or since, and it would turn both lawmen and badmen into national celebrities.

Just one week before the massacre, on June 7, 1933, an event took place that would mark another start to this riotous period in history.

On that morning, a man named Horace Grisso, walked to work along the streets of New Carlisle, Ohio, north of Dayton. Grisso was the bookkeeper at the New Carlisle National Bank and the first employee to arrive on that Saturday morning. He unlocked the bank's door and went inside, his footsteps tapping on the marble floor. He walked behind the teller's cages, and as he did, three men wearing handkerchiefs across their faces stood up in front of him. "All right, buddy, open the safe," ordered the trio's leader, a 29-year-old young man who was robbing his first bank.

He had been released from the Indiana State Penitentiary just three weeks before. He was a small, slender man, five-feet-seven, with short brown hair and a lopsided, wiseacre grin who had served nine long years for the drunken mugging of a grocer in his hometown near Indianapolis. He had promised his father that he would go straight after his release, but he couldn't do it. He had made a promise to his friends that were still doing time that he would help them escape. He just needed to raise enough money to put the plan into action.

Horace Grisso reached for the drawer where the bank's combination book was kept. The leader grabbed his hand, then allowed him to slowly open the drawer. Grisso went to the safe, fumbled with the lock, unable to open it with his shaking hands. One of the other would-be bank robbers, a teenager named William Shaw, asked for permission to shoot Grisso. "He's stalling," Shaw snapped.

But the leader raised a hand and told Grisso to take his time – just get the safe open.

Just then, the front door opened and the leader hurried to intercept the bank's clerk as she came inside. He told her that he didn't want to hurt her, and then directed her to lie on the floor. He courteously took a coat off the back of a nearby chair and placed it beneath her. He then tied her hands and feet with wire. By then, Grisso had opened the safe, and Shaw, and the third man, another teenager named Paul "Lefty" Parker, began lifting out bags of cash. The leader stayed by the front door, intercepting two more employees as they came inside. He told them, with a grin, that they shouldn't come to work so early.

Within minutes, the three men were back in their car, speeding toward Indiana. After the money was counted, they ended up with $10,600, not a bad haul. But the leader wasn't satisfied. That night, they pulled up in front of Haag's Drugstore in Indianapolis. Inside, the leader headed toward the cash register at the soda fountain, while Shaw took the main register. Guns in hand, they emptied out the registers and backed out of the door, only to find that Lefty Parker had parallel-parked the getaway car at the curb, snugly wedged between two other parked cars. As the leader fumed, Parker bumped the cars in front and behind several times before finally wheeling out and making a getaway.

But the night was not yet over. A half hour later, they stopped at a City Foods supermarket. Robbing the store was Shaw's idea. What he neglected to tell the others was that he had robbed the place once before. The minute that they entered the store, guns drawn, the manager hung his head. "Here they are again," he groaned. He told them that a company was now collecting their cash, because of past robberies, and they had just collected it a few minutes before.

There was no money left in the registers.

As the leader stomped outside, Shaw paused long enough to scoop up several boxes of cigarettes. When the leader got into the car, Parker gunned the engine and sped away, leaving Shaw inside of the store.

"Stop! Stop!" the boss called out as Parker drove up the block.

Parker hit the brakes and drove in reverse toward the grocery store as Shaw, panting heavily, ran up the street to meet them and jumped in. Parker was so rattled that he ran the next stop sign. Finally, they left town, heading for a nearby farm.

It was on that day that the criminal career of the small gang's leader, John Dillinger, began.

2. Dillinger's "Raw Deal"

As any convict can tell you, prisons are filled with innocent men, or at least with men who were "screwed over" by a lawyer, the police, a judge, or the system itself. One has to wonder what would have become of John Dillinger if he had not ended up with the overly harsh prison sentence that he received after the drunken robbery of a grocery store owner when he was, as Deputy Sheriff Russell Peterson stated, "just a kid." Would he have ended up as a farmer like his father? Or was his fate predetermined, so that he would end up just like he did – as the most famous bank robber in American history?

John Herbert Dillinger was born on June 22, 1903, in Indianapolis. He was a precocious child from a moderately well-off family that operated a grocery store and owned several rental houses. His mother, Mollie, died when he was three after an operation for an apoplectic attack. Dillinger was raised by his 15-year-old sister, Audrey, and his father, John Wilson Dillinger. Dillinger's father was strict but never had much trouble with his son, who was a quiet child with good grades and who was well liked by friends and teachers. When he was quite young, he proved to be an excellent athlete, especially excelling at baseball.

In 1912, Dillinger's father married Elizabeth Fields of Mooresville, Indiana. The couple had two children, Hubert and Doris, who Dillinger would be close to over the course of his life.

Dillinger's first brush with the authorities took place when he was in sixth grade and he was charged with stealing coal from the Pennsylvania Railroad yards and selling it to neighbors. He was released into the custody of his father and, soon after, the elder Dillinger packed up his family and moved them to a modest farm outside of Mooresville, about 20 miles south of Indianapolis. He reportedly wanted to get his son away from the corrupting influences of the city. It didn't seem to do much good, though. By then, Dillinger was becoming a problem for his father. Out of frustration, his father often beat him, but Dillinger never held it against him. Later in life, he would say that his father "didn't know any better."

Life in Mooresville was anything but idyllic. Dillinger refused to help his father on the farm. He dropped out of high school, but regularly attended Sunday School at the First Christian Church. During World War I, he tried to get a job at the Link-Belt Company in Indianapolis, but was rejected because he was too young. He soon found a position as an apprentice machinist at the Reliance Specialty Company, where he was rated as an outstanding worker. He drove back and forth to work each day on his prized motorcycle. He also used the motorbike when he worked for four months as an errand boy for the Indianapolis Board of Trade.

Dillinger spent most of his spare time in the county seat of Martinsville, where he joined the local baseball team and earned a reputation as a remarkable second baseman. He also started dating a young woman named Frances Thornton, his Uncle Everett's stepdaughter. The two of them fell in love and Dillinger asked his uncle for her hand in marriage, but he refused, telling Dillinger that they were both too young. In truth, he actually wanted the girl to marry a wealthy boy from Greencastle, Indiana.

On the night of July 21, 1923, Dillinger impulsively stole a car from the parking lot of the Friends Church in Mooresville. Hours later, he abandoned it in Indianapolis, but fearing arrest, he enlisted in the U.S. Navy. Unknown to Dillinger, the owner of the car, Oliver P. Macy, knew John and refused to press charges. Regardless, Dillinger enlisted under his real name but gave a false St. Louis address when he filled out his paperwork. After basic training at Great Lakes, he was assigned to the *U.S.S. Utah*. He went AWOL several times and was thrown in the brig, and when the ship was anchored off Boston in December, Dillinger jumped ship permanently. The Navy listed him as a deserter and posted a reward for his capture, but Dillinger went back to Indiana.

Young John Dillinger about the time that he joined the Navy

At home, Dillinger met and began courting 16-year-old Beryl Ethel Hovious, a waitress at the Callis Restaurant in Martinsville. The two of them married in April 1924, but, by all accounts, it wasn't much of a marriage. They moved in with Beryl's parents, but Dillinger spent more time playing baseball and shooting pool than paying attention to his wife.

On the night of September 6, 1924, Dillinger finally stepped completely over the line of the law. Cooking up a plan with a former convict and umpire for the Martinsville baseball team named Edgar Singleton, the two men decided to rob Frank Morgan, a Mooresville grocer who carried his week's receipts home on Saturday nights. Regretfully, it made no difference to Dillinger that Morgan had always been very nice to him, even after he caught him stealing penny candy from the store when he was a boy. Instead of turning him over to the police, Morgan had given him a lecture on honesty. Or perhaps it did make a difference, because Dillinger drank heavily to get his courage up to commit the robbery.

Dillinger hid near the Mooresville Christian Church and Singleton waited in a getaway car down the street. As the grocer was passing the church around 10:30 p.m., Dillinger whacked him over the head with a large bolt that was wrapped in a rag. He held a small .32-caliber revolver in his hand, but he didn't use it. Morgan fell, and when he got up to fight, Dillinger hit him a second time. The grocer cried out, and as neighbors ran to help him, he grabbed Dillinger's gun, which accidentally fired. Thinking that he had shot Morgan, Dillinger fled down the street, without any money, toward the spot where Singleton was supposed to be waiting for him. His accomplice, and the getaway car, was gone.

Morgan's head required 11 stitches, but he told Deputy Sheriff John Hayworth that he couldn't identify his attackers. Hayworth looked into the case, though, and came to believe that Dillinger was involved. He took Morgan out to the Dillinger farm with him and the grocer confronted John. He insisted that Dillinger wouldn't have hurt him. It couldn't be John, Morgan told the lawman. Hayworth took Dillinger in for questioning anyway, and when his father came to collect him from the county jail, the tearful young man confessed to the hold-up attempt. The prosecutor promised the elder Dillinger that his son didn't need an attorney and would receive a lenient sentence if he threw himself on the mercy of the court. The farmer convinced his son to do so and Dillinger, just 20 years old, entered a guilty plea. To his surprise, he was fined $100 and sentenced to concurrent sentences of up to 10-20 years in prison. His accomplice, through his attorney, received a change of venue and a much lighter sentence that resulted in his parole in just two years.

Dillinger was in shock, and even Morgan County, Indiana, Deputy Sheriff Russell Peterson said that he believed the young man's sentence was too harsh under the circumstances: "He was just a kid. He got a raw deal. You just can't take away ten years from a kid's life."

Betrayed and angry, he was sent to the Indiana State Reformatory with no plans to cause trouble, he said, "except to escape." Over the course of the next several years, Dillinger tried to break out over and over again, always getting caught. One night, he was found to be missing from his cell and was discovered under a pile of clothing in the laundry. Another time, he made a saw and cut his way out of his cell. He was captured in the corridor. He tried again in 1925 and was captured once more. Needless to say, Dillinger hated every minute of his incarceration at the Reformatory, but it would not be long before he would become acquainted with a group of inmates there who would forever change his life.

In late March 1925, Dillinger met a recent arrival at the reformatory named Homer Van Meter, and the two became fast friends. Barely 19-years-old when he was locked up, Van Meter was a slender, but physically strong young man with a scar across the middle of his forehead and the word "hope" tattooed on his right forearm.

Van Meter was born on December 3, 1906, in Fort Wayne, Indiana. He came from a family of railroad workers and both his parents were hard-working, respectable citizens that were well-liked in the city. His father, Cary, was a conductor on one of the fastest freight runs of the Nickel Plate Railroad, where Van Meter's uncles and nephews also worked. Associates called the stern, heavy drinker "the King" – but never to his face. He died at the age of only 47 from a "general nervous collapse" in 1918, when Homer was 11. One of Homer's uncles died in an insane asylum. Many of Homer's family members believed this trait to be hereditary and used it to explain the young man's foray into a life of crime. He began skipping school and getting into trouble at an early age, and before he entered sixth grade, he ran away from home to Chicago, where he worked as a waiter and a bellboy.

At age 16, Van Meter was first arrested in Aurora, Illinois, for shoplifting and was charged with larceny. He was booked under the false name of Kenneth Jackson, and the charge was later reduced to "disorderly conduct and intoxication." He spent 41 days in jail and was fined $200. Later in 1923, he stole a car and was caught, convicted, and sentenced to a 10-year term at the Southern State Prison in Menard, Illinois. He was allowed to attend the funeral of his mother, who died on March 30, 1924, and at that time, laid claim to a portion of his parents' estate. He was paroled in December 1924.

Homer Van Meter

It wasn't long before Van Meter was back to breaking the law. On February 26, 1925, he and Con Livingston, a 22-year-old fellow ex-convict staged a daring, but only modestly lucrative, train robbery. That night, in Toledo, Ohio, they boarded a New York Central train that was bound for Chicago. A few miles east of Gary, Indiana, the two men left the day coach and headed for the train's single sleeping car. Arriving there, they forced a flagman, Paul Fornier, and T.D. Robertson, a porter, to go with them into the sleeper car. They locked the door behind them and then proceeded to rob the passengers and crew of about $50 in cash and $500 in jewelry. The two them jumped from the train as it slowed down in the Gary rail yard. Railroad officials immediately contacted the police, but Van Meter and Livingston were already on board an electric train that was bound for Chicago.

Over the next few days, Van Meter and Livingston met up with Frank Zelinski, another former convict, and a young thug named Michael Spicuzza. They were involved in several small hold-ups and then, after stealing a car, drove to South Bend, Indiana, where they planned to rob a bank.

At 2:30 a.m. on March 6, the heavily armed group was sitting in their stolen car at the New York Central Railroad station in South Bend when Police Officer Homer Ames passed by them and went into a restaurant to call the police station and report any stolen cars he had seen. One of the men followed him inside, eavesdropped on his conversation, and then went back outside and told the others about it. When Ames came out of the restaurant, he walked toward the car and one of the outlaws opened fire on him. Ames returned the shots, and Livingston was wounded in the chest. After a cab driver and a night mail truck driver pulled their own guns and joined in the battle, Van Meter, Zelinski, and Spicuzza fled down the railroad tracks. Spicuzza was captured after being shot in the leg by two railroad detectives who had heard the gunfire. Van Meter and Zelinski escaped, but heard the next day that Livingston had died.

On March 10, the cops caught up to the pair. They were arrested by railroad detectives at the Chicago train station while waiting to board a train heading out west. Van Meter confessed to Chicago Chief of Detectives William "Shoes" Shoemaker that he and "Carl Hern," who had been killed in South Bend, had robbed the train back in February. He was returned to Indiana and on March 12, he was charged with two counts of train robbery in the courthouse in Crown Point. He was sentenced to 10-21 years on each charged and sent to the reformatory.

On the night of January 5, 1926, though, Van Meter was taken to Chicago to testify against an accomplice in federal court and the handcuffed prisoner managed to escape while his distracted guard was asking for directions to get from Union Station to the Des Plaines Police Station. Evading his pursuers for more than an hour, Van Meter, who had no money, managed to hide his handcuffs under his coat and panhandle 35-cents from a passerby. He was finally arrested near the intersection of Van Buren Street and Wabash Avenue.

A few weeks later, Van Meter and his cellmate tried to escape from the reformatory by using a saw to cut their way to freedom. They made it out of their cell, but Van Meter was spotted by a guard, whom he hit several times with a lead pipe. He ran, but guards caught up to him in the yard, where he was beaten so badly that he had to be taken to the infirmary. He spent the next two months in solitary confinement in the "hole."

Van Meter had a violent temper and a sarcastic wit that he often used to provoke the guards into hitting him. Several of his teeth were knocked out during his stay at the reformatory. He often did comic impressions of the guards to entertain the other prisoners, and would often pretend to be crippled or mentally challenged for the amusement of himself and the others. He always made Dillinger laugh and the two became close friends.

But not everyone thought Van Meter was so funny. The prison's director of research once wrote about him: "This fellow is a criminal of the most dangerous type. Moral sense is perverted and he has no intention of following anything but a life of crime... He is a murderer at heart, and if society is to be safeguarded, his type must be confined throughout their natural life."

Dillinger would be dismayed on July 28, 1926, when Van Meter was transferred from the state reformatory to the prison at Michigan City – but he would soon see his friend again.

Homer Van Meter was not the only close friend that Dillinger made at the reformatory in Pendleton. Perhaps the man who would most influence his port-prison career was a bank robber named Harry Pierpont.

The soft-spoken ladies' man had been born on October 13, 1902, in Muncie, Indiana. Pierpont's childhood was a happy and largely uneventful one. When he was three, his family moved to a farm in Marion County, near Indianapolis. Raised Catholic, he attended the Assumption parochial school, where he graduated from eighth grade and earned high marks for having good behavior and above average intelligence. He was slender and good-looking, with a light complexion, brown hair, and bright blue eyes that darkened when he was angry. He was given the nickname "Handsome Harry."

In June 1921, Pierpont was allegedly hit in the head with a baseball bat and knocked unconscious. According to a relative, who may have been looking for an explanation for Harry's subsequent life of crime, he was never quite right again. After the incident, he complained of eye problems, headaches, and stomach trouble. Pierpont became melancholy, reclusive, restless, suffered from bouts of sleeplessness, and had a poor memory. He also developed a keen interest in motor cars and for writing bad checks.

Later in the same year, Pierpont was arrested for the first time. He was

Harry Pierpont

picked up in Indianapolis for carrying a concealed weapon and jailed for 10 days. At the request of his mother, who stated in a letter that he was "dangerous to be at large and should be in a hospital," he was sent to the Central Indiana Hospital for the Insane. He was locked up there on September 21, and was finally discharged on March 14, 1922, in an "improved condition." During his time there, records said that he was moody, cross, contrary, excitable, appeared extremely melancholy, and talked incoherently at times.

During Pierpont's time at the asylum, he was often in and out of it and receiving sporadic care. On January 2, 1922, while still receiving treatment, he stole a car in Indianapolis and drove to Greencastle, Indiana, where he broke into the Cook Hardware Store and stole nine handguns. Two nights later, in Terre Haute, he tried to steal a car that belonged to Edward Devine, who caught him in the act. Pierpont fired four shots at him, but Devine was only slightly wounded. The melee ended when Devine's wife hit Pierpont over the head with a package of meat.

Pierpont was arrested, tried, and convicted of attempted car theft and assault and battery with intent to murder. While awaiting trial, he attempted to saw through the bars of his cell and almost made it out before he was discovered.

Pierpont was sent to the Indiana State Reformatory at Jeffersonville on March 12, 1922, and on November 17, he was transferred to the new reformatory at Pendleton. Almost as soon as he arrived, his mother, Lena, began pressing the superintendent to get him paroled. The superintendent wrote back to one of her many letters: "This young fellow has been as wild as a March hare... I only wish that I could write a different letter to you, but this boy has put a ten-rail fence up for me and it is hard to climb."

But Lena, a determined woman who thought her son meant no harm and deserved to be free, refused to give up. She visited the superintendent and told him about Pierpont's mental illness. At first his parole was rejected, but then he was released from the reformatory on March 6, 1924.

But, of course, he would be back.

After his release, Pierpont worked at his father's sand and gravel business in Brazil, Indiana, for a few months, but was soon back to his old ways. He became mixed up with several bank robbers, including Earl Northern. Pierpont was friends with Earl's sister, Mary, with whom he would maintain a relationship with in the years to come.

Pierpont and the others committed a series of robberies in Indiana, including banks at Marion, New Harmony, and Kokomo. On November 26, 1924, they raided the South Marion State Bank and made off with about $4,000. On December 23, the same bunch took about $2,500 from the Upland State Bank. On March 11, 1925, Pierpont and his associates hit the New Harmony Bank and stole $4,828 in cash, $4,300 in Liberty bonds, and $2,000 in negotiable securities. On March 27, it was the South Side Bank in Kokomo, which yielded $3,000 in cash and another $7,000 in Liberty bonds.

Three emergency squads of Indianapolis police armed with riot guns fruitlessly searched the roads between Kokomo and Indianapolis, but it was one of the gang's girlfriends who led to their capture. Louise Brunner, girlfriend of Pierpont's pal Thaddeus Skeer, was trailed to Detroit by detectives, and the couple was arrested when they met up at a prearranged meeting spot on April 2. Pierpont was picked up, also in Detroit, later that same day, and was shipped back to Indiana.

On May 6, 1925, he received his new sentence – 10-21 years at the reformatory in Pendleton. He arrived there on July 3, and struck up a friendship with Dillinger and his twitchy friend, Homer Van Meter. Two months later, Pierpont tried to escape by drilling through the bars of his cell. He was caught and transferred to the state penitentiary at Michigan City, the same place that Homer Van Meter ended up the following summer.

Dillinger grew bored after his friends were transferred and he soon began getting into trouble. He was caught gambling and had another 30 days added to his sentence. A disorderly charge in August 1926 led to another 30 days tacked on to his term. He was thrown into solitary confinement in December, and as soon as he was released, he got into a fistfight and was sent back to solitary. On October 17, 1928, he was charged with destroying prison property.

To get out of the horrible job of making manhole covers in the prison foundry, Dillinger poured hot iron into one of his shoes to injure his heel. Unsympathetic guards sent him right back to work. Determined, Dillinger "spilled" acid on his wound and was finally transferred to yard duty. Later, he worked in the prison's shirt factory and displaying a great affinity for it, he easily did double and even triple the amount of required work. Occasionally, he even helped slower workers make their quotas.

In 1929, Dillinger received bad news in the form of divorce papers from his wife. She had visited him often, but could take no more of having a husband stuck behind bars. Perhaps it was this sobering news that convinced Dillinger that the smartest way to get out of prison was to be a model prisoner. He cleaned up his act, steered clear of fights, and even started attending classes.

In 1929, the same year his wife filed for divorce, Dillinger came up before the parole board. He was turned down and it must have been at that moment that he came up with a new plan for his incarceration. If he was going to have to stay locked up awhile longer, he would find a way to improve his situation, or at least do his time among friendly faces.

As it happened, Indiana Governor Harry Leslie was sitting in on the parole hearing. Dillinger had once been playing baseball in the prison yard and had overheard the governor remark that he ought to be playing professional ball. When he knew that he would not be getting out of jail, he asked the board to send him to the state prison in Michigan City because it had a "real baseball team." Governor Leslie convinced the board that a move was in order, as it might help Dillinger to find work when he did finally get out.

Dillinger was shipped out to Michigan City on July 15, but he never joined the baseball team. Instead, he renewed his friendship with Homer Van Meter and Harry Pierpont, and they put together a very different kind of team.

3. Behind Bars at Michigan City

The Indiana State Prison at Michigan City was very little like the reformatory at Pendleton. The reformatory had been designed for younger men, who had not quite graduated to the degree of hardened criminals. Work and education, it was thought, might set them onto the right path when they were released. This was not the case at Michigan City. A man locked up here was going to do hard time.

The prison had a silent system – men ate, marched, and worked in silence. They had to raise their hands if they wanted to use the toilet. Inmates had to learn that if they wanted to talk, they had to do it without moving their lips. A typical cell measured just six by nine feet and had an unshaded 15-watt lightbulb. On each wall was a card that listed the prison's 22 rules – no books, magazines, or newspapers were allowed. Each prisoner was given one piece of soap, a corncob pipe, tobacco, and a towel. An inmate could smoke three times an evening in his cell, and the pipe or cigarette had to be lit by a trusty. With about 2,800 prisoners packed into the stale, crumbling building, there were too few guards and frequent escape attempts. In 1929, prison authorities increased the restrictions on the inmates, which led to a strike that was quickly suppressed.

Conditions were harsher than at the reformatory, but there were some advantages to being incarcerated at Michigan City. There were few professional criminals at Pendleton, but at Michigan City, a convict could learn the "trade" from men who were experts in forgery, bank robbery, and confidence games. With no books, magazines, or anything else to occupy the men's minds, they talked all that they could and the younger men quickly absorbed the rules, ideas, and precautions offered by the professionals.

When Dillinger arrived at Michigan City, he was reunited with Pierpont and Van Meter. He was also introduced to three other men who would someday become members of what would be dubbed the Dillinger Gang: John "Red" Hamilton, Charles Makley, and Russell Lee Clark. Dillinger was quickly accepted into the group.

Pierpont fared about as well as was expected at Michigan City. He compiled a dismal record. Known for his ability to withstand hunger and beatings, he planned four escapes and assaulted and bound a guard during one attempt. He also wrote to acquaintances on the outside, requesting that they try and smuggle guns and hacksaws into the institution. He was cited for possessing a handcuff key, making a key for his cell door, and talking in the dining room and chapel, both of which were minor offenses.

Van Meter gave prison officials almost as much trouble as Pierpont did. He smuggled saws into his cell, illegally mailed notes to friends on the outside, and made two escape attempts. Then, Van Meter decided to try for parole by becoming a model prisoner. Although he had little formal schooling, he somehow became an educated, skilled, and polished man in prison, even learning to speak German. He was able to convinced prison officials that he was sincere about changing his ways, even though the whole thing was a ruse. He wrote to a friend: "I am sure that I have not lost my formula of salesmanship." He wrote long letters to the parole board and with help from his uncle, W.E. Dowd, and his brother, Harry, he managed to get in front of the state board of pardons. He managed to get out of the Michigan City prison on May 20, 1933.

When he left, he made plans to meet Dillinger in Indianapolis as soon as he was released. Van Meter promised him that he could show him how to get rich.

Dillinger's new friends had their own questionable backgrounds and each had their own blemished records from their time at Michigan City.

John Hamilton, who would always be the most stable and level-headed of Dillinger's friends, arrived at Michigan City in March 1927. Always willing to take a dare, as a boy he had once climbed a 175-foot factory chimney for 10-cents. Another time, trying to show how fast he could move his hands through a train's speeding wheels, he lost the index and middle fingers on his right hand. As a result, some called him "Three-Fingered Jack." More often, everyone knew him as "Red," thanks to the color of his hair.

Born in Binginlet, Ontario, Canada, on August 27, 1898, to John and Sarah Hamilton, he had eight brothers and sisters. When he was three, Hamilton's

John "Red" Hamilton

family moved to Sault Ste, Marie, Michigan, and he spent his boyhood in the region, attending McKinley Public School. Like Dillinger, he was also a faithful attendee at Sunday School and he was a better than average student. He loved the outdoors and spent much of his time hunting and trapping. He was an excellent marksman, who won a number of shooting competitions, a skill that would come in handy later in life.

After leaving school in the tenth grade, Red worked as a lumberjack and a deckhand on a Great Lakes freighter. Around 1919, he joined two friends in Pontiac, Michigan, where the three worked as freight hustlers for the Oakland Motor Company.

Hamilton was in Michigan for almost a year before he returned to Sault Ste. Marie. On August 22, 1921, he married Mary Stephenson – the woman that many claim was his downfall. Mary's brother, Alvia, was part of a criminal gang and she had a taste for high living. During their marriage, the couple lived on a small farm, where Mary made a garden and kept chickens. Hamilton worked in the lumber camps – and did a lot of bootlegging on the side. The couple had two sons, Howard and Orville.

In 1923, Hamilton was driven out of town after a liquor still was discovered in his chicken coop. He was arrested, but jumped bail in 1924 and hooked up with the Mary's brother's gang. The first big robbery that Hamilton took part in occurred on July 20, 1925, when they stole a $33,000 payroll from the Lakey Foundry in Muskegon Heights.

By 1926, Hamilton was working as a carpenter and living with Mary and the children in Detroit. Red began running rum south from Canada, but was arrested in Ecorse, Michigan, later that same year. The charges were later dropped. On December 23, 1926, Hamilton tried to burglarize a safe at the Walter E. Miles Coal Company in Grand Rapids, Michigan. Along with Raymond Lawrence, a rumrunner and former police officer, they broke into the coal company's office, only to be discovered by two police officers on patrol. The officers were checking the office's outside door and saw a set of burglar tools on the floor. Thinking that they had surprised the thieves, they attempted to surround the place, only to find a high wooden fence in the way. Meanwhile, Hamilton and Lawrence, after spotting the police car, fled out a back door. They got away with only $200.

On January 3, 1927, the Stephenson gang – Hamilton, Lawrence, Clayton Powers (who was married to Mary's sister), Curtis Turner, and the Stephenson Brothers, Alvia, John, George, and Joseph – robbed the Fulton Street branch of the Kent State Bank in Grand Rapids and made off with over $25,000.

Turner was arrested on March 13, thanks to a tip to the police from a scorned girlfriend, and he admitted his role in the bank robbery, implicated Hamilton, and then told detectives that Red was planning to rob another bank in South Bend, Indiana, on March 15.

And he was right. Early that morning, two bandits slipped into the bank before it opened, tied up the employees, and waited for the 8:00 a.m. opening of the time clock on the vault. Ten minutes before it was supposed to open, however, a bank official managed to slip past the robber that was covering the door. A minute later the bandits counted their hostages and realized one was missing. They immediately fled, leaving behind $48,500 in cash and $85,000 in securities. A squad of police officers soon arrived on the scene, but the would-be robbers had vanished.

Later that day, Chief of Police James J. Hatt, having lunch at home, received a mysterious telephone call from a man who claimed to have seen a Chevrolet coupe parked in his neighborhood that morning. A few hours later, he saw a young man changing the same car's license plates from Michigan to Wisconsin tags. Hatt investigated, found the car, and discovered a sawed-off shotgun and a box of shells on the back seat. He called up six officers from the local police station to help him raid the house where the car was parked. When they entered the house, which was opened by Hamilton's brother, William, they arrested Red, Lawrence, and three unnamed men. Early the next morning, Lawrence confessed to the attempted robbery of the South Bend bank and the earlier robbery in Grand Rapids. Hamilton refused to say anything.

Less than 36 hours after the bungled bank robbery, the two bandits were each sentenced to spend 25 years at the Indiana State Prison. Both men had ended up pleading guilty to the charges as a way to avoid life sentences.

Mary didn't wait for him to get out. While he was locked up, she obtained a divorce and later married a man in Toledo. She died in childbirth in 1930, and Hamilton's two sons were sent to live with his mother-in-law in Ohio.

Red's prison record was tame compared to most of the prisoners. He was once cited for making too much noise in 1927 and for skipping rope in the shirt factory in 1932. In spite of this, his pleas for clemency were rejected because the parole board considered him to be a dangerous man. And he certainly was.

Charles Makley

Charles Makley arrived for a stay of 10-20 years at Michigan City on June 23, 1928. Always remembered as a "likable fellow" by residents of his hometown of St. Marys, Ohio, he was one of six children born to the poor Catholic family of Edward and Martha Makley on November 24, 1888. His father, a stonemason, and his mother separated when he was young. Makley was already working in a local mill by the age of 12, soon after he left school.

At 17, Makley left home and engaged in various ventures, including mining and selling cars, in Boise, Idaho, Detroit, and other places. He grew into a stocky young man, and with one leg shorter than the other, he walked with a limp.

Around this time, Makley began his criminal career, starting with petty thefts. When Prohibition began in 1920, he turned to bootlegging and became a con man. Within a few months, he stole a furnace salesman's car, traded it in on a new Terraplane, an inexpensive but powerful car that was built by the Hudson Motor Car Company. Because of its speed, the Terraplane became the car of choice for 1930s bank robbers. But Makley took it one step further. Using a pamphlet left in the stolen vehicle by its owner, sold the car dealer a furnace for cash. He got away with this one, but was arrested for the first time a year later, when he was charged with receiving stolen property.

On January 2, 1923, he and another man were arrested in St. Louis in connection to a $97,000 robbery of messengers from the Drovers National Bank in Kansas City, two years before. It had been the biggest robbery in that city's history. They had trouble hitting him with a large bond, though, especially after

Makley's lawyer found a doctor that testified that he was physically unable to run away because of a bad knee. Makley paid the reduced bond and then skipped out.

He was back at work in July 1924 when he and two other men robbed a Kansas City couple of $571 and took their car. He was arrested again in late August in Wichita, Kansas, for the hold-up of the Corn Exchange Bank in Kansas City, which snagged $13,000. Makley was charged with two bank heists and the July armed robbery, and was sentenced to 15 years in prison on September 23. He confessed to stealing the car, but denied any part in the bank robberies. Makley, under the alias of Charles McGray, was sent to the Missouri State Penitentiary on October 15, 1924, but was freed on parole on June 5, 1925, making his stay behind bars in Missouri a short one.

Back on the outside, Makley put together a small gang of bank robbers. They hit locations in Ohio, Indiana, and Missouri, using Hammond and Lafayette, Indiana, as their headquarters. They spent some time in Kansas City, until they became too "hot" there and syndicate leaders in town set them packing. Makley had a particular ruse that worked well for him prior to the robberies. He was a portly man and, when dressed in a nice suit, looked like a bank president or prosperous businessman. No one expected him to pull a machine gun out from under his overcoat and demand that tellers fill up bags with cash. He later bragged that he often addressed civic luncheons in small towns, just before robbing the local bank.

In early January 1926, the gang was in Missouri and made off with about $3,500 from the bank in Ferguson, Missouri. But they ran into trouble after grabbing $26,320 in cash and bonds from the Citizens Bank of Festus, Missouri, on September 25. They escaped from the bank, but a posse captured most of the bandits at a clubhouse near Eureka, Missouri. Another of the bandits was arrested in St. Louis. Makley was the only one of the robbers to escape, and he returned to Michigan to put together a new gang.

Around noon on September 30, 1926, Makley's new gang, wearing goggles and fake mustaches, pulled off the first bank robbery in the history of Portland, Indiana, getting away with about $25,000. Six days later, they robbed the Chickasaw Farmers Bank in Chickasaw, Ohio, of about $5,000 in cash and securities. More than two months later, on December 17, they held up a bank messenger and guard who were taking $79,000 to the Fidelity Bank and Trust Company in Kansas City, Missouri. Five men, including Makley, were convicted of the robbery and sent to prison. Makley was released on an appeal bond and quickly fled the state – and went back to robbing banks.

On March 24, 1927, with a new gang, Makley hit the Indiana State Bank in Linn Grove and escaped with about $2,500. On June 8, they stole $4,500 in cash and another $45,000 worth of government securities from the First National Bank of Ansonia, Ohio.

Makley's outfit struck again on November 1, getting away with only about $1,000 from the Tippecanoe Loan and Trust Company, located across the street from the police station in Lafayette, Indiana. During the heist, the seven heavily armed men killed police Captain Charles Arman when he tried to prevent the robbery. On March 27, 1928, the gang struck again at Linn Grove, making off with another $1,900. Just over a week later, on April 4, Makley and another man stole about $6,000 from the Bank of St. Henry in St. Henry, Ohio.

This put Makley's total to about $500,000 from banks in Indiana, Ohio, and Missouri in just over a two-year period. But his luck was just about to run out.

One of Makley's men, Eddie Meadows, was arrested by a Hammond, Indiana, police detective on June 5, 1928, for the Kansas City bank job after he was overheard boasting about the robbery. Makley, and his sister-in-law, Edith, were arrested later that day by five policemen. He was just about to get a hold of a large arsenal, but he surrendered without a struggle, despite the fact that he had always boasted that he would be taken alive. Three other members of the gang were also arrested that same day in Hammond. Obviously, Eddie Meadows had talked.

In the end, so did Makley, but only because a tearful Edith had begged him to clear her name. Thanks to this, Edith was not charged with any crime, but she did have to appear as a state's witness during Makley's trial. Makley ended up confessing to the bank robberies at Linn Grove, Ansonia, St. Henry, Chickasaw, Festus, and Ferguson, but denied any others. Other members of the gang told police that they had been the ones who robbed the banks in Kansas City and Portland.

Makley ended up with 10-20 years at Michigan City. During his time behind bars, he kept his nose clean and compiled an almost perfect record. He was too busy instructing his younger friends in the art of robbing banks to get into too much trouble.

Dillinger's other new pal was Russell Lee Clark, who entered the penitentiary at Michigan City on December 16, 1927. The man that everyone referred to as a "smooth talker" was one of seven children, born in Terre Haute, Indiana, on August 8, 1896. His parents, Dan and Minnie, were a poor farming couple and Clark lived a hard life as a child. After graduating from the eighth grade, he left home at age 16. He had gray eyes, dark eyes, stood just over six feet, and had a scar down the middle of his back.

Clark enlisted in the army in 1919, just after World War I, at Camp Zachary Taylor in Louisville, Kentucky. He only lasted four months. He received a dishonorable discharge, but no records exist to say what offense he was accused of. After leaving the service, he worked as a tailor, truck driver, and a coal miner. Later, he worked in a Terre Haute glass factory, a commercial distillery, in a tie factory, and, of course, as an armed robber and bandit.

On June 22, 1922, Clark married Frances M. Wilson (also known as Bernice Clark and most popularly as Opal Long) in Edgar County, Illinois. She was the sister of Pat Cherrington, a girlfriend of John Hamilton. She was not an attractive woman. She was a heavyset, red-haired woman, with lots of freckles, huge breasts, and large buttocks, which led to her ending up with the unflattering nickname of "Mack truck." But she loved Clark and was fiercely loyal to him. She had a hard life growing up, living with her grandmother until she was eight, and

Russell Clark

then went to live with her mother and the latter's new husband. She had little education and worked at odd jobs in restaurants and five-and-dime stores.

Clark had first been arrested in Terre Haute in 1921 on suspicion of robbery, but he was released. A short time later, he became involved with Ralston "Blackie" Linton, a local criminal who was known for robbing roadhouses during Prohibition. On November 6, 1923, Linton's gang blew the safes in two banks in Spencer, Indiana. Linton went to prison for the robberies, but refused to tell who else was involved. Clark was arrested again, but he was again released.

Clark was suspected in being part of a kidnapping plot in 1926, when bootleggers Oscar Moore and A.L. LeClerq disappeared, and a suspect in the murder of Joe Popolardo of Danville, Illinois. He was also picked up for bootlegging in the summer of that year, but the police couldn't make the charges stick. On August 22, though, Clark was one of three men who robbed the Bellevue Club in Evansville, Indiana. Unmasked and brandishing revolvers, the trio took $3,000 in cash and jewelry from the club's co-owner, Charles "Cotton" Jones. Clark was arrested on a fugitive warrant by Terre Haute police on August 30, and the next day, was picked up for the Evansville robbery. Eventually, Jones decided not to prosecute and Clark was free again.

In July 1927, Clark was living in Detroit with his wife, Opal, and decided to join up with Frank Badgley's crew after meeting Badgley at a poker game in Indianapolis. Clark and Badgley's brother-in-law, Charles Hovius, were introduced in a Detroit rooming house and Clark's brother, Edward, also joined the group and offered his Indiana farm as a hideout.

On July 21, Clark, Badgley, and another man robbed the Paragon State Bank in Paragon, Indiana. They got away with $2,238. The same three men also got $4,855 from the New Augusta State Bank in New Augusta, Indiana, on August 8.

Late in September, the Badgley gang traveled from Detroit to Whiteland, Indiana, where they held up a drugstore, and then went to Straughn, Indiana, where they robbed the People's Bank of $1,002. For some reason, Badgley went alone to try and rob the Huntertown State Bank and failed. Three days later, he was caught after another robbery in Amboy, Indiana, and was imprisoned for life as a habitual criminal.

Early in December 1927, Clark and Hovius stole an automobile in Detroit and drove it to Indianapolis to visit friends. After they left, they traveled through Anderson and Fort Wayne and decided to try and rob the Huntertown bank themselves. They made their attempt on the afternoon of December 8. While one of the bandits kept cashier Horace Tucker under guard, the other scooped $1,313 into a flour sack. As the two made their escape, Tucker fired at them with a brand new pistol that he kept under his window. The bandits returned fire and Tucker was wounded when a bullet grazed his arm.

Near Pioneer, Ohio, at the Michigan state line, Clark and Hovius abandoned their car after it blew a tire. They seized two other vehicles from passing motorists, but those cars also lost tires after short distances. Sheriff Lloyd Bly, warned that the two criminals were headed toward Pioneer, set up a trap to catch them. After seeing the men fleeing across an open field, lawmen fired at them. Clark and Hovius shot back several times. Hovius was eventually captured, but Clark made it into the woods. A posse of about 150 lawmen, farmers, and local volunteers continued the chase for six miles, with Clark and his pursuers exchanging more than 30 shots.

On the morning of December 9, a farmer near Hillsdale, Michigan, saw Clark on his property. Suspicious of the way that the stranger was acting, the farmer ordered him to leave. Clark hid in the man's barn instead and almost froze to death. When the posse approached, looking for the bandit, the farmer told them about the mysterious man. They searched the farm and Clark was found in the barn. He was arrested and taken to the county jail, where he and Hovius confessed to the Huntertown robbery – a bank that both men must have believed by this time was cursed.

They waived extradition and were turned over to Indiana authorities on December 10. After being tried and convicted for the Huntertown robbery, Clark was sentenced to 20 years. The proceedings happened so quickly that his family was never notified of the trial and he never had time to hire his own lawyer.

Nearly three years later, on November 5, 1930, Clark was taken to New Castle, Indiana, as a witness in a trial. Two days later, at about 6:00 a.m. on the return trip, he and the other prisoners tried to escape from the automobile that was being used to transport them. Other officers saw what was happening, stopped the cars, and forcefully subdued the convicts before returning them to the penitentiary. When the badly beaten prisoners arrived at Michigan City on November 8, Clark was in such bad shape that he remained in the prison hospital until November 12.

Undeterred, he attempted to escape three times during his incarceration and was one of the five leaders in the 1929 prison strike to protest the conditions of the penitentiary. Although several convicts stopped working, the strike ended quickly after prison officials punished the ringleaders. Clark was placed in solitary confinement in the "hole," a place that he was very familiar with since, during his sentence, he was sent there for escape attempts, talking, and fighting.

While Pierpont, Hamilton, Makley, and Clark schooled Dillinger and Van Meter on the best methods for robbing banks, the older men also received their own education from a more experienced bank robber named Walter Dietrich, a member of the "Baron" Herman L. Lamm gang. Lamm, a young Prussian officer, who had been forced to leave the German army just before World War I for cheating at cards, emigrated to the United States and traveled to Utah. He was arrested on robbery charges in 1917 and while doing time at the prison in Salt Lake City, developed a system for robbing banks that would prove very successful.

Lamm put his military training to good use. Planning, precision, and timing were the keys to Lamm's method. Before robbing a bank, Lamm cased it for days to determine the floor plan, the location of the safes, how the safes operated, and who was supposed to open them. Then he would rehearse the robbery with the best professional criminals that he could find. Each member of the crew would have his own job and was required to do it in a certain amount of time. Lamm had a rule that the gang would leave the bank at a scheduled time, no matter how much, or how little, money had been obtained. The escape route was planned in advance, and several dry runs were usually made before the robbery took place. For the getaway, Lamm always used a high-powered, but nondescript car, and he looked for the most skilled drivers as his wheelmen.

The gang carried out one successful robbery after another, until December 16, 1930. That day, Lamm, G.W. "Dad" Landy, Walter Dietrich, and James "Oklahoma Jack" Clark robbed the Citizens State Bank in Clinton, Indiana, of $15,567. While everything went smoothly inside of the bank, the escape turned into a disaster when, in the midst of making a fast U-turn, the getaway car jumped a curb and blew a tire. The robbers seized another car, but they were unable to get it to move faster than 35 miles an hour. Abandoning that vehicle, they took a truck that had almost no water in the radiator and soon overheated. The bandits stole another car, but it ran out of gas.

When the lawmen chasing the gang caught up with them in Illinois, a furious gun battle ensued between the bandits and almost 200 police officers and volunteers. Lamm and the driver of the getaway car were killed during the shootout, and Landy shot himself rather than be captured. Clark and Dietrich were captured and ultimately sent to Michigan City for life.

4. Bank Jobs

Since Dillinger would be out of prison before any of the others, he was cultivated as the contact man on the outside. It would be his job to hit a number of small town banks, targeted by Pierpont and Hamilton, and use the funds to finance a prison break and free the others. During his last four years inside, Dillinger was a model prisoner, which was all part of the plan. On top of his good behavior, Governor Paul McNutt received a petition from Dillinger's Mooresville neighbors, asking that he be released to help his father on the farm. Even the judge who had sentenced him, perhaps regretting his harsh decision, signed the petition. Dillinger was set free on May 22, 1933, and he immediately rushed to Mooresville, where his stepmother was seriously ill. She died just an hour before Dillinger arrived.

The following Sunday, Dillinger attended church with his father and sat weeping as he listened to the pastor give a pointed sermon on the return of the "prodigal son." When the service ended, he told the minister how much good it had done him -- and two weeks later began robbing small banks and isolated stores.

Dillinger recruited small-time hoodlum William Shaw and driver "Lefty" Parker and using the list that his friend devised, robbed the bank at New Carlisle, Indiana. They followed that up with the two robberies in Indianapolis, including the disastrous one at the grocery store.

On June 24, Dillinger and Shaw attempted to rob a Marshall Field's Thread Mill in Monticello, Indiana, but did not get any money. As Shaw wrestled with manager Fred Fisher, he lost his .45 pistol. When Fisher chased after Shaw, Dillinger, arriving in the getaway car, fired a shot into the ground to scare Fisher away, but the bullet ricocheted and hit the manager in the leg. The duo fled down a dirt road and became lost. After driving about 50 miles, they turned onto a paved highway just 12 miles from Monticello.

Things were not going well for the would-be outlaws.

While driving back to Indianapolis, the two men argued about what to rob next. They finally decided on a fruit market in the city. As they entered the market, Shaw saw a boy who lived in his neighborhood and told Dillinger that they needed to leave quickly. After grabbing $175 from the register, they ran for their car. A customer threw a milk bottle at them and Dillinger fired a shot in the air to discourage pursuit.

After leaving town for a few days to scout banks on Pierpont's list, Dillinger returned to Indianapolis on June 29. Unfortunately, he was finding that many of Pierpont's potential targets had gone under at the start of the Depression and he was often met with empty buildings rather than banks that were ripe for robbing. Dejected, he and Shaw robbed a sandwich shop. Afterward, according to some accounts, Dillinger worked with several other gangs to get a share of bank

Even after spending nine years in prison, Dillinger was still young when he was released – and still learning the robbery trade.

robberies in Muncie, Fort Wayne, East Chicago, and even Kentucky. This may have been the reason why he was flush enough with cash to go to Chicago and attend the World's Fair with a Michigan City ex-con named Frank Whitehouse and his wife.

After returning to Indianapolis, Dillinger was impatient for a big score and began casing the downtown Massachusetts Avenue State Bank. While he was doing so, Shaw disappeared. A few days later, Dillinger received a message that Shaw had taken off to Muncie, Indiana, after learning that the police were looking for him in connection with a robbery that had taken place while Dillinger was still in prison.

Dillinger drove to Muncie on Friday, July 14, and found Shaw and a group of friends in an apartment on South Council Street. The apartment's other occupant was a hard-drinking, dimwitted ex-con named Harry Copeland, who would join Dillinger for other bank jobs. That afternoon, they took Copeland and drove 10 miles west to the farm town of Daleville, which had a bank that Dillinger had scouted. They agreed to rob it on Monday.

For some reason, perhaps because they were low on cash, they decided to first rob a Muncie roadhouse, the Bide-a-Wee Tavern. A few minutes after midnight, Dillinger and a partner walked in, guns drawn, handkerchiefs over their faces, and within minutes ran out of the bar with about $70. On the way out of the bar, Dillinger encountered a couple walking in. With a grin, he pinched the woman's bottom; when her male friend objected, Dillinger punched him in the face.

Robbing the tavern turned out to be a mistake. The next morning, Dillinger and Copeland had just left the boarding house to move Dillinger's car into a garage out back when they heard someone yell, "Hands up!" It was a pair of Muncie detectives, backed by two patrolmen, who had Shaw and the others in an alley behind the house. The detectives, following up on the previous night's robbery, had easily traced Copeland's car, a green sedan with yellow wire wheels. Dillinger encountered the scene as he turned his car into the alley. Without a word, he slammed on the brakes, threw the car in reverse, and raced backwards down the alley. The policemen never saw him. Shaw and the others were taken to the Muncie jail, where Shaw confessed to more than 20 robberies and named his accomplice as "Dan Dillinger," a name that meant nothing to detectives.

Dillinger shrugged off the arrest of his companions, and went forward with the plans to rob the small Commercial Bank in Daleville with Harry Copeland. After parking the car in front of the bank, Dillinger entered first, pulled his gun, and walked up to the 22-year-old teller, Margaret Good. He asked for the bank president, but Miss Good said he wasn't in. She was the only employee in the bank at the time. Dillinger smiled and slid a pistol through the teller cage. He said, "This is a stick-up. Get me the money, honey."

Margaret, who had been robbed twice in the preceding years, pointed at the open vault and raised her hands. As Harry Copeland herded the customers against the wall, Dillinger leapt over the five-foot railing with ease, went into the vault, and scooped up an estimated $3,500 in cash and two diamond rings that belonged to the daughter of the bank's owner. When he was finished, Dillinger led Margaret and the customers into the vault, shut the door, and strolled out to the getaway car. The two men were in and out of the bank in less than 10 minutes.

Dillinger's style was now established, and soon, lawmen all over the state would be looking for him.

5. "Baby Face" Nelson

At the same time that Dillinger was working to collect enough money to break his friends out of prison, another man who would eventually become "Public Enemy #1," and would partner with Dillinger in 1934, was arriving on the scene. His real name was Lester Gillis, but history would come to know him as "Baby Face" Nelson.

In the early 1930s, Nelson was a bit of an enigma. In hindsight, as the number of robberies and hold-ups that he committed became better-known, it became plain that they were often accompanied by senseless violence. He was a small man, standing just under five-feet, five inches, and had the stereotypical short man's need to prove how powerful and dangerous he was. Much of his dubious celebrity would stem from his association with Dillinger, and yet, Nelson was a feared criminal in his own right.

Born Lester Joseph Gillis in an apartment building on Chicago's West Side on December 6, 1908, he was the youngest of seven children. His Belgian immigrant parents came from respected families. His mother, Mary, had been a teacher in the old country and believed in the importance of a good education. His father, Joseph, was a skilled tanner, who eventually became the assistant superintendent of a local leather company. Joseph was also a heavy drinker and, in 1925, he committed suicide by gas while drunk.

Lester (who, from this point on, will simply be referred to by his commonly-known name of George Nelson) was a bright boy who made good grades during his first years of public school. But when his parents sent him to the parochial school, also attended by his sisters, behavior problems and truancy issues began to appear. His mother, Mary, could never bring herself to believe that her son was bad, starting in childhood and continuing all of the way to the end of his life. Even when he began skipping school, started stealing cars, and once found a gun in a neighbor's car that he fired and injured another boy when the bullet ricocheted off a fence post, she always made excuses for him.

Nelson grew up in an area known as the Patch, on Chicago's Near West Side. It was a jumble of ethnic European families and he had many friends from different backgrounds. Although Nelson lived in the same neighborhood as future bank robber and kidnapper Alvin Karpis for a time, the two did not meet growing up. Both were familiar with the West Division Street, North Street, and Sacramento Boulevard areas, and even knew some of the same kids, but they would not become acquainted until later.

In 1922, Nelson was arrested for auto theft while attempting to sell some car accessories that he had stolen. Because of his bad attitude and failure to cooperate with the police, he was shipped off to a reform school in St. Charles, Illinois. His record was exemplary, and in April 1924, he was paroled for good behavior. Five months later, though, he was sent back for parole violations. He finally got out in July 1925, but remained free for a short time before being sent back again in

October. Some nine months later, in July 1926, he received his final release from St. Charles. He was now too old for reform school. While there, however, he received an excellent education for a criminal, learning about car thefts, safe cracking, and armed robbery.

At 17, Nelson returned home and initially appeared to be interested in honest work – but that didn't last long. He threw in with a gang that specialized in stealing tires, which included George Ackerman, Jack Perkins, and Albert Van de Houten, who owned a tire shop. Ackerman was a "well-known police character," but he had never been convicted of a crime. Perkins was Nelson's best friend, and another friend, Arthur N. Johnston, ran a racetrack book, taking bets on local horse races.

Lester Gillis, who despite many aliases, would eventually become best known as George "Baby Face" Nelson

Nelson soon found himself back in trouble. In early 1927, he was arrested by the Chicago police for smashing store windows and grabbing merchandise. He was sentenced to a year's probation.

In 1928, Nelson met a pretty young salesgirl at a Chicago Woolworth's store named Helen Wawrzyniak. The petite 16-year old was just five feet, two inches tall and weighed less than 100 pounds. The daughter of poor Polish parents who had settled in Chicago, Helen was a graduate of Harrison High School. The two of them promptly fell in love and soon married. She retained the name Helen Gillis throughout their marriage. She stuck with him no matter what happened and would be with him until the very end of his life.

Ten months after their marriage, Helen gave birth to a son, Ronald, on April 27, 1929, and a daughter, Darlene, on May 11, 1930. The children ultimately proved to be difficult for the couple to care for, as Nelson's "business" kept them constantly on the road, so they were sent to live with relatives. Both were initially with Nelson's mother in Chicago, but Ronald was later sent to Washington to live with Helen's sister.

From March 1927 to August 1928, Nelson worked as an auto repairman's helper and driver in the transportation department of the Commonwealth Edison Company in Chicago. He also worked at a gas station at Sacramento and Grand Avenue, in a garage on the West Side, and another garage that sold Chrysler automobiles. Nelson loved cars and was constantly working on them to make them

Nelson's wife, Helen, who used her husband's real last name of Gillis throughout her life.

go faster. He was an exceptional driver and actually drove in a few dirt-track races at Chicago's Robey Speedway around 1930.

It was during this period that he began using the name George Nelson, one of several aliases he would eventually employ. Another commonly-used alias was Jimmie Nelson, which many of his underworld contacts knew him by. Nelson was widely feared, both by criminals and members of law enforcement. He had a lethal temper and while he had a young face – which spawned his famous nickname – and a small stature that led some to believe he could be bullied; Nelson was a vicious fighter who often killed for the thrill of it.

Unhappy with just getting by on his low wages, he got some of his friends together and began a series of robberies. On January 6, 1930, he and four accomplices took $25,000 worth of jewelry from the home of Charles Richter on Chicago's Lake Shore Drive. On January 22, Nelson and three others stole $5,000 in jewelry from the Lake Forest, Illinois, home of attorney Stanley J. Templeton. Two months later, on March 31, Nelson, Stanton Randall, and Harry Lewis, robbed "Count Enrique Von Buelow" (who was actually a German gigolo named Henry Dechow) and his wealthy wife, making off with only $95 in cash, but over $50,000 in jewelry.

Nelson and two others even robbed the wife of Chicago Mayor William Hale "Big Bill" Thompson in front of her apartment building. The trip forced Mary Thompson to hand over a six-carat blue diamond ring, a diamond bracelet, and a brooch set with 14 small stones – all valued at over $18,000. She told police that one of the robbers had a "baby face. He was good looking, hardly more than a boy, had dark hair, and was wearing a gray topcoat and a brown felt hat, turned-down brim."

In October 1930, Nelson, Lewis, and Randall turned to bank robbery. That morning, two smartly dressed young men entered the First National Bank of Itasca, Illinois, just after it opened. Both pulled out revolvers and ordered the two employees – assistant cashier Ray A. Frantzen, the son of the bank's owner, and clerk Emma Droegemueller – to raise their hands and "make it snappy." After forcing them to lie down on the floor, the bandits made off with $4,678 and ran out the door. Although Frantzen notified the sheriff and police in nearby towns, the robbers vanished.

A month later, on November 7, Nelson and an accomplice tried to rob the State Bank of Plainfield, Illinois, but bulletproof glass in the cashier's cages prevented the bandits from getting to the bank employees or the cash.

On November 22, Nelson and two others hit the Hillside State Bank in Hillside, Illinois. Shortly after the bank opened, three men came through the front door, one of them firing shots into the ceiling to get everyone's attention. Two of the bandits forced the three employees and a young customer to line up against the lobby wall, while the third man rifled through the cashier's cage and the vault. When a teller tried to set off an alarm, one of the bandits yelled at him to stay away from the device. Nelson and his partners escaped back to Chicago with $4,155 to split between them.

In the wake of the robbery in Hillside, one of the bank employees told police that one of the bandits was a "young man with a baby face." As law enforcement officials scrambled to solve the string of robberies, this statement, along with a tip from an informant about a young bandit known as "Baby Face," had the cops searching for Nelson. The press picked up on the "Baby Face" nickname, which Nelson hated, but which Helen thought was "kind of cute."

During the early morning hours of November 23, Nelson and seven other masked bandits hit a roadhouse owned by Harry Goetz in Hillside, Illinois. At 1:00 a.m., the roadhouse was only slightly busy. There were about 15 people inside, most of whom were dining, when Nelson and the others burst inside with shotguns and pistols. They marched the bartender and two patrons into the rear room, where several people were eating, a male pianist was playing a jazz tune, and a woman was singing.

One of the robbers yelled, "This is a stick-up! All hands up! Everyone get over and face the wall!"

As the crowd hurried to the wall, James Micus, a police lieutenant with the Indiana Harbor Belt Railroad, walked out of the bathroom. He was forced into line with the others, who were being relieved of their valuables by three of the gunmen. As Micus approached the wall, he whipped out a pistol and fired two shots at Nelson. Panic ensued, and soon all of the lights went out except for a few dim bulbs at the back of the room. When one of the bandits tried to turn the ceiling lights back on, he turned off all of the lights by mistake. The roadhouse became a hellish scene of roaring guns and muzzle flashes as the bandits returned the policeman's fire. In the confusion, they successfully escaped, but left behind a ghastly scene: two wounded men, one mortally wounded woman, two dead women on the floor, and a cluster of terrified customers screaming for help. The haul from the robbery amounted to only $300.

Three days later, Nelson and several others raided a tavern north of Chicago and stole $125. Nelson got angry when a customer, Edwin R. Thompson, nervously smiled at him and Nelson shot him.

After the Hillside bank robbery, Nelson and Helen, who were living in Cicero, Illinois, went on a spending spree. Nelson should have known better, because his lavish purchases were drawing attention. Informers passed along rumors about the couple to the police, and on February 14, 1931, officers arrested Nelson and he was charged with armed robbery. He was identified as one of the men who robbed the Hillside bank, but Nelson refused to name anyone who was with him. Meanwhile, police picked up Powell and Randall.

Nelson, Powell, and Randall were each indicted on a single count of robbery on February 20. Even though some of his pals provided alibis for him, a jury convicted Nelson on June 25. On July 9, he received the maximum sentence of one year to life at Joliet Penitentiary and was behind bars again on July 17.

Nelson's rebellious nature didn't serve him well in prison, and he made enemies among both prisoners and guards. Convict Ray Miller assaulted Nelson, and on December 6, 1930, he was placed in solitary for calling a guard "obscene names."

Meanwhile, investigators decided that Nelson fit the description of one of the robbers in the Itasca bank robbery, and on January 6, he was taken to Wheaton, Illinois, to be formally charged. In February, after a three-day trial in Wheaton, during which Nelson was locked up in the DuPage County Jail, he was found guilty of the Itasca robbery and sentenced to another one to 20 years in Joliet.

At this point, Nelson knew that he would be spending the rest of his life in prison if he didn't figure out a way to escape from custody. On February 17, 1932, handcuffed to a guard and in leg irons, he boarded a train at the Wheaton depot that would take him back to the penitentiary. Arriving at the station in Joliet, the guard hailed a cab to taken them to the prison, which was the policy since there was no prison car available.

The taxi cab traveled through town and as it was drawing within sight of the penitentiary's main gate, Nelson suddenly pulled a pistol and forced the guard to remove his handcuffs while telling the cab driver to keep going. When the cab passed a secluded cemetery in the suburbs, Nelson yelled for the driver to stop and then forced both men to get out. He clubbed both men with his gun and left them on the ground unconscious. Nelson got back into the cab and drove toward Chicago, making his escape.

To this day, it remains a mystery how Nelson got the weapon. Someone attending the trial could have given it to him at the courthouse or could have slipped the gun to him on the crowded train, or on the station platform. The guard and cab driver were never considered as suspects. Since Nelson had no money to bribe anyone to help him, it was likely a friend or relative, like Helen or his loyal sister, Leona.

After his escape, Nelson staged a series of movie theater hold-ups to raise some cash and then fled west to Reno, Nevada, where he had underworld contacts. In Reno, he worked for a short time as a chauffeur for gambler William J. Graham. Graham and another gambler, James C. "Red" McKay, sent Nelson to San Francisco to see bootlegger Joe Parente, who controlled most of the criminal activities in the wide-open city.

Nelson, using the name Jimmie Burnett, found a house in the small town of Sausalito. He went to work as a liquor truck driver and guard. As soon as he had the money, Helen joined him with their daughter, Darlene, in the spring of 1932.

Through his association with Parente's organization, Nelson met two men whose fates would ultimately become entwined with his: John Paul Chase, a tall, handsome bootlegger with a trim mustache who would become his closest friend and comrade, and Joseph "Fatso" Negri, a minor criminal who was useful mainly because he would gladly run just about any errand for money.

Chase was born in California in 1901 to a family who had come from Nebraska. After dropping out of school, he worked on ranches and farms and eventually ended up in Reno, where he worked for gamblers. Since 1926, though, after he was fired from a position as a machinist in a railroad shop, he had earned a living as a bootlegger. Although he was likable, popular with women, and a hard worker, he was never really smart enough to succeed on his own.

John Paul Chase

In Nelson, Chase found a leader who could help him become someone important. Impressed when the gangster revealed his real name and told him about his prison escape and bank robberies, Chase was excited by Nelson's big plans.

Like Nelson, the chunky Negri, who had been involved in crime since his teenage years and served a four-year stretch in San Quentin for armed robbery, had also recently become involved with Parente and his organization. Nelson did not reveal his true identity to Negri, but he did gain some respect for him when Negri showed strong nerve during their first job together, which also included Chase. The way that the three men accomplished their assignment pleased Parente, who began using them as security for most of his liquor shipments.

Near the end of the summer of 1932, Helen became ill, and as her stomach pain worsened, a friend of Nelson recommended that he take her to a private hospital in Vallejo, California, operated by Thomas "Tobe" Williams, a former bank robber, burglar, and safe cracker. For exorbitant fees, his hospital discreetly provided such medical services to criminals such as bullet removal, plastic surgery, and fingerprint removal. He also treated common ailments, as well. Helen was admitted on September 12, and underwent an appendectomy. Nelson visited often over the next five days, joined by Chase and Negri. After her recovery, the couple returned to Sausalito on September 17.

In October, Negri received a shock when one of Parente's men showed him a detective magazine that included a mugshot of escaped bank robber Lester Gillis, also known as Baby Face Nelson, who looked just like his pal Jimmie. As others became aware of the photograph, Nelson learned that his identity had been exposed and he, Helen, and Darlene fled to Reno, where he went back to work for William Graham.

By April 1933, Nelson had grown restless in Reno. He bought a new car after New Year's and in April, he, Helen, and Chase drove to St. Paul, where the Nelsons rented an apartment. In May, they rented a summer cottage along the shore of Lake Michigan, just outside the underworld haven of Long Beach, Indiana. With the repeal of Prohibition slated for December, Nelson knew that he needed to find a line of work that didn't include bootlegging. He began recruiting members for a new gang that would target Midwest banks during the coming summer and fall months.

Among those who joined up with Nelson were Homer Van Meter, Dillinger's pal who had recently been paroled from Michigan City; Tommy Carroll, an expert machine-gunner who had once been a promising boxer; and "jug maker" Eddie Green, a specialist in selecting the best banks to rob.

Van Meter, after his parole, had been laying low and planning new jobs when he met up with Nelson. Eventually, he would join forces with Dillinger again. Later in 1933, he met Marie "Mickey" Conforti, a 20-year-old brunette who worked at Scott's discount store in Chicago. She would also play a role in the drama to come.

Tommy Carroll

Tommy Carroll was born in Red Lodge, Montana, in November 1900. He came from a poor family. His father was a day laborer and was frequently unemployed, and to make ends meet, the family took in boarders. When Tommy was very young, the family moved to Council Bluffs, Iowa, where Tommy's mother, Emma, died in 1906. His father died two year later. This left Tommy and his brother, Charles, as orphans and they were raised by their maternal grandparents, Levi and Lucinda Zentz. Levi was also a laborer, and the two children were forced to take menial jobs, such as selling newspapers on the streets, to help the family survive. They also joined a local gang of neighborhood toughs and began skipping school. Both boys would become criminals as adults, but in time, drifted apart.

Tommy left school after eighth grade, and with World War I raging in Europe and sentiment rising across the country for America to enter the conflict, Carroll enlisted in the U.S. Army on September 1, 1917. He served in the Quartermaster Corps and Signal Corps as a private, but when he went overseas he became a motorcycle dispatch rider and highly proficient with a machine gun. Tommy Carroll would not be the only gangster who made use of his military training and skills with firearms to become a better bank robber.

Carroll was discharged from the army in New York in June 1919. After returning to Council Bluffs, the young man, who all his friends described as "happy-go-lucky," worked as a taxi driver, hotel clerk, boilermaker, boxer, and did odd jobs. He also had a few brushes with the law and by the 1920s, had done some prison time. Despite the scars on his jaw and neck, he was a good-looking man with chestnut hair and blue eyes. By the 1930s, he was sporting a mustache, adding to his rakish persona.

With his post-military career doing very little to put cash in his pockets, Carroll began compiling a lengthy police record. He joined a car-theft ring and on January 24, 1920, was arrested by police in Omaha, Nebraska, in the act of stealing a car. It was his first arrest and he was sentenced to 60 days in the county jail. As soon as he got out, he went right back to work with the gang.

On May 24, 1921, Carroll, James Durick, and Dick Fernley stole a car in Council Bluffs and hid it in a barn in Florence, Nebraska, near Omaha. A snitch told the police about the theft and the authorities staked out the barn. At 11:00 p.m. on May 26, a vehicle with the three car thieves in it drove up. As they got out and approached the barn, the officers surprised the trio and Durick and Fernley were arrested. Carroll, however, escaped down a path that ran next to the barn. One of the policemen fired shots at him, but missed.

On October 21, 1921, Carroll landed in jail again in Council Bluffs, this time for auto theft and public drunkenness. He was sentenced to spend five years at the State Reformatory at Anamosa. He spent the next 16 months locked up and was released on June 18, 1923. After his release, he took a job at a piano manufacturing business in Bellevue, Iowa, where he worked until his parole ended in 1924.

Four months later, though, he was arrested again, this time for a grocery store robbery in Kansas City, Missouri, but the case was dismissed. The following year, he was arrested on suspicion of murder in Kansas City, but that charge was also dropped.

After that, Carroll went east to the St. Louis area. On August 11, 1925, he was arrested on suspicion of robbery. He was released five days later because of insufficient evidence. In November, he was back along the Mississippi River because he married a drug addict named Viola in East St. Louis on November 25. But he didn't stick around for long.

In September 1926, he was arrested in Tulsa, Oklahoma, for having concealed weapons when he was found sleeping in a brand new Nash sedan. He had stolen the vehicle 11 days earlier in St. Joseph, and when investigators made the connection, they released Carroll to their counterparts in St. Joseph. They turned Carroll over to the U.S. marshal in Kansas City, who charged him with violating the Dyer Act, which made it a federal crime to transport a stolen car across state lines. He was released on a $2,500 bond and promptly skipped town.

In February 1927, he was back in Kansas City. On February 19, he attempted to rob a grocery store that was owned by John and Catherine Gunter, but a city detective named Frank Rogers was in the store at the time and fired two shots at the bandit. Both shots missed as Carroll was fleeing without any of the cash from the register. On February 28, with James Roark and Martin Wilson, Carroll robbed a Kansas City soda shop proprietor named Joseph Soebel of $3,340. Later that day, the three were arrested. While in custody, Carroll was charged with the attempted robbery of the grocery store two weeks earlier. On March 24, after a jury had been impaneled, Carroll decided to plead guilty to the soda shop robbery and was sentenced to five years in the state prison at Jefferson City. Roark and Wilson were tried and sentenced the following week.

Carroll served three years of his sentence and was released on April 26, 1930. Less than a month later, on May 21, he was arrested again for stealing the Nash in St. Joseph and was charged with violating the Dyer Act. Tried and sentenced, he was given a sentence of 21 months at Leavenworth. He worked as a plumber while he was there and racked up numerous violations of prison rules, mostly for loitering and talking. He was released on October 26, 1931 – and it was the last time that he ever saw the inside of a prison.

In February 1932, Carroll and Viola opened a restaurant in Mankato, Minnesota, briefly trading in his gun for an apron. However, by July, Carroll had become tired of hard work and little money, and he abandoned his wife when he fell in love with a 20-year-old nightclub singer known as "Radio Sally" Bennett. She was great at singing Irish tunes like "Danny Boy" and playing song requests on her ukulele at the Boulevards of Paris club in St. Paul. Carroll was immediately smitten on the night that he came in with some pals and asked her to sing at his table. He came back every night for the next three weeks and told her that he was a gambler and a bootlegger. Although she refused to get married, Sally agreed to live with him.

For six months during the spring and summer of 1932, the couple lived in a second-floor apartment in St. Paul. Pete and Mary Vogel, a foundry worker and a schoolteacher, were their landlords and lived on the first floor. The Vogels had two sons, Jim and John. Whenever Sally asked Carroll what he was doing, or who his friends were, he would tell her that it was none of her business. They went to the movies three times a week, to parties at Lake Gwasso, and to the Green Lantern, a popular tavern for underworld characters who drifted into St. Paul, a city that offered protection for criminals.

Many of Carroll's gangster friends met at the apartment to discuss possible crimes. They were always respectful to the Vogels and their relatives. Loretta Murphy, a Vogel aunt, later recalled that "Carroll was a relentless flirt. He'd come to me and say, 'Don't you think we should have a drink, you know, before you go to bed?'"

Pete and Mary Vogel thought of him as a well-dressed gentleman, who often ate with them. After a dinner of plain fare like hamburgers and potatoes, he would often give them $10, a tidy sum during the Depression.

One night, Carroll saw police officers enter the Vogel home and, thinking they had come for him, climbed out of a window to escape. However, the police had been called to the home after local thugs had stolen $10 from John Vogel when he was on the way to the grocery store. Carroll told the young man, "Next time that happens, you let me know and I'll give you the money. We don't want the police here."

It was obvious that Carroll was on the wrong side of the law, but the Vogels overlooked it because he was both generous and kind to the family. But even so, they had no idea just how far on the wrong side of the law that Carroll actually was.

During the time that Carroll had been living in their apartment, postal inspectors had been looking for him, along with gang members Otto V. Shreck, William L. Schepers, Richard Pyes, and Charles Fisher in connection with a series of 38 mail and postal burglaries in Minnesota, Iowa, and Wisconsin. Most of the crimes involved blowing safes and stealing government property, stealing cash, stamps, and postal savings certificates.

Carroll stayed one step ahead of the inspectors until May 17, 1933, when his luck finally ran out. He was arrested on May 17, 1933, with burglary tools in his possession. They were able to link him to only one of the robberies and he was released on a $15,000 bond on June 12, but skipped out of St. Paul. He eventually hooked up with Nelson in Indiana and became part of his new gang of bank robbers.

Eddie Green, who also joined up with Nelson, had a flair for planning successful bank robberies and setting up escape routes. The "jug maker" was born in Pueblo, Colorado, on November 2, 1898, to John and Margaret Green, who had four other sons. His father, a steelworker, died when Eddie was three, and in 1906, the family moved to St. Paul. All of the boys would eventually get into trouble with the law.

Up until 1913, Eddie attended Franklin School, where he graduated eighth grade. His first job after school was as a credit department clerk and he later worked as an ironworker. During World War I, he served in Britain's Royal Navy and served on a ship transporting troops.

Green's first brush with the law occurred on August 11, 1916, when he was arrested by the police in Milwaukee for driving a stolen vehicle while intoxicated. He spent six months in jail. After his release, and his stint in the Royal Navy, Green seemed to live a law-abiding life until late in 1921, when he joined the large, shotgun-wielding John C. Ryan gang, which robbed the Crane & Ordway Company payroll on December 23. Green's brother, Francis, who was employed by the company, was suspected of providing inside information to the gang.

On July 17, 1922, Green was arrested by the St. Paul police for robbing the Park Theater and for a burglary that netted only $354, but he was released. On August 8, Green and another man were picked up by police in Des Moines, Iowa, on suspicion of being auto thieves and fugitives from Minneapolis. Green's stolen car contained safecracker tools. Four days later, Green was turned over to the sheriff in St. Paul.

He was one of several prisoners in the Ramsey County Jail when a dozen members of the John C. Ryan gang, impersonating federal Prohibition agents, attempted to free Green and Ryan from the facility. Newspapers called it "the most daring jail delivery ever perpetrated in an American city."

Eddie Green

Gang members stormed the building, scooping up keys, and going in search of Green. They found him on the second floor, but none of the keys would work. However, they were able to find the keys to the jail's hospital, where Ryan was recovering after being wounded in the leg during an attempted robbery of St. Paul's Park Theater in July. Ryan, on crutches, fell down the stairs but still managed to join his men, who fled in a large touring car after locking the jailers inside of the building. Since the bandits had cut both telephone lines to the jail, the captive law officers had to set off the fire alarm to be rescued.

The next day, Ryan and six of his gang, including Green's brother, were arrested at a rooming house of Mrs. Emma Powers, an aunt of the Green brothers.

Meanwhile, things were getting worse for Green, who was still in jail. He was identified by two of the victims of the December 23 payroll robbery as one of the bandits. He was found guilty of first-degree robbery, despite claiming that he was sick in bed at the LaSalle Hotel in Minneapolis at the time of the heist. Dr. Clayton E. May testified that Green was telling the truth, but the jury wasn't impressed. He was sentenced on two counts of robbery to terms of 40 years and five years at the Minnesota State Reformatory in St. Cloud.

Green's high-strung personality ended up getting him sent to solitary confinement several times for a variety of offenses, including striking other inmates and "imitating ladies singing" after a chapel service. According to the prison physician, Green was "the type with criminal tendencies, selfish, impulsive, and hard to manage." His bad record got him transferred to the Minnesota State Prison at Stillwater in July 1923. He was released on July 1, 1930, and returned to Minneapolis, where he completed his parole in January 1932.

By September of that year, Green was living with a divorcee Bessie Skinner. Bessie had a reputation in the underworld for being exceptionally smart. She had grown up in North Dakota and moved to the Twin Cities, where she worked as a waitress and a hostess in a nightclub called the Hollyhocks Inn in St. Paul, which was owned and operated by St. Paul crime boss Danny "Dapper Dan" Hogan. He was slain by enemies in 1927.

Bessie was also friendly with the next crime boss, Harry Sawyer. She later operated a haven for bandits, especially for the Barker-Karpis gang, called the Alamo Roadhouse on Highway 1, north of St. Paul, until June 1933. She met and befriended such criminals as Verne Miller and Frank Nash, the instigator and the victim of the Kansas City Massacre.

After leaving prison, Green lived a quiet, unassuming life as a shoe salesman. His neighbors in Minneapolis were unaware of his ties to the criminal underworld. On January 28, 1933, he took part in a Kansas City bank robbery that netted $14,500. Earl Doyle was the leader of the crew, which included Green, Thomas "Buck" Woulfe, and "Dago" Howard Lansdon. A North Kansas City marshal named Edgar Nall and Thomas Woulfe were both seriously wounded. On April 11, Woulfe died soon after being captured.

Green joined up with another gang on April 4, 1933. Made up of Green, Alvin Karpis, Dock Barker, Volney Davis, Earl Christman, and Jess Doyle, and armed with machine guns, rifles, handguns, and several hundred rounds of ammunition, they robbed the First National Bank of Fairbury, Nebraska, of over $15,350. Police and volunteers rushed to the bank and in the battle that followed, eight citizens were wounded and Christman was mortally wounded. The body count likely would have been much higher, but two of the gang's machine guns jammed.

Christman was taken to Verne Miller's home in Kansas City, where he died from his wounds. Green stayed at his side until his death. Miller's home was considered a safe refuge for gangsters and it would be there, it is believed, that Miller met with Pretty Boy Floyd and Adam Richetti to plan the June 16, 1933, attempt to free Frank Nash from custody at Union Station in Kansas City. After Christman died, the gang members traveled to Kansas City, where the Barker-Karpis gang was living that spring.

Soon after, Green and Bessie moved into an apartment on Kedzie Avenue in Chicago, in close proximity to the homes of other members of the Barker-Karpis gang. Later that year, they followed Karpis back to Minneapolis and arranged for the money and bonds from the Nebraska robbery to be laundered through underworld connections.

Eventually, the casual violence of the Barker-Karpis gang became too much for Green. During an August 30, 1933, robbery at the South St. Paul Post Office, in which one policeman was killed and another wounded, Green told his girlfriend "how crazy the whole plan was. Without necessity, they shot down individuals during the course of the robbery." Thanks to this, along with other overly violent events that occurred in the course of their robberies, Green began serving as an "underworld post office," acting more as a contact for various members of the gang instead of an actual participant in the bloodshed.

Green and Bessie seemingly lived a quiet, normal life, and neighbors considered them ordinary people. Green was smart enough not to make expensive purchases that would attract attention and he managed to keep his gangster pals away from his home. He used safe houses where they could meet and hide out and he left to go to these places each morning, giving the appearance that he had a regular job.

In the summer of 1933, Green hooked up with Nelson's new gang, offering advice on the best banks to hit and planning getaway maps that could be used to get the bandits out of the towns where the banks were located. It was meticulous work, but Green was highly skilled at it and was able to bring an air of professionalism to the mercurial little gangster's outfit.

In time, Nelson and Dillinger would join forces into what the newspapers would call the "Second Dillinger gang," a designation that irritated Nelson and would mark the bloodiest period in Dillinger's history as a criminal.

6. "Desperate Dan"

As the weeks passed during the summer of 1933, Captain Matt Leach of the recently formed Indiana State Police began to see the name "Dillinger" associated with an increasing number of crimes. He was notified when a confession followed the robbery of the Bide-A-Wee tavern, naming "Dan Dillinger" as one of the bandits. Leach guessed correctly that Dillinger had been involved in the Daleville robbery. Employees of the bank had described him and reporters from the Muncie, Indiana, newspaper started calling the outlaw "Desperate Dan." This marked the first time in Dillinger's criminal career that he had received notoriety in the press. It would not be the last time and, before long, they were going to start getting his name right.

Matt Leach would come to be one of Dillinger's greatest antagonists. The police captain wholeheartedly pursued the outlaw, only running into problems and roadblocks when the Bureau of Investigation belatedly decided to join the hunt for Dillinger. Until that time, it was Leach who was continuously on his trail.

The tall and wiry lawman was born in Croatia under the name Lichanin to a naturalized American mother. Adopted in the United States by a family named Leach, he worked as a wood finisher in Illinois, served in World War I, and finally became a law officer in Indiana. As a new breed of lawman, he believed that psychology should be used when dealing with criminals, and he studied and used the most up-to-date police methods available at the time. His rise in the Indiana State Police, which at that time had a force of only 42 men, including clerks, was very rapid, and he took orders directly from Governor McNutt.

Leach, author John Toland wrote, was a man of conflicts. He was hot-tempered and yet capable of unusual self-control; intense, nervous, yet one who could accept setbacks with stoicism. He was a self-educated, self-polished man whom many assumed to be a college graduate. Even Dillinger knew what a dogged lawman Leach could be. He once joked, "Someday that guy will try to have me indicted for shooting Abe Lincoln."

On July 22, Frank Hope, Dillinger's apparently clueless parole officer, drove to Mooresville, where he was told at the Dillinger farm that John was visiting his sister, Audrey Hancock, in Maywood, about 15 miles away. From Audrey, he learned that John had taken two of her daughters for a ride and might be at an Indianapolis gas station, which was run by two of her sons. Hope drove to the station, but Dillinger wasn't there either.

Thinking ahead, Hope had two deputy sheriffs stationed at the Hancock home, but when Dillinger came by to drop off his nieces, the lawmen were sleeping in their car. Hope then set up a personal stake out of the Dillinger farm, hiding in an orchard with a gun, but he never saw the outlaw.

Dillinger would never see his parole officer again.

Dillinger's next bank robbery was the smoothest one of his career so far. He, Harry Copeland, and Hilton Crouch, a professional racing driver who was good at getaways, hit the First National Bank of Montpelier, Indiana, and made off with a $10,110 on August 4, 1933. Dillinger strolled into the bank, yelled, "This is a stick-up!" and then leapt over the cashier's cage barrier, and scooped up the money.

According to one account of the robbery, two men, Al Wikel and John Fox, were leaning against the wall outside of the Kroger store, which was next to the bank, when the three robbers walked out. Dillinger and Copeland passed within 10 feet of the men, carrying bags of cash. Fox jokingly said to Wikel, "Look at the money those men have. Let's hold them up," at which Dillinger looked at them and grinned. The men then jumped in their car and drove away.

When local police learned of the robbery, they quickly set up roadblocks, but the bandits were already gone – which was particularly embarrassing since the offices of the Police Chief, the town's mayor, and an attorney were located above the bank. All contained rifles that could have been used to thwart the robbery.

The blue-green Dodge that had been used in the robbery was found abandoned near English Lake, Indiana, in the northeastern part of the state, later that same day. It had no license plates and the rear window had been knocked out so that the bandits could fire their weapons at any pursuers. Eight pounds of roofing nails were found in the back seat, which could have been tossed on the road to puncture the tires of a pursuing vehicle – if anyone had been chasing them, that is.

Dillinger's next robbery, however, did not go so well. On August 14, Dillinger, Copeland, Sam Goldstein, and two unidentified men, raided the Citizens National Bank in Bluffton, Ohio, but only gained $2,100. Two well-dressed men entered the bank around noon, while a third waited just outside the entrance, and two more stood on the street outside. One of the nattily-attired men walked to the window of assistant teller Roscoe Klinger and asked him for change for a five-dollar bill. After pocketing the bills and coins, the man pulled out a gun and shouted, "Stand back! This is a stick-up!"

Meanwhile, a customer entered the front door and was immediately covered by the man standing guard there. At this point, Dillinger vaulted over the counter and ordered cashier Elmer G. Romney and bookkeeper Oliver Locher to put their hands up. The bank employees and customer were made to lie down on the floor while the bandit shoved all of the money that he could find into a large sack.

After he had cleaned out the closest drawers, he demanded to know where the rest of the money was located. As Locher pointed to a large safe, the bank alarm went off. The other well-dressed bandit called out that they needed to leave, but Dillinger remained calm and collected. He asked again about the cash, looking for another teller window.

One of the bank robbers stationed outside panicked when the alarm went off and fired several random shots into the air to keep back the large crowd that was starting to gather to check out the excitement. Bullets struck several buildings, including a dry goods store, a drugstore, and a clothing store. Some townspeople later reported that they thought the shots that were fired were simply American Legion members setting off noisemakers while passing through town on their way home from a state convention in Lima.

Dillinger was the last to leave, taking $2,100 in cash and a .32-caliber revolver from the cashier's cage. As the bandits exited the bank, one of them began wildly swinging a machine gun toward the crowd, but luckily, he didn't fire it. They piled into their getaway car and roared out of town with a machine gun protruding from the rear window as a deterrent to anyone who decided to give chase. From start to finish, the robbery had taken less than five minutes.

Despite the alarm, the town marshal did not show up at the bank until the bandits were long gone. The automobile they escaped in was described by witnesses variously as an Essex, a Buick, a Chrysler, a Pontiac, and a Chevrolet. No one even bothered to go after them.

Still needing a substantial amount of money to break his friends out of the prison at Michigan City, Dillinger targeted a big city bank for his next heist – the Massachusetts Avenue State Bank in downtown Indianapolis, located near state police headquarters. At noon on Wednesday, September 6, Dillinger and Copeland strolled into the bank's lobby. Without a word, Dillinger, wearing a straw boater hat that was tipped jauntily to the side, scrambled atop a seven-foot-high teller cage and pointed a pistol at the assistant manager, Lloyd Reinhart. "This is a stick-up," he said.

Reinhart, deep into his telephone conversation, kept his head down and ignored the order, thinking that someone was joking with him.

"Get away from that damn telephone!" Dillinger snapped at him.

Reinhart looked up and found himself staring into the barrel of Dillinger's gun. He dropped the telephone receiver, realizing that it was no joke. Reinhart raised his hands and Dillinger hopped down and began shoving cash from the counters into a white sack. Behind him, Copeland was fidgeting, looking outside, and urging Dillinger to hurry several times. Within minutes, Dillinger and Copeland hurried out of the bank and into a waiting getaway car. Later, when they counted the take, it came to more than $24,000 – at the time the second costliest bank robbery in Indiana history.

With the number of Dillinger's successful bank robberies growing, Matt Leach launched an extensive search for the bandit. He raided several apartments, arrested several Dillinger associates, and set up stake-outs at the Dillinger family farm and at the home of his sister, Audrey, but had no luck.

On August 14, the day of the Bluffton robbery, the Indiana State Police arrested several Dillinger associates at an apartment in East Chicago, Indiana. One of those taken into custody was Clarence "Whitey" Mohler, an escapee from Michigan City who had drunk shellac to convince prison authorities that he had tuberculosis, which had earned him a temporary parole for treatment. Leach told him that, if he provided useful information, he would turn Mohler over to Kentucky authorities on a robbery charge instead of returning him to the Indiana State Prison to serve out the rest of his life sentence.

Captain Matt Leach of the Indiana State Police.

Mohler revealed to Leach that the third bandit in the Montpelier robbery had been Sam Goldstein, which was unknown at the time, and that Homer Van Meter had been working with Dillinger and that he, along with Dillinger and several others, had robbed a bank in Grand Haven, Michigan. (Note: The Grand Haven robbery was the work of Baby Face Nelson, without Dillinger or Van Meter) He also claimed (erroneously) that Dillinger had committed 24 bank robberies in the preceding 60 days, and then gave him the address of an apartment in Gary, Indiana, that the gang had been using for two weeks.

Leach quickly made plans to raid the apartment, where the state police captain was almost shot by three of his own men, who hid in the apartment, waiting for Dillinger to return. Leach knocked at the door and then stepped inside to find himself confronted by three drawn guns. They missed Dillinger, but they got Sam Goldstein, who confessed that Dillinger had been there and added that he might be staying in an apartment in Hammond, Indiana.

Police officers immediately went to the Hammond apartment, but no one was there. Nevertheless, the landlady was arrested when two .45 automatics were found on the premises. A stolen Pontiac, with its rear window broken out and a bag of roofing nails in the backseat, was discovered in the garage out back. A young neighborhood boy told Leach that several men in a Terraplane had been at the apartment just before the police had arrived. He said that he overheard one of them say that they were going to a resort in Gary and noted that three of the men looked like Dillinger, Copeland, and Van Meter. He also told Leach that he had called the Gary Police Department to report the presence of Dillinger and the other gangsters, but the police refused to believe him. When Leach raided the Gary resort, the bandits were nowhere to be found.

Three months of robbing banks had finally provided Dillinger with the cash that he needed to free his friends from the prison at Michigan City.

Dillinger recruited two women – Pearl Elliott, the owner of a nightclub and brothel in Kokomo, and Mary Kinder, Harry Pierpont's girlfriend – to help in the escape attempt. Elliott had been involved in Pierpont's Kokomo bank robbery and since Pierpont never gave her up to the cops, she was willing to help break him out of prison. Pearl's job was to give money to the person who would bribe the prison guards. Mary was to provide clothes, money, and an apartment in Indianapolis where the escapees, including her brother, Earl Northern, could hide out after the prison break.

One evening in early September, Dillinger carried out his plan. He wrapped three loaded guns in newspaper and tossed them over the 30-foot wall that was located just behind the state prison's athletic field. Pierpont was supposed to pick them up, but other inmates noticed the guns first and they turned them in to Deputy Warden H.D. Claudy. The prison break was now delayed until Dillinger could come up with a new plan, but luckily, none of his pals were blamed for the attempt. Three convicts from Chicago were believed to be involved in an escape plot and were put in solitary confinement.

A couple of weeks later, Dillinger tried again. To this day, no one is sure how he slipped the second batch of guns into the Michigan City prison.

According to some accounts, he paid a large bribe to a foreman at a Chicago thread-making factory to allow several guns to be hidden inside one of several barrels of thread that were sent to the shirt factory at the penitentiary. The top of the "loaded" barrel was marked with a large red X. According to another version, Dillinger once again tossed the guns over the prison's walls. Whatever happened, the guns finally ended up in the hands of Dillinger's pals.

By the time this happened, though, Dillinger was in hot water of his own.

Back in July, Dillinger had driven to Dayton, Ohio, to visit a married girlfriend named Mary Longnaker. The two of them, along with Mary's friend, Mary Ann Buchholtz, traveled to Chicago to attend the World's Fair. While they were there, Dillinger amused himself by having his picture taken with a police officer that

Mary Longnaker and Dillinger at the 1933 World's Fair in Chicago. Dillinger thought it was funny that he had a police officer snap this photo of them together at the fair.

was patrolling the fairgrounds. He thought it was even funnier when he got the lawman to agree to take a picture of himself and Mary.

On the way home, on July 24, they stopped in Michigan City so that Mary could see her brother, Jim Jenkins, who was serving time at the state prison. The two women went inside while Dillinger waited in the parking lot. Dillinger was infatuated with Mary, and had recently threatened her husband, whom she was in the process of divorcing. The two men had gotten into a scrap at the village pumping station where Howard Longnaker worked and they had to be separated by Town Constable Orth Stocker and others.

Unfortunately for Dillinger, the police had been watching Mary, for her brother was a friend of Dillinger and Pierpont's at Michigan City. Dillinger also didn't know that, when her divorce became final, Mary was planning to marry a young man that she had recently met. Dillinger was only a fling to her.

On August 25, the Dayton police received a tip from the Pinkerton Detective Agency that Dillinger was seeing a local woman. Mary's rooming house was staked out and her landlady, Lucille Stricker, was asked to be on the lookout for Dillinger. She finally called when Dillinger showed up on September 22.

"He's here," Mrs. Stricker told the night sergeant, W.J. Aldredge.

"Who's here?" he asked.

"John Dillinger, you dumb flatfoot!"

Within an hour, the police had the boarding house surrounded. Sergeant Aldredge and two detectives, Russell K. Pfauhl and Charles E. Gross, met the landlady at the backdoor. She told them that Dillinger was upstairs, in Mary's room. Pfauhl, armed with a shotgun, and Gross, carrying a machine gun, crept up the stairs and knocked on Mary's door. She opened it a moment later and the two men pushed into the room. Dillinger, wearing an undershirt and gray pants, was standing in the living room. He had been showing Mary snapshots from their trip to the World's Fair.

Pfauhl aimed his shotgun at Dillinger's head and ordered, "Stick 'em up, Johnnie. We're police officers!"

Dillinger dropped the photographs on the floor. For a second, his hands wavered.

"Don't, John," Pfauhl warned him," I'll kill you on the spot."

7. The Murderous Jail Break

On Thursday evening, October 12, Dillinger sat in the bullpen of the Lima, Ohio, jail, playing pinochle with three other prisoners. After his capture in Dayton, armed officers had brought him to Lima, a crossroads town in northwestern Ohio, to stand trial for an unremarkable bank robbery that he had pulled off in Bluffton that August. It wasn't an imposing jail, just a stone wing at the rear of Sheriff Jess Sarber's house on the town square. Sheriff Sarber was an overweight, kindly man, a former used car salesman who turned to law enforcement when the Depression put him out of business. His wife was a fine cook, serving the prisoners meals of pork chops, ribs, and mashed potatoes.

It was just another night in the Lima lockup. After dinner, Dillinger had joined the card game. Down the hallway, Sheriff Sarber was in his desk chair, reading the newspaper. His wife, Lucy, sat across from him, working a crossword puzzle. Around 6:00 p.m., the deputy, Wilbur Sharp, came in, loosened his gun belt and tossed it on a spare desk. He sat down to rest on the davenport.

At 6:25, the jail's outside door opened and three men in suits walked in. Mrs. Sarber, concentrating on her puzzle, never even looked up. "What do you need?" Sheriff Sarber asked the first man, who wore a dark gray suit, and overcoat, and light felt fedora.

"We're from Michigan City. We want to see John Dillinger," the man replied.

"Let me see your credentials," Sheriff Sarber said.

"Here's our credentials," the man said. It was the last thing that Sarber heard before the man raised a pistol and fired straight into his chest.

On September 24, two days after Dillinger's arrest in Dayton, his friends at Michigan City finally received the three automatic pistols that had been smuggled into the prison. Walter Dietrich saw the marked barrel containing the hidden weapons on a truck that was loaded with thread for the shirt factory. After removing the guns and hiding them in one of the factory's button boxes, he told Pierpont and the others that Dillinger had come through for them. At that point, they had no idea that Dillinger had been locked up in Ohio.

Among those who were part of the escape party were Pierpont, John Hamilton, Charles Makley, and Russell Clark. A few others planning to escape with them were Joseph Burns from Chicago, who was serving a life sentence for murder; Edward Shouse, who received a 25-year sentence in 1930 for robbery of the Grand Theater in Terre Haute; James Clark, serving life for robbery; and Jim Jenkins, brother of Mary Longnaker, serving a life sentence for murder. Mary Kinder's brother, Earl Northern, was also supposed to take part in the escape, but he didn't reach the rendezvous in time and was left behind.

The prison at Michigan City, from which Dillinger helped his friends escape.

On the day before the planned breakout, Pierpont, Clark, Makley, and Hamilton talked about the escape during exercise period. In August, Pierpont had been denied parole, even though the judge, prosecutor, and 11 of the original jurors (the 12th had died) had recommended his release. He was determined – as were the other three – not to be captured alive.

At 1:30 p.m. on a cloudy and chilling September 26, they decided to make their break. Pierpont and Clark approached the superintendent of the shirt factory, G.H. Stevens, and told him that he was wanted in the basement. As Stevens went downstairs, Pierpont and Hamilton each pulled one of the smuggled pistols, while the others involved in the escape seized him. Hamilton told him, "Turn around, Stevens. We're going home, and you're going to lead us out. There won't be any rough stuff if you just come along and mind your business."

Meanwhile, Dietrich lured Assistant Warden Albert Evans into the basement by telling him there was a jug of wine there. Evans was also taken prisoner when he reached the basement. Pierpont stuck a pistol in his stomach as he snarled at him, "We're going home, and you're going to do what we tell you. If you try anything, you're dead where you stand."

One of the other convicts suggested that they kill Stevens and Evans, but Makley came to their defense. "We need 'em," he said. "They're going to take us out. Ain't you fellows?"

The convicts and their captives walked casually outside and across the yard. Stevens and Evans led the way, followed by three inmates carrying automatic pistols under stacks of shirts. The others followed, carrying concealed iron bars. They also had with them a heavy, five-foot-long steel shaft that could be used as a battering ram, if they needed it. No one was suspicious of the strange procession. One guard on the wall was even asleep. Hamilton tried to get the attention of a friend in hopes that he would join them, but the convict walked past without noticing him or any of the others.

At the first of the three steel gates that separated them from the outside world, Evans whispered to a guard, Frank Swanson. "They've got guns. Open the gate or they'll kill us."

Swanson unlocked the metal barrier and was forced to join the group. The guard at the second gate, Guy Burklow, opened it and fell in line without making a fuss once the guns were pointed at him. Fred Wellnitz, the guard at the third gate, however, was beaten unconscious when he tried to grab his rifle. Evans was also slugged when he complained about the beating. Using Wellnitz's keys, the escapees opened the gate and entered the administration building, where they spotted Lawrence Mutch, superintendent of prison industries. Two of the inmates grabbed him and hustled him out of the room, forcing him to take them to the prison arsenal. When he refused to open the arsenal door, he was beaten severely.

The prisoners rounded up eight clerks, including two women, and Warden Kunkel, who they did not recognize, and forced them into the vault. When Finley Carson, age 72, moved too slowly, one of the convicts cursed him and shot him in the stomach. Chief Clerk Howard Crosby hid under a desk, grabbed a telephone, and called the local police. He whispered, "There's trouble out here at the prison! Send policemen and guns!"

Jenkins grabbed one of the guards that he particularly disliked and asked Pierpont for a gun. He told the trembling man that he was going to kill him.

"We're out of here. Why kill anyone?" Pierpont asked.

It was pouring down rain when 10 convicts fled through the main entrance at the same time that Harrison County Sheriff Charles Neel was delivering a prisoner. Dietrich, Burns, Fox, and James Clark forced Neel into his car and drove away. The other six men, led by Pierpont, ran to a Standard Oil station across the street from the prison's main gate. One of the convicts fired several shots at the prison.

The owner of the station, Joe Pawleski, was standing next to his car when the men came running across the street. Two of the convicts, both armed, demanded his keys, threatening to "blow his brains out" if he didn't hand them over. Terrified, Pawleski began to run with the keys still in his pocket. He was running toward a neighbor's house, where he knew he would find a gun. One of the convicts started shooting at him, while another screamed "Give it to him! Give it to him!"

Pawleski later told reporters, "They acted like crazy men, and I guess that's why their aim was so poor."

Three more shots were fired. One bullet passed through the service station owner's jacket sleeve. He finally made it to safety and the convicts began looking for another means of escape.

They quickly flagged down a passing automobile driven by Herbert Van Valkenberg of Oswego, ordered Van Valkenberg, his wife, and 89-year-old relative Minnie Schultz out of the car, and drove it away. A few minutes later, the general alarm at the prison was sounded, sending the region into a state of panic.

Roadblocks were set up as radio broadcasts alerted everyone to the escape. Volunteers were called out throughout the state and a 500-man posse was organized. There were countless reports of fugitive sightings, however, most of them turned out to be false. After prison officials locked down the remaining convicts, the prisoners cheered and rattled their cell doors in celebration.

Dillinger's pals – along with a few hangers-on – were free from Michigan City.

The two autos carrying the fugitives sped west on State Route 12 toward Chicago, until the driver of the car carrying Sheriff Neel turned south onto a side road. Going too fast, the driver lost control and plowed into a ditch. Unable to get the car to move, the four convicts, dragging Neel along with them, walked to a nearby farm owned by Carl Spanier and forced Spanier to drive them south in his car. When the auto ran low on gas and they stopped to refuel, the farmer escaped. The fugitives abandoned Spanier's car and took Neel into an area of thick underbrush and woods, where they hid, plagued by rain and a lack of food.

When they'd finally had enough, the escapees decided to leave Neel tied up in the woods. However, Clark argued that the elderly sheriff might die if he was left in the rain. Burns, Fox, and Dietrich agreed and told Clark he could stay with Neel while the others moved on.

The other men left and Clark waited until about 3:00 a.m. before pulling Neel to his feet and walking to Highway 6, where they caught a ride to nearby Hobart, Indiana. The lawman bought food for himself and Clark, and even gave the convict his topcoat to wear so that he could hide his prison uniform. Afterward, the two took a bus to Gary, where Clark released Neel, who hiked over to a local police station. Everyone at the station thought Neel had been killed by the escaping convicts, since three state militias had been searching for him but no one had seen or heard from the sheriff since the breakout.

After arriving in Gary, Clark hailed a taxi and made his way to Hammond, Indiana, where he was arrested later that day after the police questioned taxi drivers about suspicious passengers. Clark had managed to elude the authorities for three days.

The other six fugitives, who fled in the second car, made their way to Indianapolis. At about 3:00 a.m. on the morning after the escape, they knocked on Mary Kinder's door. Pierpont insisted that Mary, who was not expecting them for another day, provide them with a place to hide out. Since her parents were in her apartment, she had to take them elsewhere. Still in their prison uniforms, they went to the home of Ralph Saffel, a young man that Mary had been dating, and forced him to shelter them before sending him downtown with Mary to buy them some clothes.

Pearl Elliott was at Saffel's home when the two returned. Mary had called her before going downtown and had told Pearl to bring money. For the rest of the day, the fugitives bathed, shaved, changed clothes, and divided up the money that Dillinger had left for them with Pearl. Harry Copeland came by late that night, and everyone except Saffel left for a new hiding place that Copeland had found. Saffel was warned to keep quiet, or else.

That same day, two detectives showed up at Mary Kinder's apartment. Her sister, Margaret Behrens, told them that Mary had not been home since the previous night. Margaret was known as "Silent Sadie" because she had not talked about a bank robbery her husband had committed in 1927 and for which he was jailed. She had been arrested during the investigation of the robbery, but was released after a short stint in custody.

But the Indianapolis police had received a tip that the convicts were in the home of a local woman and Mary was suspected, but they could find no trace of her. More tips came in, stating that the convicts had been seen in Brownsville, south of Indianapolis, the next day. A getaway car and prison jackets belonging to Shouse and Makley were found by police at about 7:00 p.m. Two hours later, the fugitives commandeered a sedan in Franklin, Indiana, owned by Frank M. Ratcliffe, and forced him to drive them several miles east of the city before releasing him.

Mary Kinder

Meanwhile, Matt Leach heard a report on radio station WIND about a woman who claimed she had been questioned by two escaped convicts about the location of a certain auto garage. In the background were the sounds of sirens and gunfire, leading Leach, like most listeners, to believed that the fugitives had been cornered and were shooting it out with police. Leach hurried to the scene of the "gun battle," only to find a director and a troupe of actors. Angry, he had the director arrested when the group admitted that they had merely been performing a crime drama.

Lawmen in Brazil, Indiana, spotted Ratcliffe's stolen auto at about 8:45 p.m. on September 29, but the fugitives got away. At 1:30 a.m., on September 30, state police Sergeant Bert Davis, in a patrol car near Indianapolis, saw a suspicious-looking car heading for the city. With siren screaming and red lights flashing, he chased after the auto at speeds up to 80 miles per hour and was very close to the vehicle as it entered the western suburbs. The driver of the fleeing auto suddenly screeched to a halt at an intersection, and Davis roared past.

The driver whipped around the corner and a bizarre accident took place. The auto made a wide turn and struck a light pole and when it did, the rear door of the car flew open and James Jenkins fell out. He scrambled to his feet, but with Sergeant Davis turned and closing in, Jenkins was left to fend for himself. The car continued to speed west and the next day, Ratcliffe's car was discovered abandoned in Greencastle.

Jenkins fled into the night. As he ran away, Edward Watts, a local jeweler, fired at him but missed. A few hours later, Jenkins came upon Victor Lyle, a young man just getting home from a late date. Jenkins asked him for a ride, telling Lyle that he was in bad shape because he had been in a fight "over on Route 40." Lyle agreed and let the bandit into his car. Once inside, Jenkins pointed a gun at him and told him to drive south and keep away from the main roads.

When Lyle told him that he was low on gas, Jenkins directed him into a filling station. While the fugitive was trying to get the attention of the attendant, Lyle threw the car into gear and sped off. He contacted the police in Bloomington around 3:00 a.m. Despite the early hour, a group of armed volunteers soon formed. It was made up of state police, deputies, farmers, and men from a local Civilian Conservation Corps camp.

Somehow, Jenkins managed to elude them and reached the village of Bean Blossom, Indiana, later that day. He asked a man named Will Altop if there was an auto garage in town, explaining that his car had broken down. Altop was suspicious of the man and found three friends – storekeeper Herbert McDonald, Ivan Bond, and farmer Benjamin Kanter – and together, they drove around looking for Jenkins so that they could ask him some questions. They soon found him and offered to help him if he could show them that he was unarmed.

Although Jenkins called to him, "Don't get out!" McDonald walked toward him with a shotgun. Jenkins jerked out his revolver and fired twice, hitting McDonald in the right shoulder. Standing just 10 feet away, Kanter fired at Jenkins with a shotgun, somehow missing him with the first blast. He quickly fired the second barrel and this time struck the bandit on the side of the head. Jenkins spun around and fell to the ground. He was taken to a doctor in Nashville, Indiana, where he died.

The state police and Jenkins' father, George, a Pentecostal minister, identified the body. Reverend Jenkins said, "I'm glad it's like this. Better this than that he'd killed somebody else."

After Jenkins' death, Pierpont, Makley, Russell Clark, Dietrich, Shouse, Copeland, and Mary Kinder hid out at a farm that belonged to Pierpont's parents near Leipsic, Ohio. For whatever reason, the police didn't get around to raiding the farm for several days. By then, the fugitives had fled to another hideout in Hamilton, Ohio.

From the moment that Mary had told them that Dillinger had been arrested, there was never any question that Pierpont's band wouldn't try and free him. After finding their new hideout, they began laying plans for Dillinger's rescue. To put their plan together, they needed money and for that, of course, they decide to rob a bank. Makley suggested that they hit the First National Bank in St. Marys, Ohio, his hometown.

On October 3, Pierpont, Makley, Hamilton, Clark, and Shouse drove to St. Marys, which was just south of Lima, where Dillinger was being held. They arrived in town just before 3:00 p.m., the bank's closing time. As it turned out, the bank had been officially closed by the U.S. Treasury Department for a bank holiday and was not scheduled to reopen for several weeks. Fortunately for the bandits, though, the bank had just received a large shipment of cash from the mint and was allowed to make change for local merchants, although it was not allowed to conduct any other business.

When the car belonging to the five bandits pulled to the curb in front of the bank, there was a large crowd across the street listening to a radio broadcast of the World Series. While one man remained in the car and another took up position in the bank's doorway, Makley, Clark, and Pierpont entered the bank. Pretending to read a road map, Pierpont approached the window of teller Roland Clausing. He then lowered the map and pointed a .45 automatic at Clausing. "Just stand still," he ordered the teller as he went behind the cage.

Ed Shouse

While one bandit watched the teller, another forced three employees and a customer into the director's room. When two more customers walked in, Makley, standing near the front door, pulled a gun, and took them to the director's room, as well. He returned to his post at the door.

Pierpont cleaned out all of the cash at the counter and then asked bank employees to open the small safe inside of the vault. But they told him that only conservator W.O. Smith could open the safe. At this point, Smith, who was an old friend of Makley's but did not recognize him at first, walked into the bank. Makley greeted him and then took him to the vault, where he explained to Pierpont that the safe was on a time lock. A few minutes later, the lock clicked off and the bandits forced him to open it up. Once it was emptied out, they herded a total of eight captives into the vault. As Pierpont was closing the door, Makley called out from the front, "Wait a minute – here's another one!" This final customer was also ushered into the vault.

Pierpont left the captives with a final warning: If they made any noises before the bandits had gone, they would "blow the side of the building in with submachine gun fire." An alarm was turned in, but no one heard it.

The robbery went off without a hitch, or as the newspapers said it, "with a nonchalance which amazed their victims." The outlaws drove back to Hamilton, Ohio, with an easy $14,000. The money, though, was too new to spend, and Mary Kinder spent several days washing and ironing the bills to make them look worn.

Once the money was safe to pass, they began reconnoitering Lima. Despite Matt Leach's warning that they might attempt a rescue of Dillinger, Pierpont could see no additional guards around the jail. They decided to launch their breakout on Columbus Day, October 12.

Sheriff Jess Sarber

When they arrived at the jail, Pierpont and Clark parked in front, while Makley, Copeland, Hamilton, and Shouse parked a Terraplane a block away. The six bandits gathered in front of the courthouse, then Pierpont, Makley, and Clark headed for Sheriff Sarber's office at the jail, while Copeland returned to the Terraplane. Shouse walked over to stand near the jail, and Hamilton moved into position by a theater behind the building. At the time, there were 16 prisoners being held at the jail, including Dillinger.

At 6:25 p.m., it was starting to get dark. The prisoner's dinner of pork chops and mashed potatoes had been served and the sheriff, his wife, and Deputy Wilbur Sharp were in the office. Both Sarber and Sharp were unarmed. Sharp's weapon was in its holster, on the spare desk, and Sheriff Sarber had a gun in the middle drawer of his desk.

When Pierpont, Makley, and Clark walked into the office, Sarber asked what they wanted. Pierpont replied that they were officers from the state prison and had come to see Dillinger. When Sarber asked for their credentials, Pierpont shot him with a .38 revolver. He fired twice, one of the bullets striking Sarber in the lower abdomen, and the other lodging in the wall. Falling to the floor, Sarber made an effort to rise, but Makley hit him in the head with a pistol, which accidentally discharged, making a deafening sound and filling the room with gunsmoke.

Sheriff Sarber was mortally wounded. Blood spilled from the hole in his abdomen and Pierpont leaned down and demanded the keys to the cells. Pierpont hit him twice more with the butt of his gun.

"Don't kill him!" Clark shouted.

"I'll get the keys," Lucy Sarber screamed. "Don't hurt him anymore!" She scrambled to her husband's side and grabbed the keys from the desk and handed them to Pierpont, who walked over to the barred door of the cell block. When one of the inmates peeked his head around the corner, Pierpont raised his pistol and fired a shot into the bullpen area. Pierpont yelled, "Get back, you motherfuckers! We only want John!"

At the sound of the first shots, Dillinger knew that his friends had arrived. Pierpont, grinning, unlocked his cell door. Dillinger asked his cellmate, Art Miller, if he wanted to escape with him, but when Miller refused, he said goodbye and shook his hand. Dillinger picked up his coat and hat and followed Pierpont out of the cellblock. Dillinger paused as they reached the office and he saw the dying sheriff, who had been kind to him during his imprisonment at the jail. He said nothing, but took Sarber's gun, which Pierpont handed to him.

Sarber called out from the floor. "Oh men, why did you have to do this to me?" he moaned. He turned to his wife, who hovered above him. "Mother, I believe that I'm going to have to leave you."

Although Mrs. Sarber begged to stay with her husband, Pierpont forced her and Deputy Sharp into the cellblock and locked the door. As the gangsters were leaving, they were seen by a policeman and a young man, Lowell Cheney. They fled the scene in two cars. After breaking a cellblock window with a chair, Sharp shouted to Cheney for help. The young man ran into the jail office and called the local police.

An ambulance soon arrived to take Sheriff Sarber to the hospital and he died 90 minutes after the escape. Sirens echoed through the streets of Lima that night, as police and volunteers arrived to man roadblocks that accomplished nothing. Early the next morning, the Pierpont home near Leipsic was raided, but no one was found. Fred Pierpont – who admitted that his brother and the other fugitives had used the farm as a hideout – was arrested and a stolen car was recovered on the property.

Meanwhile, Dillinger sped away with the gang, arriving at the rented house in Hamilton that night. At that point, Dillinger faced a decision. He could have left the gang and fled to parts unknown. He had accomplished what he set out to do – raising the money and making good on his promise to break his pals out of prison. They had returned the favor, so they were square. He could have walked away. Instead, he decided to stick with his friends and become a full-time bank robber.

8. Up North with Baby Face Nelson

While Dillinger and his friends were busy escaping from prison and the Lima jail, Nelson was also having a busy late summer and fall in 1933. On August 18, he and his cohorts robbed the Peoples Savings Bank in Grand Haven, Michigan, of $14,000. The holdup crew included Edward "Eddie" Bentz, an expert bank robber who schooled Nelson in the art of finding the perfect bank, organizing the robbery, and creating the perfect getaway map. Bentz only signed on to help case the bank and set up the robbery, but at the last minute, Nelson convinced him to be involved in the actual heist. The rest of the crew was made up of Nelson, Earl Doyle, Chuck Fisher, Tommy Carroll, and "Three-Fingered Jack" White. When the bank alarm was triggered, a number of townspeople rushed to the bank to see what was going on and spotted White waiting with the getaway car at the rear of the bank. When White saw the crowd, he drove off, leaving the rest of the gang behind.

When the bandits came out of the bank, using hostages as shields, they discovered the getaway car had vanished. During the gunfight that followed, Earl Doyle was wounded and captured, and four hostages – two locals and two bank employees – were wounded. The gunmen commandeered a passing auto and forced two women and four children out of the vehicle before fleeing town in it. The car was later abandoned, and the gang took another one, until it blew a tire and crashed into a tree. The bandits stole yet another vehicle and managed to elude the massive manhunt that followed in the wake of the robbery. Nelson swore that he would kill White for deserting them.

The next month, Carroll thought that the Union Bank in Amery, Wisconsin, a town that he had visited many times, would be easy to rob. Fisher, Thomas Gannon, and Van Meter joined him in the robbery on September 13. When assistant cashier Clifford Olson came to work early that morning, the four masked men came up to him carrying a shotgun, rifle, and two handguns. They forced Olson inside and then locked the door behind them.

Olson was told to open the vault, but he was unable to do so on the first try. A nervous Van Meter gave him several hard kicks to get him to focus his attention. Just as the vault was finally opened, head cashier Vincent Christenson walked through the bank's rear door, calling out to Olson that the lock on the door appeared to have been tampered with.

"That's all right," one of the bandits said, stepping toward Christenson and pointing a pistol at the cashier's head. "Come and lie down on the floor."

The bandits loaded two black satchels with $11,000 in cash and $35,000 in securities and escaped across the Minnesota state line.

In October, Nelson and the gang split into two groups and hid out in cabins at the Debago Resort on Round Lake and Louge Lake, both about 15 miles from the central Minnesota town of Brainerd – and its First National Bank. Nelson had scouted the bank himself and put together the plan. Early on the morning of October 23, Nelson, Homer Van Meter, John Paul Chase, Tommy Carroll, and Chuck Fisher left their cabins and headed for Brainerd.

Just after 6:00 a.m., three of the bandits surprised the bank's janitor as he arrived for work and they forced him to let them into the building. Two of the other men stood guard outside, with a machine gun hidden under a bushel basket. The crew inside, waiting for the time lock to open at 8:45, herded together the 14 employees who arrived for work and locked them in a washroom. The bandits chatted with their hostages and even allowed them to smoke as they waited.

But as time passed, things began to spin a little out of control.

About 8:00 a.m., Nelson, who was standing near the front door, grabbed 17-year-old employee Zane Smith as he entered the bank. For no discernible reason, he took hold of the young man's collar, swung him around, and punched him in the jaw. He then dragged him across the bank lobby floor and shoved him into an office with the bank guard and the janitor.

When the time lock clicked open, the bandits snatched up $32,000 in cash and vacated the bank. But as they fled, they sprayed the interior of the bank with machine gun fire. Some claimed that the outlaws laughed maniacally as chunks of plaster rained down onto the bank's marble floor.

9. The First Dillinger Gang

In October 1933, the "Terror Gang" as the press would dub them, set up their base of operations in Chicago. Not the leader of the group, but a member among equals, Dillinger was able to promote trust, loyalty, and confidence among the gang's members. He was also a "peace maker," always managing to smooth tempers and settle arguments when the others argued.

Pierpont was considered the "thinker" of the gang and he was more experienced than Dillinger, even though he often encouraged Dillinger to take the role of the leader. Most of the decisions made for the group were made by those two, or by Hamilton, who was the "old pro" among them. Mary Kinder often described Hamilton as being "nice and quiet as could be." Opal Long, who was married to Russell Clark, added that "somebody forgot to give John a memory. He'd forget the addresses of the places where we were staying, and he'd even forget the aliases he was using. He'd stumble into trouble and stumble out of it somehow."

The idea that there was an actual "Dillinger gang" was a product of the newspapers of the day. It was really more of a criminal community that included several robbers that Dillinger worked with when possible and when the law and luck allowed. The group lived in twos and threes in several apartments on Chicago's North Side. None of them drank hard liquor, sticking only to an occasional beer, so as not to draw attention to themselves.

In general, the bank jobs the gang pulled were well-planned and precisely timed. While scouting a bank for a robbery, two of the gang posed as journalists and were given a red-carpet tour by the bank's president, who took them around and bragged about the institution's security arrangements.

The female members of the entourage began to play an important role in the organization of the gang. Mary Kinder, Pierpont's girlfriend, became more widely known than most of the women who were referred to as "molls." Initially, a "moll" referred to a female pickpocket in the 1920s, but it evolved into a "gun moll" during the Depression era. At first, these women were a shadow of the men. They were unknown save for an occasional description furnished by an informant. There were no photographs. People assumed they were sexual creatures, basking in a sordid limelight. But, in time, as many of the women of the Dillinger gang were arrested, their stories dominated the front pages. They were easier to capture than their boyfriends and they often had to be left behind. Once in custody, they were photographed, often during or immediately after attempts to apprehend their companions, while emotions ran high. When news photographers were able to shoot high-speed photographs of the women going into custody, their subjects hid their faces. Designed to discourage later identification, these gestures were exploited by the press as physical signs of contrition – showing fear, shame, and modesty. It was a cheap thrill for newspaper readers. For three cents – the cost of a newspaper – they could get a look at the sleazy glamour of fallen women. Sex was an unapproachable subject in American in the early 1930s and this served as a juicy substitute.

They were not the usual humdrum stories about the proper women of Midwestern society. Yet the reporters took their cue from the style employed by those reporting on the ladies' auxiliary or church socials. These women, usually referred to as "girls," were described in terms of their tears, laughter, or confidential revelations. They were girls, but they were America's bad girls, even though some of them hated to be referred to in such a manner. Jean Delaney Crompton, sweetheart of Tommy Carroll, asked news reporters, "Please, don't call us molls."

And there is no question, they were much more than that. The women cooked or slipped out covertly for take-out meals when their men couldn't show their faces in restaurants. They bought and rented cars, rented apartments, and opened safe deposit boxes under assumed names. The girls learned to never leave behind too much money into a hideout, because a "bump out" by the police meant a lost deposit. This and other strategies became part of their domestic lives. Ironically, they had been raised to perform household chores and very little else by school systems unwilling to train girls into full employment possibilities. They had spent years in useless "homemaking" classes, but the girls managed to twist their lessons into becoming support staff for the gangsters they loved.

For the most part, the police viewed these women with contempt. They saw them as whores because sex without marriage, it was believed in the 1930s, must offer some sort of material benefit for the women. In the case of Mary Kinder, materialism might have been one motivation that stood out of the complex set of circumstances that drove her to Harry Pierpont. She had a photographic memory for the amounts spent on everything she acquired. She would recount, years later, these amounts to the penny.

Other factors spurred the hatred of policemen, who were outraged that a moll would have sex with killers. They saw them as accessories after the fact to every murder these men committed. Often judges and prosecutors shared this view, as did the Bureau of Investigation under the leadership of straight-laced J. Edgar Hoover. He fought a heated campaign against the Dillinger gang's women, writing, "She is more dangerous to society than the desperado himself. It is she and her kind who makes him seek a life of crime." Even years later, he continued to attack the women, long after they had served their sentences, writing essays that accused them of carrying venereal diseases, a largely erroneous claim. The "moll," he claimed, authored the moral collapse of the men around her.

Hoover's wild accusations about the women of the Dillinger gang were largely untrue, although they were essential to the organization of the gang. Mary Kinder had the strongest personality of the women, assuming a sort of leadership role among them. She was outspoken, aggressive, and the kind of women that

Opal Long (left) and Patricia Cherrington, two of the young women law enforcement referred to as Dillinger "molls."

Hoover would have undoubtedly been terrified of, either as a gangster's girlfriend or as a woman in legitimate business. The other women connected to the gang in late 1933 were Opal Long, Hamilton's girlfriend, Patricia Cherrington, and Evelyn "Billie" Frechette, Dillinger's pretty, dark-haired girlfriend, who was part Menominee Indian and had high cheekbones and large, brown eyes. Pat Cherrington had recently introduced Dillinger to Billie, who was a hatcheck girl at the Chicago nightclub where Pat was a dancer.

Billie Frechette was born in 1907. Her father was French and her mother was a Menominee Indian and she was born and raised on a reservation in Wisconsin. She lived there until she was 13, and then spent the next four years at a Catholic-run Indian school in Flandreau, South Dakota. She graduated in 1924, lived in Milwaukee for a time, and eventually drifted to Chicago. By 1932, she was a quiet young woman with a taste for whiskey, working as a hatcheck girl at the same club where her best friend danced. Brassy and melodramatic, red-headed Pat Cherrington was a party girl from Texas who dropped out of school at 13, was married by 15, and a divorced mother by her early twenties. She and Billie worked in a series of nightclubs and dated a number of questionable men. In June 1932, they were arrested with their boyfriends, a pair of stick-up men named Weldon Spark and Arthur Cherrington. The women were released but Spark and Cherrington were sent to Leavenworth for robbing a mailman. On the eve of their departure, the women impulsively married them.

In the summer of 1933, Billie and Patricia, never to be reunited with their husbands, were drifting through life, dating bad men, and living in rundown hotels. A gallbladder infection had ended Pat's dancing days, and she was rooming with her younger sister, Opal Long. No one knows precisely how the three young women became connected to Dillinger and his pals, but Billie would claim that she never forgot Dillinger's first words to her. He was standing beside her at the table and looked down at her with a grin. "Hey baby," he said to her, "Where have you

Evelyn "Billie" Frechette

(Left) Billie and Dillinger together

been all my life?" They danced. Dillinger was polite, which was enough for Billie. If she needed any further convincing, it was his cavalier attitude – and the large roll of bills in his pocket. After that night, she didn't want anyone else. "Why should I?" she later said. "He treated me like a lady."

Russell Clark found his wife, Opal, through friends in Chicago. Opal would later write kind things of their life together. "I'd had a pretty rocky time of it when he was gone," she said. "I was glad to see him, and I was scared of what was going to happen to him." Often Makley and Shouse stayed with them and they moved around to four or five different addresses in the Uptown neighborhood on the North Side.

Hamilton and Billie's friend, Patricia Cherrington, became involved during the summer of 1933. Pat, who had been born in September 1903, had a short-lived union with Chester Young, whom she had married at 15. In 1930, she met Bob Cherrington and he was sent up for a life sentence two years later. She took up with Harry Copeland for a time and then with Hamilton later on. Pat worked as a waitress and then as an interpreter of Russian and Egyptian dance. While working as a dancer in a nightclub, she was introduced to Hamilton by Dillinger. After a brief courtship, Hamilton asked her to marry him. Although she didn't want to get married – in part because she was still legally married to Bob Cherrington – she did agree to move in with Hamilton. She never did it for the money, she said, since she made over $100 a week as a dancer. She did it because she loved him.

In Chicago, Dillinger and Pierpont lived with Billie and Mary Kinder, renting a four-room apartment at 4310 Clarendon Avenue on the city's North Side. The bellman later recalled that the luggage that belonged to the two couples was always very heavy – machine guns and ammunition add weight, you see. Most mornings, everyone slept late, finally getting up around 10 or 11. Dillinger kept the guns locked in a closet and often handled the cleaning chores, wrapping a towel around his waist while he washed the dishes or mopped the floor. Mary and Billie liked to watch him, bemused. He explained that cleaning was a habit that he had picked up in prison and it helped him to clear his mind. They had a telephone, but never bothered to hook it up. Delivery boys rang the bell at all hours, arms filled with food from neighborhood restaurants and the delicatessen downstairs. When they arrived, Dillinger never answered the door.

Most afternoons, the couples went out driving, stopping at shops on State Street to buy new clothes. Dillinger bought several blue suits and a brown one, making sure that no one bought anything that was too flashy, or attracted attention. Although he did spend $149 to get a new winter coat for Billie. Dillinger took care of his clothes, always keeping his suits pressed and his hats dusted. Mary Kinder was impressed that he changed his underwear every day. With money in their pockets for the first time in their lives, all four of them spent a lot of time in the dentist's chair, enduring days of caps and fillings.

The evenings were for fun. They went to a movie theater almost every night. Dillinger, who had entered prison before the advent of talking pictures, was a movie fanatic. He pushed the group to see a new picture three or four nights each week. Soon, they had seen every movie on showing on the North Side. After the movies, they had dinner and then went to a nightclub, usually the College Inn or the Terrace Gardens. All of them stayed away from hard liquor, mostly drinking beer, and Dillinger drank less than the others. He really couldn't dance, but reluctantly allowed Billie to show him a step or two. Pierpont laughed from their table, refusing to step foot on the dance floor. Mary later wrote that she watched how kind Dillinger was to Billie on their nights out. Both had lived rough and disappointing lives and she could see that they were falling in love.

They saw little of the others during this period in Chicago. But every once in a while, Dillinger would have Clark, Makley, and Hamilton over to play poker. For a group of ex-cons, bandits, and killers, they were an amiable lot. Opal Long later stated, "They were all friends. They were like old graduates getting together, only their school was prison and the things they had to talk about were not football games and parties, but the way they 'snitched' on jail keepers and the weeks they spent in the 'hole' on bread and water. Those were the things that kept them together at a time when it would have been a lot safer to split up and go their own ways."

The one exception to this feeling of camaraderie was Dillinger's dislike of the gang's sixth member, Ed Shouse, a slick character that Dillinger was sure was trying to seduce Billie. The other men noticed the sarcastic comments that Dillinger aimed at Shouse, but it was the discovery that Shouse planned a bank robbery on his own that finally led to his exile. Mary Kinder overheard him trying to get Hamilton to join him. "You ain't going to do a damn thing!" Mary snapped at him. The other gang members voted to kick Shouse out that same night. The next morning, when he arrived at Dillinger's apartment, they each tossed him a roll of bills. Dillinger said to him, "There's your money. Now get your ass out."

With several new robberies planned, Dillinger and Pierpont decided that they needed more weapons – not just pistols but Thompson machine guns and bulletproof vests. On October 14, Dillinger, Pierpont, and Makley traveled just across the state line and raided the Auburn, Indiana, police station, surprising Fred Krueger, the officer on front desk duty at the time. He had just sat down to eat a bag of popcorn when two men in suits walked in. Both of them had a pistol in each hand. One of them spoke up, "You might as well sit still. We don't want to kill anyone unless we have to. Have you got any guns?"

"Yes," Krueger replied and slid his hand toward the weapon holstered on his belt.

"Oh no," the man said politely. "I'll get it."

Krueger and another officer on duty were disarmed and locked in a cell. Taking the keys to the gun cabinet, Dillinger, Pierpont, and Makley lugged a small arsenal out to their car: a Thompson machine gun, a .38 caliber Smith & Wesson, a .401 Winchester rifle, a .45 caliber colt, a 44-40 Winchester rifle, several hundred rounds of ammunition, and three bulletproof vests.

From Auburn, they returned to Chicago and their rented apartments. On October 20, they were back on the road, looking for more guns and ammunition. That Friday night, they walked into the city hall in Peru, Indiana, an hour north of Indianapolis, and put guns in the faces of the desk officers. "I haven't plugged anyone for a week," Pierpont said, "and I would just as soon puncture one of you cops as not."

Pierpont covered the officers while Dillinger and one of the others broke into the gun cabinet, emptied the contents onto a blanket, and then lugged it out to the car. The evening's take came to six bulletproof vests, two sawed-off shotguns, two Winchester rifles, and a half-dozen .38 caliber pistols. Before they left, they stripped the officers of their guns and badges, never knowing when a police badge might come in handy.

Armed to the teeth and with a solid plan, Dillinger and Pierpont felt ready to take on their first bank. They decided on the Central National Bank in Greencastle, Indiana, west of Indianapolis. It was home to DePauw University and that Saturday was Homecoming, which meant, Makley insisted, the bank would be flush with cash. At 2:45 on October 23, 1933, a black Studebaker eased along Jackson Street in downtown Greencastle and parked in front of the bank. Five men got out of it – Dillinger, Pierpont, Makley, Hamilton, and Clark. All wore overcoats with guns

Central National Bank in Greencastle, Indiana

hidden beneath them. Clark remained with the car and Hamilton waited at the bank's entrance. The other three men walked inside.

Stepping up to the fifth teller window, Pierpont, who with Dillinger had scouted the building a few days before while posing as news reporters, asked Assistant Trust Officer Ward Mayhall to change a 20-dollar bill. When Mayhall told him to go to a different teller, Pierpont opened up his coat and produced a machine gun instead.

Dillinger, pistol in hand, made a flashy leap over the railing that separated the bank's lobby from the teller's area, and herded the tellers into the vault room. Pierpont followed, and the pair quickly stuffed more than $18,000 from the cashier's cage into a sack. They also took bonds valued at over $56,000. Later, bank employees and customers would all comment on how calm and methodical the robbers were. The gang cleared the cash from drawers and counters into muslin sacks so efficiently that no one from the sheriff's office across the street ever realized that a robbery was in progress.

"It's five minutes!" Makley called, signaling an end to the agreed-upon time for the heist.

Dillinger jumped back over the railing. When he saw a farmer standing in front of the teller's cage and a small amount of money on the counter, he asked him, "That your money or the banks?"

"Mine," the farmer replied.

Dillinger grinned at him. "Keep it. We only want the bank's."

Seven words. That's how many it took to earn Dillinger a place in Depression-era American history. As news of the robbery made the newspapers, and Dillinger's comment to the farmer at the counter spread, many people across the Depression-ravaged country began to look at him as some sort of latter-day "Robin Hood," believing that he only wanted to steal from the rich. Of course, the only poor people that Dillinger and the others were giving money to were themselves, but to many, hit hard by bad times, they cheered the idea of anyone who struck back at the banks and the government, who they saw as the real villains of the day. After an editorial appeared in an Indiana newspaper that called for Dillinger's capture, a reader sent a letter that read, in part: "This person [the editorial writer] calls Dillinger cheap. He isn't half as cheap as a crooked banker or a crooked politician because he did give the bankers a chance to fight, and they never gave the people a chance."

Of course, what occurred as the bandits left the bank, but didn't get applauded because the newspapers didn't cover it, was that a customer who entered the bank as they were leaving was slugged in the face so hard by one of the robbers that he was knocked to the floor.

By the time the police finally did arrive, the outlaws were long gone. They easily avoided roadblocks by traveling a planned escape route all of the way back to Chicago.

In the wake of the gang's raids in Auburn and Peru, and the robbery in Greencastle, the state of Indiana entered a state of almost frenzied hysteria. Criminals and escaped convicts were certainly nothing new, but the Midwest had never seen anything like the heavily armed bandits who were now raiding police stations and robbing banks at will. These were stories that the people of Indiana were used to reading about from Texas or Oklahoma, where bandits like Bonnie and Clyde and Pretty Boy Floyd were wreaking havoc. Such things weren't supposed to happen in Indiana.

Scrambling to look like he was doing something, Governor Paul McNutt stationed 700 National Guardsmen at armories across the state. Guard officials announced that they were prepared to deploy tanks, airplanes, and lethal gas to fight the gang. They put up roadblocks all over the state, so many that the head of the State Police had to issue a statement to Halloween partygoers, warning them of anything that might cause Guardsmen to mistake them for Dillinger. American Legion members from Indiana volunteered to have 30,000 of its members deputized to patrol the highways. We can assume that they would not be armed with tanks or poison gas.

The editor of the *Indianapolis News* telegraphed the owners of the newspaper in Washington, D.C. He wrote: "Convict gang running wild. Can you have Homer Cummings offer federal aid to Indiana? One sheriff dead, one kidnapped, two police stations robbed of arms, bank raided." The attorney general passed the request on to J. Edgar Hoover, whose response was a cool one. Even if he had jurisdiction, which was unclear, Hoover knew the limitations of the Bureau. He preferred cases that he could win. A manhunt like this one, requiring a vast commitment of men toward an uncertain outcome, was a guaranteed loser. The Bureau was still fumbling around with the Kansas City Massacre investigation, which was going nowhere. To make matters worse, Bureau agents had recently botched the chance to arrest Verne Miller, the lead suspect in the massacre, in Chicago. Hoover had been incensed. He wanted nothing to do with the hunt for Dillinger. He noted in a memo: "I told [the attorney general's assistant] we had offered assistance with reference to fingerprint matters but in so far as helping to catch them is concerned, we were not [going to]."

With no help from the Bureau — which was likely for the best in those days — the responsibility for apprehending the gang fell to Matt Leach and the year-old Indiana State Police. Unfortunately for Leach, the State Police was soon regarded as being as comical as the Bureau. The *Indianapolis News* ran a cartoon featuring an armed gunman chasing a group of troopers around the state. The caption read *Happy Hunting Ground*. Leach pleaded for more weaponry, and Governor McNutt agreed, getting them $10,000 to buy bulletproof vests, machine guns, and 10 new patrol cars. To use them, though, Leach first had to find Dillinger. With no clue where he was hiding, or where he might strike next, he came up with a new ruse — to drive a psychological wedge between the gang's members. We have to assume that he did not consult with an expert on psychology before attempting this. If he had, he definitely would have been advised against further embarrassing himself.

Always a magnet for reporters, Leach gathered together a group of Indianapolis reporters and asked them for help. Leach said, "The real rascal that we have to deal with is Pierpont. He's a super egoist. We'll offend him deliberately and start jealousy in the gang. We'll name it the Dillinger Gang. That will cook Pierpont. He'll blow his top. After a lot of people have been killed and banks robbed, we'll wind it up and Pierpont will get the works."

Needless to say, the harebrained plan drew chuckles from Pierpont and Dillinger as they sat reading the newspapers in Chicago, far away from the Indiana roadblocks and state troopers. That time period was probably the happiest days of Dillinger's life. His profile was still low enough that he could live in the open, he had money in his pocket, his pals were gathered around him, and he and Billie were in love.

But it would be the last quiet time in Dillinger's career — a career that would be over in just eight months of blood, violence, and death.

10. High Speed Pursuit

As the days passed, Dillinger and the others began to grow wary of making new contacts in Chicago. Word on the street had it that Dillinger needed to be worried that the police search for him might bring heat on the Chicago Outfit and anger Frank Nitti, who had taken control of Capone's organization after his boss had been sent away to federal prison. As it would turn out, Dillinger had good reason to fear this.

The few people that the gang did see tended to belong to the many Indiana State Prison alumni who were also living in the city. The ex-cons bunked in crowded apartments, in rundown hotels, or with girlfriends, and were always looking to make a quick dollar. It was through this group, who were always under the eye of the Chicago police, that word of Dillinger's presence in the city filtered back to the growing number of lawmen and private detectives who were hunting him.

It was into this conglomeration of ex-cons that an insurance investigator named Forrest Huntington was able to insert a paid snitch and former Michigan City acquaintance of Dillinger's named Art McGinnis. In Chicago, McGinnis spread the word that he was working as a fence, looking to buy stolen bonds. Dillinger and Pierpont already had a contact who was trying to move the bonds from the Greencastle and St. Mary's banks. Each week, McGinnis passed on a number of rumors to Huntington, few of which he could verify. There were stories that Dillinger was trying to buy mortars at an army depot, scouting banks in Indianapolis, or planning to rob the Federal Reserve.

Matt Leach fought with Huntington over McGinnis, who he wanted to control himself. Huntington balked. He saw Leach as a publicity-hungry civil servant and blamed him personally for the bungled attempts to capture Dillinger that August. He was convinced that information he had given to Leach should have resulted in Dillinger's arrest. But since Leach had antagonized police officials all over the state, no one wanted to work with him, and so Dillinger had eluded capture.

Huntington's control over McGinnis was further complicated by the Chicago police, who placed the informant under surveillance as part of its own attempts to track down Dillinger. Huntington was obliged to sit down with Lieutenant John Howe, head of the department's Secret Squad, and strike a deal to get them to ignore McGinnis. If they did, he promised, they could handle Dillinger's arrest. Huntington pressed McGinnis to set up a face-to-face meeting where Dillinger could be captured.

On Monday, November 13, McGinnis called the investigator in an excited state. Dillinger had just been in McGinnis' apartment, McGinnis told him, looking to pass eight $1,000 Liberty Loan bonds. They had agreed to meet in a downtown parking lot that afternoon. But there was a glitch – McGinnis now wanted rewards he had been promised for capturing *all* of the gang members, not just Dillinger, and he refused to reveal the address of the parking lot until Huntington promised that the

Chicago police would *not* arrest Dillinger that day. He didn't want word getting out that he had been the man who ratted out Dillinger.

Huntington telephoned Lieutenant Howe, who checked with his superiors. They told him to use his best judgment. Howe told Huntington that they would just watch. There would be no arrests.

That afternoon, Huntington and Howe were sitting in a cafeteria in the Chicago Loop when a car driven by a man who looked very much like Dillinger picked up McGinnis on a nearby corner. Three hours later, McGinnis telephoned. He had driven around the city all afternoon with Dillinger and had dozens of stories to tell. Almost offhandedly, he mentioned that Dillinger was suffering from a case of barber's itch, an inflammation of hair follicles, which he had contracted in the Lima jail. McGinnis set up an appointment for him with a doctor named Charles Eye, who had an office on Keeler Avenue, just below Irving Park Boulevard. Once again, McGinnis insisted that Huntington refrain from anything that would lead to Dillinger's arrest.

Two of Matt Leach's men were in Lieutenant Howe's office when Huntington arrived to relay the news. They immediately telephoned Leach in Indianapolis, who, within minutes, began an angry series of calls with Howe and Huntington. Leach demanded that Dillinger be captured that night because they might not get another chance to take him. But Huntington, like his snitch, was eager to capture the whole gang, and Howe backed him up on this. However, the two men did reluctantly agree to allow Leach's men to accompany them that night.

At 7:15, Huntington, Howe, and Leach's men waited in a darkened car and watched as Dillinger arrived at Dr. Eye's office in an Essex Terraplane sedan. A man and woman, likely Pierpont and Mary Kinder, remained in the car while Dillinger went inside. A few minutes later, he came out and drove off. The officers let him go.

The next morning, when McGinnis checked in with Huntington, he told him that Dillinger had a follow-up appointment at Dr. Eye's office that night. McGinnis urged that this time the officers follow Dillinger to wherever he was living, where they could find the rest of the gang. By later afternoon, Lieutenant Howe was again refereeing an argument over what to do. Huntington agreed with his informant and wanted Dillinger followed. Leach, who had driven up from Indianapolis, wanted him captured, or better yet, dead. The argument was ultimately won by an officer who walked into Howe's office that day from Lima, Ohio. He argued that Dillinger should be killed to avenge the death of Sheriff Sarber.

By 7:00 that evening, three squads of Chicago police had gathered on a side street two blocks from Dr. Eye's office. The morning had seen a cold front blow into the city, driving temperatures down to close to the single digits. Leach was there, as were Huntington and Howe. Because Dillinger was wanted in Indiana, the squads had been placed under Leach's supervision. A short time later, Huntington and a Chicago office crept forward to watch Dr. Eye's office. At 7:25, Dillinger drove up in the Terraplane. Billie was with him. As the two men watched, Dillinger hurried into the building, leaving Billie waiting in the car.

Huntington hurried back to where the others were waiting and briefed them. Everything was set. The men piled into four cars and drove to their positions. Three of the cars pulled to the curb on Keeler, a quiet street, facing Dillinger's car. A fourth car, driven by a Chicago detective named Howard Harder, parked across Irving Park Boulevard, about 50 yards behind the Terraplane. Dillinger was now boxed in. Leach had taken aside one of his men, Art Keller, and told him that he had no interest in taking Dillinger alive. If Keller got the chance, Leach told, he should kill him.

As the clock ticked off the minutes, the men shivered in the unheated squad cars. They all saw Dillinger as he emerged onto the sidewalk and they saw him glance over at their cars, all parked so that they were the wrong direction on the street. He knew something was amiss. He opened the driver's-side door, slid behind the wheel, and told Billie to hold on tight. Before any of the police officers could react, Dillinger threw the powerful Terraplane in reverse, tires squealing, and roared backwards into Irving Park Boulevard traffic. Horns blared and cars slammed to a stop as Dillinger fishtailed into the busy street.

At the curb on Irving Park, Detective Harder yelled for his driver to ram Dillinger's car, but in his haste, he flooded the car's engine. Dillinger put the Terraplane into first and the car shot forward, heading east on Irving Park, narrowly missing several cars. Behind Dillinger, only one of his pursuers, a car driven by a Chicago detective named John Artery, managed to give chase. In Artery's passenger seat was Art Keller, the officer with orders to kill Dillinger. Artery pressed the accelerator to the floor and began catching up to Dillinger's car. Narrowly missing streetcars, autos, and pedestrians, both cars careened down Irving Park Boulevard at speeds approaching 80 miles an hour. Finally, able to draw even with Dillinger, Keller leaned out the window and fired at Dillinger's fleeing Terraplane. "Get down!" he shouted at Billie, who scrunched down on the floorboards.

Keller emptied a .38 and then a shotgun into Dillinger's car. Dillinger screeched right onto Elston Avenue. Keller managed to stay with him. The chase was short, lasting just over a mile, but it was a frantic one. Keller continued to fire at Dillinger and Billie, but neither were hit. At one point, Dillinger swung a sharp right off Elston, then swerved into a dead-end street. Behind him, Artery didn't react in time. He raced past the street as Dillinger reversed the Terraplane, tore off in the opposite direction, and made his escape. "That bird sure can drive," Keller muttered.

Dillinger and Billie abandoned the bullet-riddled Terraplane on the North Side and took a cab to Clark's apartment, where the gang was holding an impromptu party, dancing to music on a radio. Mary Kinder heard someone pounding on the door, opened it, and was surprised when Dillinger and Billie hurried in. Dillinger was sure that it had been a mob assassination attempt. It was not until he saw the morning papers that they were certain their pursuers had been police officers. Front page stories about the incident introduced Dillinger to thousands of Chicagoans who had never heard of him before. The *Chicago Tribune*, which claimed that Dillinger's "prowess in crime has been compared to the James boys

The bullet-riddled Terraplane was found abandoned the next day. The newspapers told about Dillinger's daring gunplay — even though he never fired a shot.

and Harvey Bailey," featured a breathless account of how police traded bullets with a machine gunner who fired at them from an unseen portal in Dillinger's car. In fact, the shoot-out, was not a shoot-out at all because Dillinger never fired a shot; he was too busy trying to drive.

While everyone had an idea about who had betrayed them, Dillinger and Pierpont were certain that it was Art McGinnis. They quickly moved out of the Clarendon Avenue apartment, and moved across town to Russell Clark's place. The Chicago police were close behind them, raiding the Clarendon Avenue flat the next day. Coincidentally, Dillinger's old partner, Harry Copeland, whose heavy drinking caused Dillinger to steer clear of him because he was a liability, was arrested the following night, after he pulled a gun on a woman with whom he was arguing in a North Side bar. Soon after, Pat Cherrington took up with Hamilton. Her sister, Opal Long, was already occupying Russell Clark's bed.

Dillinger refused to let the police disrupt his plans. Gang members had been trying to pass their stolen bonds through a fence in Milwaukee and, en route, had scouted the American Bank and Trust in the small town of Racine. That weekend, the gang rented an apartment in Milwaukee and drove around downtown Racine, studying the bank and creating an escape route. They had burned through a lot of their money and Dillinger had expensive dreams, including Florida vacations, buying an airplane, and planning for one last big job that could get him out of the bank robbing business for good. He and Pierpont made a plan to hit the bank on Monday.

Meanwhile, in Indianapolis, Leach received a package in the mail. When he opened it, he found an 1896 paperback book called *How to Be a Detective*. Many thought that Dillinger had sent it to him, but it was actually a prank by two local reporters.

Dillinger would have thought it was funny, though.

11. Robbery in Racine

On Monday, November 20, a car cruised to stop near the American Bank and Trust Company in Racine, Wisconsin. The brutal cold spell that had plagued the region during the previous week had passed, but a cool wind was blowing in off Lake Michigan. Russell Clark was likely the driver of the car, but records don't say this for certain. Witnesses to the robbery would count five bandits, but a man named Leslie Horner later confessed and was convicted of taking part. If this was true, then Clark was not along for the robbery. Whoever the driver was, he dropped off the others on downtown corners before parking in a lot behind the bank. The idea was that the outlaws could vacate the bank through the back door and have easy access to the getaway car and the escape route out of town.

One problem, though: the bank had no back door.

Pierpont was the first man into the lobby. He unfurled a Red Cross poster and without a word, hung it up in the bank's front window, blocking the view of the bank's interior from outside. Dillinger, Makley, and Hamilton walked inside a few moments later. At the cages, the head teller, Harold Graham, was counting a stack of bills. He had just placed a NEXT WINDOW, PLEASE sign in front of the window when Makley said, "Stick 'em up!"

Graham kept his head down, intent on his task and ignoring the order, thinking that someone was joking with him.

"I said, stick 'em up!" Makley repeated.

Graham still didn't look up. With a whiff of impatience, he said, "Next window, please."

Without a word, Makley shot him. The bullet went through Graham's right arm and lodged in his hip. He fell backward, stunned and bleeding, but as he did, he managed to press the alarm button. Outside, the alarm began to clang loudly, plainly heard up and down Main Street. On the sidewalks, passersby quickly looked toward the bank. Two more alarms rang at police headquarters. It was time to move.

Dillinger and Pierpont rushed past the teller cages, ordering all of the employees to lie down on the floor. Dillinger shoved the bank's president, Grover Weyland, ahead of him to the vault. He hustled him inside and then began shoving stacks of bills into a bag. Pierpont kept an eye on the front door.

At police headquarters, the police had a lackadaisical response to the alarm. The bank had suffered a series of false alarms in recent weeks, and Officer Chester Boyard just assumed that this was another one. He grabbed two men, strolled out to a squad car, and drove down the street to the bank. A few minutes later, Boyard was the first one out of the car at the bank. The moment that he entered the lobby, he heard a voice yell out, "Stick 'em up!" Before he could react, one of the robbers leveled a machine gun at him. Sergeant Wilbur Hansen was next inside, carrying a machine gun that was pointed at the floor. From the back of the bank, Pierpont shouted, "Get that cop with the machine gun!"

The American Bank and Trust Company in Racine, Wisconsin, located on the corner in the center of the photo

Makley, who was covering the lobby, turned and fired. A bullet grazed Hansen's right hand and tore through his side. He pitched forward to his knees, stunned by the shot. A woman fainted, collapsing onto the floor, and knocking over a vase of flowers, which shattered. Makley stepped over and tried to rip Officer Boyard's pistol from its holster. It wouldn't come free. He took a moment to unbutton the holster and take the gun. Outside, a third officer ran away down the street, looking for help.

By this time, a haze of gunsmoke was hanging over the lobby. Outside, a crowd was starting to form. The manager of Goldberg's Shoe Store, four doors north of the bank, hurried down to investigate. Officer Boyard made eye contact with him through the front door and vigorously shook his head at him. He ignored the policeman's warning and climbed onto the bottom sill of the window to peer into the bank. Makley saw him and fired a rattling burst from his machine gun, shattering the glass and sending the manager scrambling for cover.

Dillinger was nearly finished in the vault. By this time, he knew there was no back door to the bank and one glance out the back window told him that it was a long drop to the parking lot below. "We'll have to shoot our way out the front!" he yelled. He waved his gun at Grover Weyland and three female tellers who were cowering under the counter, beckoning them to come forward. When Weyland hesitated, Pierpont slapped him, sending his eyeglasses bouncing across the floor. Weyland glared at him and snapped, "If you didn't have that gun in your hand, you wouldn't have that much guts."

Before Pierpont could respond, Dillinger pointed to another police officer who had entered the lobby. Dillinger let out a laugh," Come right in and join us," he told the cop.

"What the hell is going on?" the policeman called out.

Officer Boyard shook his head at him and the man fell silent.

Each of the five bandits grabbed a hostage or two, and together, they headed out the front door. So many people had gathered outside on the sidewalk, though, that the gang literally had to push their way through them. A number of the onlookers, noticing Officer Boyard in the huddle, assumed that he had captured the bank robbers, instead of the other way around. They crowded forward to get a better look, while those at the front of the group yelled for them to get back.

As the bandits and their hostages parted the crowd, two detectives hurried around a nearby corner. When he saw them, Pierpont called out to Makley, who turned and fired a burst from his machine gun. The detectives took cover in the Wylie Hat Shop.

People were yelling, the machine gun was deafening, and yet people refused to move back off the sidewalk. They pressed forward even as the scrum of gang members and their hostages inched in the direction of the lakefront and their waiting car. In the confusion, several of the hostages slipped away into the crowd. At least one passerby found himself briefly taken hostage. With the noise and movement, the street was chaos. As the bandits finally reached the parking lot, Pierpont again saw the two detectives peering down the alley to the south. "Mack, there's that fella with the gun again, get him!" Pierpont snapped at Makley.

Makley swung the machine gun around and the weapon roared with another volley. As showers of dust, brick, and asphalt erupted around them, the detectives vaulted into the rear entrance of the Liberal Clothing store.

When the gang reached the car, Dillinger got behind the wheel. Pierpont grabbed Grover Weyland's collar, "C'mon, Mr. President, you're going with us." He turned to a teller named Anna Patzke and said, "And you in the red dress." The two hostages took positions on the car's running board beside Dillinger. Officer Boyard was placed opposite of them.

Dillinger gunned the engine and sped away, narrowly missing two running police officers. Weyland waved his arms as they passed, indicating that they should not shoot. With Hamilton reading the getaway map, Dillinger drove west across town, running two red lights before ending up in a traffic jam. They told Boyard to beat it and pulled the two remaining hostages into the car so that they wouldn't attract attention. Forced to slow down by the snarl of traffic, Makley began to curse. "Cut it out, Mack," Dillinger said, "we got a lady in the car."

Looking over at the teller, Dillinger grinned. "Maybe we oughta take you along. Can you cook?"

"After a fashion," Anna replied.

"Maybe some other time," he laughed.

The traffic jam cleared after a moment, and within minutes, they were driving on dirt roads through the open Wisconsin countryside. They stopped to change license plates, then again to fill up from a gasoline can that they had left hidden along the route. When Anna Patzke said she was cold, Pierpont lent her his coat. He gave Weyland his hat. Tensions between the two men had ebbed. Dillinger's mood turned buoyant. They stayed on country roads, passing several farms and, at one point, an old man on a tractor. Dillinger called out loudly to him and waved. The farmer waved back, happy to greet them.

Finally, they pulled over next to an opening in the forest and looked for a large tree. The two hostages were placed on opposites sides of it and their hands were tied together with shoelaces. When they realized the hostages were afraid that they were going to be shot, Pierpont soothed their worries. "Sorry, mister," he told Weyland, "I'll have to have my hat."

The gang was back in Milwaukee by the end of the day. Mary Kinder was doing laundry when they walked in, Dillinger teasing Pierpont because he had given Anna his new coat. After they divided up the loot from the bank, the take came to roughly $5,000 for each of them.

By nightfall, as lawmen and volunteers spread across southern Wisconsin in a vain attempt to track down the bandits, reporters and police from Milwaukee, Chicago, and Indianapolis descended on Racine. One of Matt Leach's men was there, and he quickly confirmed that the robbery had been the work of Dillinger. When reporters asked Grover Weyland what the gang had been like, he replied "genial." He also related the story of Makley being told to stop cursing in the getaway car because a lady was present.

This kind of small courtesy was becoming a Dillinger trademark. The bandit was an avid reader of his own press clippings. It's possible that this penchant for niceties had less to do with good manners than with an increasing awareness of his own public image. Dillinger knew how the public tended to celebrate daring bank robbers, and he craved the attention – which he got. Dillinger was being perceived by many in the Midwest as a force of retribution against the banks and politicians who had plunged the nation into a depression.

He was loving every minute of it, and this was only the beginning.

12. Meanwhile... In Old San Antonio

From June to November 1933, Tommy Carroll used the Minneapolis duplex of Sally's brother, Joseph Bennett, as a hideout, and Homer Van Meter and Nelson both visited him there. On November 11, Carroll barely escaped from two Minneapolis police officers who tried to arrest him for the Brainerd bank robbery. After kicking one officer in the face and punching the other, and then stealing his gun, Carroll fled barefoot. He left behind $1,600 in crisp bank notes, a rifle, a machine gun, and a shotgun.

With the heat cranked up, Nelson ordered everyone out of town. Leaving his baby girl with his mother in Chicago, he took Helen and his four-year-old son, Ronald, and drove south to San Antonio, where they registered at the Johnson Courts Tourist Camp on November 22. The other gang members arrived soon after, and everyone settled in for an extended vacation. Nelson spent much of his time hanging around at a neighborhood garage and in the basement workshop of a local gunsmith. The others spent most of their time in bars and whorehouses.

Trouble began two weeks later, when the madam of a whorehouse that had been frequented by Carroll and gang member Chuck Fisher saw a machine gun in their car. On December 9, she called local Chief of Detectives Audry Clark and told him that she suspected them of being "high-powered northern gangsters." The detective passed the tip on to the San Antonio Bureau of Investigation agent in charge, Gus Jones. No one realized who the two men were and even if they had, the name "Baby Face Nelson" didn't mean much to anyone at the time. The manager of Chuck Fisher's apartment building was a friend, so Jones drove over and got a look into Fisher's place. He saw nothing out of the ordinary.

Two days later, on December 11, the madam called the San Antonio police with another tip. One of the gangsters was coming to her house to take one of the girls horseback riding. Two detectives, H.C. Perrin and Al Hartman, were sitting in a car outside of the brothel when a taxi pulled up and Tommy Carroll got out and went up to the door. A moment later, Carroll and a girl returned to the taxi. As the cab drove away, the detectives followed.

Carroll glanced in the rearview mirror and quickly spotted the tail. Driving down East Commerce Street in the middle of downtown, just a half mile from the Alamo, Carroll ordered the driver to stop the car. He jumped out and ran around a corner into an alley. Detective Perrin, armed with a sawed-off shotgun, and Hartman, with his service revolver, jumped out of their own car and ran after him.

The alley was a dead end. As Perrin ran toward it, Carroll stepped out and fired several shots. The first bullet struck the detective right between the eyes and he dropped to the pavement. Carroll's next shots shattered Hartman's right wrist and elbow. Carroll ran off down the street, put his gun in the face of the driver of a pickup truck, jumped inside, and sped off.

By later that night, the Nelson gang was gone. The only member who didn't escape was Chuck Fisher, who was captured by Gus Jones at his apartment. Fisher was later returned to Minneapolis and charged with a series of post office robberies. He was sent to Leavenworth for eight years, but he told the authorities nothing. Not for four more months would anyone realize that Nelson had been in San Antonio.

The gang scattered. Van Meter and Carroll returned to St. Paul, while the Nelsons drove west, crossing New Mexico and Utah, before landing in San Francisco a few days before Christmas.

13. Holidays

After the Racine robbery, Dillinger and the rest of the gang decided to split up for a bit and let the heat die down. They would meet again in Chicago. Russell Clark and Opal set out for Texas. Charles Makley went to Denver and rented an apartment there. On December 11, he ran into someone who knew him, and fearful that the man might call the police, he abandoned his apartment and went straight to the bus station. His instincts turned out to be right, for soon after, a pair of investigators from the district attorney's office, believing that he might try and leave town quickly, also went to the bus station to arrest him. Makley managed to leave town just seven minutes before the investigators arrived at the station.

John Hamilton would not be so lucky. On December 14, a Chicago police detective was sent to investigate a tip that one of the gang's Auburn automobiles was being serviced at a garage on Broadway. Sergeant William T. Shanley and a patrolman named Frank Hopkins decided to stake out the garage in case Dillinger or one of the others showed up to get the car. The two men hunkered down in the garage, while their back-up, Officer Martin Mullin, waited in a squad car about a half-block away. About 4:00 p.m., Shanley told Hopkins to walk to the squad car and tell Mullins to take the vehicle back to the station and send out a relief team of officers. Just after Hopkins left, Hamilton and a girlfriend, Elaine Dent, entered the garage.

As they came inside, Shanley walked over and asked Hamilton if the green Auburn was his car. Hamilton replied that it wasn't, it belonged to his wife. Elaine took out a vehicle receipt and handed it to the detective, but Shanley wasn't interested. He was only interested in Hamilton. "Keep your hands out of your pockets!" he said, and began frisking Hamilton's pockets for a gun.

As he did so, Hamilton brushed the detective's arm away from him, reached into his shoulder holster, and whipped out a pistol. He fired and killed Shanley where the man stood. He fell to the garage floor with the vehicle receipt still clutched in his hand.

Hamilton grabbed Elaine by the hand and pulled her out of the garage. As he started to run, the two got separated. Moments later, Hopkins came running back and saw the fleeing pair. He managed to catch up with Elaine, just as Hamilton disappeared on the other side of a vacant lot. Hopkins seized the struggling and cursing woman and took her back to the garage. She theatrically told detectives that she was an innocent victim and had no idea that Hamilton was a criminal.

The killing of Detective Shanley was front page news and it would be the catalyst for the formation of the Chicago Police Department's "Dillinger Squad" two days later. The special unit was headed by Captain John Stege, who had 40 men under his command. Their primary task was to locate Dillinger and bring him to justice – one way or another. Two weeks later, on December 28, the Illinois Crime Commission, which had created America's first official "Public Enemies" list in April

1930, issued its latest roster of most-wanted criminals. The list contained 21 names, with John Dillinger being listed as Public Enemy Number One.

After the incident at the garage, Dillinger decided that it was time to take the Florida vacation that he had been thinking about. The gang left Chicago in four cars, with plans

Captain John Stege, head of Chicago's "Dillinger Squad," formed after the murder of Detective Shanley by John Hamilton

to meet up in Chattanooga, Tennessee, in three days. Before leaving town, Clark, who had dyed his hair brown, and Opal, bought a new car. After stowing a suitcase filled with machine guns, pistols, and ammunition in the back seat, they headed out of town.

While driving on slick roads near Evansville, Indiana, Clark hit a truck. The front of his car was wrecked and the truck was damaged. Opal was knocked unconscious and was bleeding from a large cut on her face. After the truck driver called the police, an ambulance and several lawmen arrived. Although Opal said that she would not go to a hospital, Clark insisted that she go and assured her that he would come and get her later. Opal had hidden $4,500 in her shoe and was worried that someone would find the cash at the hospital and ask questions.

Clark didn't argue when the police asked him to accompany them to the station. He took the suitcase of guns from the wrecked vehicle and put it in the back of the police car, and rode with the officers to the station. When they arrived, Clark simply left the suitcase with he and Opal's other bags on the sidewalk, walked into the station, admitted that the wreck was his fault because he had not been paying close enough attention on the icy road, and settled up financially with the truck driver. The police captain shook Clark's hand, told him he was a "square shooter," and let him go. He even offered to help Clark out if he ever needed it someday. Clark shook his hand, walked outside of the station where he had once been locked up, and quickly headed for the hospital.

Meanwhile, Opal was having a very bad day. Afraid that she might talk under anesthesia, she refused ether when the doctor sewed up the cut on her face, gritting her teeth as they patched up her wound. After treating her, the hospital staff took her to a room and wanted to put her to bed, but Opal was reluctant. When she took her shoes off and placed them on the bed, a nurse tried to put them away. Opal fought fiercely until the nurse finally allowed her to put her shoes – and the cash she had shoved under the inner sole – under her pillow.

By the time that Clark got to her room, Opal was in an anxious state. He took her out of the hospital and checked them into a hotel for the night. Since they could not wait for their car to be repaired, they boarded a plane the next morning, bound for Chattanooga. They were unable to locate the rest of the gang there, but finally caught up with them in Florida.

Harry Pierpont and Mary Kinder's trip to Florida was also eventful, but not in the same way. They stopped in Nashville along the route, where Pierpont bought Mary a diamond ring and a wedding ring from a jewelry store. Two days after arriving in Florida, the couple were in the lobby of their hotel when a swarm of police rushed through it. Pierpont almost ran for the door, but soon learned that the police were there because a guest had jumped out of an upper-level window.

Dillinger was the first to arrive in Daytona Beach, Florida, on December 19. He and Billie rented a sprawling two-story beach house with enough rooms for everyone. They spent the next week strolling the beach, fishing, playing cards, and listening to the radio. They were happy to be away from the cold weather in Chicago, and this was the first time that most of the gang had ever seen the ocean. After a few days, everyone piled into the cars and took a two-day trip to Miami, where they watched the dog races and took in a nightclub or two.

On New Year's Eve, the gang threw a rousing party. It was the only time that the others ever recalled seeing Dillinger drunk. As the final minutes of 1933 ticked away, he stepped out onto the balcony of the beach house with Mary Kinder, machine gun in hand. He pointed up toward the moon. "Think I can hit it?" he asked Mary. As the clock struck midnight, Dillinger pointed the gun into the air and fired off an echoing roar of bullets out over the Atlantic Ocean.

14. The Robbery Dillinger Didn't Do

After spending a few weeks in the Florida sun, the gang began to get bored and decided to extend their vacation by driving across country to the Southwest. For whatever reason, they decided to go to Tucson, Arizona. Makley, Clark, and Opal were going to take one car and Pierpont and Mary Kinder in the other. Right after Christmas, Billie had gone to Wisconsin to visit her family for the holidays, so Dillinger decided that he wanted to go and get her before going out west. Hamilton hoped to reunite with Pat Cherrington, so he rode along with Dillinger, heading north to Chicago.

According to Pat Cherrington, who later told her story to the authorities, Dillinger and Hamilton left Florida on Sunday, January 14. Hamilton sent her a telegram that afternoon from Savannah, asking her to meet him at a hotel in Chicago. Driving through the night, he and Dillinger reached the Windy City the next morning. That same day, maybe low on cash and maybe unable to move any more of their stolen bonds, they decided to rob a bank. It was apparently an impetuous decision. Some have credited it to Dillinger's grown belief in his own ability to do anything, others to restlessness, others claim it was a need to get back into the limelight since he hadn't robbed a bank in two months, and others claim that Dillinger didn't rob the bank at all.

Whatever the reason, the bank that Dillinger selected was in East Chicago, Indiana, the corrupt mill town where he had spent some time the previous summer. Dillinger knew certain members of the East Chicago police department, and it has been suggested that his decision to rob the First National Bank that day had been prearranged. He knew his contacts would look the other way. The problem was, if that was true, they didn't tell the rest of the police department to let the bank robbers get away.

At 2:45, Dillinger and Hamilton got out of a car that was double-parked outside of the bank. They left a driver in the car; his identity has never been established. Inside of the bank's lobby, Dillinger pulled a machine gun out from what some witnesses claimed was a trombone case. He shouted, "This is a stick-up! Put your hands up everybody!"

Walter Spencer, one of the bank's vice-presidents, pressed a silent alarm button beneath his desk and it rang a block away, at police headquarters. As the customers raised their hands and lined up against the walls, one of them left behind his cash on the counter. "You go ahead and take your money," Dillinger told him. "We don't want your money, just the bank's."

Hamilton stood by while Dillinger was dealing with the customers. "Come on," Dillinger said, "get the dough." Hamilton then hustled behind the teller cages and began clearing stacks of cash off the counters into a satchel. Just then, a police

The First National Bank in East Chicago in the 1930s

officer named Hobart Wilgus appeared at the front door, apparently unaware that a robbery was taking place.

Dillinger spotted him. "Cop outside!" he called to Hamilton, who hesitated. But Dillinger reassured him, telling him to take his time, they were in no rush.

As Wilgus walked through the bank's front door, Dillinger stepped over to him and disarmed him. He emptied the bullets from the policeman's gun and tossed it back to him. He saw Wilgus eyeing the machine gun that the bandit held in his hands. Dillinger quipped, "Oh, don't be afraid of this. I'm not even sure that it'll shoot."

As Hamilton relieved the cages of their cash, Dillinger saw men in suits hurry toward the bank. They were plainclothes detectives, answering the bank's alarm. Hamilton saw them, too. Dillinger, playing to his captive audience, continued to admonish Hamilton. "Don't let those coppers worry you! Take your time and be sure to get all the dough. We'll take care of them birds outside when we get there."

A few moments later, Hamilton was finished. Dillinger waved his machine gun at Walter Spencer, the vice president, and told him to come out with him. Spencer asked if he could grab his coat, but Dillinger shook his head and told him that he wouldn't be going far. He then grabbed Officer Wilgus by the arm. Dillinger said, "You go first. They might as well shoot you as me. We love you guys anyway."

Just as had been done at the Racine bank two months before, Dillinger shoved the hostages out of the bank ahead of him, using them as human shields. This time, though, he wasn't facing a curious crowd of civilians. Outside, behind parked cars and in storefronts on both sides of the front door, were seven East Chicago police officers. As he edged onto the sidewalk, Dillinger hunched behind Officer

Wilgus, while Hamilton kept an arm around Walter Spencer as he walked behind him.

For a long moment, as the four-man group shuffled along the sidewalk toward the getaway car, no one spoke. Dillinger locked eyes with at least one of the officers, several of which were no more than 20 feet away. They were just steps from the car, and for a few seconds, it looked as though Dillinger was going to safely get away. Then one of the officers, a 43-year-old detective named Patrick O'Malley, shouted, "Wilgus!" Officer Wilgus twisted out of Dillinger's grasp and gave O'Malley a clear shot at the outlaw. O'Malley fired his revolver four times, at least one of the bullets striking Dillinger's bulletproof vest.

A newspaper illustration of slain Detective Patrick O'Malley

Dillinger was stunned. His genial demeanor inside of the bank vanished. He shoved Wilgus out of the way, snarling, "I'll get that sonofabitch!" He raised his machine gun and fired directly at Detective O'Malley. The detective's body jerked, and then fell to the ground with eight bullet holes in his chest. He was dead by the time he sprawled onto the pavement.

When O'Malley fell, the six remaining officers opened fire. Chunks of sidewalk flew, nicks appeared in the surrounding buildings, and clouds of brick dust filtered into the air. Dillinger and Hamilton ran for the getaway car, ducking between a line of parked cars. Hamilton almost didn't make it. He was struck by several bullets. Some reports claim that he was hit seven times, with six of the bullets striking his shoulders and left arm. One bullet had passed through his bulletproof vest and passed through his body just above the pelvic bone. Hamilton fell to the ground, but Dillinger scooped him up, along with the satchel of cash, and managed to get him into the open door of the getaway car. As bullets pounded the fleeing automobile, the driver careened off down Chicago Avenue, eluding police pursuit. In minutes, they were gone.

In the wake of the robbery, witnesses swore that the leader of the bandits had been Dillinger and the evening newspaper made it official. John Dillinger, the man who many people in Indiana cheered for fighting the greedy bankers, was now a killer. For the rest of his life, some versions of the story say, the murder weighed on Dillinger's mind. He would repeatedly deny shooting O'Malley to lawyers, lawmen, and friends. More than once, he even volunteered this to complete strangers. His denials may have had less to do with the prospect of a murder conviction than with his public image. In his heart, Dillinger truly believed that he was a regular guy, making the best of bad times. Dillinger didn't want to be a bad guy. He wanted to be someone that ordinary folks and people like his sister, Audrey, and her family could cheer for. He didn't want to be remembered as the murderer of Detective O'Malley.

Was Dillinger just fooling himself, or could he have been telling the truth when he claimed that he didn't kill the police officer? The bigger question is this: did Dillinger and Hamilton carry out this bank robbery at all? Was it actually committed by other bandits, with Dillinger mistakenly ending up with the blame? As mentioned, Dillinger always claimed that he did not rob this bank, but rather than take his word for it, we will take a look at the arguments against it.

There is no question that Dillinger and Hamilton went to Chicago after leaving Florida. Dillinger wanted to pick up Billie and take her to Arizona with him. There is nothing to say that Hamilton planned to go to Arizona. We do know that he wanted to reunite with Pat Cherrington. He sent her a telegram from Savannah, asking her to meet him. The trip alone does not prove that the two men planned to rob a bank, especially in East Chicago, a town where they had contacts on the police force and which they had previously used as a hideout.

But, we should look more closely at the robbery itself. Dillinger had learned the art of robbing banks by experienced men, one of whom was John Hamilton. There is nothing about the East Chicago robbery that fits the methods that had been used by the gang. It was not planned in advance; there was no time. There was no time to scout the bank. Even if they were familiar with the layout, things could have changed since they had last been in East Chicago. At no time in the past had they taken such a risk. That's the least of the problems, though.

Based on the methods that they had used previously, Dillinger and Hamilton would not have attempted to rob a bank with just two men, or rather three, if you count the mysterious getaway driver who was never identified. It also seems unlikely the two men would have worked with a driver they didn't implicitly trust. All of those men were either in jail, or on their way to Arizona. Expert bank robbers like Eddie Bentz, who schooled Baby Face Nelson on finding the perfect bank and crew and organizing a foolproof robbery, always recommended six or seven men for an adequate crew, and no less than five. Dillinger had been taught by men who were just as savvy – including Red Hamilton – and it's very unlikely that he would have tried such a stunt with only two men and no time to prepare for the robbery.

In addition, based on the witness accounts, it seems unlikely that the robbery itself matched the style of John Dillinger. Putting aside the dialogue that witnesses claimed to hear, which sounded like it came from a gangster movie, there was the story of Dillinger carrying a machine gun in a trombone case. It's a claim right out of a newspaper cartoon, and something Dillinger had never done before. To make matters worse, there was the way that Dillinger reportedly belittled Hamilton, who was portrayed in witness reports as a bumbling and inexperienced bandit, who needed Dillinger to tell him how it was done. Not only was Hamilton more experienced than his younger friend, Dillinger would have *never* treated Hamilton in such a manner.

And then there's the question of John Hamilton's wounds. According to reports, he was hit seven times while fleeing the bank. Seriously wounded,

Dillinger allegedly took him to a Chicago hotel, where Pat Cherrington met up with them. Unable to find an underworld doctor to treat Hamilton (since the Chicago Outfit had forbid anyone to help the bank robbers), Hamilton suffered for more than a day before a "discreet" doctor could be found. The physician believed that Hamilton's condition was hopeless, but accepted $5,000 to treat him. Dillinger, Hamilton, and Pat checked into an apartment on January 15, and stayed for five days, although Dillinger would have had to abandon his dying friend so that he could leave and continue his vacation – which seems unlikely. Hamilton was then said to have been nursed by Pat at the home of a woman named Hazel Doyle, wife of gangster Earl Doyle, who Hamilton had done time with at Michigan City.

The amazing thing is that – according to this story – Hamilton had an almost miraculous recovery from his "serious wounds." In mid-January, he was near death, lucky to survive, but on March 6, he took part in a wild bank robbery in Sioux Falls, South Dakota. Even if the rest of my arguments don't seem plausible to the reader, that one should definitely be considered. The idea of anyone recovering from seven bullet wounds that fast – especially six wounds that made it impossible for him to raise his left arm – is markedly unbelievable.

What it all boils down to is that, in my opinion, the two men who robbed the First National Bank in East Chicago were not John Dillinger and John Hamilton – it was two other bandits entirely. But who was the most famous gangster in America, at a time when the average person may have only seen a picture in the newspaper? John Dillinger, of course. I don't believe that, even if they had time to do it, Dillinger and Hamilton would have robbed a bank in a city that had previously offered them protection, with no planning, without a full crew, and behaved in the manner that was reported by a group of scared witnesses.

There's no question that Dillinger was happy to lie when it made him look better, but I don't believe he was lying about the murder of Detective O'Malley. A bank robber killed him, there's no question about that, but I do feel there remains a question about whether or not it was John Dillinger.

Regardless of what really happened, John Hamilton remained in Chicago with Pat and Dillinger met up with Billie. They stayed in Chicago just long enough to visit a divorce attorney; as soon as Billie could end her ill-conceived marriage, she and Dillinger planned to wed. Afterward, they drove south to St. Louis, where Dillinger wanted to visit a large auto show. There, he bought a new V-8 Ford, checked into a downtown hotel, and spent an evening dancing in its roof garden. The next morning, they started west on Route 66, heading for the Arizona sunshine.

15. Trouble in Tucson

The sunbaked desert town of Tucson, Arizona, home to about 30,000 people, was as far away from the Midwest as the gang was likely to get. It was like another planet to them. It was a place where men wore cowboy hats and boots and mariachi music filled the evening air. There were mountains, rattlesnakes, tumbleweeds, cacti, and hitching posts on the edge of the street. For men used to the cities, farms, rolling fields – and jails – of the Midwest, Chicago seemed a world away. It was an intoxicating place and it was one that made them careless.

When Dillinger and Billie arrived in town, they found the others already enjoying the tequila-fueled nightlife of Tucson. Pierpont and Mary had checked into a motor court on the edge of town. Russell Clark was staying with Makley at the city's finest lodging, the Congress Hotel. Makley had hooked up with a local singer, and everyone was having a grand time. Dillinger and Billie checked into the same motor court where Pierpont was staying, registering as "Mr. and Mrs. Frank Sullivan" of Green Bay, Wisconsin.

After all of the outlaws got together, they devised a plan for keeping a low profile. To avoid suspicion, they would rent different houses and act like quiet, well-behaved tourists. Unfortunately, things got off to a bad start.

One afternoon, driving around town, Pierpont inexplicably stopped to chat with a pair of policemen. He introduced himself as a vacationer from Florida, then pointed out a random car and told the officers that he thought he was being followed. One of the cops chatted with Pierpont while the other followed the strange car. Pierpont proudly showed him some of the finer elements of his new Buick, like the speedometer and the power steering. They talked about weather in the desert and got so friendly that Pierpont even told him the name of the place where he was staying. When the second officer returned, he assured him that the other car was harmless and with a wave and a thank-you, Pierpont drove off. It was an idiotic thing to do, but it's almost as though he couldn't help himself. The gang was far away from home, far from trouble, and supposed to be keeping things low-key. It's almost as if Pierpont just needed the risk so that he could stay on his toes. Or maybe he just thought that nothing could touch them, but he was wrong.

During the day, the gang went sightseeing and they spent evenings in the clubs. Things went smoothly until the evening that a leaky oil furnace in the Congress Hotel's basement caught on fire. Flames shot up the elevator shaft, and filled the building with smoke. Firefighters promptly arrived and one of them, William Benedict, was puzzled to see two men propping a ladder up against a third-floor window. It was Makley and Clark, who explained to him that they were trying to retrieve their luggage. Once the fire was under control, Benedict went upstairs to Room 329, forced open the door, and carried out a heavy fabric box. He didn't know it, but it contained Makley and Clark's machine guns. Makley thanked him profusely and gave him $2.

The Hotel Congress in Tucson

Three days passed. On Friday morning, January 25, Bennett, the fireman who had helped Makley and Clark, was flipping through an issue of *True Detective* magazine and was stunned to see, staring up at him from the pages, the "Mr. Davies" whose luggage he had rescued from Room 329. When a deputy sheriff stopped by the firehouse later on that day, he showed him the magazine. By lunchtime, Benedict's story was being told at police headquarters. It got the attention of a patrolman named Harry Lesly, who had heard a strange story from a pair of tourists that same morning. The night before the hotel fire, the tourists had told him, they had shared some drinks at a nightclub with a man who introduced himself as Art Long. It was actually Russell Clark, and he'd had a few too many shots of tequila. He was soon telling the tourists that if a man had a machine gun, it made it a lot easier to weather the Depression. The tourists noticed that "Long" and all of his pals appeared to be wearing shoulder holsters under their coats.

The stories started detectives looking through wanted posters. It turned out that "Mr. Davies" was a perfect match to a photograph of Charles Makley. An officer telephoned the Congress and learned that Mr. Davies' luggage had been taken to a rented bungalow on East Second Street. By 1:30 p.m., three Tucson policemen were sitting in a car, watching the house. Not long after they arrived, Makley walked out to his Studebaker with his girlfriend. As he drove away, the squad car cautiously followed him.

The officers followed the car to downtown Tucson, where it parked outside of the Grabe Electric Company. The policemen walked inside, found Makley standing at a counter, and told him that he was under arrest. Makley protested, claiming that he was a Florida businessman on vacation. The officers told him that he could explain the mix-up downtown at the station. When he arrived, Makley insisted to Chief C.A. Wollard that he was "J.C. Davies," on vacation from Florida. All of his papers were at his house, he said, and he could clear up the confusion. The chief, after looking over Makley's mug shot, said that his fingerprints would take care of any lingering questions. Makley protested, but it didn't do any good. The chief soon ordered him locked up in a cell.

Wollard was now convinced that the rest of the Dillinger gang was somewhere in Tucson. He called in three of his best men, Sergeants Frank Eyman and Dallas Ford, and a detective named Chet Sherman. Wollard made sure that the three men studied photographs of the other gang members, and told them to keep Makley's bungalow under surveillance.

The three officers parked nearby and set up surveillance on the house. After an hour, they began to grow impatient, so they decided to check and see if anyone was inside. They devised a simple ruse. Using a letter that he had in his jacket pocket, Detective Sherman approached the house, pretending to be a messenger. He rang the bell and Opal Long, Russell Clark's girlfriend, opened the door. Sherman thrust the letter forward and said that he had a delivery. When she reached for the letter, the detective shoved his shoulder against the door and pushed his way inside. Russell Clark was in the living room. Sherman drew his revolver and ordered Clark to put up his hands. Instead, Clark lunged for the gun and managed to get hold of it by the barrel. The two men wrestled for the pistol, crashing through the living room and into a bedroom.

Spying the commotion from outside, Sergeants Eyman and Ford ran toward the house, bounding up the steps and onto the porch. When Opal saw them coming, she slammed the door, just as Ford thrust his hand forward. The door shut on his finger, snapping the bone.

Ford kicked open the door, knocking Opal aside, and burst into the bedroom to find Sherman and Clark grappling on the bed. Clark was struggling to break free and reach under a pillow when Ford hit him over the head with his pistol. Eyman pulled Clark off the bed and, in moments, they had him in handcuffs. Under the pillow that Clark had been reaching for was a loaded .38. A further search of the bungalow turned up two Thompson machine guns, an automatic rifle, two pistols, two bulletproof vests, and just over $4,500 in cash. The three officers put Clark and Opal into a car and drove them downtown. No one thought to remain behind at the house.

When they arrived at the police station, Chief Wollard ordered them back out to search for Pierpont and Dillinger. If they got wind of their friends' arrests, they could vanish into the desert and they would be impossible to catch.

The chief's instincts were right. At the same time that he was directing his officers, Pierpont arrived at Makley's bungalow. Walking up the steps, he saw drops of blood on the porch and saw overturned furniture through the window. He ran back to the car, drove back to the tourist camp where he had been staying, and told Mary to start packing. They had to get out of town and try to warn Dillinger, if they could.

Pierpont's stunt involving the police officers from a few days earlier was just about to come back to haunt him. At the same time that the couple was packing up, a patrolman walked into Chief Wollard's office and mentioned the friendly "Florida tourist" that he had recently encountered. The description matched Pierpont. The chief sent Sergeant Eyman and two patrolmen to the tourist camp where the man said he was staying. As the three men drove up, they spotted Pierpont driving off in his Buick. They followed the car for several blocks, discussing the best way to proceed. Finally, they decided to stage a routine traffic stop. Honking their horn, Eyman waved for Pierpont to pull over. He complied and the sergeant stepped up to his window and asked to see his license.

Pierpont handed over a fake identification and Eyman looked it over. He handed it back and apologized, pointing out that Pierpont didn't have a visitor's identification sticker on his car, as the law required. It was no trouble to get one, he said. If Pierpont could just follow him to the station, he would have his sticker in minutes, and could be on his way. Pierpont weighed his options and, knowing he was outnumbered, agreed. Eyman cheerfully volunteered to ride along with him and climbed into the backseat behind Pierpont and Mary.

Eyman kept up a stream of cheerful chatter on the way downtown. He talked about the weather and the local nightlife, looking casually out the window. Pierpont nodded and smiled a lot, while Mary sat frozen in the passenger seat. Unknown to the couple, Detective Eyman had drawn his gun and had placed it between his legs, out of sight of those in the front seat. He took out a pack of cigarettes and offered one to Pierpont. He declined.

At the station, Eyman led Pierpont and Mary down a flight of stairs to Chief Wollard's office. The guns collected from Makley and Clark were spread across the chief's desk, and the second Pierpont walked in, he knew that it was over. Instinctively, he went for the gun in his shoulder holster, but Eyman was too fast. His own gun was already in his hand and he pressed it to the side of Pierpont's head, ordering him to take his hand out of his coat. But Pierpont went for his gun anyway. Eyman and two other officers tackled him and the group went down to the floor.

Eyman shouted, "Drop that gun, or I'll kill you!"

Pierpont went slack. He was hauled to his feet and one officer violently twisted his arm behind his back while the other searched him. Pierpont's composure had returned and he forced a thin smile. "You're treating me pretty rough, aren't you?"

"What did you want us to do?" Eyman smirked. "Kiss you?"

The cops now needed to find Dillinger. They knew he was somewhere in the city. Night was starting to fall and with no other clues, they decided to stake out Makley's bungalow and the tourist court. A detective named James Herron and two uniformed policemen parked outside of the bungalow. The two officers slipped into the house through the back door and Herron circled around back to get the car out of sight, worried that it might spook Dillinger if he saw it.

Just then a shiny new Hudson sedan came around the corner and parked in front of the bungalow. Herron ducked behind some bushes as a man in a brown suit got out and approached the front porch, leaving a woman in the car. Herron came out from behind the bushes just as the man started up the steps. As he did, the man paused, glancing down at the bloodstains on the porch. He whirled around, as if to run to his car, and came face-to-face with Detective Herron.

John Dillinger and James Herron stood five feet apart from one another on the bungalow's lawn. Herron drew first, pistol in his right hand, and ordered Dillinger to put up his hands. Dillinger merely looked at him. Herron blustered, finally stepping forward. He thrust the gun toward the outlaw. "Up with those hands or I'll bore you!" he growled.

Dillinger slowly raised his hands. "What's this all about?"

Just then the other two officers came out of the house and Herron told them to cover the car. The two men hustled past and Herron grabbed Dillinger by the coat and shoved him forward. It was at that moment that Dillinger must have realized that he could not charm his way free. He went for the gun in his shoulder holster, but he was too slow. Herron jammed his pistol hard into his back and one of the other officers put a riot gun in his face.

Dillinger gave up.

The arrests in Tucson made front-page news across the country. The next day, crowds of curiosity-seekers swarmed the Pima County Jail, where the four gang members and their girlfriends were kept under guard. Chief Wollard's office was inundated with telegrams and telephone messages. At the local airport, every arriving plane brought reporters and photographers from Chicago, New York, and other cities.

At 10:00 that morning, all seven of the prisoners were led in shackles into a packed courtroom to be arraigned. Four states had put in claims for the Dillinger gang members. Indiana State Police Captain Matt Leach wanted custody of all four gangsters, but that decision ultimately resided with Arizona's governor.

As the prisoners were led into a courtroom before the justice of the peace, Dillinger slumped in his chair, refusing to stand up. When he was forced to stand by guards, he snarled, "I ain't Dillinger. I'm being framed."

Pierpont cracked jokes until he was ordered to be silent. When he was called, he stood, laughing and said, "That must be me." As the clerk called the name "Anne Martin," the alias under which Billie had been booked, Pierpont laughed again and snickered, "There ain't no such animal."

Charged with being fugitives from justice, bond for each man was set at $10,000. Opal, Mary, and Billie were all charged with obstructing justice and bond was set at $5,000 for each of them. Later, Mary's bond was increased because of her role in the Michigan City escape.

Flashbulbs popped wildly as the prisoners were led out of the courtroom. Billie smiled at Dillinger, who grinned back. He leaned over and kissed her.

That afternoon, a steady procession of reporters, politicians, and policemen filed past the gang's jail cells, ogling the infamous Midwestern gangsters as if they were freaks in a traveling sideshow. Dillinger warmed to the attention, finally admitting his identity, and playing the role of the genial, big-time bank robber.

Dillinger and the others waiting to be arraigned in the Tucson courtroom. Mary and Billie can be seen hiding their faces from the reporter's cameras.

"I'm an expert in my business," he told a group of reporters who hovered at his cell and wrote down everything that he said. "I can play tag with the police any time. They just dodge around on old trails like fox hounds that don't know what's going on. And the dumbest ones in the world are the Chicago kind. Right now none of these smart-aleck coppers have got a bit of evidence that I killed anyone or robbed any bank."

The others took their cue from Dillinger, smiling for the camera and tossing out smug remarks. Pierpont even traded wisecracks with the Arizona governor, B.B. Moeur. "These cops out there ain't like the ones in Indiana. They pull too fast for us," he said.

The jovial mood waned when the reporters left. By Sunday morning, when delegations of prosecutors from Ohio, Wisconsin, and Indiana arrived in Tucson to argue for extraditions, the gang members were no longer in the mood to chat and tell jokes. At the sight of Matt Leach, who had briefly jailed his mother that fall in hopes that he could force information out of her, Pierpont flew into a rage. He shouted at him, "I should have killed you when I had the chance, you dirty sonofabitch! You put my mother in jail... If I ever get out of this the first thing I'm going to do is kill you, you rat!"

Leach stared at Pierpont for a moment, and then turned to a reporter. "There's a man who loves his mother," he quipped.

When Leach walked up to Dillinger's cell, he extended his hand through the bars. Dillinger hesitated, then shook it. "Well, we meet again, John," Leach said. He took a step back and studied the bank robber for a moment, then complimented him on the mustache that he had grown. Leach asked him if he was ready to return to Indiana.

Dillinger snorted. "I'm in no hurry. I haven't a thing to do when I get there."

Dillinger was flown by plane from Tucson to Chicago.

16. Indiana's "Escape Proof" Jail

The airplane carrying John Dillinger landed at Chicago's Midway Airport at 6:10 on a dark and snowy Tuesday evening, January 30, 1934. It had been a long flight, and Dillinger's first time on a plane. His departure from Tucson came after a two-day struggle between lawyers from Wisconsin, Indiana, and Ohio, each making a case to prosecute the gang before the others. In the end, Governor Moeur ordered Dillinger to Indiana to stand trial for Detective O'Malley's murder in East Chicago. If he was convicted, he would end up in the electric chair. Pierpont, Makley, Clark, and Mary Kinder were sent to Ohio to answer for Sheriff Sarber's murder. Mary was later released. Billie and Opal were set free. They got onto a bus, bound for Chicago.

When Dillinger's plane landed, he descended the stairs into a throng of photographers and 85 members of the Chicago Police Department, which the *Chicago Tribune* noted was "a reception such as had never been accorded a criminal in Chicago." As the flashbulbs popped and reporters pushed and shoved to get a glimpse, two officers shoved Dillinger into the backseat of a waiting car.

The Chicago police, many outfitted with machine guns and bulletproof vests, were taking no chances. Thirteen automobiles and a dozen motorcycles, with their sirens blaring, were part of a caravan that traveled from the airport and onto city streets that were lined with the curious. It crossed the border into Northwest Indiana, headed for the town of Crown Point, the seat of Lake County, where Dillinger was to be tried.

There were more than 500 people waiting when Dillinger arrived at the jail. Many of them were Indiana National guardsmen and heavily armed volunteers, who were on the lookout for any of Dillinger's pals, who might try and break him out of prison. These men were tense and ready for trouble, but things inside the jail were much different. A crowd of reporters and photographers had already gathered when Dillinger arrived at 7:40 p.m. He was led into Sheriff Lillian Holley's office, about whom Dillinger remarked, "Mrs. Holley seems like a fine lady." She had become sheriff after her husband was murdered by a drunken farmer, thrusting her into a role that she would soon prove to be unprepared for.

An almost festive atmosphere developed inside of the jail as the huge throng of reporters, and even many of the lawmen, drank beer and chatted with the friendly and talkative bank robber. Dillinger gave interviews, answered questions that were shouted to him with friendly quips, and gave some of his most famous quotes to the newspapermen who eagerly jotted down every word. Dillinger was making the most of his reputation of the "noble bank robber," striking back at the banks and politicians who had plunged the country into the Depression.

The jail in Crown Point, Indiana, where Dillinger was held.

(Below) The scene on the street outside of the jail when Dillinger arrived.

"Are you glad to see Indiana again?" one of the reporters asked.

"About as glad as Indiana is to see me," Dillinger joshed.

Another reporter spoke up. "You're credited with having smuggled guns into the Indiana State Penitentiary just before the big outbreak of September 26."

Dillinger grinned. "I'm not denying it."

"How'd you get them in?" a reporter yelled.

"You're too inquisitive," the bank robber remarked with a laugh.

Among those gathered around the office were Sheriff Holley and Lake County Prosecutor Robert Estill, who had accompanied Dillinger from Arizona and had experienced firsthand his disarming friendliness. After being cajoled by reporters to have their photograph taken with the famous prisoner, Sheriff Holley reluctantly stepped into the frame. Robert Estill, however, actually got chummy with the gangster. When the newspapers published photographs of Prosecutor Estill with

Dillinger posing for reporters at the Lake County Jail. To his left was Prosecutor Robert Estill, who would be widely criticized for his friendly interaction with the bandit. Sheriff Lillian Holley is to the far left.

Dillinger leaning on the man's shoulder, people around the country were outraged, including J. Edgar Hoover, who condemned him in writing.

Dillinger, though, sensing a receptive audience, began unspooling his life story for the eager reporters. He said, "I was just an unfortunate boy. Back in Mooresville, the old hometown, I got drunk ten years ago and help up a grocery. I got $550 and then I got caught… In the prison I met a lot of good fellas. I wanted to help them out. There's no denying that I helped fix up the break at Michigan City last September, when ten men got away. Why not? I stick to my friends and they stick to me."

One of the reporters called out, "How long does it take you to go through a bank?"

Dillinger let out a chuckle. "One minute and forty seconds flat," he replied.

The casual and relaxed way that Dillinger spoke, his easy jokes, his crooked grin, his obvious charisma – it made a powerful impression on a group of reporters who were used to dealing with menacing Outfit gangsters. Dillinger had a star quality like none of them had ever seen before. A reporter from the *Chicago Daily*

News wrote the next day, "He had none of the look of a conventional killer – none of the advertised earmarks of the crook. Given a little more time and a wider circle of acquaintances, one can see that he might presently become the central figure of a nationwide campaign, largely female, to prevent his frying in the electric chair for the murder of Policeman Patrick O'Malley."

For a national press that uniformly painted criminals as "rats" and "cold-blooded killers," the stories that were published about Dillinger after his impromptu press conference at the Lake County Jail were unprecedented. It was a turning point in Dillinger's career and the moment that he stopped being just a Midwest bank robber and became a true national figure – an accessible, jovial, down-to-earth fellow that readers and radio listeners, who were unaccustomed to identifying with criminals, would soon find themselves rooting for.

The half-hour that Dillinger spent spinning yarns for the reporters in the Crown Point jail set the tone for the press coverage that was still to come: Dillinger the accidental bank robber, the misunderstood farm boy, the loyal friend who only committed crimes to help his pals. Dillinger seemed to understand how well he was doing that night and cleverly played it for sympathy. As the deputies finally led him away, he tossed out one last statement, "I am not a bad fellow, ladies and gentlemen. I was just an unfortunate boy who started wrong." In the *Chicago Tribune* the next morning, a reporter who was present noted "something like a tear glistened in one eye as interviewers left."

It was the performance of Dillinger's lifetime. Many assumed that it would be his last, though. Arrested for murder, set to go on trial, and likely ending up in the electric chair, they thought this was the end of Dillinger's career.

But John Dillinger was just getting started.

On Monday morning, February 5, Dillinger was brought into the courtroom at the Lake County Criminal Courts building, his hands and feet in shackles, and a grin on his face. There were 40 deputies on duty for the initial hearing. Newspapers were carrying stories that John Hamilton, the only gang member still at large, was going to stage a raid to rescue Dillinger. Hundreds crowded the hallways, trying to get a look at Dillinger, and deputies searched every person who entered the courtroom.

Dillinger listened quietly as a one-armed attorney that his father had hired, Joseph Ryan, argued for more time to prepare his case. Ryan spoke in a low voice, so low that many struggled to hear him. Dillinger looked a little dejected, unhappy with the representation that had been hastily arranged. Judge William Murray listened and gave Ryan four days. Dillinger would be arraigned on Friday, February 9.

Among those in the courtroom that day was a white-haired, 49-year-old Chicago attorney named Louis Piquett – the stereotypical gangland mouthpiece. The melodramatic, arm-waving former bartender had worked his way through Democrat cronies to become Chicago's chief prosecutor in the early 1920s, until his indictment on corruption charges in 1923 ended his tenure in that position. Even though the charges were later dropped, Piquett went into private practice

Dillinger is handcuffed and guarded as he smokes during a court recess while Deputy Sheriff R. M. Pierce, left, looks on during Dillinger's hearing at Crown Point.

with client's that were the lowest of the Outfit's ranks, abortionists, bootleggers, and killers. In his spare time, Piquett engaged in a variety of minor stock market swindles. Like a host of Chicago criminal defense attorneys, he saw Dillinger as a ticket to fame. He managed to have one of his cards slipped to him the week before. When Dillinger agreed to meet him, the two sat down twice inside the jail. They were perfunctory conversations with both men feeling the other out, but the meetings ended when Dillinger's father hired Joseph Ryan.

After the Monday morning hearing, the head jailer, Lewis Baker, tracked down Piquett outside the courtroom and told him that Dillinger wanted to meet with him. They met in a cell at the jail. Worried that their conversation might be overheard, Piquett loudly tapped a coin throughout their talk. Dillinger was worried. Ryan wasn't going to keep him out of the "hot seat." He wanted Piquett to represent him, but the wily attorney warned him that it would cost a lot of money. Dillinger promised to raise the lawyer's fee and Piquett agreed to represent him.

Piquett, very quickly, became the most important person in Dillinger's life. Publicly, he was Dillinger's staunchest defender and the flamboyant leader of what was becoming the bank robber's "admiration society." But it was in secret that Piquett served Dillinger best, doing everything from ferrying secret messages to fielding book offers. Dillinger's relationship with Piquett, and with Piquett's investigator, an easy-going man named Arthur O'Leary, became the foundation on

Infamous underworld attorney Louis Piquett, who essentially became an accomplice to Dillinger's ongoing crimes.

which his future exploits were built. In time, the two men became Dillinger's secret partners, enablers, and the fixers who handled his every need.

On Friday morning, Piquett took center stage at Dillinger's arraignment. It was another packed courtroom. The walls were lined with deputies armed with machine guns. Reporters and photographers jostled for space. In the crowd were two of the Arizona policemen who arrested Dillinger. Both said they were mulling over offers for movie roles and vaudeville shows, but were holding out for more money.

Dillinger was shackled again, but looked much more content with having Louis Piquett as his side. As soon as Judge Murray took the bench, Piquett was on his feet with an opening volley. "Your honor! Are we to have a hearing in accord with the spirit of the laws of this state and of this nation, or are we to witness a mockery in the name of justice? Is the state to be permitted to continue inciting an atmosphere of prejudice and hatred? The very air reeks with the bloody rancor of intolerant malice. The clanging of shackles brings to mind the dungeons of the czars, not the flag-bedecked liberty of an American courtroom. I request the court to direct that those shackles be removed."

It was clear that Piquett was in his element and the prosecutor, Robert Estill, was no match for him. "This is a very dangerous man, Your Honor," he squeaked.

Judge Murray sighed. "Remove the handcuffs from the prisoner."

Piquett got what he wanted, but he was just getting warmed up. "Thank you! May I also point out that this is a civil court, and not a military court-martial. Could anything be more prejudiced than machine guns pressed into the defendant's back, and an army of guards cluttering up the room? May the court direct that all guns be removed from the courtroom?"

Sherriff Holley's nephew, a deputy named Carroll Holley, stood up from his seat. "I'm responsible for the safe-guarding of the prisoner," he said.

Piquett whirled around. "Who are you?" he demanded. "Are you a lawyer? What right have you to address the court?"

Judge Murray, likely with another sigh, ordered the guns to be removed from the courtroom. Piquett then launched into an argument for more time. He wanted four months to prepare Dillinger's defense. Estill said that it should only take 10 days. Piquett shouted, seemingly in pain. "To go on trial in ten days would be a legal lynching of this poor lad! There is a law against lynching in this state!"

"There's a law against murder, too," Estill snapped back.

"Then why don't you observe it?" Piquett thundered. "Why don't you stand Dillinger against a wall and shoot him down? There's no need to throw away the state's money on this kind of mockery. Your Honor, even Christ had a fairer trial than this!"

Estill was about to reply when Judge Murray told both attorneys to calm down. Piquett apologized to the court and motioned to Estill. "Bob and I respect each other," he said.

Judge Murray couldn't help himself. "He'll be putting his arm around you soon," he joked. A ripple of laughter went through the crowd. After a few more arguments, the judge gave Piquett a month: Dillinger's trial would begin on March 12. Estill was unhappy. "Your Honor, why don't you let Mr. Piquett take Dillinger home with him, and bring him back on the day of the trial? You've given him everything else that he's asked for." He shook his head and sat down.

Dillinger watched the whole thing wearing his trademark grin. As the handcuffs were placed back on him for the return to the jail, he leaned over to Piquett and whispered, "Atta boy, counsel."

On Monday, February 12, Piquett was back in Crown Point. Rumors persisted that Red Hamilton was preparing to break Dillinger out of jail. Sheriff Holley had asked that Dillinger be moved to the prison at Michigan City. Dillinger urged Piquett to block the move, and Piquett laughed the whole thing off, telling him not to worry. He would not be moved to Michigan City.

In Judge Murray's chambers, Piquett listened as Sheriff Holley argued that the prison was the only place that they could guarantee Dillinger could not escape from. But Piquett knew how to handle the situation. "I think that's a very nice jail you have here," he said to Sheriff Holley. "What makes you think there's anything wrong with it?"

Mrs. Holley snapped at him. "There isn't anything wrong with it. It's the strongest jail in Indiana."

Piquett nodded his head. "That's what I thought. But of course, I don't want to embarrass Mrs. Holley. I appreciate that she's a woman, and if she's afraid of an escape…"

Sheriff Holley cut him off. "I'm not afraid of an escape! I can take care of John Dillinger or any other prisoner."

And that did the trick. But to make sure, Piquett added that if Dillinger was transferred, then he would request a change of venue for the trial. Judge Murray, liking all of the press attention that he was getting as he presided over the famous prisoner's trial, didn't want to lose that so he quickly ruled that Dillinger would remain at Crown Point.

Piquett returned to the jail three days later, on February 15, bringing Art O'Leary with him so that he could meet Dillinger. Piquett was planning to send O'Leary to Florida to establish Dillinger's alibi. He was claiming that he was still in Daytona Beach when eyewitnesses put him at the East Chicago bank robbery. As the two men rose to leave, Dillinger stopped them. He wanted to pass on a note to Billie.

Piquett and O'Leary looked at the folded note on the way back to Chicago. Dillinger had drawn a floor plan of the Crown Point jail and a suggestion to Hamilton (who he clearly knew was not laid up, nursing all of those bullet wounds) as to how he could break him out. The note instructed Hamilton to dynamite a corner of the jail, then use blowtorches to cut through the steel walls into the cell block where Dillinger would be waiting. This was the first hint that the two men had that Dillinger had no intention of waiting around to stand trial. It was also a frightening one. It was a ridiculous scheme and one that would, no doubt, get everyone involved killed. Nevertheless, after some discussion, Piquett passed the note to Billie, who got it to John Hamilton.

Piquett's investigator, Art O'Leary, who offered assistance to Dillinger in the months to come, and never betrayed him.

Hamilton had been hiding out with Pat Cherrington since he had gotten word about the others being arrested in Arizona. To get Dillinger out of jail, he was going to need help. Desperate, he reached out to a man that he knew he could trust – Homer Van Meter. At the time, Van Meter was in St. Paul, where he had hooked back up with Baby Face Nelson.

Nelson was already preparing for "bank robbing season" in the spring, when the back roads of the Midwest would be open and free of winter snow and ice. He sat down with ex-con Eddie Green to discuss the best banks to hit and came up with three: one in Sioux Falls, South Dakota, and two in Iowa, in Mason City and Newton. The problem was manpower, because at the time, Nelson only had three men. There had been a number of recent arrests and the number of trusted men for new jobs was in steep decline. No one was eager to work with strangers.

A solution came with the telephone call from John Hamilton, asking if Nelson's gang might be able to free Dillinger from the Crown Point jail. By all accounts, Nelson was interested in the idea. Hamilton, likely knowing the dynamite and blowtorch plan was out of the question, suggested that they smuggle Dillinger a gun. Nelson didn't know how, but he knew Alvin Karpis did. Karpis had once told him that he had smuggled a gun to Harvey Bailey in a Kansas jail. The gun was discovered, but at least they got it inside. Nelson sent word to Karpis in Chicago and he and Van Meter met up with him to discuss ideas.

Karpis wasn't eager to get involved. He was dealing with enough heat already. On January 17, he and other members of the Barker-Karpis gang had kidnapped a banker and beer baron's son named Edward Bremer from the streets of St. Paul. They drove him to a house in Bensenville, Illinois, where he was restrained and forced to provide the names of people who would act as intermediaries in getting a $200,000 ransom. Bremer's father refused to pay unless he saw some proof of life, so Bremer was forced to write a note, pleading that he be returned to his wife and children. When Adolph Bremer also tried to reduce the

Barker gang leader, Alvin Karpis, who would play a role in the future of the Dillinger Gang, and his part in the Bremer kidnapping would keep his gang in the headlines, along with Dillinger.

ransom money, Fred Barker became enraged and suggested they should kill Edward. His brother Arthur and Karpis overruled him. In the end, the ransom was paid by dropping off a bag full of cash, which was collected by George Ziegler. Bremer was driven to a deserted road by Ziegler and released on February 7, left on the empty road with a small amount of cash. He had to make his own way back home. Ever since the kidnapping, Bureau agents had been all over St. Paul, looking for the gang members.

Nelson and Van Meter left with some ideas, but not much else. Back in Chicago the next day, Karpis mentioned the brewing rescue attempt to Fred Barker, who said that he hoped they had better luck than they had with Bailey.

"I don't know," replied Karpis. "I got a feeling that Dillinger'll get killed there in that jail. I don't think he's gonna make it, but they're goddamn sure gonna try."

Dillinger was quiet and well-behaved in the Crown Point jail. He spent most of his time stewing about how to escape. Billie had passed along the news that Hamilton had rejected the dynamite idea, and Dillinger couldn't blame him. It was a suicidal plan. Hamilton had been in contact with Van Meter and Nelson, who offered to front Dillinger the money for bribes, which could be put to good use.

Through Piquett, and using the money provided by Nelson, Dillinger managed to bribe one of the jail officers (most accounts implicate Deputy Sheriff Ernest Blunk) to smuggle a wooden gun into the facility, and Edwin J. Saager, a garage mechanic, who was to provide a fast car for the escape. By bringing a fake gun into the jail, a cover story could be devised that Dillinger had gotten a razor from a piece of wood, which he then darkened with shoe polish to make it look authentic.

With the bribes distributed, the breakout was originally planned for Friday, March 2. However, Piquett had not yet tracked down a wooden gun. It showed up at the office around noon that day and someone subsequently passed it to Blunk. Early on the chilly, gloomy morning of March 3, Blunk gave the wooden gun to Dillinger, who then began looking for his chance to get out of the "escape proof" jail.

A hard rain was coming down on Crown Point that morning. It was a raw and gusty day and low gray clouds hung ominously over the brick jail. Just after 9:00 a.m., Sam Cahoon, a 64-year-old janitor, passed through the receiving room and trudged up to the criminal cell block, where Dillinger was held. After gathering his mops, Cahoon hollered for a guard named Win Bryant to let the prisoners out of their cells so he could clean. Together, the two men entered a metal box on the corridor wall and threw the lever that opened the cells, allowing Dillinger and 14 other prisoners to roam the wide corridor between the barred cell block. A few minutes later, after doing some other chores, Cahoon returned, and with Bryant looking on, pulled the lever to open the barred door, letting in two jail trustees, who carried a box of toilet paper, soap, and cleanser.

Cahoon had just stepped into the cell block, passing by Dillinger, when the bandit thrust his wooden gun into Cahoon's side and took him hostage. He turned Cahoon around and faced Bryant. "C'mon Sam," he said, "we're going places. You're gonna be good, aren't you?"

As Cahoon mumbled something in reply, a hulking black prisoner named Herbert Youngblood, who was in jail while he was awaiting trial for murder, appeared at Dillinger's side. He was carrying a wooden toilet plunger handle as a weapon. He was the only inmate that Dillinger had been able to talk into helping him. "You got a gun?" Youngblood asked Bryant. The guard shook his head. It was jail policy; no one carried guns near the cell block.

Dillinger motioned toward an open cell. He made Bryant and the two trustees get inside. Cahoon started to follow them, but Dillinger stopped him before he closed the cell door. "No, I got use for you," he said. "You're going to get me out of here."

Dillinger pushed the janitor outside the cell block. The only way out was down a 70-foot concrete corridor that led to the warden's office. At that time of the morning, the warden and a group of guards were sipping coffee and preparing for the day. It was the only way out. A flight of four steps bisected the corridor, dividing the old jail from the more recent addition. It put Dillinger just above the group's line of sight.

"How many doors between me and the outside?" Dillinger asked Cahoon.

The janitor thought for a moment, then answered, "Four."

Dillinger didn't have long, maybe only minutes, before someone came into the cell block. He demanded the location of guards, doors, and guns from Cahoon, using a pencil to draw a diagram of the jail on a shelf. Cahoon told him all that he could. Then Dillinger, his wooden gun still in the older man's back, led Youngblood slowly along the corridor, stopping at the top of the steps. Bending down to peer along the hallway, they saw a man cross between rooms. "Who's that?" Dillinger demanded.

Cahoon replied, "Ernest Blunk." Blunk was a 32-year-old deputy sheriff and, according to some sources, was the man who had been bribed to bring Dillinger's gun into the jail.

Herbert Youngblood, the only inmate at the jail who was brave enough to go along with Dillinger's escape plan.

Dillinger told Cahoon to call to him and Cahoon hollered, "Blunk! Come here a minute!"

When Blunk approached, he looked up the steps and saw Dillinger. He quickly surrendered and when Cahoon refused to help Dillinger any further, he shoved the janitor into the cell with Officer Bryant and the trustees. He took Blunk along in the man's place.

Using Deputy Sheriff Blunk to summon Warden Lou Baker and several guards, Dillinger locked them in cells. One by one, they were surprised and locked in the cell with the others. One of them, Kenneth "Butch" Houk, reached for Dillinger's gun, but Dillinger overpowered him and shoved him into the cell. As they left the cell tier, they encountered trustee John Kowaliszyn, who offered no resistance and was taken prisoner.

After Dillinger took a full set of keys from the trustee, he, Youngblood, and Blunk entered the jail office, where guns and ammunition were stored. He took the warden's two machine guns, keeping one and handing the other to Youngblood.

With Youngblood, trailing behind, he swept through the first floor of the jail and released the prisoners, forcing them to march in front of him. When they encountered an Indiana National Guardsman on duty, he was relieved of his .45-caliber pistol. With too many hostages to handle, he sent the prisoners back to the cellblock. He, Youngblood, and Blunk went into the kitchen, where three more

Deputy Sheriff Ernest Blunk, who most suspect smuggled the wooden gun into the jail for Dillinger. He made a convenient — and easygoing — hostage during the jailbreak.

guards, the warden's wife, and her mother, Mary Linton, were taken prisoner. Dillinger put on a hat and overcoat that was hanging on the wall and took his captives back to the cellblock, after assuring the women that he wouldn't hurt them.

The women were locked in the basement laundry, and the guards were taken to the cellblock where Dillinger had left his other captives. A search of the jail turned up another five guards, who were locked in with the others. Dillinger, Youngblood, and Blunk went into the jail garage, where there were two cars, but the keys were missing. They went back inside and Dillinger went through the warden's desk and then returned to the cell where he had locked up the guards. He told them that he needed some money for his escape and took up a collection of $15. He then laughed and rapped the wooden gun on the cell doors so that they could see what he had used to escape. He told Warden Baker, "I'm sorry to have to do this to you, Mr. Baker. But you can see how it is."

The warden sighed. "Yes, John, I can see how it is."

After Dillinger locked several doors behind him, he, Youngblood, Blunk, and three trustees who had joined the group walked through the kitchen door and into a side yard. Dillinger and Youngblood, each still armed with machine guns, led the group through the yard and entered the back door of the Main Street Garage. No guards were around. They had apparently all been stationed in front of the jail, and yet, did not hear the clamor of more than 30 jail employees yelling from the windows to be let out.

On an interesting note, the sister of the garage's owner, Clyde Rothermel, was married to the brother of Dillinger pal John Hamilton. Rothermel knew there was going to be an escape attempt, but he wanted nothing to do with it, since he would be an obvious suspect, so he stayed home. Oddly, no one seriously investigated him in the wake of the escape. Mechanic Edwin Saager and Robert Volk, a mail truck driver, were the only people inside of the garage. Although Volk had a pistol, he offered no resistance when Dillinger walked in and demanded the fastest car in the garage.

Saager showed him to Sheriff Holley's Ford, which was gassed up and ready to go. Dillinger allowed the trustees to return to the jail, while he got into the car's

The garage from which Dillinger escaped in Sheriff Holley's car. It was located next to the courthouse. The jail is on the far right side.

passenger seat and forced Blunk to drive. Youngblood and Saager climbed into the back. Holding a machine gun across his lap, Dillinger ordered Blunk to drive out of the garage. He laughed, "Maybe I ought to go back and tell Mrs. Holley I'm leaving. She seemed like an awfully nice lady, and I don't want her to feel hurt about all this."

As the car sped away from the jail, Blunk came close to hitting a passing motorist and drove through a red light. He was moving so fast that Dillinger later said that he was tempted to rob the local bank with the officer as his getaway driver.

Meanwhile, mail truck driver Edwin Volk immediately called the police, then ran out of the garage and yelled at a volunteer guard who was stationed across the street, telling him what had happened. He was met with skepticism. He then hurried next door to the prosecutor's office, where numerous guards had been stationed to prevent a raid on the jail. Once again, no one believed him. But Volk was insistent and so several of the volunteers went next door and tried to get into the jail. The doors were all locked. It took more than 10 minutes for them to get inside and free the imprisoned jail employees. Sheriff Holley was first told of the escape by John Hudak, a trustee, and immediately notified the state police. She thought the escape was "too ridiculous for words." She couldn't believe that it could happen. The sheriff denied a report that she had a job that was too big for a woman. "Oh, hell's fire, of course not," she scoffed, adding, "If I ever see John Dillinger again, I'll shoot him dead with my own pistol."

As the escapees left Crown Point behind, Dillinger worried about roadblocks and sent Blunk off onto gravel roads. He had him stop once to remove the red light from the front of the sheriff's car, and instructed him to keep his speed down to 30 miles an hour so they wouldn't attract attention. Dillinger sang as they drove along muddy back roads. Along one muddy track about two miles from Peotone, Illinois, the car skidded into a ditch filled with water. It took Saager half an hour to put chains on the rear wheels so that the vehicle could get out of the ditch.

Once he was finished, Dillinger set his two captives free, giving them $4 for food and carfare. Dillinger apologized and told them that he would have given them more if he had it.

Suspecting that a white man and a black man traveling together would draw too much notice, Dillinger told Youngblood to hunker down in the back seat. Then, waving at the two men he'd left on the side of the road, he drove off toward Chicago – never realizing that by driving across the state line in a stolen car had finally caused him to commit a crime that the Bureau of Investigation actually had jurisdiction over. Hoover and his agents could now join the hunt.

A farmer later picked up Saager and Blunk and took them back into town, where they explained what had happened and called Sheriff Holley. Blunk later said, "I was never scared of Dillinger. I knew he wouldn't hurt me. He was too nice for that."

Since there was no extensive radio system that could quickly alert police throughout the region about the escape, Dillinger and Youngblood reached Chicago without incident. It didn't hurt that the authorities in Crown Point had given out the wrong license number for the sheriff's stolen car. The police were slow to find out what had happened. In fact, officials in Indianapolis learned about the escape from local newspapers.

No one knew where Dillinger was, but he was now the most wanted man in America.

Louis Piquett learned of the escape from a telephone call that morning, while Billie was in his office. One of Piquett's nephews called him to tell him that he had heard it on the radio. The attorney called the Crown Point jail warden, Lou Baker, to confirm the story. It was true, Dillinger had "just left us," Baker told him resignedly.

The gin flowed freely for the next couple of hours while Billie, Piquett, O'Leary, and Meyer Bogue, an ex-con gofer, celebrated the escape. Bogue ran out and grabbed some of the newspaper extras that were already appearing and they read them between drinks.

Outside, the police were swarming the streets, taking positions at the main entry ways to the city from the south. Acting Police Commissioner Ira McDowell warned that, "If Dillinger sticks his head inside Chicago, he will be shot at first sight. Those are my orders."

Piquett knew that his office would be watched. He thought of a former secretary, a woman named Esther Anderson, who lived on Wellington Avenue, on the North Side. He sent Billie over, then followed in a taxi. O'Leary stayed behind, waiting for Dillinger's call. The telephone rang around 3:00. Dillinger only spoke a few words, "Where will I go?" O'Leary gave him the address and told him that Piquett would be waiting.

Piquett was leaning against the building at 434 Wellington Avenue, hat pulled down, and hands stuffed in his pockets, when Dillinger drove up. He greeted the lawyer with a wave. Piquett walked over to the car and found Herbert Youngblood lying flat on the backseat, two machine guns clutched in his hands. "Is this the place I'm going to stay?" Dillinger asked, eyeing the building.

Piquett shook his head. "No, I just want to bring you up here for a few minutes so we can talk."

The home of Billie's sister at 3512 North Halsted

The two men walked into the lobby, where Billie leaped into Dillinger's arms. Upstairs, Esther Anderson took one look at Dillinger and told them to get out. Dillinger returned downstairs to the car with Billie, and Piquett came down a minute later. Billie suggested that they go to her sister's house on Halsted. Dillinger asked Piquett to come over later that evening. "And I need some money," he said to Piquett. "Let me have whatever you've got on you."

Piquett fished in his pocket and pulled out a roll of bills, handing Dillinger about $300.

On the way to the apartment, Dillinger put Youngblood on a streetcar, handed him $100, and thanked him. Youngblood wouldn't last long on the outside. He was killed in a police shoot-out in Michigan two weeks later.

Dillinger and Billie went to her sister's place, a second-floor flat at 3512 North Halsted. That night, Piquett visited and listened as Dillinger told them what had happened at Crown Point. During the story, Piquett asked him when he could expect to be paid. A dark cloud passed over Dillinger's face. His previous attorney was supposed to have given Piquett the $500 he had initially been paid, but hadn't earned. He promised to sort out the fee right away.

The next day, Dillinger stayed in the apartment, speaking at one point with John Hamilton, who told him about arrangements with Nelson and his gang. That night, Tommy Carroll drove up in front of the building in a green Ford. Dillinger and Billie came out a side entrance, carrying suitcases, and climbed into the backseat. They headed northwest out of the city, toward St. Paul and a meeting with Dillinger's new partner, Baby Face Nelson.

17. Meanwhile... in Ohio

Dillinger's escape from the supposedly "escape-proof" jail caused a sensation across the country.

Even President Franklin D. Roosevelt, in his radio "Fireside Chat," told the nation that he was "shocked by the public adulation of a vicious criminal... It permits police to be corrupted and intimidated, and romanticizes men who are nothing but insane murderers." J. Edgar Hoover called the event a "damnable outrage," and said, "Someone is guilty either of nonfeasance or malfeasance. Either negligence or corruption must be at the bottom of this. That is true of nearly all jailbreaks. Escape from a good jail is impossible if the jail authorities are both diligent and honest." Republicans used it as an opportunity to criticize the Democratic governments of Indiana and Lake County. Many thought it was humorous, suggesting that perhaps Crown Point should be re-named, "Clown Point."

The *Chicago Tribune* told its readers that Dillinger, "aided only by his desperate courage and a little toy pistol he had made himself escaped yesterday morning from the heavily guarded jail. Colonel Henry Barrett Chamberlain, the director of the Chicago Crime Commission, was "speechless." He added that, "There should have been a competent, trustworthy, proven guard assigned to watch Dillinger day and night. I can't understand it."

Dillinger's relatives and friends were relieved. His father in Mooresville said, "It makes a fellow feel a little better, but of course they may catch him. Guess I'll start listening to the radio again now. When he was out before, that's about all I did when I wasn't working." Mary Kinder was delighted to hear the news – and relieved that she could prove that she had nothing to do with it.

Clarence Marley, the Mooresville justice of the peace who had arranged for Dillinger to be held for trial for the robbery of Mr. Morgan years before, put a notice on a bulletin board in the city hall, which read: "Johnnie isn't with them anymore."

Many letters to the editor continued to support Dillinger. One writer suggested, "Governor McNutt, why not give Dillinger a gold medal and a pardon? He deserves both. Hurray, for you, John. May you never be caught!" Only a few letters criticized the bandit and disagreed with the idea of Dillinger as some sort of Robin Hood-like folk hero.

Many investigations were made into the escape, but nothing was ever proven. However, the *Crown Point Register* snarkily noted, Dillinger's escape had caused an "unwholesome fear of the toy pistol as a dangerous weapon. What would have been just a plank in the hands of an ordinary prisoner helped to bring an instant compliance to Dillinger's commands."

Things weren't going so well for the outlaws in Ohio.

On February 13, some three weeks before the Crown Point escape, Harry Pierpont, Charlie Makley, and Russell Clark, were taken from Michigan City to Lima, Ohio, to be arraigned for the murder of Sheriff Sarber. After Leo M. Larkins, police chief of Findlay, Ohio, who was serving as a volunteer guard, refused to loosen Makley's handcuffs at the Indiana State Prison, Makley would not come out of his cell. Larkins was forced to drag the gangster out. On the trip to Lima, Larkins had Makley shackled to him. The two men practically snarled at one another during the entire trip. Makley promised to "get" Larkins when he got out. If he didn't, he would have some of his friends get the police chief. Larkins, a former football player, wasn't impressed. He told Makley that if he saw him again, he'd give him "the licking of your life."

Makley loudly protested his treatment at the county jail. He complained to reporters that he was unable to communicate with the outside, referred to the jail as a "dungeon," and said that the prisoners had been treated like "a pack of wolves."

On February 17, they were arraigned in Lima. All three were granted trials and entered not-guilty pleas to charges of killing Sarber.

When Dillinger escaped from Crown Point on March 3, the three men, expecting to be rescued soon, put on their best clothes and waited – and then waited some more. Residents and town officials in Lima, terrified that an attempt would be made to break out the prisoners, called in the National Guard. The number of guards at the jail was doubled, and sandbag emplacements containing heavy machine guns were set up outside. Based on information from an unknown source, Ohio Guard Brigadier General Harold M. Bush announced that Dillinger was on his way to Lima.

But he never came. Dillinger would have needed an army to break his friends out of the jail and he was too busy running for his life, trying to get as far away from Indiana and Chicago as he could

On March 8, Harry Pierpont became the first of the indicted outlaws to go on trial for Sheriff Sarber's murder. The atmosphere of the trial was a like a carnival, set up in a state of panic. Special passes were required to enter the courtroom, which was kept locked when the trial was in session, and even the jurors were searched when they entered. Armed guards stood outside the courtroom and Pierpont was shackled hand and foot. He didn't have a lawyer as clever as Louis Piquett, although his attorney, Jessie Levy, did question the jurors about whether or not they were influenced by the "veritable fortress" that the courtroom had become. Prosecutor Ernest Botkin objected, stating that the "career and character of John Dillinger" justified the precautions. He demanded the death penalty because "it was necessary, to accomplish their purpose in a few minutes, that they act viciously, cruelly, murderously, as they did, to secure possession of the keys so that John Dillinger could be liberated. Death was part of the plan for this crime."

The testimony of Pierpont's mother, Lena, that the outlaw was "at my house eating supper" at the time of the murder carried little weight when measured against Mrs. Sarber's and Deputy Sharp's identification of Pierpont as the sheriff's killer. According to Mrs. Pierpont, when the police raided her home at midnight on the day of the killing, all of the gang had left except for her son, Harry, and his "wife," Mary, who were hiding in a secret room above the kitchen.

Pierpont testified that Sarber's gun, which had been found on him when he was arrested in Tucson, had been given to him by Dillinger on Christmas in Daytona Beach. He insisted that Edward Shouse, the bandit who had been kicked out of the gang and who now testified against Pierpont, was insane. When the prosecutor declared that Pierpont had stolen more than $250,000, the gangster replied that if he had, "at least I wasn't elected president of a bank first." The courtroom, of course, roared with laughter.

But the jury didn't find it so amusing. On March 11, he was found guilty of murder in the first degree, with no recommendation of mercy, which meant that a death sentence was mandatory.

When Pierpont walked past Makley's cell after the trial, Makley asked, "Well, what was it?"

"Well, what would it be?" Pierpont sighed.

Makley's trial began on March 12. As he left the jail for court, Pierpont called out, "Good luck, Charlie!" Makley's sisters, Florence and Mildred, and his half-brother, Fred, the only defense witness, attended the trial, during which Judge Emmitt E. Everett ominously stated, "We have received direct word that Dillinger is on his way here with armed men." This sent a ripple of terror through the courtroom, and it must have thrilled Makley at the defense table.

Governor White and his daughter, who were on hand for the trial, were placed under guard when the idea came into someone's head that Dillinger might kidnap them and use the two to ransom his fellow gangsters. Three heavily armed men, led by Dillinger, were reportedly seen driving in northwestern Ohio, someone announced. More armed men poured into the courthouse, upsetting Makley's attorney. He entered a motion for a change of venue, because the heavy police presence was prejudicial to his client, but the judge overruled it.

During the trial, which lasted six days from jury selection to verdict, Makley, like Pierpont, was handcuffed and shackles were placed on his feet as soon as he sat down. Ed Shouse refused to testify against Makley. After the closing arguments, the jury deliberated throughout the night of March 16. They found Makley guilty of murder in the first-degree, making the announcement the next morning. There was no recommendation of mercy, meaning that Makley would also receive the death penalty.

Russell Clark was the last to be tried. Opal paid Louis Piquett to help defend him, but when the boisterous attorney showed up in Lima, he was harassed and even jailed by the local police. He never got close to the courthouse and, eventually, he just gave up.

Clark's trial began on Monday, March 19. Jury selection took two days, and testimony began on Wednesday. Clark's attorney, Jessie Levy, asked Judge Everett for a directed verdict of not guilty on the basis that Clark "doesn't believe in capital punishment."

It was a desperate move and the judge had no patience for it. Everett snapped in reply, "This is utterly silly for you to say, because he is on trial for murder, that he doesn't believe in capital punishment." Despite more arguments from Levy, the judge ruled against him.

Ed Shouse testified against Clark, but insisted that he had only fired one shot on the night of the jailbreak and murder, and had injured himself. Clark's mother, May, insisted that her son had been in Detroit on the night of the murder. A brother-in-law, Andrew Stracham, and a sister, Mrs. Beulah Stracham, also testified on Clark's behalf.

Clark had little hope for the trial. He often yawned and dozed off, believing that a death sentence was a foregone conclusion. But while the jury found him guilty of first-degree murder on March 24, there was a recommendation for mercy, which his friends had not received. The verdict caused Clark to be affected for the first time during the trial and he cried at the defense table.

That same day, both Pierpont and Makley were sentenced to die on Friday, July 13. The date was later changed to October 17. The death sentences were the first ever handed down in Allen County, Ohio, and newspaper accounts described Pierpont as "brazen and defiant." Clark received a life sentence on March 26.

On March 27, 1934, as sleet pelted them from the sky, the three bandits were taken from Lima to the Ohio State Penitentiary in Columbus. They were transported in a caravan led by 45 armed officers. National Guardsmen in two trucks kept machine guns aimed at the crowd of spectators outside of the prison.

It was the last home that all of the men would ever know.

18. The Second Dillinger Gang

While Indiana politicians and prosecutors were squabbling over who was responsible for Dillinger's escape, the bandit had managed to finally come to the attention of the Federal Bureau of Investigation. The agency officially became involved in the hunt when Dillinger drove Sheriff Holley's stolen car from Indiana to Illinois. By crossing the state line, he had violated the federal Dyer Act, also called the National Motor Vehicle Theft Act, which was enacted in 1919 to impede the interstate trafficking of stolen vehicles by organized thieves.

After the escape, Hoover called Melvin Purvis, the special agent in charge of the division's Chicago field office, to express surprise that the office "had done practically nothing in this matter," although Hoover had previously ordered that they were "not to take the initiative," and had turned down previous requests for assistance from Indiana. But now, he insisted that there would be no more inaction and told Purvis to "take immediate steps" and "put forth every effort" to apprehend Dillinger.

Melvin Purvis was a boyish agent from South Carolina who was not yet 30-years-old when Dillinger first started making headlines. Unhappy as an attorney in his hometown, he had enrolled at the Bureau in 1926 and swiftly moved up the ranks. He became Hoover's favorite Special Agent in Charge and their correspondences struck up a more familiar tone than the director's letters to other agents. In many early letters, Hoover admonished the handsome young man to stop referring to him as "mister," and he often commented on Purvis' attractiveness to women. Staff members in the Chicago office always believed that Purvis was one of Hoover's favorite agents and some would later speculate that it was romantic in nature. But if so, it was unrequited. Purvis was a dedicated lady's man who would later marry.

In the first days of the Bureau's involvement in the hunt for Dillinger, Purvis still had Hoover's every confidence – but later, that would change, and he would find himself demoted and berated right out of the Bureau.

The hunt for John Dillinger would become the most important case in the Bureau's history. More than anything else, it would validate the Roosevelt administration's push for a national law-enforcement authority and make the Bureau a real American institution. It would seem natural for Hoover to eagerly join the manhunt, but this was not the case. In fact, he saw the Dillinger case as a potential quagmire and he long resisted allowing the Bureau to be drawn into it, as evidenced by the way that he had stayed clear of the hunt after the death of Sheriff Sarber.

And Hoover was no more eager to chase Dillinger in the hours after his escape from Crown Point. The Kansas City Massacre, as well as the Barker-Karpis gang's kidnapping of Edward Bremer, were still unresolved at that point, and drew the daily attention of dozens of agents, including 14 on Bremer in Chicago alone. Purvis drove down to Crown Point to survey the situation, but reporter's calls to the Bureau were met with indifference and the callers were informed that "Dillinger was not a federal prisoner."

But when Dillinger's escape began dominating national newspaper headlines, Hoover telephoned Purvis. He did not immediately order Purvis onto the case. Instead, FBI records indicate that he attempted to gauge the Bureau's chances of success if it joined the manhunt. Specifically, Hoover asked Purvis what information his informants could give them that might lead to Dillinger's arrest.

But Purvis had little, or nothing, to offer. He had no informants in place and was unsure how to proceed with any information that he might gather. In fact, his questions to Bureau headquarters suggest someone who was badly out of his depth. Purvis thought he might want to tap some telephones, but he was unclear about the legality of wiretaps in Illinois. He twice called Sam Cowley, the agent who served as the Bureau's investigative chief, and asked whether he needed to bring Chicago police along with him on a raid. By law he did, Cowley reminded him, personally believing that Purvis only wanted the police along to buoy his confidence.

Purvis hired a confidential informant – a source he had used before, at $5 a day – and mounted a raid with Chicago police officers a few days after Dillinger's escape. They stormed the apartment of a woman named Anne Baker, whom the informant erroneously charged with hiding Dillinger after his jail break. The raid was a disaster. No one named Baker lived in the apartment. It wasn't until the next morning that Purvis learned he had raided the wrong address.

But the headlines kept appearing, finally forcing Hoover's hand. He sent a wire to all Bureau offices, directing agents to "give preferred and immediate attention" to the Dillinger case. As mentioned, the rationale for the Bureau entering the case

Agent Melvin Purvis – He would soon be the most famous G-man in the country, whether J. Edgar Hoover liked it or not

was that Dillinger had crossed state lines with a stolen car, but this was a thin excuse. Hoover was forced into the Dillinger case by his own ambitions – if the Bureau wasn't hunting the country's most wanted man, what was the point of it?

With no evidence that Dillinger had left the Chicago area, the impact of Hoover's directive fell heavily on the overwhelmed Purvis. Unsure where to begin, Purvis sought guidance from John Stege from the Chicago Police Department's Dillinger Squad, but Stege stonewalled him. Since the Bureau had been unwilling to help anyone else with the case, why should anyone else help the Bureau?

Stuck, Purvis had to start from scratch, pulling five agents off the Bremer kidnapping case to look for Dillinger. It's difficult to say whether the questionable quality of the Bureau's work in the weeks that followed was due to the Bureau's indifference, or Purvis' lack of experience. Agents headed for the Crown Point jail, taking statements from everyone involved in the escape, and visited the prison at Michigan City, where onetime gang member Ed Shouse gave them Billie Frechette's name. For the next 10 days, as Dillinger sightings poured in from cities as far away as Los Angeles and Seattle, Purvis and his men looked into Billie's background and searched for the relatives of Dillinger's jailed partners.

The investigation went precisely nowhere.

Dillinger was, of course, where no one was looking for him.

The bank robber was busy fleeing from Chicago while his pals were getting ready for their trials in Ohio. He arrived in Minneapolis just 36 hours after escaping from Crown Point, and ended his trip at the Santa Monica Apartments on South Girard Avenue. Eddie Green had rented the place for Dillinger and Billie under the name "Mr. and Mrs. Olson." Billie gave the janitor a $50 deposit, and they wired the shades closed.

There is no record to say what happened at Dillinger's meeting with Lester Gillis, a.k.a. Baby Face Nelson, the following day. The two outlaws likely knew one another. There are unconfirmed accounts that they met in East Chicago the previous June, and there had been talk of teaming up for a train robbery that autumn. The two men had friends and contacts in common, and they certainly knew one another by reputation. Dillinger was grateful to Nelson for fronting the money for his escape bribes, and grateful for accepting him into a new bank robbery gang. For weeks afterward, he remarked to people about what a huge favor Nelson had done for him.

For Nelson, working with Dillinger meant instant respect and prestige, two things that Nelson craved – one year before, the 24-year-old had been a gangland chauffeur. Now he was running a gang that included the nation's most wanted bank robber. Dillinger gracefully accepted a secondary position in "Nelson's gang," but the press certainly didn't see it that way. When the two were eventually linked, the newspapers dubbed them the "Second Dillinger Gang," which angered the hot-headed Nelson.

There is no record of what happened at that first meeting just as it is always unknown whether or not Dillinger realized that he was joining forces with a psychopath.

On the night that Dillinger arrived in the Twin Cities, Nelson was driving through Minneapolis with John Chase when the two cut in front of a car driven by a paint salesman named Ted Kidder, who was returning from a birthday party with his wife and her mother. Irritated that Nelson had cut him off, Kidder sped up and cut back in front of Nelson. This enraged the gangster. Nelson pulled alongside Kidder's car and attempted to force it to the curb. Kidder pulled ahead, but Nelson stayed directly behind him as they neared the Kidder home in the St. Louis Park section of Minneapolis. Not wanting to lead the angry driver to his house, Kidder headed toward a drug store, where he could call the police. When he reached the store, he quickly got out of the car just as Nelson drove up and shouted something at him. A moment later, three shots rang out. Two bullets struck Kidder in the midsection and he fell to the pavement.

Baby Face Nelson was thought by many to be a psychopath, but he was unquestionably afflicted with "small man's syndrome" and the need to always prove himself. He chose to do so through violence.

His wife, Bernice, ran to his side. "You've killed him!" she screamed.

Nelson snapped, "Keep your damn mouth shut, or I'll let you have it, too." He backed up the car and drove off.

On the cold Tuesday morning of March 6, a green Packard sedan pulled to a stop in front of the Security National Bank & Trust Company in Sioux Falls, South Dakota, one of the targets on the list that Nelson had recently put together. Six men in dark overcoats got out of the car and stepped onto the sidewalk. Looking around with their fedoras pulled down low on their heads, they made for an ominous scene. A bank stenographer saw them through the window. She joked to the clerk, "There's a bunch of hold-up men." And she was right.

Just three days after he had escaped from the Crown Point jail, Dillinger was about to rob a bank. One of the men remained by the car as Tommy Carroll took his position next to the front door, a machine gun hidden under his coat. Dillinger and Nelson led John Hamilton and the others inside. As soon as they walked into the lobby, Nelson threw open his overcoat, pulled out his machine gun, and shouted, "This is a hold-up! Everyone on the floor!"

As a dozen or so employees and customers inside the bank lay down on the floor or backed against the walls, a clerk managed to push a button that caused

Security National Bank & Trust Company in Sioux Falls, South Dakota

an alarm to begin loudly ringing outside of the bank. Nelson flinched as it began to clang, but Dillinger, accustomed to working at the sound of an alarm, walked coolly to the tellers' cages and, with Homer Van Meter, began sweeping stacks of cash off the counter and into bags. Nelson became more agitated as the alarm continued to ring. In contrast to the others, who remained calm, he began to pace the lobby nervously, sticking the muzzle of his machine gun into the hostages' faces. He began to shout, "I'd like to know who set that alarm off! Who did it? Who?"

As Dillinger and Van Meter shoved the bank president toward the door to the vault, Nelson was working himself into a frenzy. He pointed his gun at one employee after another. "If you want to get killed, just make some move!" he yelled at them. "If you want to get killed, just make some move!"

Within minutes, the first police officers arrived outside. A traffic cop, Homer Powers, was the first to answer the alarm. Tommy Carroll met him with his machine gun, and in moments Powers was standing on the sidewalk with his hands above his head. The police chief, M.W. Parsons, and one of his detectives, arrived next on the scene. They were also disarmed and joined Powers on the sidewalk. A crowd of townspeople started to gather, drawn by the sound of the alarm and the sight of the three policemen with their arms raised in surrender.

In the lobby, Nelson was still pacing nervously. Just then, a motorcycle cop named Hale Keith drove up outside of the bank. Spotting him through the large front window, Nelson jumped over a low railing, scrambled onto the loan officer's desk, and let loose a deafening barrage of gunfire through the plate-glass window. Women screamed as Keith fell, hit by four of the bullets. According to accounts, Nelson laughed maniacally and shouted, "I got one! I got one!"

As Dillinger and Van Meter finished in the vault, the crowd outside continued to grow. People were leaning out of second-story windows, watching Carroll, who had managed, without firing a shot, to disarm most of the city's police department, pace up and down in the street. There were now hundreds of spectators watching the scene, chuckling and laughing – why was no one reacting? They were under the impression that a Hollywood movie was being shot in their town and that the bank robbery was just part of the action. Just the day before, a movie producer had been in town spreading the word that he would be filming in Sioux Falls the following day. The "movie producer" had been Homer Van Meter.

Inside, Dillinger and Van Meter were finishing up. Just as Dillinger had done in Racine, they grabbed a bank manager and four tellers and herded them out onto the sidewalk to the car. As they left, Nelson shot out the bank's front windows.

By this time, other police officers had taken up position on the street, hoping to get a shot at the bank robbers as they made their escape. The scattered gunshots that rang out as they emerged from the bank were real – this was no movie.

The bandits loaded the bank manager, Leo Olson, and the tellers onto the Packard's running boards. The car had just started to move when a policeman fired a shot into its radiator. Steam began hissing out from under the hood. The car stopped and the hostages jumped off. One of the women began to run, but she was stopped in her tracks by a shout from the bandits. A minute later, the hostages were back on the running boards, and the Packard again moved forward slowly through the city streets, and south toward the cold prairie at the edge of town.

Once they hit Route 77, Dillinger ordered the car stopped again. He and John Hamilton got out and sprinkled roofing nails all over the road, which would slow down any pursuit. With the Packard's engine coughing and sputtering, they continued their escape. A few miles later, though, the car finally began to falter. Everyone jumped out, hailed an oncoming Dodge, and sent the frightened owner running out into the fields. The bandits shoved the hostages onto the highway and began transferring a set of gas cans to the new car.

Just as the gang was switching cars, Sheriff Melvin L. Sells, in pursuit with three men in a squad car, spotted the cars parked on the highway. Sells stopped about 100 yards back, not wanting to jeopardize the safety of the hostages. Nelson, spotting the police car, fired a volley of machine gun fire their way. The officers saw Dillinger grab Nelson and pull him into the car and the gang sped off to the south.

Years later, Sheriff Sells insisted that he chased the gang for two hours, giving up only after he lost them somewhere in Iowa. However, the next day, the morning newspaper reported that the sheriff turned back the moment that the robbers opened fire on them. The gang's fleeing car was last seen in southwestern Minnesota, heading toward St. Paul, but the local sheriffs who gave chase were unable to catch up to it.

The following day, the newspapers, the eyewitnesses, and even the bank president swore that it had been Dillinger that robbed the bank, but almost no one believed them, including Hoover's Bureau. The idea that Dillinger could rob a bank three states away, only three days after escaping from Crown Point, was considered ridiculous. A St. Paul agent arrived in Sioux Falls the next day, but the Bureau investigation never went any further.

The gang returned to its apartments in the Twin Cities to split the haul. It came to roughly $46,000, nearly $8,000 per man. What Dillinger thought of

Nelson's crazed behavior is unknown, but the events of the day were a clear indication of the two gang leader's different styles. Whatever he thought, Dillinger needed Nelson's gang. For the first time, he had bills to pay, to Piquett, and to attorneys representing Pierpont, Makley, and Clark, who were then still on trial for Sheriff Sarber's murder in Ohio. He needed more money and he needed it fast.

19. Robbery in Mason City

A week after the robbery in Sioux Falls, the gang moved on to its next target – the First National Bank in Mason City, Iowa. Eddie Green and Homer Van Meter spent a weekend in town, studying the layout of the bank and staying in a room at the YMCA. On Tuesday, March 13, the others drove down from St. Paul and they met at a sandpit at the southern edge of town. The party that met up with Green and Van Meter was made up of Dillinger, Nelson, John Hamilton, and Tommy Carroll.

They all knew this was a high-risk job. A year of robberies had turned many Midwestern banks into small fortresses, and the bank in Mason City, located on the town's square, was said to be the strongest in Iowa. A guard sat in a steel cage behind bulletproof glass on the second floor of the lobby. He was armed with tear gas and a rifle. But, dangerous or not, Green assured the others, the payoff was huge. He estimated that the vault held more than $250,000. If everything went according to plan, they wouldn't have to work again for months.

Around 2:00 p.m., the guns were loaded into the blue Buick that Green and Van Meter had been driving, and headed into town with Carroll at the wheel. They drove down Pennsylvania Avenue and stopped in front of the towering, seven-story red-brick façade of the First National Bank. A freelance cameraman named H.C. Kunkleman was on hand as the Buick came to a stop. Standing next to his tripod, Kunkleman watched, curious, as five well-dressed men got out of the car. One of them noticed Kunkleman's camera. The man called out to him, "Hey you! If there's any shooting to be done, we'll do it. Get that thing out of here." Kunkleman, startled, stop filming.

According to author Bryan Burroughs, Mason City historians have no idea of who Kunkleman was, or why he was filming that day. His footage of the robbery's prelude and aftermath was later developed and shown in a local theater. It then disappeared. For decades, locals tried in vain to locate Kunkleman or his film. It was finally found by a Mason City camera-store owner in 1996. The five-minute film, which shows scenes inside of the bank before and after the robbery, details the bullet holes and broken glass left in the wake of the raid, and features some of the bank officials, customers, and onlookers who witnessed the robbery taking place. It can now be found preserved online. Regrettably, Kunkleman stopped filming before he could capture the images of Dillinger, Nelson, or the other bank robbers on film.

Carroll was the man who remained in the car, cradling a rifle. Nelson walked up the sidewalk beside the bank, taking a position at the head of its rear alley. Dillinger, wearing a gray fedora and overcoat with a striped scarf, lingered outside the front door as Van Meter, Hamilton, and Green hurried into the bank.

The lobby was filled with customers, about two dozen of them, standing in lines in front of the tellers' cages. To get everyone's attention, one of the bandits raised a machine gun and fired a deafening volley into the ceiling. As chunks of

The First National Bank in Mason City, Iowa, the second target of the new Dillinger gang.

(Below) The bank's interior

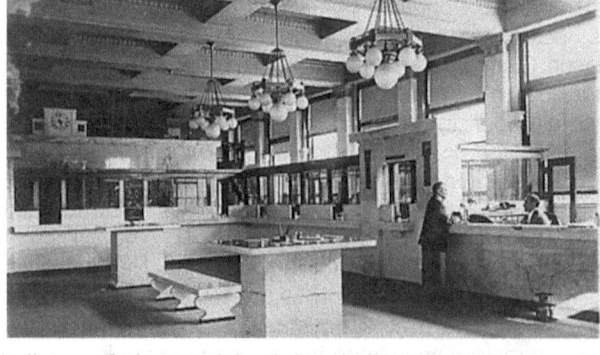

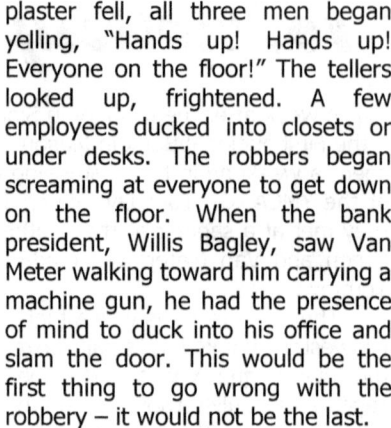

plaster fell, all three men began yelling, "Hands up! Hands up! Everyone on the floor!" The tellers looked up, frightened. A few employees ducked into closets or under desks. The robbers began screaming at everyone to get down on the floor. When the bank president, Willis Bagley, saw Van Meter walking toward him carrying a machine gun, he had the presence of mind to duck into his office and slam the door. This would be the first thing to go wrong with the robbery – it would not be the last.

Van Meter thrust his machine gun forward, preventing the door from closing. Bagley threw his weight into the door as Van Meter, after struggling for a moment, pulled the gun free. Stepping back, he fired a number of bullets through the door. Women screamed. Bagley, a bullet creasing his chest, sprawled behind his desk with his hands over his head. Van Meter gave up trying to break in and stormed through the lobby, ordering everyone onto the floor.

As he rushed across the lobby, still yelling, the guard in the steel cage above the front door, Tom Walters, recovered from his initial surprise and jammed a canister into his tear-gas gun. He aimed it through a gun slit in the bulletproof glass and fired the shell at Eddie Green, who was directly below him. It struck Green in the back and he was knocked to the floor, on top of a tangle of prone customers. A man on the floor kicked away the canister, which was spewing gas, and it skidded toward another man, who kicked it back.

Green got back to his feet with a dense cloud of tear gas forming around him and he looked up at Walters, who was struggling to clear his gas gun. The gun was jammed and nothing he could do would get it to fire again. Green grabbed the collar of a bank executive named R.L. Stephenson, held him up as a shield, and opened fire on Walters. The bulletproof glass cracked and splintered, and one bullet slipped through the gun slit, creasing a bloody line across the guard's chin and right ear. Furious, Green fired some more, but bullets ricocheted off the glass once again and he demanded to know how he could access the cage. "Get that sonofabitch with the tear gas!" Green yelled at Hamilton, who was busy scooping money off the counters.

Hamilton looked up and saw Walters struggling with the tear-gas gun, even as he was grabbing his Winchester rifle. For a few moments, the two men looked at each other. Hamilton could see that it was of no use to fire at the bulletproof glass, and Walters knew that he couldn't fire the rifle without hitting a civilian. Hamilton tried to provoke Walters to come out from the cage, or to shoot at him, but Walters later recalled, "I couldn't because I would've plugged half the people in the lobby."

Billowing clouds of tear gas floated through the bank, and more was coming. From a position on the mezzanine, a bank officer named Tom Barclay grabbed a tear-gas candle and tossed it down into the lobby. Gas was filtering into the second floor when a switchboard operator, Margaret Johnson, crawled over to a window and opened it. Looking down, she spotted a small man in a camel-hair overcoat standing in the alley. She begged him to call for help – the bank was being robbed.

The short man was Nelson. "Are you telling me, lady?"

By now, everyone in the bank was coughing, their eyes watering badly. The gas was so thick that it was difficult to see. As Green and Van Meter prowled the room, keeping everyone on the floor, Hamilton turned his attention from the bank guard to the assistant cashier named Harry Fisher. Hamilton, carrying a white cloth bag filled with money from the tellers' cages in one hand, he pressed a pistol into Fisher's back and shoved him toward the vault. Fisher was frightened, but he was also very aware that there was over $200,000 in cash inside of the vault. The cashier was dragging his feet and Hamilton gave him a boot to the backside to get him moving along.

When Fisher reached the barred door leading to the vault, he fished a key from his pocket, then opened the door and stepped inside. The gate snapped shut before Hamilton could enter behind him. There was now a barred door between the two men. Hamilton kept his gun trained on Fisher through it, but he was unable to enter, and Fisher claimed that he could not open the barrier from his side. Hamilton told him to shove the money through the bars and Fisher, determined to move as slowly as possible, walked into the vault and grabbed an armload of bags containing one-dollar bills. He plodded back to the barred door, sliding them one by one to Hamilton. When he was finished, he plodded back into the vault and grabbed more bags of ones. Hamilton growled at him, "If you don't hurry up, I'm gonna shoot you."

While Harry Fisher was cleverly slowing the robbery to a crawl, a huge crowd was gathering outside of the bank. People came out of stores and homes all around the square, drawn by the sound of the gunfire inside of the bank. For a few minutes, it was a festive affair with people laughing and joking. A few, spotting H.C. Kunkleman's tripod-mounted camera, thought a movie was being shot.

Dillinger was standing on the sidewalk by the bank's front entrance, smiling a little as he kept the crowd at bay, when Van Meter pushed 10 hostages out to join him. The two lined the group up in front of the bank, using them as human shields. Dillinger then ducked into the bank to see what was taking so much time. "Gimme three more minutes!" Hamilton called out to him.

Dillinger grabbed six or seven other people and pushed them toward the front door. "Stand close to me," Lydia Crosby, a bank stenographer, heard him say. Outside, Dillinger lined up these hostages with the others. There were now more than 15 bank employees and customers standing on the sidewalk in front of the bank, hands raised above their heads. Van Meter went into the shoe store next door and forced a half-dozen shoppers out onto the sidewalk to join them.

Then, from the right, came gunshots. It was Nelson, of course, firing off a volley of bullets at a reporter from the *Mason City Globe Gazette* who had heard shots and hurried to the scene. The reporter ducked into the Yelland and Hanes Book Store as the brick wall over his head was chipped by the flying lead. A moment later, a large Hudson sedan drove by. Nelson yelled, "Get back!" and then shot at it, too, bullets striking the radiator. The auto squealed to a stop, reversed direction, and sped back into the square, narrowly missing some bystanders. A little girl in the crowd began crying hysterically.

Nelson swung his machine gun left and right, apparently looking for any further "threats." As he waved the Thompson around, several eyewitnesses stated that he began laughing. He fired a barrage of shots at a row of parked cars, then another at the second floor of the hardware store. Several of the bystanders later admitted that they thought he was deranged. He was nothing like the calm, collected men in front of the bank, patiently reassuring the hostages that they meant them no harm.

Just then, a man named R.L. James, secretary to the Mason City school board, strolled up the sidewalk to the bank, somehow unaware that a robbery was in progress. "Stop right there!" Nelson screamed at him, but James, who was hard of hearing, kept walking. Nelson opened fire, hitting James in the leg, and he fell bleeding to the sidewalk. Nelson trotted up to him, snatched up a portfolio that James was carrying, and searched it. "I thought you were a cop, you sonofabitch," Nelson swore at him.

James moaned, "I'm not a cop."

Dillinger took a few steps down the sidewalk, likely regretting getting mixed up with the little gangster at all, and gestured at James. "Did you have to do that?" he asked.

Nelson snapped at him. "I thought he was a cop!"

As Dillinger turned away in disgust and walked back toward the hostages, an elderly judge named John C. Shipley was peering down from a third-floor window

A still from the Kunkleman film that was being shot just before the robbery took place in Mason City. The ad to the left is from the local Globe-Gazette newspaper and featured five minutes of film from just before the robbery. It was shown at the Cecil Theater on March 1?, 193?.

directly above him. Shipley had fished an old revolver from his desk drawer and, drawing a bead on Dillinger, he pulled the trigger. He winged Dillinger on the arm and the bank robber whirled around and fired a pistol several times up at the window. The bullets bounced off the front of the building and Shipley ducked away unhurt. Turning back, he spotted a city patrolman darting across the square. The officer, James Buchanan, ducked behind a large boulder that was used as a Civil War monument. Dillinger raised his gun and fired, the bullet ricocheting off the boulder. Dillinger could see that things were getting out of hand. He sent Van Meter to get the others and Van Meter hurried into the bank, waving away the tear gas, and yelled to Hamilton, "We're leaving!"

Hamilton was still having problems with Cashier Fisher and demanded more time from Van Meter. Hamilton could see the stacks of bills on the shelves inside of the vault. The cashier's speed had gone from slow to glacial. He demanded that Fisher bring him bigger bills, but Fisher continued to load stacks of one-dollar bills into the bandit's bag. Hamilton was enraged when Van Meter came inside and told him that they were leaving as he had only about $20,000 in his bag and there was over $200,000 still sitting in the vault. But he finally decided that he couldn't wait. A moment later, he turned from the vault door, grabbed a bank employee, and pushed him toward the front. In a minute, all six gang members were on the sidewalk outside, surrounded by about 25 hostages. Each man shoved a group of people toward the Buick. Their moods had rapidly turned sour. When Eddie Green spotted a man staring from behind a parked car, he yelled, "Pull in that damned turtleneck! I'll cut your head off!" He fired a single shot as the man ducked behind the car.

As the herd of bank robbers and hostages were making their way toward the getaway car, Judge Shipley returned to the overhead window and started shooting again. This time, spotting Hamilton with the money sack, he aimed in his direction. A shot from his revolver clipped Hamilton in the shoulder and the bandit lurched forward, stumbling toward the car. The wound was not serious, nor was Dillinger's.

Five hostages were shoved onto the running boards, two more on the front fender, and several more on the car's rear fender. Several women were pushed into the backseat. The car's windows were jammed with arms and legs. The bank robbers also piled inside and Tommy Carroll inched away from the curb and began slowly driving away, the car groaning and creaking under all of the extra weight. Witnesses counted anywhere from 20 to 25 people inside and outside of the car.

The overloaded automobile crept along at about 15 miles an hour as it zigzagged through city streets toward the edge of town. At one point, as they passed the Kirk Apartments, a woman named Minnie Piehm called out, "Let me out! This is where I live!" Unbelievably, Carroll stopped the car and Miss Piehm untangled herself from the backseat and trotted off to the apartment building. An assistant cashier was about to follow when one of the gang said, "Get back here, you."

As comical as the escape sounds, it wasn't funny to the hostages who were clinging to the car's running boards and fenders. "Stop looking at me or I'll kill you," one of the gang members snarled several times.

The police were unable to shoot or try and stop them with all of the hostages on the vehicle and so they were forced to follow at a distance. The slow pace made it easy for the police chief, E.J. Patton, to catch up. He was in one of the two squad cars that followed the Buick as it turned south on Highway 18 and began to pick up speed. At one point, as the getaway car crested a rise, Nelson said to Carroll, "Wait till they come over the hill and then I'll pop them off." Sitting in the front seat, Nelson struggled to the window and fired several wild shots at Chief Patton's car.

The chase continued. A few miles out of town, the Buick stopped. Nelson climbed out of the car and fired off a volley of machine gun fire at the chief's car, which had also stopped. He grabbed a bag of roofing tacks and began tossing them out by the handful, hoping to blow the tires on the pursuer's autos. Dillinger watched as several bounced under the Buick. In a calm voice, he said, "You're getting tacks under our own car."

When Nelson jumped back into the Buick, Carroll headed south once more, speeding up to about 30 miles an hour. It was snowing, and several of the hostages outside of the car were freezing. One of the tellers, Emmet Ryan, gave a woman his jacket. For some reason, this angered Dillinger, who gave him a cold stare. Most likely, Dillinger wanted to be the one who came to the woman's "rescue" and offered her a coat; it was better for his image. Ryan again irked Dillinger when the car turned onto a dirt road to release several hostages. Ryan started to walk away. Then, realizing how cold another hostage was without a coat, he suggested that the other man leave instead. "Who the hell is running this show?" Dillinger snapped at him.

Meanwhile, Chief Patton was still in pursuit. He pulled to the roadside when the car stopped, but Nelson was waiting for him. He opened fire, hitting the police car, but missing the chief. He told the departing hostages that they needed to pass on a message to the law. "Tell 'em if they don't stop following us we're gonna kill everyone in the car!"

The Buick continued on, weaving down old country roads for the next 45 minutes or so until they finally found the sand pit where they had left their second car. Most of the hostages were left there, but two accompanied the gang as they drove north. They were eventually released when Chief Patton turned back to Mason City. When they were certain that they had gotten away, the gang stopped to clean and bandage Dillinger's and Hamilton's shoulder wounds.

Dr. Nels Mortensen, the respected doctor who treated Dillinger for his gunshot wound. He was later arrested and spent a year in jail for his good deed — but maintained to the end of his life that he had no idea the wounded man was Dillinger.

They were back in St. Paul by nightfall. Bleeding and exhausted, the gang went looking for a doctor for Dillinger and Hamilton. Their first stop was Harry Sawyer's Green Lantern tavern, the infamous underworld haven. Sawyer wasn't there, but the bartender sent them to a local doctor named Nels Mortensen, a prominent physician with shady friends. He was president of the state board of health but he was also a friend of Harry Sawyer's and had treated Fred Barker for syphilis and took out the tonsils of one of Alvin Karpis's girlfriends.

When the gang arrived at his home, the Green Lantern bartender told the doctor that the two men had been hurt in a fight downtown. Mortensen said that he didn't have his medical bag with him, but he let the men into the house. Standing in his foyer, he took off Hamilton's bandages and checked the wound; it wasn't serious. Dillinger almost fainted when he stripped off his shirt. He stumbled into a chair, and Mortensen gave him a glass of water. Dillinger's wound was deeper, but only slightly more serious. He told the men to come to his office the next morning if they needed further treatment. As they left, the doctor caught a glimpse of a machine gun under Van Meter's coat. He went back to bed without telling anyone about the nocturnal visit.

A month later, though, when Bureau agents learned about the incident, Hoover decided to make an example out of Dr. Mortensen. He received a prison sentence of one year. When Mortensen died in 1971 at age 87, he still insisted that he had no idea that his patient that night was John Dillinger.

After returning from the doctor's house, the gang divided up the money. Despite cashier Fisher's attempts to bungle the robbery, they still got away with about $52,000. It wasn't the score that they had hoped for, but there were no complaints. The division of spoils that night offers a glimpse into the dynamics between the gang members. Later, after Pat Cherrington was arrested by Bureau agents, she spoke about that night and the way that Nelson "was very much disliked by all members of the mob." Everyone seemed to be on edge around him and on this night – as well as other nights after a bank robbery – they would invariably have Nelson sit in the middle of the room, although he was not aware they were arranging things in that way, and allow him to count off each person's share. All of the others surrounded him, facing Nelson, "as they expect at any time that Nelson would shoot them and take the entire amount."

After the money was split up, the gang scattered. Van Meter and his girlfriend, Mickey Conforti, settled into a new apartment on Girard Avenue in St. Paul. Dillinger and Billie had already moved into a new place on South Lexington Avenue, since they had to leave their Minneapolis apartment after Hamilton's gun accidentally went off and Dillinger didn't want to take the chance that they had been noticed. In the new place, Hamilton slept on the couch with Pat Cherrington.

On the Wednesday morning after the late-night visit to Dr. Mortensen, Dillinger took Billie to Chicago. Art O'Leary was in Louis Piquett's office when the phone rang. It was Dillinger, instructing the investigator to be in front of the office, on the Wacker Drive side, in 15 minutes. It was a short meeting in the car. O'Leary listened as Dillinger talked and drove. He wanted Piquett to help Billie arrange a divorce so that they could be married. O'Leary promised to pass on the message and Piquett sighed when he did so. For the trouble of representing Dillinger, he had yet to be paid anything at all.

That night and the next, Dillinger and Billie bunked in the basement of Louis Cernocky's Crystal Ball Room in Fox River Grove, a notorious spot that often offered overnight stays for underworld figures looking to keep a low profile. They had another quick meeting with O'Leary on Sunday afternoon, when O'Leary had the unpleasant chore of telling Dillinger that Piquett couldn't help with a divorce. He didn't do that kind of work.

The next morning, Dillinger dropped off a package of money for O'Leary. It contained $2,300, including $1,000 each for Piquett and Pierpont's parents. He then took Billie to the airport, where she took a flight to Indianapolis to see Dillinger's father. In Mooresville, she gave the elder Dillinger several bundles of cash and the wooden gun that Dillinger had used to escape from the Crown Point jail. He also sent along a letter to his sister, Audrey, telling her that he hoped to visit when the weather was warmer and instructing her not to worry about him. He was safe, he said, and "besides I'm having a lot of fun."

While Billie was spending the night at the Dillinger home in Indiana, Dillinger was on his way east to the Pierpont's house in Ohio. He sat on the front porch and made sure that the family received the money that he sent for his friend's defense. Afterwards, he returned to Chicago, where he was reunited with Billie.

Unbelievably, the Bureau still hadn't put the Dillinger or Pierpont homes under surveillance.

While Dillinger was driving back and forth between Minnesota and Ohio, Nelson was on his way to Reno, Nevada, where he became mixed up in a murder that would not be solved for many years. Reno's two crime bosses, Bill Graham and Jim McKay, were in the middle of fighting a federal mail-fraud case involving their support for a gang of con men that operated in the city. Somehow, the two men learned that the government's star witness against them was Roy Fritsch, the controller of a Reno bank that Graham and McKay owned.

On Thursday, March 22, Fritsch disappeared after parking his car near his home. An eyewitness later reported that he had seen two men hit Fritsch over the head and drag him to a waiting car. The crime has never been officially solved. But according to informants who spoke to the FBI many years later, the killers were Nelson and his friend, John Chase. They claimed that Nelson murdered Fritsch and dumped his body in a mine shaft. To this day, it's never been found.

While all of this was taking place, the Bureau was still bumbling their way along in pursuit of Dillinger. By the end of March, Melvin Purvis and his men had spent four weeks on the case, yet had failed to unearth even a single lead on the gang's whereabouts, nor any hint that they were behind the robberies in Sioux Falls and Mason City. As the publicity about the Crown Point escape died down, the Bureau's investigation lost what little momentum that it had. In hindsight, Purvis's lack of planning seems inexplicable. He didn't bother placing the Dillinger farm in Indiana under surveillance; had he done so, agents might have been waiting for Billie when she visited there.

The only solid lead that the Bureau managed to come up with came from Matt Leach's men, who had discovered that Russell Clark's girlfriend, Opal Long, was in Detroit with her mother. The Bureau's Detroit office forced the Indiana men to withdraw and took over surveillance in hopes that Opal might contact Dillinger. There was a slim chance of this happening, it seemed, but Purvis managed to squander even this minor lead. On Thursday, March 29, agents in Detroit followed Long to the downtown train station, where she boarded a train to Chicago. When she arrived, Purvis had his men follow her to the Commonwealth Hotel, where Hoover approved a tap on her phone.

But Opal realized that she was being followed. That night, she got into a taxi, looking out the rear window as a pair of agents trailed behind her. The cab took what Purvis described in a report as a "zigzag course" through downtown streets, easily eluding his men. Weeks later, agents learned that Opal had gone straight from Chicago to St. Paul, where she joined Dillinger.

By the end of March, Hoover was growing impatient. Irritated by the newspaper coverage that Dillinger's robberies were getting in Chicago, the director sent Purvis a harsh letter, demanding results. But Purvis had no updates to offer him. There had been no developments. After a month of searching, Purvis and the Bureau agents had no idea where Dillinger could be found.

And then, oddly enough, Dillinger found them.

20. Shootout at the "Hellman" Apartment

While the Bureau's half-hearted pursuit of him was continuing, Dillinger hid out and allowed his wound to heal in a new set of rooms at the Lincoln Court Apartments, a small, 32-unit building, in a nice part of St. Paul. The place was cramped with Hamilton and Pat sleeping on the sofa, but they got along well. The good news was that Nelson was gone, away on a jaunt out west. Van Meter came and went without warning, always checking the license plates of cars parked on the surrounding streets, insuring that they were not government cars.

There was a movie theater down the street, which Dillinger and Billie visited several nights each week. On Friday night, March 31, he took Billie to see *Fashions of 1933*, a review of the latest designer clothing from New York and Paris. That same night, Opal arrived from Chicago, having ditched her Bureau tail there. She assured Dillinger that she hadn't been followed. Dillinger went to bed happy that night, unaware that events had already been set into motion that would shatter the peaceful period in St. Paul.

Earlier on the same Friday that Dillinger took Billie to a fashion show, a woman named Daisy Coffey walked up the snow-covered steps of the Federal Courts Building in St. Paul and entered Room 203, the local Bureau office. The special agent in charge, Werner Hanni, and his men were focused on the Bremer kidnapping case, but Hanni stopped what he was doing long enough to take her statement. Mrs. Coffey, who said that she managed the Lincoln Court Apartments on South Lexington Avenue, told Hanni that she was suspicious of the couple renting Apartment 303. The new tenants, "Mr. and Mrs. Carl P. Hellman," had frequent guests, always used the rear door, and kept their blinds down until at least 10:30 every morning. Hanni was unimpressed. He wrote in a memo, "She says that she just has a feeling that there is something mysterious and questionable" about the Hellmans.

After Mrs. Coffey left, Hanni gave her statement to a pair of young agents, Rosser "Rusty" Nalls and Rufus Coulter, with orders to look into her claims. Later that day, the pair drove uptown and showed Mrs. Coffey photographs of the only men that the St. Paul office was interested in – Alvin Karpis and the Barkers. Mrs. Coffey couldn't identify any of them. But she had written down Mr. Hellman's license plate number. After returning downtown, Nalls ran a check and found the car registered to Carl Hellman of North St. Paul. But when he called the post office to ask for Hellman's address, he found that there was none. The name appeared to be fictitious.

That night, Nalls and Coulter drove back to the apartment building and parked on a side street. The Lincoln Court was a three-story, red-brick building. There

The Lincoln Court Apartments in St. Paul

was a paved alley behind it and it was surrounded by a quiet residential neighborhood. From their car, they could see that the blinds in Apartment 303 were lowered. It seemed like a normal thing to do; otherwise anyone could see right in. In the space below the shade, they could see a man and a woman moving about inside the apartment. After three hours of sitting in a cold car, they returned downtown and made a note of seeing nothing out of the ordinary.

Nonetheless, they returned the next morning at 9:00 a.m. to question the occupants of the apartment. They were still bothered by what appeared to be "Mr. Hellman's" false name. Bureau officials decided that they needed a police escort so Coulter volunteered to find a patrolman while Nalls drove ahead to start surveillance. Nalls reached the building a little before 10:00 and parked beside it. A few minutes later, he saw two women leave through the back entrance. They walked to a parked car, talked to a man inside of it, and then drove off. Nalls, following routine, wrote down their descriptions and no one would realize until later that he had seen Opal Long, Pat Cherrington, and John Hamilton. They were going out for breakfast and grocery shopping. Nalls didn't recognize them. He was still focused on Karpis and the Barkers.

At 10:15, Nalls saw Coulter and a policeman drive up and then go into the building. A minute or two later, Nalls watched as a thin man drove up in a green Ford sedan, got out, and also walked inside. Nalls was still sitting in his car a few minutes later, watching the front entrance, when he saw Coulter running toward him across the building's front yard, holding his pistol, and stumbling in the snow. Coulter then spun around and exchanged gunshots with the thin man, who was chasing after him.

Just minutes before, Agent Coulter and a St. Paul police detective named Henry Cummings had knocked on the door of Apartment 303. After a wait of nearly a minute, the door opened a few inches and a young women peered out over the chain. Detective Cummings identified himself and asked to speak with Carl.

Billie forgot Dillinger's alias. "Carl? Carl who?"

"Carl Hellman."

Billie suddenly recalled who she was supposed to be and quickly replied. "He's just left and won't be back until this afternoon. Come back then."

"Are you Mrs. Hellman?" Cummings asked.

Billie nodded and the policeman said that they would just talk to her then.

"I'm not dressed," Billie replied. "Come back this afternoon."

"We'll wait until you get dressed," said Coulter.

Billie said that it would take a second and she closed the door. Coulter heard a second latch snap closed.

Dillinger was still in bed and Billie ran into the room. "It's the cops!" she cried. "What should I do?"

Dillinger jumped out of bed and began getting his clothes on. He told her, "Keep your shirt on, and get some things into the large bag."

As Billie tossed their clothes and meager belongings into the bag, Dillinger opened a dresser drawer and pulled out the parts of a machine gun. It would take only moments to fit them together. He was rapidly doing so as he walked to the door.

Outside, Coulter and Detective Cummings were still waiting in the hallway. Coulter was getting anxious. He whispered to the police officer. "We'll have to call for some help. You can go or I will."

"What do you want?" Cummings asked. "Your department or ours?"

Coulter answered, "I want to get our department."

Coulter hurried downstairs to the manager's office to telephone the Bureau. When he returned upstairs, Cummings was still standing in the hallway. Together they waited, nine more minutes by Coulter's estimate.

It was then that Homer Van Meter, after parking his green Ford sedan out front, appeared at the top of the third floor's back stairwell. He knew there was trouble as soon as he saw the two men standing outside of Dillinger's door. Van Meter walked right at them, shouldered past, and then stopped at the top of the front stairwell. He turned back and looked at Coulter. "Is your name Johnson?" he asked the agent.

"No," Coulter said.

As Van Meter turned and started down the stairs, Coulter stepped toward him and asked, "What's your name?"

Van Meter stopped on the lower landing. "I'm a soap salesman."

"Where are your samples?"

"Down in my car."

Coulter asked if he had any identification and Van Meter said no, that it was also in the car.

Van Meter then turned and disappeared down the staircase. After a few moments, Coulter decided to follow him. He walked down to the lobby and looked outside. The "soap salesman" had vanished. Coulter had just turned to walk back upstairs when he saw Van Meter standing in the shadows at the top of the basement stairs, a pistol in his hand.

Van Meter shouted, "You want this, asshole? Here it is!"

As Van Meter raised the gun to fire, Coulter jerked backwards, crashing through the front door. He turned and ran across the snowy yard, and Van Meter chased after him, firing wildly, each shot throwing up a small explosion of gray, dirty snow. As Coulter raced across the snow, he pulled his own pistol, spun back, and returned fire. Van Meter ducked back into the building.

Upstairs in Apartment 303, Billie begged Dillinger not to start a gunfight. But the moment that he heard the shots outside, he snapped the ammunition drum into the machine gun and fired a burst through the door. Wood splintered and cracked as the heavy bullets slammed through the door. Dillinger pushed the broken door open a few inches, stuck the Thompson's muzzle outside, and began firing down the hallway. Detective Cummings pressed himself back into an alcove as bullets whizzed past his face. The moment that Dillinger stopped shooting, Cummings ran down the front stairs. Inside of the apartment, Billie came out of the bedroom and found Dillinger with a grin on his face.

"Keep your shirt on," Dillinger repeated when Billie begged him not to shoot again. "You're coming with me. Snap that suitcase together and follow along." Dillinger stepped to the door and fired another thumping round down the hallway. Billie followed, lugging the heavy suitcase, which had more guns inside, with two hands.

Outside, the neighborhood was in chaos. Cars were stopped on the street, and people were leaning out of their windows, trying to see what was going on. Recognizing Coulter's assailant as the man from the green Ford, Agent Nalls pointed out his car, and Coulter promptly shot out one of its tires. Nalls ran to a nearby drugstore to telephone for reinforcements.

For whatever reason, neither agent even considered the building's rear entrance. Dillinger and Billie came out that way, followed by Van Meter about a minute later. He jumped on a horse-drawn delivery wagon that was parked at the curb. He donned the driver's cap and whipped the horses down the street.

Dillinger, walked casually down the alley, carrying the machine gun close against his right leg. He handed Billie the car keys and took the suitcase, watching over his shoulder as he walked. Billie hurried ahead to the garage where they stored their black Hudson and backed the car out. Dillinger tossed the suitcase into the backseat and climbed in. Billie stomped the accelerator and they roared down the alley. "Slow down!" Dillinger urged. "You'll attract attention.

None of the Bureau agents or police officers who descended on the neighborhood had any idea who was doing the shooting. One agent telephoned Washington to say that the suspects didn't match the descriptions of anyone in the Barker gang.

It wasn't until two hours later, when agents finally stormed Apartment 303, that the Bureau realized who they had found. Inside, amid an arsenal of pistols, machine guns, men's suits, and ladies undergarments, they found three photographs. One showed a baby boy, another a teenager. The third was a Navy sailor with a crewcut and a familiar crooked smile. It was Dillinger. Fingerprints that were taken from a Listerine bottle confirmed it. From the drops of blood that were found in the hallway outside the apartment, they guessed he had been hit.

And they were right, but it had not been by a bullet fired by a Bureau agent or cop. He had been hit by a ricochet, one of his own bullets. It stuck him high on the left calf, passing through his leg just below the knee. As sirens sounded all over St. Paul, Dillinger told Billie to drive straight to Eddie Green's apartment. He needed a doctor.

Green sent them to an office building in downtown Minneapolis, and a doctor named Clayton May, a general practitioner whose practice included $50 abortions and treating venereal diseases among the St. Paul underworld. When Green said he had a friend injured in the explosion of an illegal still, May followed him outside. Dillinger was in the backseat with Billie. They drove to an apartment on the south side, a place where the doctor treated his shadier clients. Billie threw an arm around Dillinger and helped him limp inside.

Dr. May later insisted that Dillinger threatened his life, but in truth, the roll of cash that he carried was all the persuasion that May needed. The wound wasn't serious. It was cleaned with a mercury solution and bandaged. He gave Dillinger a tetanus shot and told him to rest; it would take several days to heal. After May left, Dillinger drifted off to sleep.

21. The Last Gasp of Eddie Green

J. Edgar Hoover was in a rage. As the initial reports of the St. Paul gunfight landed on his desk, he demanded answers. Nothing about it made sense. Why had only two men carried out a raid, and why was one of them an officer from the notoriously corrupt St. Paul police department? Why were his men armed with pistols, and not machine guns? Why had no one informed him of the raid? And why, most of all, had his agents allowed Dillinger to get away? During a telephone call with Purvis, Hoover condemned the St. Paul office for their "atrocious bungling of the raid." From that point on, Hoover said, all information on Dillinger – no matter how trivial it seemed – was to be relayed to his office in Washington. And, as Hoover repeated to agents in St. Paul, the local police were never again to join in with Bureau raids.

The shoot-out in St. Paul had a tremendous effect on Hoover. From the memoranda that he penned in its wake, he seemed amazed that Dillinger had the nerve to actually fire on his men. It was this offense, which Hoover took personally, that caused him to make Dillinger's apprehension the Bureau's highest priority. He ordered all of the Midwest offices to give Dillinger precedence "over all other pending cases." New agents hurried to St. Paul. Cots were sent up in the Bureau office and at the post office, where the men grabbed short naps between calls.

Hoover would get Dillinger, no matter what it took.

On the Monday after the shootout, the Bureau got its first break. The Lincoln Park's manager, Mrs. Coffey, telephoned the St. Paul office with another tip. Her husband had found the address of one of Dillinger's visitors – the man who had exchanged shots with Agent Coulter. The man rented an apartment at 2214 Marshall Avenue. Agents had surrounded the building within an hour. By daylight, there was no sign of Dillinger, or anyone else, but the manager identified a man who matched the description of the shooter. He had lived in Apartment 106. The unit had been rented two weeks earlier by another man, who gave his name as "D. Stevens." The manager had not seen either man for several days.

As Bureau agents surveyed the place, they saw that all of the windows were closed. From the outside, the apartment looked vacant. They waited as long as they could and then, betting that the suspect was too smart to return, they had the manager unlock the door around 7:30 a.m. Inside they found what was clearly a bank robber's hideout: a Thompson machine gun stock, a two-foot dynamite fuse, road maps and airline schedules, license plates, three notebooks filled with getaway maps, and enough ammunition to outfit a small military unit. After dusting

The apartment building on Marshall Avenue

for fingerprints and collecting receipts and laundry tags, all but two junior agents returned downtown.

A few hours later, just before noon, the agents left behind were pacing the apartment, machine guns in hand, when they heard a key clicking in the front latch. The agents leapt to the door and jerked it open to find a startled "negress" – as the Bureau report later called her – facing the muzzles of their guns. She said her name was Lucy Jackson, and she was a maid whose sister had asked her to clean the apartment. The sister, Leona Goodman, was waiting in a car outside. The two agents brought her in.

The story that Leona Goodman told would prove as important as any the Bureau heard all year. She said that she worked for a man she only knew as "Mr. Stevens." He had arranged for her to clean the homes of a number of his friends – friends that the Bureau would later discover were everyone from Home Van Meter to Frank Nash to Harry Sawyer. Just that morning, she said, Mr. Stevens had visited her home, handed her a key, and asked her to clean out this apartment. She wasn't feeling well, so she had asked her sister to do it for her. She had promised to pack some clothes into a tan suitcase and bring it to her house. Mr. Stevens had promised to come and get it later on that day.

The agents took Mrs. Goodman downtown, where the tan suitcase was emptied and refilled with stacks of Wanted posters. An agent named Ed Notesteen was told to take Mrs. Goodman, the bag, and two agents to Mrs. Goodman's home to await the arrival of the mysterious Stevens. As he left, Notesteen asked Inspector William Rorer what to do if Stevens appeared. According to Noseteen's report on the day's events, Rorer's reply struck him as unusual. "Shoot him," he was told.

By early afternoon, Notesteen and the other two agents were waiting at Mrs. Goodman's house. From the tone of his memos, it's clear that Notesteen wasn't comfortable with his orders. Agent George Gross, who sat in a window with a machine gun across his lap, noticed several suspicious cars driving by. Notesteen called Rorer and requested reinforcements and, a little later, was relieved to see several agents driving nearby streets. While on the telephone, Notesteen pointedly asked Rorer to restate his earlier orders. Rorer replied that it all depended on Mrs. Goodman's identification of Stevens. "If she says that's the man, kill him."

Notesteen fretted throughout the afternoon, still unhappy about his orders to shoot "Stevens" on sight. They had no idea who the man was. For all they knew,

The home of Leona Goodman, where Eddie Green came to pick up belongings left behind at the Marshall Avenue apartment. This illustration from a true crime magazine shows the positions of Bureau agents who were waiting to ambush him, and Green's car. Green was killed in cold blood as he walked up the house.

he could simply be a real estate agent or apartment owner. He could be anyone. Notesteen repeatedly asked Mrs. Goodman, who sat in the kitchen, whether she could be certain if she saw Mr. Stevens. "I'll know him," she assured him.

Three hours passed and then, at about 5:30, Agent Gross saw a Terraplane sedan pull to a stop out front. "There's a car," he told Notesteen. "It's stopping across the street."

A man in an overcoat got out of the car and walked toward the house, heading to the kitchen door. Mrs. Goodman saw him coming. She quickly got up from her chair, shoved the suitcase outside, and slammed the door in the man's face without saying a word.

As the door closed, Notesteen hurried into the kitchen. "Is that the man?" he asked her.

Mrs. Goodman nodded. "Yes, that's the man who came by this morning, and that's the man from the apartment."

"Let him have it!" Notesteen then shouted to Agent Gross, apparently no longer hesitant about carrying out orders that amounted to cold-blooded murder.

There was a sudden rattle of machine gun fire and shattering glass. Notesteen went to the window and looked out. A man was sprawled face down on the sidewalk. The suitcase was lying next to him and blood was starting to seep through his overcoat. To Notesteen's surprise, a woman appeared from the shadows and was crouched over the fallen body, sobbing. Now, what was this?

He looked over at Mrs. Goodman, who had begun crying hysterically. "Are you positive this was the right man?" he asked her.

"Yes, it was," she choked out between sobs.

Notesteen telephoned Inspector Rorer and told him what had happened. Then, he slammed down the receiver and ran outside, where he saw other agents starting to appear, looking over the body in the yard. The fallen man had been shot in the head and was either dead, or dying. No one knew who the wounded man was and the crying woman wouldn't say. It wasn't Dillinger, they could see that. A driver's license, which turned out to be fake, identified him as Clarence Leo Coulter.

The next day, the Bureau was able to identify him as Eddie Green. The crying woman was his wife, Beth. And neither of them knew where Dillinger was hiding.

Eddie Green was still alive when ambulance attendants wheeled him into Ancker Hospital in St. Paul. In fact, he was more than just alive. While thrashing about and babbling incoherently, he lapsed in and out of consciousness. A bullet had entered the back of his skull through the brim of his hat, traced a half circle around his skull, and came to rest above his right eye. After he was settled into a hospital bed, doctors pronounced his condition grim – he didn't have long to live. A pair of Bureau agents took positions by his bed, writing down everything he said.

Throughout the night, Green screamed for someone named Jim, who agents later learned was one of his brothers. He asked for Fred, then George, then someone named Lucy, then demanded, "Honey, back the car to the door." Near sunrise, the agents began asking him questions about Dillinger. Most of what he said was unintelligible, or was obviously confused. At another point, he said, "I've got the keys, he wants them."

"Whose keys are those?" an agent asked.

"John's."

"John who?"

"Dillinger."

Green said nothing more about Dillinger, refusing to say where Dillinger could be found. At one point, however, he mentioned a doctor he had paid. The agents asked if anyone had been shot at the Lincoln Court Apartments and Green said, "Jack... in the leg." They pressed for the address of the doctor where "Jack" had been taken and Green murmured, "Wabasha Street." When they pressed him for the address on Wabash Street, he said, "980, I guess." There was no 980 Wabasha Street.

As the morning wore on, Green remained alive. In fact, he stabilized, but his information remained gibberish. By nightfall on Wednesday, April 4, he was still rambling. A new set of agents had arrived. In an effort to focus Green's utterings, they decided to question him while pretending to be doctors and gang members. To the surprise of the skeptical among them, this new plan seemed to work. At one point, Agent Roy Noonan, posing as a doctor, asked Green if he knew the man who drove the green Ford and fired on Agent Coulter at the apartment building.

Green snorted, "Doc, you sure are a nosy fella. Give me a shot so I can sleep."
Noonan replied, "I will if you tell me who drove the green Ford."
"You know as well as I do."
"No, I don't know."
"What do you want to know that for?"
"I just want to know. Did Jack drive it?"
"Yes."
"Jack who?"
"You know without asking me."
"No, I don't know. Who was he?"
"Dillinger," Green said impatiently. "Now will you give me that shot?"

And the melodrama continued. A little at a time, agents coaxed more information from the dying man. The best lead came around 11:00 p.m., when an agent tricked Green into naming an address in Minneapolis where he said Dillinger was hiding out – 635 Park Avenue.

At the Bureau's downtown office, this information sent everyone into high gear. Agents scrambled to Park Avenue, but found no 635. An agent at Green's bedside telephoned a few minutes later. Green was now saying the address was 1835 Park Avenue, Apartment 4. They found this address. It was a two-story rooming house in a run-down area where, agents would later learn, a doctor named Clayton May kept a secret office where he performed abortions.

That same day, Hugh Clegg, the Bureau's assistant director, had arrived from Washington to supervise the hunt for Dillinger. He stepped in to hunt down the Park Avenue address. He ordered every man to the building and, by midnight, they had the building surrounded. They waited, but nothing happened. The building was quiet. The only light came from a single apartment downstairs. An agent knocked on its door, saying he was looking for someone who had just moved into the building. The man who answered the door said that everyone there had been living there for at least six months. They were working folks and most had children. To the agents, it looked like a dead end. Clegg returned downtown, leaving a group of agents to watch the place. At daylight, another shift arrived. They watched the building's tenants come and go, but none looked familiar. No one was stirring in Apartment 4.

Finally, late that afternoon, Clegg decided to raid the apartment. After positioning men around the building, he and three agents armed with machine guns knocked on the door. As Clegg later described the operation: "We knocked on the door and a man about 45 to 50 years of age came to the door; upon opening the door machine guns were punched right in his stomach, and he was ordered to 'stick 'em up'; he did not stick 'em up, but he seemed to be amused. His wife, a small woman, was quite excited and wanted to shoot us. No shooting was done. There was a little girl in the place."

It was the wrong apartment.

Several days later, agents would learn that Dillinger's hideout was downstairs. It didn't matter, though. Dillinger had left the previous night at 6:00 p.m., about five hours after the delirious Eddie Green revealed where he was hiding.

Green lasted for a week. The Bureau agents hammered at him for days, even after his face and arm became partially paralyzed. He contracted meningitis, with his temperature reaching 105 degrees, and still the questions were asked over and over – until he could answer no more. On the night of April 10, he slipped into a coma and he died at 12:55 the following afternoon.

Eddie Green had been an expert at picking just the right bank to rob, but he made a fatal mistake when he returned for a suitcase that he should have left behind.

22. Indiana Road Trip

Dillinger had skipped out of St. Paul just hours before Bureau agents surrounded his hideout. The bullet wound in his left leg had been bandaged and he drove Billie south to Iowa, across Illinois, and into Central Indiana. A few hours after agents raided the apartment at 1835 Park Avenue, Dillinger parked his car behind his father's farmhouse outside of Mooresville. It was a little after midnight on Friday, April 6.

Unbelievably, the Bureau had still not placed the Dillinger farm under surveillance. There just seemed to be too many moving parts in the Dillinger case for the Bureau to keep up. The head of the Cincinnati office, Earl Connelly, whose territory covered Central Indiana, hadn't actually joined the hunt for Dillinger until Hoover's directive had been sent out earlier in the week. Connelly was considered one of the Bureau's best investigators. He had joined the Bureau in 1920 and had been a special agent in charge since 1927, and after running offices in St. Louis, Seattle, and New York, he took over the Cincinnati office in 1933. Connelly's men had already spread out across Ohio and Kentucky, checking dozens of leads. But no one thought to check Dillinger's family farm. Connelly would blame this mistake on the fact that he just didn't have enough agents – sadly, though, he probably just didn't think of it.

Hubert Dillinger, the bandit's 20-year-old half-brother, was delighted to see that John was home. He was surprised when he walked into his father's house on Friday morning and Dillinger jumped out from behind a door, pointed a finger at him, and cried "stick 'em up!" There were hugs and grins all around; both Hubert and his father were happy to see him. He introduced Billie to Hubert as his new wife and seemed anxious to convince the young man that the two of them were married. He repeated it several times. Dillinger parked his Hudson in a barn out back and, after breakfast, Hubert went out and helped him remove the tires, clean them, and paint them black.

When darkness fell, Dillinger announced that he and Hubert were going on a quick trip – they would be back by daylight. Getting into the Hudson, Hubert drove them east across Indiana to Ohio. On the way, Dillinger described his escape from Crown Point and St. Paul and the brothers chatted most of the way. Around midnight, they reached the farm of Harry Pierpont's family outside of Lima, which was also still not under surveillance by the authorities. Hubert stayed in the car while Dillinger went inside and gave the Pierponts some money to cover their legal fees. They stayed less than 15 minutes.

On the way back to Mooresville, Dillinger fell asleep. About 3:00 a.m., as they passed Noblesville, east of Indianapolis, so did Hubert. The Hudson sideswiped a pickup truck that was carrying a load of horseradish, swerved off the highway, smashed through a wire fence, and came to rest in some trees. The car was a wreck, but neither man was hurt. The horseradish truck was demolished. The driver, a man named Joe Manning, limped over to Dillinger's car in time to see

Dillinger remove the front and rear license plates. Hubert rushed the man away, telling him that they were okay. Dillinger then removed his machine gun from the car and wrapped it in a blanket, then took Hubert and they started off across the fields. They walked about three miles, until they reached a road. At that point, Dillinger told his brother to hitchhike to Indianapolis, get another car, and come back for him. He pointed out a haystack and told Hubert he would hide in it until he returned.

By the time a state patrol car arrived at the accident site, the Dillingers were long gone. They did find a machine gun clip in the car, though, which aroused their suspicions. A call was placed to Matt Leach when they returned to their post later that morning. As it happened, two Bureau agents were in Leach's office at the time. They drove out together to look at the wreckage. The car's engine number was relayed to Cincinnati, and agents there checked it with St. Paul. To the surprise of almost everyone in the Bureau, who assumed Dillinger was still in Minnesota, the number matched that of a car "Carl Hellman" had purchased two weeks before. Leach immediately ordered roadblocks to be put up all over Central Indiana.

The Bureau's focus was now switched to Indianapolis. Earl Connelly set his headquarters at the Spinks Arms Hotel, and asked Hoover for 10 more men. They began arriving at the Indianapolis airport over the weekend and began showing up in Connelly's temporary office in ones and twos. For the first time (amazingly), the Bureau began studying Dillinger's family. By Saturday afternoon, Connelly and his men had searched out the homes of Dillinger's father, his sister, Audrey Hancock, and the Indianapolis filling station where Hubert worked. Until he could arrange surveillance posts, Connelly established a regular circuit that agents could drive to watch them all.

While federal agents were arriving in Indiana, Hubert returned to the farm with Dillinger, who had spent several nervous hours hiding in a haystack. If he was worried that the Bureau was back in Indiana, he gave no sign of it. He lay down on the living room couch to rest his sore leg, keeping his machine gun resting next to him, under a blanket. His biggest concern was getting a new car. Later in the morning, he gave Hubert and Billie some money and sent them to Indianapolis to find one. They bought a new Ford for $722 and stored it in a Mooresville garage.

On Sunday, Dillinger was still on the couch, reading about himself in the newspapers that his father had saved, when family members began to arrive after church. His beloved sister, Audrey, who had raised him, was the first to arrive with her husband, Emmett, their teenage daughters, a plate of fried chicken, and three coconut cream pies, which she knew were her brother's favorite. Dillinger walked outside when they came up the driveway, trading kisses with his sister and her girls. A little later, two of Audrey's sons, Norman and Fred, arrived as well.

Although none of the Dillinger men were demonstrative by nature, it was a warm reunion with hugs and arms around the shoulders. There was a sadness, too. It didn't take much for anyone to consider that this might be the last time that any of them saw "Johnnie." To Audrey's relief, her brother seemed unchanged by his life on the run. He had the same easy smile and was always quick to make a

A Dillinger family reunion occurred in April 1934. Shown here is Audrey, Dillinger's beloved sister, John, half-brother, Hubert, John Dillinger, Sr., and Audrey's teenage daughters.

joke. Everyone watched Billie closely. She was quiet, but it was obvious that John loved her. She was pretty, but Audrey could see the scar hidden under her makeup.

With children in the room, they didn't talk about Dillinger's exploits at first. The conversation was mundane: a cousin's trip to Texas in search of work, Hubert's job at the gas station. While the adults talked, Dillinger's favorite niece, 18-year-old Mary, gave him a manicure. When she accidentally bumped his leg, she saw him wince. At one point, Emmett took Dillinger aside and asked him what had happened at Crown Point.

Dillinger didn't reply at first. "If you don't know anything, you can't tell anything, can you?"

"No," Emmet shook his head.

Two more snapshots from April 1934 at the Dillinger farm: Dillinger poses with the wooden gun from the Crown point jail break; and with Billie outside of the house.

"Let that be a lesson to you."

He was more forthcoming when Audrey took him aside, though. He described the jail break in detail and sketched her a map, which he burned with a match when he was finished.

They ate chicken sitting on the ground outside the back door. It was a beautiful spring day with a lot of sunshine and a nice breeze. Afterward, they walked across the fields and into the woods. Dillinger held hands with Mary. He told her, "You believe what's in the papers if you want to, but take it from me, I haven't killed anyone and I never will. Take about half a grain of salt, believe half of what's left, and you've got it made." He smiled at her.

They walked back to the house and Dillinger posed for snapshots, clowning around with his machine gun and with the wooden gun from Crown Point. When a plane appeared overhead – it was simply a stunt flyer, but no one knew it at the time – Dillinger went back into the house. It was the first time that the family saw him worried during the short trip. But the illusion of the carefree, Sunday picnic was shattered.

After that, Dillinger seemed on edge. He kept going to the window and watching the airplane. Hubert and Fred Hancock took the younger children to go and fly a kite in the yard. A little later, around 3:00, Mary walked into the living room and said, "There's a car out there with a couple of fellows in it and it looks suspicious." With the mysterious plane still buzzing around overhead and cars going past the house, Dillinger announced that it was time to leave. He asked Hubert to take Fred and go and get the Ford that he had purchased the day before.

The car with the two "suspicious" men inside of it was not the only one that passed by the Dillinger house that day. Unlike the Bureau, the general public had already tracked down the childhood home of the infamous bank robber and it had become something of a tourist attraction. Curiosity seekers, Sunday drivers from Indianapolis mostly, craned their necks as they passed by on Route 267, hoping to get a glimpse of the homestead.

The two "suspicious" men that Mary saw, though, were likely a pair of Bureau agents named J.L. Geraghty and T.J. Donegan. Records indicate that they were out looking for the Dillinger farm that day. They had just arrived in Indiana. Donegan had come in from Cincinnati the night before and had been given a whirlwind tour of the area at 2:00 a.m., but he didn't remember much of what he had seen in the darkness. He was working on about two hours of sleep and doing his best not to get lost. His partner, Geraghty, was even more out of his element. He had arrived in Indiana from New York City that morning and one farmhouse and barn looked just like another to him.

As they cruised past the Dillinger farm that afternoon, the agents spotted three cars in the driveway: two sedans and a Chevrolet coupe that matched descriptions of Hubert's car. This was good news since their orders had been to find Hubert and to keep an eye on him. Two miles past the farm, they turned around and headed back. When they passed a second time, they saw several children and two men outside of the house.

They went down the road and turned around again. They were trying to find a spot from where they could watch the driveway entrance to the house, but weren't having any luck. When they passed the farm a third time, they noticed that Hubert's car was gone. They immediately set off for Mooresville, trying to find him. As they entered the small town, they saw the car, driving toward them, back toward the Dillinger farm. A black Ford was driving just ahead of it. A few blocks later, the agents turned around and headed back toward the farm, taking their time so that they didn't arouse suspicion – or at least not more than they already had.

Hubert saw the agent's car and assumed that the men inside were Bureau agents, or police officers. He returned to the farm, left the car, and told Dillinger they were being followed. He and Fred then drove off in Hubert's Chevrolet, promising Dillinger that they would see him later that night. By the time that Geraghty and Donegan passed the farmhouse for the fourth time, the two young men were gone. When they saw that Hubert's car was missing again, they got worried. They drove faster, hoping they could overtake Hubert farther down Route 267. They made it as far as Plainfield before giving up. Thinking that Hubert must have turned off on a side road, they returned in the direction of the Dillinger farm.

By that time, Dillinger had concocted a plan to evade anyone watching the farm. He had hoped to leave after it got dark, but between the airplane and the men following Hubert, he decided that sooner would be better than later. He arranged for everyone to leave at the same time, going in different directions, and hopefully confusing anyone who might be watching. As it turned out, Dillinger gave the Bureau way too much credit.

Audrey and her husband drove out first, turning left toward Mooresville. Dillinger's father drove the next car, turning right. Billie got behind the wheel of the third car, the new Ford, along with the two teenage girls. Dillinger slid down onto the rear floorboards with a machine gun, and pulled a blanket over his head. No one saw them leave as Billie turned right on the road and drove toward Plainfield.

When Dillinger thought it was safe, he told her to stop the car. Just as she did, the two Bureau agents, Geraghty and Donegan, approached from the south. They saw the car sitting on the side of the road and recognized it as the car they had seen earlier. As they neared the Ford, they saw three women and a man inside. Just as they passed, the man climbed out of the passenger side and began to walk around the rear of the car. Both agents got a good look at him. He was average height, well-built, wearing a gray summer suit and matching hat. It was John Dillinger.

They didn't recognize him.

Later, they would swear to their superiors that it could not have been the infamous bank robber, but it was – the most wanted man in America. Dillinger turned and watched over his shoulder as they drove on past. Later that night, he and Billie headed for Chicago.

The following week, local newspapers confirmed the rumors about Dillinger's weekend visit. The story made national headlines. When she was confronted by reporters, Audrey spoke freely of the happy reunion. There was speculation that federal agents had been in the area, but the Bureau never said a word. It wouldn't be until many years later, when records were finally made public, that anyone would become aware of how badly Hoover's men had fouled up that day.

They drove past Dillinger, who was standing on the side of the road, and they never even knew it was him.

23. Women Behind Bars

The next morning, Dillinger and Billie slept late. She later recalled that, as they lay there in bed, he spoke about the future and getting out of the criminal life. They could find a quiet place, somewhere far from the Midwest, where they could settle down and live like normal people. Billie told him that she would love that. It was not the first time her "Johnnie" had spoken of such things, and it would not be the last.

It was around noon when they reached Chicago. Dillinger telephoned Piquett's investigator, Art O'Leary, who would become his most trusted contact in the coming weeks. They met at 3:00 p.m. at the corner of Sacramento and Augusta, then drove around while Dillinger described what happened in St. Paul and Mooresville.

O'Leary later stated that Dillinger asked him about a doctor who did plastic surgery work in the city. O'Leary said that Dillinger wanted to have him work on him so that he could "live like other people." He and Billie wanted to get married and settle down somewhere, he told him. O'Leary promised that he would ask Piquett about it. Later, the FBI would seize on this information and claim that Dillinger went through with the surgery, which was why his corpse didn't really look like him. Of course, no one could change their eye color, but that's getting ahead of the story.

After dropping O'Leary off, Dillinger drove downtown to the U Tavern on State Street, where Billie went inside and talked to one of Opal Long's old boyfriends, a man named Larry Strong. She needed a place to stay. Strong said that he could find something and arranged to meet her at 8:00 that night at a bar called the Tumble Inn. Billie thanked him and left.

What she didn't know when she walked out the door was that Strong had already been questioned by agents from the Bureau. When she left, Strong – or someone he talked to – telephoned Melvin Purvis.

The Bureau immediately went after this new lead and later that night, Purvis himself walked into the dim, dingy confines of the Tumble Inn at a little past 8:00 p.m. He had dressed down for the stakeout. Larry Strong was sitting at the bar, half-drunk, talking to the bartender. The only other people in the tavern were an elderly man and a young boy. Purvis took a seat on a barstool and made small talk with Strong and the bartender. Neither man knew or recognized him.

Outside, a dozen agents waited in the streets. About 8:30, Dillinger turned his Ford down Austin Street and pulled up to the curb beside the Tumble Inn. Standing down the block, Agent James J. Metcalfe saw the car arrive. The quiet man, born in Germany and raised in Texas, was one of the few members of the group of agents who came to be known as the "Dillinger Squad" who would achieve prominence after his FBI career. He wrote poetry, and after leaving the Bureau, he became a journalist and a syndicated poet, with his verse appearing in newspapers all over the country.

Unfortunately, though, Metcalfe was a better writer than a federal agent. Studying the car in the dim light, he couldn't make out the face of the man behind the wheel. When he saw the woman get out of the car, he decided to get a better look. As Billie went into the Tumble Inn, Metcalfe casually strolled down the sidewalk past the parked car. Dillinger was behind the wheel, a machine gun across his lap. Metcalfe passed no more than five feet from him – and didn't recognize him.

Inside, Purvis saw Billie when she walked in. She went up to the bar, standing between him and the inebriated Larry Strong. Purvis offered her a stool, but she shook her head no, ordered a beer, and leaned toward Strong to talk. Purvis strained to hear the whispered conversation, but he couldn't. After a minute, he left his seat, went outside, saw one of his men, and nodded. Agent Ralph Brown, pulling a machine gun out from under his coat, rushed inside, followed by several other agents. In seconds, Billie and Strong were arrested.

Unbelievably (again), no one said anything about the man in the car outside. Instead, for reasons that have never been explained, Purvis took two agents and searched the tavern's basement. Only after returning upstairs did Purvis realize that he had never asked how Billie had arrived. In a car, someone told him. Several agents dashed outside, but Dillinger was long gone.

When Billie was arraigned several days later, she openly mocked the Bureau to reporters, saying that Dillinger was inside the Tumble Inn when she was arrested. Purvis dismissed this "ridiculous statement," but failed to mention the fact that Dillinger might as well have been in the car – he was only a few feet away from the front door in full view of a dozen agents. Two of the agents said that they had seen the man, but it was too dark to say that it was Dillinger. Agent Metcalfe, who had walked within inches of the car, said that he hadn't gotten a clear look inside "due to the fact that the car stood beside a curb of unusual height, so it would have been necessary to stoop very low in order to look into the car from the sidewalk." Of course, these excuses never explained why the man wasn't arrested anyway. Bureau agents in St. Paul had mercilessly executed Eddie Green without even knowing who he was. Since they knew Billie was Dillinger's girlfriend, why not arrest the man – or as the Bureau was in the habit of doing, machine gun him to death – just to be safe?

It was another Bureau screw-up that didn't make the newspapers.

Art O'Leary was at his apartment that night when his telephone rang. It was Dillinger. "The G's just picked up Billie," he said.

"How did it happen?"

"I was sitting in my car right around the corner. There were too many of them for me to take her away. It was that Larry Strong. Where's Mr. Piquett? Is he still in Washington?"

O'Leary said that he was and Dillinger asked O'Leary to get in touch with him as soon as possible and see if there was any way that he could get Billie out.

Meanwhile, Billie was taken in handcuffs to the Bankers Building, where the Bureau had its Chicago offices. Agents pushed her into a chair beneath a bright light in the conference room. All that night and into the next day, they hammered her with questions. She wasn't allowed any breaks, any water, or anything to eat. But as the hours passed, she still refused to say anything about Dillinger. She begged them to let her sleep, but the agents refused. At one point, Doris Rogers, Purvis's secretary, took her a sandwich and was appalled at the condition that she was in. She immediately went to Purvis's office and told him that their treatment of Billie was "inhumane."

"What do you think we should do?" Purvis asked her, obviously inexperienced with not only interrogation techniques, but with how to handle some of the agents that he had working for him.

"Let her sleep," Doris replied.

"Where?"

"I'll take her to the ladies' room."

The Bankers Building downtown, where the Bureau had their offices

She didn't give Purvis much of a choice but to agree. She returned to the conference room and asked Billie to come to the ladies' room with her.

"I can't," Billie told her. "They won't let me."

Doris eased her out of the chair that she had been in for almost 24 hours and took her to the women's lounge. There was a leather sofa in the room and Doris poured Billie a glass of water and told her to lie down. She fell asleep. An hour later, Doris woke her up and Billie cried and begged not to be taken back to the conference room. She would tell Doris everything, but the secretary had no choice. Billie was taken back to the room, to the chair, and to the questions under the hot, overhead light.

While Billie was being grilled in Chicago, Assistant Director Hugh Clegg pulled up a chair in the Bureau's St. Paul office and began talking to Eddie Green's wife, Beth. The newspapers in the area were filled with rumors that federal agents had

Assistant Director Hugh Clegg

captured the mysterious red-headed woman, but to Clegg's annoyance, Beth Green wasn't telling him anything. At least, not at first anyway.

Clegg was not one of Hoover's rough western agents. He was a 25-year-old attorney from rural Mississippi who was just getting started with a long, distinguished career with the FBI. He was trained as an agent, but he was a bureaucrat, the very model of the yes-men who surrounded Hoover in his later years. He idolized Hoover, called him "my hero," and Hoover, in turn, prized Clegg for his unwavering loyalty. Clegg had been promoted to the role of assistant director after Hoover received glowing letters from the vice president, whom Clegg had escorted on a West Coast trip the previous year.

Clegg would later remember Beth Green as the only criminal he ever liked. They had several long talks, but Beth was still reluctant to discuss Dillinger. Then, on Tuesday, April 10, Eddie Green lapsed into his final coma, and died the following afternoon, seven days after he had been gunned down outside of Leona Goodman's house. When she heard the news, Beth began telling Clegg everything she knew. She spoke of places and filled in names. It was from Beth that the Bureau first learned the names of Dillinger's gang: Van Meter, Tommy Carroll, Red Hamilton, and the vicious young man named George "Baby Face" Nelson, who Beth said was "just a kid."

But Beth's knowledge wasn't limited to Dillinger. Eddie Green did business with the Barker gang and Alvin Karpis, as well. She quickly filled in the sizable gaps in the Bureau's knowledge about how and where the gang operated. She also described a place in Chicago owned by Louis Cernocky as a rendezvous point for both gangs.

At first, Beth Green's vast knowledge did the Bureau little good, in part because Hoover simply didn't have enough men to chase down leads, and many of the men that he did have were incompetent at best. The Bureau's resources were stretched to the breaking point. Hoover had no choice but to put his trust in Melvin Purvis. Hoover sent him a handwritten note: "Son, keep a stiff upper lip and get Dillinger for me, and the world is yours."

Louis Cernocky's ballroom and tavern in Fox River Grove. The tavern and restaurant were the building to the right.

Dillinger was heartbroken by Billie's arrest. For days afterward, he tried to figure out a way that he could rescue her. She was too heavily guarded at the Bankers Building, he knew that, but the newspapers said that she was going to be transferred to St. Paul to face charges for harboring a fugitive. He decided that he would attempt a rescue while she was en route. It would be a gun battle, and for that, he needed new bulletproof vests.

On the night Billie was picked up, Dillinger fled to Louis Cernocky's tavern in Fox River Grove. Cernocky grilled him a steak and handed him a bottle of whiskey, which Dillinger took downstairs to the basement hideaway. The gang had agreed to relay messages through Cernocky, and the next day, the Nelsons, who had reunited with Tommy Carroll, arrived. By the next evening, April 11, Van Meter and Hamilton also showed up, bringing along Pat Cherrington. None of the men were thrilled with Dillinger's plan to rescue Billie, but Van Meter knew where they could find bulletproof vests.

During the early morning hours on Friday, Dillinger and Van Meter showed up in the small town of Warsaw, Indiana, about 35 miles west of Fort Wayne. A 54-year-old police officer named Judd Pittenger was standing on a street corner when he was approached by two men in raincoats. They were pointing machine guns at him. He immediately recognized both of the men.

Dillinger spoke, "We want your vests and we mean business."

Pittenger grabbed the barrel of Dillinger's gun and struggled with him for a moment, until Van Meter rammed the barrel of his machine gun into the policeman's back.

"Let loose," Dillinger said. "We don't want to kill you."

Van Meter snatched Pittenger's pistol from its holster and smacked him over the head two times with it. "Don't hit me anymore!" the officer cried out.

"Don't hit him," Dillinger said. He ordered Pittenger to take them to the police station. They wanted access to the department's weapons closet. Pittenger said that he didn't have the key and when Dillinger asked him who had it, he lied and said that he didn't know.

Dillinger shook his head. "Don't be a fool. We don't want to be forced to kill you."

"I don't want you to kill me. I have a couple of kids at home," Pittenger replied.

"That's the reason we don't want to kill you."

With a sigh, Pittenger reached into his pocket and handed over the key. They marched him to the silent police station and up the stairs to the weapons closet. While Van Meter watched the policeman, Dillinger took out three bulletproof vests and two pistols. They let Pittenger go without further injury and made their escape.

Within hours, Matt Leach had roadblocks up all over Northern Indiana. Volunteers sprang out of bed to man them, but all of their efforts were in vain. Dillinger was back in Chicago by daybreak. But the daily newspapers brought some alarming news: Billie was going to be transferred to St. Paul at any moment.

Locked away in the conference room on the nineteenth floor of the Bankers Building, bathed in sweat from the hot lights and interrogated around the clock for two days, Billie refused to talk. Purvis was happy to send her to St. Paul and let her stand trial there. In Indiana, Earl Connelly was having no better luck with Dillinger's family. He rounded up and browbeat Hubert and several of the cousins, but none seemed to know where he was hiding. Fred Hancock helpfully suggested that they go check in Arizona.

Purvis followed every lead (although apparently not Fred's) and sent men to Muncie, Fort Wayne, South Bend, and Louisville, Kentucky. Men hung around the Dillinger filling station, but found out nothing. Purvis talked to Washington and suggested that they post a $5,000 reward for information leading to Dillinger's capture, but Hoover vetoed the idea.

The robbery of the police station in Warsaw made Purvis believe that Dillinger was still nearby. He didn't believe that he would take another trip to Florida without Billie. That weekend, Purvis drove to South Bend and then to Muncie, checking more dead-end tips. By Monday, April 16, Hoover was getting impatient. Bureau agents were running all over the Midwest without any plan. They needed an orderly system for tracking down leads. That Wednesday, Hoover told Purvis to stop going to Indiana and to stay in Chicago. Connelly and the other agents were to clear all leads through Purvis and telephone him at least once a day. Hoover agreed with Purvis in his belief that Dillinger was still near Chicago.

And then the very next morning, they got word that he had been seen in Sault St. Marie, Michigan.

Purvis and Hoover had been right, at least initially, Dillinger had been in Chicago while Bureau agents were scouring Indiana in a pointless search for him. On the Saturday morning after the Warsaw robbery, Art O'Leary went to meet him at the corner of Belden and Campbell Avenues. When O'Leary saw Dillinger standing across the street, he tipped his hat to signal him that he hadn't been followed. When Dillinger did the same, the investigator crossed the street and got into his car. Dillinger climbed behind the wheel with his hat tugged down so low to keep away the morning rain that his face was obscured. Two men that O'Leary didn't know were sitting in the backseat and, for a moment, he wondered if he had walked into a trap. He asked Dillinger to take off his wet hat and show his face.

Dillinger laughed and doffed his hat and introduced O'Leary to John Hamilton. O'Leary shook his hand, noticing the missing fingers. Dillinger didn't bother to introduce him to Van Meter, the second man in the backseat. It was a short meeting. Dillinger wanted O'Leary to find out how Billie was going to be taken to St. Paul. He said that he would call him on Monday for details.

No one thought Dillinger's plan to rescue Billie was a good one. Both Hamilton and Van Meter had tried to talk him out of it. O'Leary and Louis Piquett were even less enthusiastic. The two men agreed between themselves that they were not going to try and find out how Billie was being taken out of the city. This made for a nerve-wracking meeting on Monday for O'Leary. He and Dillinger met at the corner of North and Kedzie Avenues. Pat Cherrington climbed into the backseat of Dillinger's car so that O'Leary could get in the front. Hamilton sat with her, a machine gun covered by a blanket on his lap. When Dillinger said he was disappointed that O'Leary had come to him without the information that he needed, O'Leary urged him to have faith in the courts.

"Will Mr. Piquett go to St. Paul and help defend her?" Dillinger asked him.

"I'll have to speak with him, but I'm sure he will."

Dillinger produced a roll of bills. "That's fine, Art, give him this $500. And say, did you hear anything more about the doctor that does plastic surgery?"

"Yes, Lou says his name is Dr. Ralph Robiend." O'Leary told him that the surgery would cost Dillinger as much as $5,000. Dillinger was shocked and asked him if he thought that was high. "Not when you consider how dangerous it is. Hell, don't you realize that you're the hottest person in the whole United States?" Of course, O'Leary would have warned Dillinger if he had known that the Bureau, acting on an anonymous tip, was already looking for Dr. Robiend.

Dillinger reluctantly began to accept the fact that Billie was out of his reach. There was no way to rescue her. The Bureau soon sent her to St. Paul, where Piquett arrived to defend her. Alone now, the woman that he loved stolen away from him, Dillinger fell into a deepening depression.

Dillinger's days looked bleak, but John Hamilton's mood was even worse. With each passing day, he grew more fatalistic. He kept saying that he was sure that he was going to die soon. On several occasions, he told Dillinger that he wished that he could see his sister in his hometown of Sault St. Marie just one more time. Dillinger tried to dissuade him, but the more Hamilton stewed about it, the more he wanted to go. With a sigh, Dillinger agreed to go with him.

On Tuesday, April 17, Dillinger put on one of the new bulletproof vests, put on his shoulder holster and pistol, and got into his Ford with its powerful V-8 engine. That morning, watching for speed traps, he followed Hamilton's car out of Chicago into Indiana. He drove north into Michigan with a pair of binoculars and a thermos of cold water in the passenger seat where Billie usually was. Gun cases filled the back seat.

At nightfall, the two cars stopped for gas at a station outside Sault St. Marie, at the northern tip of Michigan. At the attendant filled his tank, Dillinger stood in the light rain with his hat pulled down low. It was the last place that he wanted to be. "You're a long way from home, the attendant said to him, gesturing to his Minnesota license plates. "What line of business are you in?"

"Clothing salesman," Dillinger replied. He paid the man and left behind Hamilton.

When the gas station attendant was later questioned by Bureau agents, he said that he thought he recognized Dillinger, but he didn't call the sheriff because he didn't believe it could be true. The attendant should have asked the agents for a job application; he was certainly Bureau material.

It was dark when they drove into town. They arrived at the home of Hamilton's sister, Anna Steve, at 8:30. Pat Cherrington, who had ridden along with Hamilton, tapped on the kitchen door of the frame house at the top of a steep hill on 14th Street. "Are you Mrs. Steve?" Pat asked.

Anna nodded in surprise.

"Now don't be afraid, don't say a word. I've got a surprise. I've got someone here who wants to see you," Pat explained.

A moment later, Hamilton appeared out of the darkness, carrying a machine gun that he had carefully concealed in a blanket. Dillinger was right behind him. He gripped a rifle and nervously scanned the dimly lit neighborhood.

At the sight of her brother, whom she hadn't seen in seven years, Anna began to cry. Hamilton held her and said they couldn't stay long. Wiping away her tears, Anna said she wanted to go out and buy some steaks to celebrate, but Dillinger shook his head and convinced her to just cook what she had in the house. Sending her three children upstairs, Anna put together a supper of eggs, bacon, and toast, and ate it with the three at the kitchen table as they reminisced about their childhood. When they were finished, both men shaved and Anna gave them quick haircuts. For the first time in weeks, Hamilton seemed happy.

Around 10:00, the kitchen door opened, startling both men, who grabbed their guns off the table. But it was only Anna's 18-year-old son, Charles. Dillinger lowered his gun. "Charles, this is Johnnie," Hamilton introduced him. He didn't have to say anything else. The awestruck young man immediately recognized the family's visitor.

Everyone went out to the sitting room, where Charles watched the two men closely. His uncle seemed to have a hard time breathing, the result of earlier wounds, and Dillinger was walking with a limp. He remained on edge, sitting near the window and saying little. He read the newspaper in between taking looks outside. After a bit, Hamilton sent Charles to fetch one of his boyhood friends, a man named Paul Parquette, who came over and was stunned to find himself face-to-face with Dillinger, America's most wanted man. It was an awkward moment and no one really knew what to say. Hamilton decided to show his old friend how a machine gun worked.

Finally, around 11:00, Dillinger got up and said that it was time to leave. Hamilton begged for one night to sleep at his sister's house, but Dillinger insisted that it wasn't safe. He was sure the Bureau was aware of the place where Hamilton grew up. They would soon be on to them. But Dillinger gave the Bureau far too much credit. Even though they knew the identities of Hamilton and Van Meter, Purvis had made no effort to place their families under surveillance.

But there was no way for Hamilton and Dillinger to know that. As they gathered up their things, Anna started to cry. Hamilton held her for a long moment and kissed her cheek. "Bye," he said, "I hope we see you again."

According to most accounts, though, they didn't. The last time that Anna admitted seeing her brother, he was walking down a muddy hill from her house. Hamilton left his car behind in town for her as a gift. He and Pat got in with Dillinger and they drove to the town of St. Ignace, only to find out that they had missed the last ferry across Lake Michigan. Dillinger found a hotel where they could spend the night, and Pat signed them in.

As it happened, Purvis's men were alerted to Dillinger's presence by one of Anna's neighbors, but by the time agents reached Sault St. Marie the next day, he was gone. The agents, accompanied by local deputies, raided the Steve home and led Hamilton's sister and her son away in handcuffs. Hoover had no sympathy for them and wanted to send a message to anyone who would harbor dangerous criminals. For Anna, the price for a supper of bacon and eggs, two haircuts, and three hours with her brother was three months in a federal women's prison.

If Hoover couldn't capture and punish the criminals, he would punish their families instead.

While Anna Steve was being questioned that Friday, Dillinger returned to Chicago and hid out at a place that no longer should have been safe: Louis Cernocky's Crystal Ballroom in Fox River Grove. It had been a week since Beth Green had told the Bureau all about Cernocky's hideout, how it served as a meeting spot for both the Dillinger and Barker gangs, and how Dillinger had just used the place to hide out a few weeks before.

As it happened, the Bureau had actually been looking into Cernocky since the previous summer, when they heard about gangsters frequenting the place. Cernocky's name had come up in the investigation into the Bremer kidnapping and Hoover had, in fact, approved a wiretap on his telephone. Agents had interviewed Cernocky's neighbors and a squad of agents had searched for the house where Edward Bremer was held during the kidnapping near the tavern just that weekend. But with all of the tips that had been coming in lately about Dillinger, Purvis had never found the time to order the place to be put under surveillance. If he had, Dillinger's story would have ended a lot sooner than it did.

On Thursday night, April 19, all of the Dillinger gang gathered at the tavern. It was the first time that the men had met since scattering in St. Paul three weeks before. Everyone agreed that they needed a spot to regroup, relax, and decide their next move in relative safety. The weekend was coming and they needed a getaway. Cernocky told them that he knew just the place, a country inn in northern Wisconsin that was run by an old friend who could be trusted. No one, Cernocky assured them, would look for them there. Cernocky scribbled an introductory letter for the owner of the place, sealed it in a white envelope, and gave it to Nelson.

By that point, there were definite signs of tension among the gang members. Not surprisingly, most of it was coming from Nelson. There is little information about how most of the gang members felt about one another. Many of those involved would be dead within the next year. What little is known came from Pat Cherrington and a few others and were comments made many months later. But from the comments, it appeared Nelson's problem with Dillinger was equal parts envy and resentment. Nelson felt that Dillinger owed him more respect than he had been given. It was Nelson who had sheltered Dillinger after Crown Point, who invited him along for the Sioux Falls and Mason City robberies, and who arranged for Cernocky to offer them a hideout. He got nothing for his trouble. All the newspapers wanted to write about was Dillinger. Nelson considered the outfit the Baby Face Nelson Gang, but to the public, he remained largely unknown. But envy was only part of the problem. Both Nelson and his wife, Helen, felt Dillinger was reckless. Anna Steve's arrest had made the papers that Friday, and the Nelsons feared that it was only a matter of time before Dillinger led the cops right to their door. That would be a high price for doing a man a favor, and Nelson resented it.

To Dillinger, he saw Nelson as unstable. The only time he spent with him was planning and carrying out robberies. As Pat Cherrington later said, "all the gang knew Nelson as a vicious character and one who loved blood, and had a great desire to kill anyone in his path. None of them desired Nelson's company but it was often necessary to have him on the job, when they had one to perform."

But for that moment, everyone was getting along. Cernocky woke the gang early on Friday morning, fed them breakfast, and had them out the door by 7:00. The timing turned out to be perfect. A few hours later, a group of Chicago cops, unaware of Cernocky's role as a hideout for Dillinger, stopped by for lunch.

The gang drove north through Wisconsin in four cars. Dillinger's group left first, followed by Van Meter. Nelson and Carroll brought up the rear.

The trip was uneventful until Nelson passed east of Madison. Driving north on Highway 51, he ran a red light and a car slammed into his driver's side door, caving in the Ford's left side. Everyone involved was lucky. Nelson and Helen were shaken, but unhurt, as was the driver of the second car, which was owned by a local cannery. Best of all, Nelson kept his temper and this time, no one got shot.

Tommy Carroll soon arrived on the scene, and worried that the police might soon show up, Nelson got his car started and talked the other driver into following him to a nearby garage. There, Nelson shoved $83 into the man's hand and drove off.

With Carroll following, Nelson managed to reach the next town north, Portage, and he left the Ford at a garage. When the manager walked inside for a pencil and paper, he discovered that the polite young man with the wrecked auto had vanished.

Van Meter was the first to reach their destination, an isolated area of connected lakes and thick pine forests. Just before the village of Manitowish, he turned left off the oil and gravel Route 51, with its numerous potholes, and drove beneath an imposing cement arch with white letters painted on it to announce the name of the secluded lodge: Little Bohemia.

24. Death at Little Bohemia

The tourist resorts in the pine forests around Manitowish, Wisconsin, came about with the waning days of logging in the North Woods. The region had been settled by loggers in the late nineteenth century and as the industry began to fade in the 1920s, the locals, many of whom were second generation French-Canadian or Scandinavian immigrants, decided to turn to tourism. Small resorts, many of them no more than a cluster of rustic cabins perched on the edge of lakes, began appearing as early as 1908, drawing people from as far south as Chicago, who arrived in the summer months to fish, swim, and hunt.

In the spring of 1934, Manitowish was a small backwoods village where everyone knew everyone – and their business – everyone married someone's sister, and every little lake had at least one illegal still that worked overtime.

The first family of the Manitowish area was the LaPortes. The oldest daughter, Ruth, married a Milwaukee printer named Henry Voss, who started building tourist cabins in 1912. In 1928, the Vosses opened the area's premier resort, the Birchwood Lodge, on Route 51, which boasted an immense kitchen, grand dining room overlooking Spider Lake, and a mammoth lobby fireplace that was the envy of nearly every other lodge in the state. There were three LaPorte sons: Lloyd, a fishing guide; George, who ran the grocery store; and Louis, a bootlegger who kept two stills running on Grants Lake during the Depression.

The youngest LaPorte daughter, Nan, transported her brother's moonshine downstate, selling it to speakeasies there. In Racine, Nan met Emil Wanetka, a short, gregarious Hungarian who ran a variety of restaurants. The two married and moved to Chicago, where they ran a little bar that became a favorite for local underworld characters called Little Bohemia. In 1926, the couple returned to Manitowish and Emil bought land on White Star Lake, not far from Birchwood Lodge, for a lodge and resort of his own, which was completed in 1931. He called the new place Little Bohemia, after the bar the Wanetkas had owned in Chicago.

Although more a roadhouse than a lodge, the new Little Bohemia was a two-story log cabin with a barroom, kitchen, and dance floor downstairs, a row of bedrooms above, and a cottage next to the back porch. It was located just out of sight of the road, a couple of hundred yards down a tunnel of huge pines from Route 51. Wanetka borrowed heavily to build the place, forcing him to keep it open all winter. He ran daily dinner specials to lure in the locals, which kept the lights on during the lean months.

Wanetka was working in the bar that Friday afternoon when Homer Van Meter walked in and greeted him by name. He explained that he had a party of 10 on their way from Duluth and they needed a place to stay. Wanetka told him that he

Little Bohemia Lodge

had the room available and would get everything worked out. Van Meter asked for lunch and then went out to the car to get his girlfriend, Mickey Conforti, and Pat Reilly, a St. Paul gangster who worked as a bartender at the Green Lantern. The three of them ate a pork-chop lunch while Mickey's bulldog, Rex, lapped at a saucer of milk. Van Meter spent the rest of the afternoon walking around the grounds of the resort, making a mental getaway map while Mickey and Reilly tried their luck at the lodge's nickel, dime, and quarter slot machines. The lodge was remote and had no other guests. It would do just fine, Van Meter believed.

Around 5:00 p.m., the Nelsons and Tommy Carroll drove up. Carrol had his girlfriend, Jean Crompton, with him. Dillinger arrived a little later with Hamilton and Pat Cherrington. Dillinger was introduced as Johnnie, and Nelson used his usual nickname of Jimmie. There were now six men and four women, and they were the lodge's only guests. At first, Wanetka was thrilled by the off-season business, but he wasn't stupid. He saw how Nelson ripped up the introductory note from Cernocky after letting him read it. He could see what hard-edged, dangerous men his new guests were. He had seen plenty just like them during his days in Chicago. All Wanetka could do was hope that they didn't stay long. Wanetka's wife, Nan, also sensed that there was something sinister about them.

The lodge's 16-year-old waiter, George Bazco, carried the gang's luggage to their rooms and noticed that the bags seemed very heavy. He joked to Wanetka, "There must be lead in this one. What are these guys, hardware salesman?"

Everyone was given rooms upstairs, except for Nelson and Carroll, who unpacked their bags in the cottage out back. Nelson was, of course, irked that Dillinger got a better room.

The cabin behind the lodge where Nelson and Carroll stayed. Nelson was, of course, irked because Dillinger had a room inside of the lodge.

Later that evening, Nan served a steak dinner to the group and Tommy Carroll set up a poker game in the bar with some of the gang members and Wanetka. Carroll and Nelson were talkative, but Dillinger, Hamilton, and Van Meter didn't say much. There was tension among the gang members, which even Emil Wanetka could sense. Oddly, George Bazco and the three girls who worked in the kitchen liked Nelson the best of anyone in the group. He joked with them and gave them big tips. He even bought drinks for others, mostly regular customers, who came into the bar. Dillinger simmered. He knew that Nelson did it to draw attention to himself – and attention was the last thing they needed.

While playing cards, Wanetka noticed that the men did not remove their jackets and were carrying guns in shoulder holsters. He also noticed that "Johnnie" resembled a certain newspaper photograph that he had seen. Later, while everyone was taking a break from the game, he ducked into the kitchen and glanced at the *Chicago Tribune*. Sure enough, his new guest was John Dillinger!

At one point in the evening, Nan's sister, Ruth, brought her daughter over from Birchwood Lodge to chat. Dillinger asked Wanetka who they were, then bought them drinks.

Around 10:00 p.m., Wanetka feigned exhaustion and announced that he was going to bed. As soon as he got upstairs, Nan was pestering him for information about their guests. He shushed her and told her that he was sure that one of them was Dillinger. After that, they lay in bed, staring at the ceiling for a long time. Eventually, Emil drifted off, but Nan lay awake, listening, for most of the night. She was startled by every noise that she heard.

The next morning, Wanetka was the first one stirring in the house. Tommy Carroll soon greeted him and asked about breakfast, which Emil promised to have ready once everyone was awake. Carroll went upstairs to rouse the others, and before long, the rest of the gang came downstairs, yawning, and all of the women in their robes. When they were finished eating, Wanetka asked Dillinger if he could speak with him privately. He told the gangster that he knew he was John Dillinger.

Dillinger's expression remained unchanged. "You're not afraid, are you?"

"No, I'm not," Wanetka lied. "But everything I have to my name, including my family, is right here, and every policeman in America is looking for you. If I can help it, there isn't gonna be any shooting match."

Dillinger placed a hand on Emil's shoulder and spoke earnestly, "Emil, all we want is to eat and rest for a few days. We'll pay you and get out. There won't be no trouble."

After this encounter, the mood at Little Bohemia sharply changed. It's likely that Dillinger told the other gang members that Wanetka knew who they were. From that morning on, Dillinger or Nelson kept a watch on the lodge telephone and made an effort to listen in on conversations. Whenever a car came down the drive, Wanetka was asked who it was.

Later that morning, Dillinger sent Pat Reilly on a run to St. Paul. They were low on ammunition, and Van Meter wanted some cash that Harry Sawyer was keeping for him. Pat Cherrington volunteered to go along with him and they left, promising to return the next day. Before Pat left, Hamilton told her that if something should happen at the lodge, she should remain in St. Paul until he contacted her.

After they left, Dillinger got out a .22 rifle, and he and Van Meter and Nelson did some target shooting. They were aiming at a can about 100 yards away, and Dillinger asked Wanetka to take a few shots as well. For years after, Wanetka would brag that only he and Van Meter could hit the target. Van Meter grabbed a machine gun, and everyone shot that too. A little later, Wanetka's eight-year-old son, Emil, Jr., came out with his baseball glove. Dillinger and Nelson played catch with the boy until he quit, complaining that Nelson threw too hard.

It was probably the game of catch that pushed things over the limit for Nan Wanetka. She did not want her son around such men. She had read in the newspaper about Anna Steve's arrest and knew well that they could all end up in jail for allowing the gangsters to stay with them. After lunch, Nan announced that she was sending Emil, Jr. to a birthday party with her husband. Dillinger gave the boy a quarter to buy some ice cream, but as father and son got ready to leave, he decided to send Van Meter with them, just in case. By evening, Dillinger had gang members watching all of the Wanetkas. When Nan went into town to buy groceries, she was sure she saw Nelson watched her from the parking lot.

By Sunday morning, Nan was nearly frantic. She had taken her sister aside and talked to her about calling the authorities. That morning, she wrote a note to her brother-in-law, Henry Voss, and slipped it into a pack of cigarettes. It read: Henry, you can go to Rhinelander and call as planned. Not a word to anyone about it. Tell them to line up the highways. There will be more here tomorrow and don't let anyone know where you are going or why. We want to be protected by them as best as they can. Tell them that."

Around 10:00 a.m., Dillinger gave Wanetka $500 and told him that the gang would be leaving the next morning, on Monday. A little later, Lloyd LaPorte, the fishing guide brother, showed up in the barroom. Nan saw Dillinger and Nelson over at a table, listening to them. LaPorte told Nan that he had left his cigarettes at home and wondered if she had any. Nan gave her brother the pack with the note in it. He walked back to his car and drove to Birchwood Lodge, where Henry Voss read the note. The telephone was a party line, and neither man trusted it. They headed south, toward Rhinelander, where they planned to call the authorities.

In Chicago, Melvin Purvis was at home that Sunday morning, enjoying a rare day off. He was reading the newspaper when his manservant, President, brought him the telephone. It was the U.S. Marshal's office in Chicago, relaying an urgent message from someone in northern Wisconsin named Henry Voss. Purvis dialed the number he was given and was soon talking to Voss, who said to him, cryptically, "The man you want is up here."

"You mean Dillinger?" Purvis blurted.

Voss refused to say. Purvis pressed him, thinking that this could be a crank call, and finally, Voss admitted it: Yes, he said. Dillinger and four other men were hiding out at the Little Bohemia Lodge at Manitowish. Purvis questioned him and Voss told him that the closest airport was at Rhinelander, about 50 miles south of the lodge. Purvis told Voss to meet him there that evening at 6:00. So that he could identify him, he told Voss to wear a handkerchief around his neck.

Purvis's next call was to Washington. He briefed Hoover, who agreed that the call sounded authentic. The director ordered Purvis to round up every available agent and head immediately to Rhinelander. Purvis then called St. Paul and passed on Hoover's orders to Hugh Clegg, who began getting his own men together. Both offices were plunged into chaos. Telephone calls bounced back and forth between agents, rousing those who were at home. Several of them leapt into cars half-dressed, hurrying to the office. Calls were made to airports, looking for planes to carry men to the North Woods. Agents unlocked their weapons closets and they hauled out every piece of heavy equipment they had, including tear gas and machine guns.

In St. Paul, Clegg arranged a 35-cent-per-mile charter from Northwest Airways. He would take Inspector Rorer and three agents and fly north. Agent Werner Hanni and three others, who admitted a fear of flying, threw their weapons into a car and drove off. In Chicago, Purvis chartered two planes and chose 11 men to fill them. Rhinelander was a three-hour flight and it took an hour just to get everyone to Municipal Airport. As they got into the plane, hurriedly finding their seats, Purvis happened to see that the pilot had only a highway road map to guide them to the remote landing strip.

He could only hope for the best.

As that Sunday afternoon dragged on, the gang members began to get restless. They all sensed that something wasn't right. All of them had been living the outlaw life for too long to know that things were off. There were too many people coming and going, too many people had seen them. That night there would be a couple of dozen more – Wanetka was having one of his dollar-a-plate dinners, which drew a good-sized crowd from the local residents. Dillinger had gotten their cars out of sight in the lodge's garage, but there was no way to avoid the people coming to the restaurant. A local man had come into the barroom after lunch, planted himself on a stool, and started drinking. Once or twice, he tried to convinced Hamilton to have a drink with him. At one point, as the day dragged on, Van Meter asked Wanetka if he knew of a place to which they could move, somewhere more private.

Dillinger decided that it was all too much. Around 4:00, he told Wanetka that there had been a change in plans. The group would be leaving that night, as soon as Pat Reilly returned from St. Paul. He asked Wanetka for an early dinner, steaks with garlic butter.

Nan Wanetka was nervously preparing the meal when her sister came to the kitchen door. Ruth started to tell her that her husband had driven to Rhinelander to call the police, when Nan shushed her. She brightly spoke up, and told Ruth that she wanted her to take home some extra meat. Emil had bought too much for the weekend. It was actually a ruse to get Ruth into the meat locker where they could speak in private. As soon as the door closed, she whispered, "They're leaving tonight, as soon as Reilly gets back!"

When Ruth left, Nan left the kitchen and poured herself a drink from the bar. Emil was stunned. "Nan, are you drinking?" he asked. She started to reply when her eyes met Nelson's. The gangster was sitting at the bar, watching her. Nan gulped and Emil tried to smile. Nelson said nothing, but it was obvious that something was wrong. Nan returned to the kitchen. Nelson started after her, then apparently changed his mind, and sat back down next to his wife.

At the same time that Nan was returning to the kitchen, Pat Reilly returned to Little Bohemia with Pat Cherrington. Dillinger and the others, busy with their steak dinners, didn't see them. Reilly was unsure of what to do. There were no cars in the driveway – Dillinger had hidden them in the garage – and Reilly worried that the gang had already fled.

Nan Wanetka was watching through the window as Reilly and Pat turned around and drove away.

Hugh Clegg and his four agents reached Rhinelander first. The plane touched down a few minutes after 5:00. He was met on the runway by George LaPorte and Henry Voss. A crowd had started to form, attracted by the airplane, so Clegg took the two men aside and produced photographs of all of the Dillinger gang members.

The only one that Voss could identify was Tommy Carroll, but they were gangsters, he said, he was sure of it.

Voss drew a rough sketch of Little Bohemia, noting all of the buildings and landmarks on the grounds. There was no way to escape across the lake behind the lodge, he assured Clegg. There was no boat and the lake was only partially frozen. There was a small, gravelly beach between the lodge and the water. The Wanetkas had even passed along a possible plan of attack. The gang was going to depart the next morning. The family and staff would hide in the cellar at 4:00 a.m., just before sunrise. It was then that the authorities had to attack. Clegg was impressed by Voss's enthusiasm.

But first, the feds needed cars. Voss drove Clegg into Rhinelander to a Ford dealership, where Clegg spoke with the manager and asked to rent three cars. The manager couldn't help him. He had no license to rent cars, and besides, only had one old coupe he could spare anyway. He asked if Clegg was raiding bootleggers in the area, because if he was, he could forget the whole thing. If word got around that he was helping such a raid, the man said, he would lose most of his customers. When Clegg said that he wasn't after bootleggers, the manager asked if it was Dillinger. Clegg must have been fuming by this time and he ignored the question. He told the man that they needed cars, and they needed them now. The manager finally agreed to help, but it would take an hour or two.

As they talked, Clegg spotted another plane coming in – Purvis had arrived. He met him at the airport. Purvis was a little shaken by a rough landing – the plane had actually spun around twice when it landed on the runway – but they were ready to go. It was a 50-mile drive to Little Bohemia, but they had plenty of time, which they needed. While they waited for the cars, Purvis decided to send Agent Ray Suran ahead with Henry Voss to Manitowish to look things over. The men headed north, but on the outskirts of Rhinelander, they ran into Voss's wife, Ruth, who had come to alert them that Dillinger was leaving tonight, after dinner. They had to move fast.

This changed everything and they returned to the airport. Purvis was speaking to some of his men when he saw Voss running toward him, shouting his name. He told Purvis about Dillinger's change in plans and the Bureau agents decided to move immediately. By then, cars were ready, and Purvis persuaded a 17-year-old boy to lend them his car, giving them five vehicles in all. At 7:15, the Bureau caravan started toward Little Bohemia.

As they left Rhinelander behind, the roads turned bad. They were unpaved, muddy from the spring thaw, and clustered with numerous potholes. The cars bumped, thudded, and slid along until one, then another, careened into a ditch. They had no time to push them out. Quickly, the eight stranded agents grabbed their guns and climbed onto the running boards of the remaining three cars. As temperatures dropped down into the thirties, they struggled to hang on with their freezing fingers.

The drivers tried in vain to pick up speed. It was getting late and it was going to be close.

The Bureau cars finally arrived at Birchwood Lodge, a mile down Route 51 from Little Bohemia, just before 9:00 p.m. Nan Wanetka and her daughter were there. She had slipped out of the lodge in anticipation of the raid. She said that Dillinger was still at the lodge, or had been a half-hour earlier. But she urged Clegg to move fast; the gang was leaving at any moment. Clegg decided to head to Little Bohemia and devise a plan of attack after they had gotten a look at the place. He told the men to toss their cigarettes and check their guns.

A few minutes later, the caravan pulled away from Birchwood Lodge, inching through the darkness up Route 51. They passed several homes, their lights shinning in the gloom, until they reached the entrance to Little Bohemia's driveway.

There is no question that the agents were nervous, if not downright terrified. The Bureau had never attempted a raid of this size before, and none of the agents had been trained for massed gunfights. Few of the men had ever even fired their guns in the heat of battle before. Everyone knew the Bureau's terrible record in gunfights. Three times in the preceding six months, agents had managed to engage armed outlaws and only one had ended with an arrest. One outlaw, Wilbur Underhill, even escaped from a house that Bureau agents had surrounded before he was captured. In St. Paul, Dillinger had literally just walked out the back door of an apartment building and had driven away. That memory reinforced the fact that this was the fourth time in 23 days that agents had been within a baseball's toss of Dillinger without actually catching him.

The night was black when the three cars turned into the muddy driveway beneath the tall pines. There was no moon. The only sound was the wind, whispering through the trees. In the dim light, they could see patches of dirty snow at the edges of the road. Ahead of them, the back porch of Little Bohemia was illuminated by the light of a single, pale yellow bulb. It was reflected off the fenders of a row of parked cars. At that moment, Purvis believed that conditions were perfect for the raid. If Dillinger was still in the lodge, they possessed the element of surprise. Most of the way down the driveway, but still in the shadows of the looming pines, Clegg stopped the lead car and got out. Purvis stopped behind him.

Just as the agents opened their car doors, though, dogs began to bark. No one had told them anything about dogs. As he sloshed into the wet driveway, Purvis saw four of five men appear on the porch. As he watched, three of the men got into a Chevrolet coupe. His heart sank, knowing that the raid had just taken a bad turn with barking dogs, an alarm raised, and gang members hurrying to their getaway car. But, as it turned out, this was just the beginning of the debacle.

In the years after that cold night in northern Wisconsin, everyone involved went to great lengths to try and explain their actions that night. The best explanation was that it was "business as usual" for the Bureau during that era. As files eventually made clear, there was never any real plan of action for that night, other than the vague idea that the lodge would be surrounded. Inspector Rorer later told Hoover that they "had been unable to make plans because of the lack of time, but expected to do so upon their arrival." Worse, though, Assistant Director

Clegg was the senior agent on site that night, there was considerable confusion about who was actually in charge. At various times, Clegg, Purvis, and Rorer were all issuing orders. The Bureau agents should have had the tactical advantage that night, but poor planning, the speed at which they had to move because they believed Dillinger was leaving, and the commotion raised by the dogs ruined any chance they might have had to surround the lodge before anyone could escape.

And things were just about to get even worse.

As the men on Little Bohemia's porch got into the Chevrolet, Inspector Rorer called out to Purvis, "Hurry! Hurry!" Hoping to get men all of the way around the lodge, Purvis told him to take two men and head into the woods on the left. Clegg told other men to get into the trees on the right. As they were scrambling into position, the Chevrolet's headlights flashed on. Music could be heard from the car's radio, eerily floating off into the forest. The car began to back up towards them. Then the driver quickly threw it into a forward gear and made a sharp U-turn, causing the headlights to swing around to where Clegg and Purvis were standing frozen in the driveway.

There was certainly no time to come up with a plan now – there was not even time to think. Although no one seems to have issued an order, Clegg and Purvis, along with an agent named Carter Baum, jogged toward the car with guns drawn. As the Chevrolet started toward them, Purvis and Clegg yelled, "Police! Stop! Federal agents!" Other agents, running wildly through the trees, joined in the chorus, "Stop the car! Federal agents!" The car surged forward. Two men appeared on the lodge's porch and began yelling, but with everything going on, no one could hear what they were saying.

The car didn't stop. As Purvis and Clegg ran forward, the car was coming right at them. "Fire!" Purvis and Clegg both shouted and shots began to ring out from all over the clearing. Purvis's machine gun jammed, but Agent Baum opened up. His tommy gun rattled and boomed, raking the car with slugs. Glass shattered, tires exploded, and the shadowy figures inside of the car danced wildly as bullets tore into them. Finally, the car sputtered to a stop.

At that moment, a figure darted out of a cottage from the right side corner of the lodge. The figure fired a pistol at Purvis – the bullets struck the ground at his feet – and then disappeared into the woods. In the confusion, no one bothered to chase him.

According to the reports after the raid, all of this happened in barely 10 seconds. As the firing began, Rorer and two agents, T.G. Melvin and Lew Nichols, trotted off into the trees on the left side of the lodge. As they went, Rorer told the two agents to keep space between them. Just as he spoke, Rorer rounded the side of the building, where he glimpsed the shadowy figure of a man about to jump from a second-floor window. "Police! Stop!" he yelled, then opened fire.

His shots were answered by a burst of machine gun fire from the window. Bullets shook tree branches and took chunks out of pine trunks. In the light from the machine gun's muzzle flash, Rorer could see two men at the window. Agent Melvin fired three blasts from his shotgun in the window's direction. A moment later, the men inside were gone. Rorer was certain they had been forced back inside of the lodge.

In the driveway, the shooting had stopped. Purvis and Clegg began shouting for the men inside of the damaged Chevrolet to come out with their hands up. The driver's door creaked open. "Hold your fire!" a man yelled. Before anyone could react, a man stumbled out of the car and ran off into the woods on the right, where a half-dozen Bureau agents were running toward the lake. Several of them had already passed the lodge's garage and became tangled in a barbed-wire fence, from which they were attempting to free themselves in the darkness.

The upper window of the lodge, where machine gun fire pinned down the Bureau agents in the woods

Agent Harold H. Reinecke was right behind these men, running toward the lake, when the fleeing man from the car nearly collided with him. "Halt!" Reinecke yelled, but the man turned again. Reinecke yelled again, but when the man kept running, the agent raised his shotgun and fired twice, missing with both shots. As the man slipped away into the darkness, he fired once more, but missed again.

As Reinecke was chasing the unidentified man into the woods, a second man emerged from the car. He moved slowly, swaying as he got to his feet, and then slumped to the ground, obviously wounded. "Hands up!" Clegg roared at him, and Purvis demanded that the man identify himself.

The man in the ground groaned loudly. "John," he managed to say.

Purvis and Clegg both ordered the man to come toward them, but he didn't move. It was dark and at a distance of almost 50 feet, Purvis couldn't see the man's face. He called for Agent Sam Hardy to run back and bring the third Bureau car up the driveway, so that they could shine the lights on the man. Hardy hustled

Bureau agents opened fire on a car that was leaving the lodge, believing that gang members were inside. They later discovered the occupants were three men from a local Civilian Conservation Corps camp.

to the car, but the keys were missing. The driver, Agent Arthur McLawhon, was somewhere out in the woods on the right. Hardy called for him to bring the keys. Several minutes passed before McLawhon appeared and handed over the keys. Hardy pulled the car up the driveway.

Purvis waited anxiously to see who the fallen man was, but as the headlights reached him, they could see that "John" was not Dillinger – or anyone else they were looking for. The man was elderly and heavyset. Purvis shouted for him to come forward and surrender. The man tried. Getting to his feet, he took a step or two in Purvis's direction, then he staggered backward, fell heavily on his rump, fished a whiskey flask out of his pocket and took a long swig. Purvis yelled at everyone to hold their fire.

The lodge was still quiet. The agents had taken up positions in the woods on the left and to the right, where they could see the lake behind the building. Word was passed along from both sides – no one had gotten through.

The old man in the driveway finally got to his feet again, staggered onto the porch, and went inside the lodge. As Purvis and Clegg watched, unsure of what to do, they could see the man inside, stumbling past the windows.

Purvis was still trying to decide what to do when the headlights of a car turned into the driveway behind them. It drove right up behind the two parked Bureau cars. The two agents standing with Purvis, Carter Baum and Sam Hardy, called out to the driver to identify himself. Suddenly, the car's engine revved and it shot backward, roaring back down the driveway toward Route 51. Baum opened fire with a machine gun. Purvis ran after the car, firing at the tires and hitting the radiator. But the car never slowed. It blasted out of the driveway, hit the highway, and vanished into the darkness. They could hear the engine running hard for a short time and then the sound faded away – but it would be back.

Purvis finally took a breath and realized that he needed to get control of the situation. His agents were shooting at anything that moved, not having any idea who they were shooting at. At this point, it was lucky that the inexperienced agents hadn't shot each other. Thinking clearly, Purvis called out for every agent on the grounds to shout out his identity and position. As he did, Agent Hardy ran up to him. He said he had spotted the headlights of the retreating car and it was moving slowly out on the road behind them. Purvis told Hardy and two other agents to sneak into the woods and try and take the car by surprise.

The three agents made it to the end of Little Bohemia's driveway at almost the same time that the car did. They ran out and called for the occupants of the car to get out and identify themselves, but again the car sped away. All three men opened fire. There was a loud pop as one of the tires exploded. As the car disappeared down the highway – this time for good – they could hear it running on one rim. There was no way to stop the car, though. In the rush to reach the lodge, no one had thought to arrange for roadblocks. The local sheriff had no idea that the Bureau was even in his jurisdiction.

Back in the driveway, Inspector Rorer came out of the woods and discussed with Purvis and Clegg what to do. They had now fired on at least five different cars and people, and no one had a clue about who any of the targets actually were. And now there was a sixth. By this point, everyone could see a man sitting in the bullet-riddled Chevrolet, which was still running. The car radio was still tinkling out melancholy tunes. Purvis called out to the man in the car, but he wasn't moving.

Rorer was told to go and check out the car. As Purvis covered him, Rorer dropped to his hands and knees and crawled through the mud and wet grass to the Chevrolet. In the front seat, he found a young man with his head leaning forward. His chest and shoulder were covered with blood. Rorer felt for a pulse, but there was none. He reached over and clicked off the radio, then turned off the motor. He then slipped his hand into the man's pocket and found a wallet. Rorer returned to where Purvis and Clegg were waiting and told them that the man was dead.

He opened the dead man's wallet and lifted out his driver's license. The man they had killed had not been an outlaw at all. He was a 35-year-old worker at a nearby Civilian Conservation Corps camp named Eugene Boisneau.

Purvis and Clegg stood in the driveway. They waited. Other than the wounded "John," who was still staggering around inside of the lodge, nothing was moving. Even though the Bureau had apparently just shot and killed an innocent man, Purvis tried to put it out of his mind. Dillinger and his gang were trapped inside of the lodge and, eventually, they would have to try and make a break for it. For now, Purvis and Clegg decided against storming the place. There weren't enough bulletproof vests, the tear-gas guns had been left behind, and, frankly, they had no idea what they were doing. The minutes ticked by. All around the lodge, agents hid behind trees, blowing on their hands and stomping their feet to try and stay warm.

An hour passed. Then, around 11:00 p.m., a new set of headlights appeared in the driveway. It was an ambulance from the Civilian Conservation Corps camp. Purvis was surprised because no one had called for it. The camp doctor, S.X. Roberts, got out of the ambulance and told Purvis that he had received a call that the camp's chef, John Morris, had been wounded. Purvis realized that Morris must be the wounded "John" who had retreated into the lodge.

The situation was getting worse by the minute.

When the ambulance arrived, another man emerged from the trees. It was a gas station attendant named John Hoffman, the third man in the Chevrolet coupe, and the one that Agent Reinecke had tried to gun down in the woods. He had a gunshot wound in his right arm and glass cuts all over his face. Together, Hoffman and Dr. Roberts called for John Morris to come out of the lodge. He stumbled out a few moments later. To Purvis's surprise, Morris was followed by three other men, who came out with their hands up. It was Emil Wanetka, the bartender, and bus boy. Wanetka said that Dillinger and his men were still inside the building, hiding in an upstairs room on the left side of the building.

Word was passed among the agents hidden in the trees that the Dillinger gang was trapped inside of the lodge. It was just a matter of time before they got them. That was the good news. The bad news was that someone, apparently a civilian, had been killed in the Chevrolet. This news was taken hard by Carter Baum, the 29-year-old agent who had fired the fatal shots. Baum retreated to one of the Bureau cars, where he sat, brooding and trying to stay warm.

Agent Ken McIntire joined him. "I think there's a man in that car," he said, "and I think he's dead."

Baum sighed. "Certainly he is. I killed him."

McIntire tried to ease the other man's guilt. Several agents had fired at the car. It was dark, and Baum couldn't be certain that he had killed the man. He urged his friend to try not to think about it.

But Baum couldn't stop thinking about it. He had killed an innocent man. His hand rested on the machine gun in his lap and he told McIntire, "I can never shoot this gun again."

That statement would later turn out to be a fatal one.

Meanwhile, Purvis and Clegg were still trying to decide whether or not to storm the lodge. Agent Werner Hanni was on his way from St. Paul and he was bringing tear-gas guns. Dillinger wasn't going anywhere. They should wait for Hanni to arrive. Purvis collared Agent Jay Newman and told him to drive over to Birchwood Lodge, telephone the Rhinelander airport, and leave a message for Hanni to hurry to Manitowish as soon as he arrived. Newman, a devout Mormon, noticed Carter Baum's plight and asked to take him along so that they could talk. Purvis agreed.

Newman drove Baum to Birchwood Lodge, where he called an agent left at Rhinelander and passed on the message for Hanni. When Newman finished the call, the operator told him he had just heard about a Packard being stolen in Manitowish. Newman, worried that a member of Dillinger's gang might be escaping, took Baum, and drove back past Little Bohemia and on into town, where they spotted a local constable named Carl C. Christiansen. The constable jumped in the car and accompanied them back to Birchwood Lodge, hoping to assemble some volunteers to comb the woods and nearby roads.

When they made it back to the lodge, they were greeted with more news. The switchboard operator, Alvin Koerner, who lived between the two lodges, had just telephoned, saying that a suspicious car was parked outside of his house. Newman decided to investigate. Newman, along with Baum and Christiansen, returned to the car and sped off toward Koerner's house, which was less than a minute away. As they came close, they saw a car parked along Route 51.

Newman told the other two men to have their guns ready.

As they approached the car, they could see that it was empty. Baum jotted down the license number. They turned into the gravel lane leading to Koerner's house. A Ford was parked in front and when their headlights swept over the car, they could see that it was filled with people. He pulled up behind it and rolled down his window. "I'm looking for Mr. Koerner," he called out.

No one answered.

"Who's in that car?" Newman asked suspiciously.

A small young man in a brown suede jacket got out of the passenger's side door and walked over to Newman's open window. "I know you bastards are wearing bulletproof vests," the man snarled, "so I'll give it to you high and low!"

More words were exchanged and then Baby Face Nelson raised his gun and fired into the car.

It was far too late when Purvis and Clegg finally realized that every assumption they had made about the evening was terribly wrong. While the two men were standing in the driveway at Little Bohemia, looking for a glimpse of the gang they believed trapped was inside, Dillinger was already long gone – and so were Van Meter, Hamilton, Carroll, and Nelson. Each of them had made his escape in the opening minutes of a disaster that would haunt the Bureau for years to come.

It would be some time before everything was pieced together, but the escape began almost when the three Bureau cars entered the Little Bohemia driveway. The gang was already packing when the agents arrived, Nelson in the cottage and the rest of them upstairs. The only guests left in the barroom were John Hoffman, the gas station attendant, and two of his friends from the CCC camp, John Morris and Eugene Boisneau. The three men had just put on their coats and stepped out onto the porch when the Bureau cars pulled up. The bartender and busboy had followed them out to say goodbye.

The three men got into Hoffman's Chevrolet, and when he turned the ignition, the radio came on. None of them saw the Bureau cars in the dark driveway. Hoffman put the car into gear and started up the driveway, still unable to see the agents, who began shouting for him to stop. Hoffman couldn't hear them over the car's radio. In fact, none of the men in the car knew what was happening until bullets began slamming into the car and shattering the windshield. On the porch behind them, the bartender and busboy began shouting, "Stop! They're our customers!" But no one heard them over the sound of the gunfire.

At the sound of gunshots, Dillinger and the men upstairs grabbed their weapons, opened a window in back, and prepared to jump out. It was then that Rorer and his men came around the left side of the lodge, saw them, and opened fire. Dillinger fired back with his machine gun.

The critical mistake in the raid belonged to Rorer. He believed that his shots had driven the gang members back into the lodge – but they hadn't. When Rorer and his men ducked to avoid the return fire, Dillinger, Hamilton, Van Meter, and Carroll had each jumped from the second-story window onto a huge mound of snow that was piled behind the lodge.

By the time that Rorer looked back, they were already gone. If he looked over toward the lake, he would have seen no one escaping because there was an eight-foot incline between the backyard and the beach. Henry Voss had not included this feature on the map that he had drawn for the agents that afternoon. Dillinger and the others, hidden behind the incline, sprinted down a set of wooden steps to the beach, turned right, and ran along the edge of the lake and into the woods.

As for Nelson, he had been the shadowy figure that had emerged from the cabin, fired at Purvis, and disappeared into the trees. By the time the agents fought their way through the barbed-wire fence, he too was gone, disappearing in the darkness.

The car that entered the lodge's driveway after the initial shooting was driven by Pat Reilly, returning to the lodge once again with Pat Cherrington. Pat had just opened the door when she heard a voice yell, "Halt!" She replied, "Go to hell," jumped back in the car, and told Reilly to step on it. When he reached the highway, Reilly paused for a moment, unsure of what to do. When shots rang out, he lost control of the car, running over a tree stump. As he fought to get the car moving, he tossed two pistols into Pat's lap and told her to start shooting. She also told Reilly to go to hell.

When the car was freed from the stump, they passed the lodge a second time, drawing more gunshots. These shots blasted out one of the car's tires and the door swung open, dumping Pat out onto the road, fracturing her shoulder. Later that night, after replacing the punctured tire at a filling station, the two hapless fugitives drove their car into a mud hole. Stuck, they sat in a field drinking whiskey. They would not reach St. Paul until the following day.

Meanwhile, Dillinger and the others were thrashing through the pines, looking for a house with a car they could steal. In the darkness, Tommy Carroll got lost and wandered off on his own. In the end, it was Carroll who had the easiest escape. He made his way to Manitowish, stole the Packard that Agent Newman heard about, and drove off to St. Paul. Dillinger, Hamilton, and Van Meter emerged from the woods about a quarter mile north of Little Bohemia. If the Bureau had established roadblocks, or even patrolled Route 51, they likely would have been spotted. As it was, Van Meter was free to attempt to flag down a passing car, but the car, driven by Nan Wanetka's brother, George LaPorte, was following the ambulance to the lodge and didn't stop.

Across the road, Dillinger spotted a wood-frame house with several cabins behind it called Mitchell's Rest Lake Resort. The men quickly crossed the road and Hamilton went to the door and knocked. Inside, the resort's owner, 70-year-old Edward J. Mitchell, was trying to explain something to his German handyman. His wife was lying on the couch, sick with the flu. When Mitchell opened the door, Hamilton asked for water and the man allowed him inside. Hamilton then casually walked across the room and pulled the telephone off the wall. The Mitchells had heard rumors about gangsters at Little Bohemia and, a short time before, heard gunshots in the woods. Now, they were seeing those gangsters face-to-face.

By this time, Dillinger had followed Hamilton into the house. Mrs. Mitchell recognized him right away. "You couldn't be Dillinger, could you?" she asked.

Dillinger grinned. "You couldn't have guessed better," he replied, then noticed the look of fear on Edward Mitchell's face. "Now don't worry, old timer, I'd never harm a hair on your head."

"My wife is just getting over the flu," said Mitchell.

Dillinger, always remembering to play the role of the bank robber with a heart of gold, took a moment to drape a blanket across the older women. "Here you are, mother," he said.

Dillinger explained that they needed a car. Mitchell told him that they had an old Model T, but it had been up on blocks all winter. Van Meter went outside and saw a Model A truck, but it wouldn't start. He asked Mitchell who owned the green couple parked next to it and he was told that it belonged to his carpenter, who lived in one of the cabins.

The carpenter, Robert L. Johnson, was awakened by a knock at his door. He dressed, grabbed a flashlight, and went to the door in his slippers. Outside, he found Dillinger, Hamilton, and Van Meter. Dillinger said that they needed a doctor for Mrs. Mitchell – and the .45 in his hand made it clear that the situation was more urgent than that. Johnson led them to his car.

Nelson was having a tougher time of it. Cut off from the rest of the gang, he ran the opposite direction, going south along the lakeshore, stumbling through thick underbrush for a half hour before seeing the lights of a cabin about a half-mile beyond Little Bohemia. The cabin was owned by an elderly couple, Mr. and Mrs. George W. Lange. Nelson didn't bother to know. He barged in the front door with a pistol in his hand. "Now, don't get excited," he told the startled couple. "I won't harm you, but this is a matter of life and death."

Nelson slumped down onto the couch, clearly exhausted, and began petting the Langes' dog, which began barking. After resting for a few minutes, he pointed his gun at the couple and said that he wanted Mr. Lange to drive him away in his

Alvin Koerner's home, near Little Bohemia

car, a 1932 Chevrolet coach. Mrs. Lange began to cry. Nelson needed her to calm down, but he was no John Dillinger. "Come on now, shut up!" he snapped at her.

The Langes put on their coats and got in the car, with Mr. Lange driving and Nelson sitting next to him. The headlights wouldn't turn on, but Nelson told him to drive anyway. Lange edged out onto Route 51 and turned right, toward Birchwood Lodge. The car had only gone a few hundred yards when it stalled.

Now what? Nelson was in a predicament. He was sure that a carload of cops was going to come around the curve at any moment. On the left, he saw a house with all of the windows filled with light. "Who lives there?" he asked Lange.

Lange replied, "Alvin Koerner."

Koerner was the switchboard operator who had been passing information to Agent Newman at Birchwood Lodge. At that moment, he was sitting in his living room with his wife, worried about the sounds of gunfire at Little Bohemia and about the call that he had taken from the wounded John Morris. His maid and two children were asleep in another room. Peering out the window into the dark, he saw the Langes' car outside. He couldn't see who was inside of it, so he hurriedly telephoned Birchwood Lodge to report it.

With his gun trained on the elderly couple, Nelson marched the Langes up the muddy drive to Koerner's front door. Koerner, not seeing Nelson behind them, let the group inside. Once he was in the living room, Nelson grabbed Koerner and told him that he needed him to drive him to the town of Woodruff. Koerner argued with him. He had children to take care of, he said. Nelson put his gun in his face and told him that it didn't matter. They were still arguing when a car drove up. Nelson demanded to know who it belonged to, but Koerner didn't know.

The car belonged to George LaPorte and he had a friend named Carl Christiansen (no relation to the constable) with him. After declining to pick up the hitchhiking Homer Van Meter, LaPorte had stopped at Little Bohemia, where Emil Wanetka and his two employees had also gotten into the car. Wanetka's group needed coats and they decided to come to Koerner's to get some. Leaving Christiansen in the car, the others walked to the house. Nelson opened the door and ushered them in.

"Hello, Jimmie," the bartender said to Nelson. The two men had gotten along well that weekend; Nelson had been a great tipper.

Nelson produced a pistol. "Never mind the bullshit, just line up against the wall."

Wanetka reached out to push the gun away. "Put that gun down, Jimmie. These people are friends of mine."

Nelson stepped back. "Who's in that car out there?"

"Nobody," Wanetka shrugged, forgetting about Christiansen in the backseat.

"Are there any G-men in that car?"

"No," Wanetka assured him.

"I'm getting out of here," Nelson said, motioning to Wanetka and Koerner, "and you two are going with me."

Nelson waved the gun at them and they walked outside. Mrs. Koerner began to cry. Nelson ordered Wanetka to drive and he climbed in next to him on the front seat, keeping the pistol at his side. Koerner got into the backseat with Christiansen.

Wanetka raised his hands. "Jimmy, I have no keys for this car."

Just then, a car drove up behind them. Agent Jay Newman was at the wheel. Nelson got out of the car and walked up to Newman's window, where he issued his threat to shoot the men. "I'll kill you!" he said to Newman, his gun inches from the agent's face.

Newman leaned back in his seat, hoping that Carter Baum, who had a machine gun in his lap, or the constable, Carl Christiansen, might take a shot at the man in his window. When neither man moved, Newman slipped a hand inside of his coat, reaching for his own pistol.

Nelson saw the movement. "Don't reach for that gun! I'll kill you! Now get out of the car!"

Newman stopped. Next to him, Baum, the agent stricken with guilt over shooting an innocent man at Little Bohemia, ducked his head behind Newman's shoulder, as if to hide. He made no move for his gun. Christensen hid behind Baum. Slowly, Newman opened the door and started to step out into the driveway. Before he could get all of the way out of the car, Nelson opened fire.

His first bullet struck Newman in the head, a glancing wound above his right eye. He fell facedown into the mud, dazed but alive. Nelson then fired wildly into the car. Baum and Christiansen both tumbled out of the passenger door, Baum landing on top of the other man. Baum then got up to run, but Nelson shot first. Three slugs tore into Baum's neck. He fell over the white picket fence that ran alongside the driveway, landing on his face. A thick gurgling sound was coming from his throat, and then it stopped. Baum was dead. He really never fired that machine gun again.

Constable Christiansen got halfway to his feet and fell forward into the headlights of the car. Nelson turned and fired at him. Two bullets struck the constable in the hip, knocking him back down. As he fell into a ditch, Nelson just kept firing and hit him three more times.

When the shooting started, Emil Wanetka ran. Nelson, seeing the blur of motion, swung around and fired in his direction. Wanetka threw himself into a snowbank and the shots went wild. Bullets kicked up gravel, sent up showers of snow, and took chunks of wood out of the house. Alvin Koerner, keeping his head low as he ran through the melee, made it back to the house and locked the door.

With nothing moving around him, Nelson jumped into the Bureau car, threw it in reverse, and floored it. The spinning wheels sent a shower of gravel against the house. As Nelson was backing out of the drive, Agent Newman regained his senses. He raised his gun and opened fire, empting the clip of his automatic at the fleeing Ford. The bullets missed their mark and Nelson disappeared down Route 51.

Newman stood up, staggering on his feet. The bullet had creased his forehead and blood was running into his eyes. He made it to the other car and saw LaPorte's friend, the other Carl Christiansen, hiding in the backseat. "Come out with your hands up!" Newman ordered him.

"Please don't shoot me," Christiansen begged him. "I'm a resident."

Newman heard a moan and he saw the fallen bodies. He pushed Christiansen toward Koerner's front door. Even as shaky as he was, he could see that they needed immediate medical attention at the scene. Christiansen banged on the door, calling for Koerner to open up, but Koerner refused to answer the door. The two men went around to the back of the house, where they could see people in the kitchen. Newman banged on the window and even put his badge up to the glass. No one came. After yelling for a minute or two longer, Newman gave up and told Christiansen that he was going to Voss's and he was taking the other man with him.

"The hell I am," Christiansen objected. "I'm staying here."

"Goddamn you," Newman swore and put his pistol to Christiansen's side. "You're going with me."

The two men climbed into the car and drove out onto the road.

Just moments after Nelson sped away from the Koerner house, the car that was carrying Werner Hanni and three other agents from St. Paul made it to the area. Speeding along Route 51 near the lodges, Hanni saw a black Ford approaching from the opposite direction. He dimmed his headlights and peered at the car, thinking that it might be other Bureau men.

Suddenly, a spotlight flashed from the oncoming car and momentarily blinded Hanni as the cars passed each other. Several of the agents turned quickly to see if the other car would stop, but it didn't. A minute later, Hanni pulled into the driveway at Birchwood Lodge to see if the car would return, but there was no sign of it. Later that night, Hanni would realize that the car with the spotlight had been driven by Baby Face Nelson.

As Hanni and his men stood at the roadside, another car drove up. Two deputy sheriff's got out and looked around. They had been called because locals had reported some shooting. A minute later, a third car arrived on the scene. "Are you officers?" a man shouted from the car.

"This is Hanni!" the agent called back.

A man got out of the car. There was blood all over his face. "This is Newman," he said. "Where's the nearest doctor?"

Back at Little Bohemia, Purvis was still in the driveway, studying the lodge and looking for any sign that the gang was still inside. The first indication that he had about how bad things were about to get was when Emil Wanetka came running out of the woods. He had jogged all the way from Koerner's place and was so winded that he couldn't raise his hands when an agent ordered him to. He finally gasped to Purvis, "All your men are dead. At Koerner's."

Purvis didn't believe him. He asked Wanetka for his name and address and when Wanetka was unable to spell "Manitowish," Purvis became hostile with him.

"Who'd you come here for?" Wanetka sniped back. "Me or Dillinger?"

Purvis told a pair of agents to drive to the Koerner house and check out Wanetka's story.

Werner Hanni's men reached the Koerner house first, a half-hour after the shooting. They found the wounded constable, Carl Christiansen, sitting up, leaning against the fence. Agent Thomas Dodd took Christiansen's flashlight and after a minute, found Carter Baum lying face down in a pool of blood. He was dead. No one had come out of the house to check on anyone outside. The family was too frightened.

As the wounded were taken to the hospital, Purvis and Clegg remained at Little Bohemia, convinced that, despite all evidence to the contrary, at least some of the gang members were still in the lodge. An hour passed. After midnight, they got so cold that they opened up the garage and took up positions inside, still watching the lodge. The rest of the agents were still standing in the woods, shivering in the cold, until the rising sun started to lighten the eastern sky.

Around 4:00 a.m., word reached Clegg that the local sheriff and a group of deputies were down the road and wanted to join them. Clegg called them up. The locals wanted to storm the lodge, but Clegg insisted that they fire tear gas grenades inside first, but even that didn't go smoothly. There was only a single gas gun, and despite all their efforts, the agents couldn't get it to fire a grenade through the lodge's window screens. The grenades kept hitting the windows, bouncing off, and falling to the ground, hissing out ribbons of gas. A group of five agents stood behind the garage debating what to do next. It was decided that the only way to get tear gas into the lodge was for someone to run up and throw one through the door. If Dillinger was still inside of the lodge – and they all were sure that he was – it might be a suicide run for the agent who tried it. Finally, Agent

John T. McLaughlin volunteered. He was the only single man there, he said, and should be the one to do it.

A few minutes later, McLaughlin ran forward and lobbed gas grenades into the lodge. One or two of the deputies opened fire on the building until Clegg told them to stop shooting. As streams of gas began rolling out from inside of the building, a woman's voice called out: "We'll come out if you stop firing."

Purvis shouted back, "Come out and bring everyone with you, with your hands up!"

A moment later, all of the gang's women — Jean Delaney, Helen Gillis, and Mickey Conforti, hugging her bulldog — walked out onto the porch. Agents rushed past them into the lodge, but found no one inside. On the beach behind the building, they discovered footprints leading into the woods.

For the first time, the enormity of the disaster hit Purvis. As the women were led away, he stood and stared, completely stunned, replaying the events of the night through his mind, as he would do many times for the rest of his life.

Two men were dead — and Dillinger had gotten away again.

25. Desperate Flight

As Hoover, Purvis, and Clegg were trying to figure out what had gone wrong at Little Bohemia, the five men of the Dillinger Gang struggled to get to safety. None of them had an easy time of it. By daylight, the police had put up roadblocks all across Wisconsin and Minnesota. Hundreds of volunteers, shotguns in hand, piled into cars, and scoured the back roads in search of the gang.

Tommy Carroll was the first to escape. His car bogged down on a muddy logging road, but after striking out on foot, he managed to hitchhike back to St. Paul.

Nelson drove south until his stolen auto quit on him at Squaw Lake, Wisconsin. Abandoning the car, he walked north through the woods and entered the Lac Du Flambeau Reservation, where he stumbled on a cottage. In the kitchen, a 15-year-old girl named Dorothy Schroeder gave him a cup of coffee and a slice of buttered bread, for which he gave her $3, despite her objections. Nelson was sipping the coffee a few minutes later when Dorothy's aunt and uncle, Ole "Ollie" Catfish, and his wife, Maggie, arrived. Catfish, an elderly Chippewa man who spoke broken English. They lived at the cottage while tapping maple trees. Nelson told them that he was a game warden and would need to stay with them for two or three days. Catfish didn't object and Nelson settled in.

The three days passed smoothly. The women cooked meals for Nelson and he passed the days mostly in silence, watching the woods. Around noon on Friday, a trapper showed up and talked with Catfish. Nelson hid in the kitchen, watching, and when the man left, he demanded to know who he was. Nelson grew more nervous throughout the afternoon and, around 6:00 p.m., he told Catfish that it was time to leave and he ordered the old man to lead him to the next town.

Catfish protested, saying that he was sick. Nelson put a gun in his face and told him to start walking. They walked down an old railroad bed and Maggie followed them until Nelson waved her back. They trekked through the woods as night began to fall. Catfish complained that his heart was weak, and they stopped several times to rest. When night finally fell, a bright full moon rose above them.

Around 9:00 p.m., after walking about six miles, they spotted a campfire. Three fishermen that Catfish knew were seated around it. Nelson walked up to the fire and warmed his hands. A few minutes later, a car appeared and parked a short distance away. "Come on, let's go see who those fellows are," Nelson told Catfish.

As they walked closer, they saw two Indians standing next to a 1928 Chevrolet sedan. Another car, this one a Plymouth, drove up as Nelson approached. Two local men, out for an evening of night fishing, were inside. As the men stood, swapping small talk, Nelson walked over to the Plymouth and looked at it. "Is that yours?" Nelson asked the driver.

One of the men gave Nelson a hard look. He asked Nelson what authority he had to be fishing on the reservation. Nelson, not surprisingly, whipped out his gun. "This is my authority," he snapped. "You line up with those Indians over there."

Nelson popped the hood of the Chevrolet parked nearby and yanked the distributor cable, disabling it. He told Catfish to get into the Plymouth, but Catfish doubled over, as if in great pain, telling Nelson that he was sick. Nelson prodded him with the pistol, again telling him to get into the car. Nelson slid behind the wheel and they took off.

Catfish guided the little gangster to an intersection with State Highway 70, at which point Nelson let him out of the car and drove off, heading south. He drove the entire length of Wisconsin, and into Illinois. He soon arrived at Louis Cernocky's tavern in Fox River Grove. Cernocky welcomed him inside and got him something to eat. Nelson's luck held – he had safely gotten away.

Despite the information from Beth Green, despite the fact that Emil Wanetka had told the Bureau that it was Cernocky who had sent Dillinger to Little Bohemia, despite wiretaps and interviews with Cernocky's neighbors, Purvis still hadn't put the tavern in Fox River Grove under surveillance.

While Nelson was hiding out and making his way back to Chicago, Dillinger, along with Van Meter and Hamilton, drove their stolen Ford south, dropping the car's owner off outside of the small town of Park Falls, Wisconsin, around 9:00 the following morning. After that, they also headed for St. Paul. Sticking to back roads, they dodged the roadblocks and posses that were looking for them and crossed

The Mississippi River bridge at Hastings, where Dillinger, Van Meter, and Hamilton eluded the police – with Hamilton being shot in the process.

into Minnesota without incident. Assuming that the northern approaches to the city would be carefully watched, Dillinger circled around to the south.

At 10:30 a.m., the three bandits approached a bridge over the Mississippi River at Hastings, about 20 miles below St. Paul. A policeman named Fred McArdle, along with three deputy sheriffs, were parked at the southern end of the bridge, checking license numbers against a Bureau bulletin that had been sent out. As Dillinger approached the bridge, McArdle was startled to see that the plates on the car matched a set on the list. He pulled out to give chase, but just as he did, a cattle truck cut him off. By the time that McArdle reached the other side of the bridge, Dillinger was gone.

But McArdle wasn't going to give up easily. He and the three deputies continued northward, toward St. Paul, hoping to catch up to the car. They had no radios, so there was no way to alert anyone that Dillinger was heading into the city. Ten miles north of the bridge, McArdle spotted the Ford, which was being driven well under the speed limit in an effort to avoid attention. Deputy Norman Dieter leaned out the window with a .30-30 rifle and fired at the Ford's rear tires. He missed and the Ford surged ahead of its pursuers. Dieter fired again and this slug punched through the thin body of the automobile between the fender and the spare, tore through the rear seat, and drilled into John Hamilton's back. He screamed in agony and slammed forward against the front seat of the car.

Dillinger smashed out the window behind Hamilton and returned fire with his .45, shattering the windshield of the police car just above Deputy Joe Heinen's head. For the next several minutes, the two cars engaged in a wild running gunfight at speeds of more than 80 miles per hour. The two cars traded shot after shot, but Van Meter, who was driving, managed to get ahead of the pursuing officers, spun to the right, and veered onto a dirt track called Cemetery Road. After losing sight of the car, Officer McArdle drove past. By the time he realized the Ford was no longer in front of him, it was gone.

Van Meter found a secluded spot and pulled over. Hamilton was losing a lot of blood from the gaping wound in his back and he needed a doctor. First, though, they would need a faster and less-recognizable vehicle. The local cops were surely on to them by now. They cruised the back roads south of the city for almost an hour without spotting one. Finally, around noon, Van Meter parked near the intersection of City Road 10 and Fifth Avenue. A few minutes later, a 1934 Ford V8 Deluxe approached. It was driven by power company manager, Roy Francis, his wife, Sybil, and their 19-month-old son, Robert. Francis was on his lunch hour, taking his wife and son for a drive to help the baby sleep. Ahead, Francis saw a man in the road and pulled over.

Van Meter approached with a gun in his hand. He was almost apologetic. "Sorry to trouble you," he said, "But I've got to have your machine." Francis stepped out and began to raise his hands. "Keep your hands down, we won't shoot you," Van Meter added.

Mrs. Francis, carrying the baby, got out of the car as the bandits tossed their belongings into the flashy roadster. Dillinger helped the wounded Hamilton into the car next, gently easing his friend into the backseat.

"What do you do?" Van Meter asked Francis.

"I work at the power company."

Van Meter smiled sadly. "You're lucky to have a nice job and a family."

Sybil Francis recognized Dillinger right away, but he smiled at her reassuringly and patted the baby on the head. He told her, "Don't worry about the kid. We like kids."

The bandits wished them well and Dillinger drove off in the Francis's car and Van Meter followed. The bullet-riddled Ford was dumped at Robert Street and Willy Road. The Francis family walked two miles to a service station and called for help.

Hamilton was in terrible pain and Dillinger feared that he might not survive the trip to Chicago. St. Paul was now off limits. After the police chase, they would have cops and federal agents scouring the city for them. The best thing to do would be to find a safe place to hide out down south, where they could find a doctor for Hamilton.

They turned south toward Chicago with the dying man in the backseat.

26. The Mystery of John Hamilton

On Tuesday morning, Dillinger managed to make it back to the Chicago area. He was desperate to find a doctor for Hamilton. The wound in his back, which was the size of a silver dollar, was festering and starting to stink of gangrene. Blood was all over the inside of the car. They had bought bandages and medicine in Dubuque, Iowa, but if Hamilton was going to have any chance at all to live, he needed a doctor. They had a set of stolen plates on the car, but Dillinger knew he couldn't drive around Chicago for long with a bleeding man in the backseat before someone noticed.

Dillinger was searching for the unscrupulous Dr. Joseph Moran, the greedy practitioner who was known for treating underworld characters. He was always willing to lend his services, for a price, of course. But this time, Dillinger couldn't find him and so he went to the Hi Ho Inn, a Cicero nightclub that was operated by brothers Bobby and Joie O'Brien. They wanted nothing to do with him. Dillinger was too hot and word had come down from syndicate leaders that no one was supposed to help Dillinger. They sent him away, but they did promise to try and find Dr. Moran and would rendezvous with him later that night.

Dillinger's visit started a series of telephone calls. The O'Brien brothers called Elmer Farmer, the man who owned the safe house were the Barkers had hidden the kidnapped Edward Bremer, who they believed could find Moran. In turn, Farmer called Dock Barker, who tried to reach Moran, but couldn't. Meanwhile, Joie O'Brien drove to Aurora, Illinois, and retrieved Volney Davis, who had been living in a safe house in Aurora for several weeks. Davis was a bank-robbing pal of the late Eddie Green and worked with the Barkers and Alvin Karpis.

Everyone gathered that night in a parking lot behind the Seafood Inn, a restaurant in suburban Elmhurst. It was the first time that Dillinger met members of the Barker Gang, but there was little time for them to get acquainted. They lifted Hamilton out of the car and put him in the back of Volney Davis's Buick. Dillinger and Van Meter then followed Davis back to Aurora and the safe house, which was located at 415 Fox Street. Davis had sent his girlfriend, Edna "Rabbits" Murray, to stay with friends. Hamilton was carried inside and put to bed, but no one believed that he could last very long. His agony was increasing by the hour.

Members of the two gangs tended to Hamilton all that night and for two more days, doing their best to ease his pain. He finally died on the afternoon of Thursday, April 26.

At dusk, Dock Barker and Volney Davis drove to a quarry near Oswego, Illinois, and dug a grave. After dark, they loaded Hamilton's body into a car, drove him to the quarry, and laid him on the ground. Davis had purchased several cans of lye to hide his features. Dillinger bent down over his friend and delivered the eulogy: "Sorry, old friend, to have to do this. I know you'd do as much for me." And then he poured a can of lye over Hamilton's head. Barker and Van Meter filled in the grave and Davis found a roll of barbed wire to place over it as a marker.

John "Red" Hamilton was left there in that shallow grave to rest in whatever peace he was able to find – or so the official record claimed. Legend, however, tells many different tales about Hamilton's eventual fate.

John Hamilton died in the Aurora safe house where Volney Davis had been staying. When the men returned after the burial, the place was a mess and so Davis said he called Edna Murray to come over and help him clean it up. He said that she nearly fainted when she arrived. White disinfectant powder covered the bedroom floor. The sink was piled high with dishes, medicines, and bloody bandages. The whole house stunk of gangrene and death.

Volney Davis, bank robber pal of Eddie Green and the Barkers, sheltered Dillinger and Hamilton after Little Bohemia.

Or that's what Volney Davis later claimed. Edna Murray had a different story. She had been ordered out of the house before Hamilton and Dillinger ever arrived there, and she later stated that she did not hear about Hamilton's death or the Oswego burial until she reunited with Davis much later. She never saw the blood-soaked safe house or the mess left behind by his final days of suffering.

The Bureau also knew nothing of his death. Despite the blood that was splashed all over the backseat of the car that Van Meter and Dillinger had abandoned, Hamilton's death was considered uncertain. Reports of it were based on informant's stories, which were second- and third-hand accounts. No one who talked had actually been there to see Hamilton die, and all of them told a different version of the story. One rumor claimed that he had been buried in the sand dunes of northern Indiana. Another claimed that he had been weighted down and dropped into an abandoned mine shaft in Wisconsin. It was not until Volney Davis had been arrested, escaped, and arrested again that Bureau agents learned of the unsuccessful efforts of Dillinger and Van Meter to get medical treatment for Hamilton from Dr. Joseph Moran.

One version of the story had it that Dillinger tracked down another doctor. In late July 1934, Dillinger girlfriend Polly Hamilton, (no relation to John), told federal agents that Chicago madam and Dillinger friend, Ana Sage (who will soon play a larger part in the story), told her that Red Hamilton was then being treated for a "badly infected wound" by Dr. Harold Cassidy. If this was true, then Hamilton was still alive as of July 1934, and possibly later.

There were others who also wondered about Hamilton's demise, including Dillinger's attorney, Louis Piquett, and his investigator, Art O'Leary. If Dillinger truly had been desperate to find help for Hamilton, why did he not try to contact them? There is no indication that Dillinger ever attempted to get in touch with them during this period. In later conversations with the two men, in fact, Dillinger repeatedly lied about what happened after Little Bohemia. He told them that he and Van Meter had hidden in Wisconsin and later buried Hamilton next to Lake Michigan. He never mentioned the Barkers, Davis, or anything else that allegedly occurred. Could he have been covering up the fact that Hamilton didn't die?

Volney Davis, however, stuck to the story that Hamilton had died in agony in Aurora, and he provided a general description of the burial site. There were inconsistencies of the actual time and place of Hamilton's death and the persons involved in the burial, but more than a year later, on August 28, 1935, federal agents who went digging in an Oswego gravel pit found a badly decomposed body.

But before the body was found, the Bureau had been receiving reports from police and individuals claiming that Hamilton was alive and hiding out in northern Indiana. Since he had been reported killed on other occasions, the search continued until the body was found in Oswego, minus a hand and so corroded from the lye that had been poured over the remains that the agents had little to identify the corpse with besides some strands of hair and a belt size. The best they could do was to pull a few molars from the skull and send them to the physician at the Indiana state prison. He compared them to Hamilton's dental chart, which showed some fillings, and declared that the Bureau had found their man. This satisfied J. Edgar Hoover, who proclaimed the belated discovery of the last member of the Dillinger gang to every newspaper in the country. The case of John Hamilton was now officially closed.

The body that was taken from the gravel pit was buried in the Oswego cemetery and the funeral service was paid for by Hamilton's sister, Anna Steve. Rumors spread around Oswego, and some of them still linger today. According to some stories, Hamilton did not die in Aurora at all, but right there in Oswego. One story even pointed to a house in town where Dillinger and his gang allegedly holed up while Hamilton slowly died in agony. Past owners of this house reported to me first-hand that the house was definitely haunted and they believed the lingering spirit was that of John Hamilton.

But was Hamilton really dead at all?

The FBI continued to received reports that stated that Hamilton was still alive. They arrived on a regular basis, but were apparently disregarded. Most of the sightings could likely be written off as mistaken identity, but there was at least one that was convincing. The arrival of the letter was recorded by the FBI on August 24, 1936, a year after Hamilton's body was supposedly found. It was sent by a former prisoner who was identified as "Happy." The informant knew some of the gang members, as well as Art O'Leary. Most believe that "Happy" was an associate of Dillinger named Fred Meyers, who lived in Chicago. The letter read:

Dear Sir:

Will you kindly advise how much you will guarantee in cash secret and confidential information about the movements of John Hamilton?

There are three people who know that he is still living and happen to know the details concerning him.

If interested please make offer through personal column of Chicago Tribune *as follows, HAP * Will buy ,000 bushels, meaning of course that many thousand dollars for this information and place ED after the word bushels.*

If this offer is OK you will be supplied with an amazing detailed report on his present physical condition and movements. Money must be on deposit at your Chicago Office but will not have to be paid until this man is captured or killed or both. This information must be kept strictly confidential between you and I and must be kept out of the newspapers except code transmissions between you and I. I am a hard working electrician and took considerable time and money to get this data and do not want to risk my life for the deal. Everything will be handled by correspondence and code in the Chicago Tribune. *If your offer is accepted, I will make you proposals which must be guaranteed by you as a strictly gentlemen's agreement.*

The FBI received the letter, but there is nothing to indicate that J. Edgar Hoover ever saw it. There was likely no follow-up ever done because by the time that the body believed to be Hamilton was found, Hoover had won the national "War on Crime," appeared on the cover of *Time* magazine, and was turning his attention to the communist threat.

Could the letter writer have been telling the truth? There are many who believe so. One of those who became convinced that John Hamilton survived his wounds and was never buried in Oswego was a nephew, Bruce Hamilton. Many years after the fact, he described a trip that was taken by family members in 1945 that resulted in the collection of a large amount of money. He was later told that the money had been stashed away by the Dillinger gang – the whereabouts of which was known to the gang's only surviving member, John Hamilton.

After the trip was over, Bruce's father, Wilton Hamilton, paid off the mortgage on his home in South Bend, Indiana, bought a new house, and purchased the family's first new car.

Less than a year later, Wilton planned a trip to Sault Sainte Marie on the Canadian border to see relatives at the home of Hamilton's sister, Anna Steve. The journey was made by Wilton and his wife, Harriet, their older son, Douglas, their daughter, Jane Margaret, and Bruce, who was then 15 years old. It was during this trip, which centered around a gathering of about a dozen relatives, that Bruce met the man that he was told afterward was his relative, John Hamilton. He and his brother and sister were told not to discuss the trip with anyone.

Around this same time, Hamilton's brother, Foye, who was recently released from prison, came into a great deal of money. He used it to build a machine shop in Rockford, Illinois, and he also purchased Turtle Island in the Great Lakes area, near Sault Sainte Marie, as well as boats and a seaplane to use getting to and from the island. Bruce suspected that a large cabin on the island provided a hiding place for his uncle, John.

Bruce's interest in John Hamilton increased with age and he learned more details about what had happened to him from his father. Apparently, the wounded Hamilton, after stopping at the safe house in Aurora, was then taken to Chicago, where he received treatment from Dr. Cassidy. While he recuperated from his wound, he hid out with his brother, Sylvester, in East Gary, Indiana. Dillinger left Red in Indiana and then returned to Aurora, while Sylvester took John to the home of William Hamilton, Bruce's grandfather, in South Bend. William helped get him to a hideout previously used by the Dillinger gang, a nearby place called Rum Village Woods. Hamilton recuperated well enough to go to work as an electrician at a family-owned bowling alley in South Bend in 1936 and 1937. According to an elderly aunt of Bruce Hamilton, John later moved to Canada and died in the 1970s.

But if John Hamilton didn't die in Aurora in 1934, then whose body was disinterred in Oswego in 1935? One possibility is that the body belonged to Dr. Joseph Moran. At the same time that Dillinger was hunting him so that he could treat Hamilton, he was supposed to be busy laundering the money from the Bremer kidnapping for the Barkers. But no one could find him. When the drunken doctor finally turned up, he was demanding a share of the ransom as payment for performing a fingerprint removal "surgery" for Dock Barker. It is believed that Dock and his brother, Fred, killed Moran and dumped the body.

The FBI had searched for Moran for months after he vanished, and later officially declared that he had been killed and dumped in Lake Michigan. Alvin Karpis later would only say that Moran had been murdered, and was buried, but he would not say where.

Was Moran the decomposed corpse that was found in the gravel pit? And if so, could he be the spirit – not John Hamilton -- who haunts the nearby house? These mysteries, like the death of John Hamilton, will likely never be solved.

27. On the Run

The days that followed the death of John Hamilton – or Hamilton's trip to Chicago for medical treatment, depending on the version of events – were angry days for Dillinger. Much of his anger was directed at Louis Cernocky, who he believed had led the feds to Little Bohemia. He and Dock Barker, who spent a lot of time at the Davis safe house, talking and listening to the radio for news, agreed that it must have also been Cernocky who betrayed Frank Nash, triggering the Kansas City Massacre. Dillinger and Van Meter kept their bulletproof vests on and machine guns close at hand. They were tired, tense, and dirty.

More bad news arrived in the newspapers on Friday evening. An aging former state legislator named "Boss" John McLaughlin had been arrested by the Bureau. McLaughlin was a crony of Dr. Joseph Moran and had been mixed up in the Bremer kidnapping. That was bad enough, but even worse, he knew that Davis lived in Aurora. Dock Barker explained the situation to Dillinger. If McLaughlin talked, the feds could be at their door within hours. Dillinger talked things over with Van Meter. They couldn't leave until they had a new car. For the moment, they decided to stay. If the cops showed up, they would be ready for them.

As night fell, Dillinger, Barker, and Van Meter took up positions with machine guns in the living room, arranged around the three large windows at the front. Volney Davis lingered outside in the street, keeping a close eye on passing cars.

An hour went by, then two. Edna Murray was sitting in the bedroom, worrying, when Davis suddenly burst through the front door. "They're here!" he cried to Barker. "A car pulled up on Fourth Street and parked and two men got out and walked up the street. There's another car on Fox Street. Three men got out of that!"

Davis ran to a closet, pulled out a suitcase, and threw it in the middle of the living room floor. Davis called out to Edna, "Rabbit, you get out of here – get in my car!"

But Dock Barker's voice was even. "Rabbit, you stay right where you are," he said. "You don't leave this apartment. If fireworks start, you get behind me and this tommy and I'll take you out of here."

But Barker's attention was soon drawn to the street. He uttered an oath and aimed his machine gun toward a pair of men who appeared across the street from the house. One of them lit a cigarette. Barker thought it was a signal for the feds to attack and his finger tightened on the trigger.

But Dillinger harshly whispered at him. "Don't do that, Dock! Wait till we're sure we're right. Then we'll give it to them!"

The room went silent. The two men in Barker's gun sights walked on, disappearing around the corner. Barker carefully lowered the gun. The moment passed – it wasn't the Bureau.

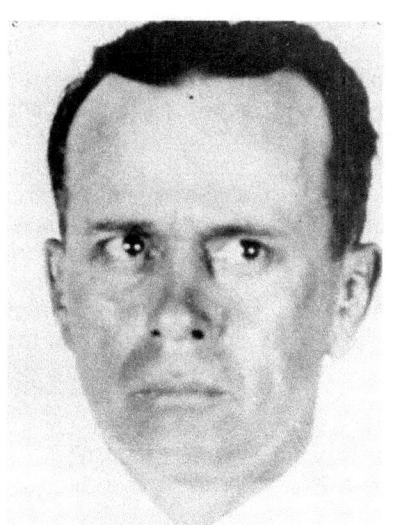
Dock Barker

They remained like that, hands tight around their weapons, standing at the windows, until later that night, when a pal of Dock's named Russell Gibson pulled up in front. He came to the door and was startled when he found himself staring into the muzzle of Dillinger's machine gun. Inside, Gibson assured them that everything was okay. McLaughlin wasn't talking – not yet anyway. He didn't know how long that would last, though, so if they were smart, they would leave as soon as possible.

Dillinger talked it over with Van Meter and they decided to stay one more night.

At the Cook County Jail, Melvin Purvis was trying to pay attention to reports from the men who were questioning McLaughlin, who wasn't telling them anything useful, and sift through the deluge of new information that was coming in after the disaster at Little Bohemia. They were buried in paper. New leads, most of them worthless, were pouring into the office. Dillinger was dead, he was in California, he was in Canada, and the list went on and on. By now, reporters had created a permanent encampment in the hallway in front of Doris Rogers's desk. Purvis couldn't go to the bathroom without one of them shouting questions at him.

Almost as troublesome were the lawmen in Indiana. Each of them was sure that Dillinger was hiding out in his jurisdiction and all of them wanted help from the Bureau. Every day that week, while Dillinger was sitting in Aurora, Purvis dispatched agents to a new town to check out another tip, from East Chicago to Muncie, to Fort Wayne to South Bend. None of them led anywhere.

The three Dillinger Gang women captured at Little Bohemia, and taken to jail in Madison, Wisconsin, were all but useless. Facing charges of conspiracy and harboring a fugitive, they gave false names and told outlandish stories and initially resisted all efforts to question them. After a few days, Jean Delaney and Mickey Conforti finally talked, but they said little that the agents could use. Conforti gave them her correct name, but said she had no idea that her boyfriend "Wayne Huttner" was really Homer Van Meter. Agent's found Conforti's invalid mother in a Chicago-area asylum and fired questions at her as she drooled and stared off into space. Just the fact that the women were in Bureau custody was a cause for mockery. Coming on the heels of Billie's arrest, newspapers mocked that while the feds may not always get their man, they always got his woman.

But what Purvis did have was cars. The found the ones that Nelson and Tommy Carroll used to escape. Both of them were found abandoned on dirt roads, mired in the mud of the north woods. They found the car that Nelson had wrecked on the way to Little Bohemia. They also ran checks on the two cars that Dillinger had left behind in the Little Bohemia garage. None of it led anywhere.

Purvis was hopeful that something found in the 16 pieces of luggage the gang had left behind would yield clues. But other than a very large collection of guns and license plates, the bags only proved that most of the gang were bad dressers. And that one of them had an overdue book from the St. Paul Library. The best lead was a business card found in Nelson's bag from a priest named Phillip Coughlin, an old family friend that agents tracked down in Wilmette, Illinois. Coughlin cooperated with them, adding to the Bureau's growing file on Nelson, who Purvis had only been aware of since the robbery in Mason City, Iowa, when a bank employee identified his photograph. Purvis had no idea at the time that Dillinger had been at Mason City, too, and it wasn't until Little Bohemia that the Bureau belatedly realized the two were working together.

On Saturday night, Volney Davis drove into Chicago and stole a car for Dillinger. Dillinger and Van Meter left on Sunday morning. After thanking Dock Barker and Davis for their help, they drove to East Chicago, where they waited for two days to reunite with Tommy Carroll.

The next evening, Wednesday, May 2, the three men arrived at a home in Fort Wayne, Indiana. The house was owned by Audrey G. Russ, a construction worker who was a friend of the Van Meter family. Even though he was startled to have America's most wanted man show up on his doorstep, Russ agreed to let them spend the night. His wife and 11-year-old daughter looked on, amazed, as Dillinger carried in four machine guns, several bulletproof vests, and a bundle of two dozen stolen license plates.

There was little to do that night but talk and Dillinger was in a chatty mood. He sat in the Russ's kitchen and regaled the family with details of his escapes from Crown Point and Little Bohemia. He laughed at the police who were hunting for him, calling them "a lot of clucks." It was the feds that he was worried about, he told them, because they could go anywhere and spend anything, even rent airplanes. One has to wonder, if had Dillinger known how badly the Bureau had bungled every recent chance they had to capture him, would he have been as nervous about them as he seemed to be?

The next morning, Dillinger and Van Meter asked for steaks for breakfast. They were hungry and had a big day ahead of them. For the first time in two months, they were going to rob a bank.

Meanwhile, in another part of Indiana, SAC Earl Connelly was increasing the pressure on Dillinger's family. His men had been following, badgering, and questioning Hubert Dillinger and other relatives for weeks. The bandit's nephew, Norman Hancock, proved to be the one who bent the most to pressure. Connelly convinced Norman to drive out to the Dillinger farm and help John, Sr. to build a fence. If Dillinger was hiding on the farm, Connelly told Norman to take out a handkerchief and wipe his face with it. Two dozen Indianapolis police officers were waiting to move if the signal was given. Connelly and a half-dozen agents were hiding in haystacks and outbuildings when Norman drove up and went into the house. At 2:10 p.m., he and Mr. Dillinger appeared on the porch. Hancock took out his handkerchief and wiped his face with it two times.

The men stepped down from the porch and starting down the road to build the fence, and as they did so, a number of Bureau cars screeched to a halt next to them. Agents jumped out and surrounded the two men at gunpoint, hauling them to the cars for questioning. Norman Hancock appeared dazed. Once they were out of Mr. Dillinger's earshot, he told Connelly that it was a mistake. Dillinger wasn't at the house. That morning, Mr. Dillinger had received an anonymous letter from someone in Minnesota, telling him that his son was safe. He had given the signal, Norman explained, only to tell the Bureau about the letter.

Special Agent in Charge Earl Connelly, who harassed the Dillinger family, with no results

Connelly was enraged by the mistake. The agents got back into their cars and the Indianapolis police returned home. By the following day, Matt Leach was complaining to reporters that Connelly's ham-handed raid had ruined any chance that they might capture Dillinger in Indiana. The bad feelings between the Indiana State Police and the Bureau were increasing by the day.

On Wednesday, May 2, while Dillinger was arriving in Fort Wayne, the car that the bandit had stolen outside of St. Paul was found on the North Side of Chicago. From the dried blood that was all over the backseat, Purvis could see that one of the gang members had been wounded. Headlines in all of the city's evening newspapers that day claimed that Dillinger was back in the city, probably with a gunshot wound. But Melvin Purvis wasn't so sure. He thought that the car might be a plant to trick Bureau agents into concentrating the hunt for Dillinger in Chicago.

For once, Purvis was right.

On Thursday, May 3, Dillinger, Van Meter, and Tommy Carroll drove east into Ohio. They stole another car in Toledo and then headed for Fostoria, which was about 40 miles to the south. Van Meter knew of a bank they could rob there that would give them a much-needed injection of cash.

We have to wonder if Van Meter knew that the people of Fostoria, a railway hub, considered the banks in town to be robbery-proof. They were so many slow-moving trains that crisscrossed the area that police believed they would dissuade any bandits from trying to put together a getaway map. But Van Meter didn't think he needed a map. He knew the town from boyhood vacations. They didn't spend any time scouting the First National Bank, or worrying about the getaway – they just needed money.

Just 10 minutes before the bank was set to close at 3:00 p.m., two men walked into the lobby with machine guns hidden beneath the overcoats that were draped over their arms. Carroll waited in the car while Van Meter and Dillinger went inside. The lobby, although almost empty of customers, presented an immediate problem. There was a mezzanine above and two side entrances. One of them led directly into the O.C. Harding Jewelry Store and the other opened into a drugstore.

Van Meter laid his overcoat across a railing and pointed his weapon at the teller cages. "Stick 'em up!" he shouted.

Dillinger went to work, but he was not the jovial criminal that so many read about in the papers. There were no smiles or small jokes that anyone would remember. He didn't leap over the teller cages or make sure that old farmers held onto their cash. His movements that day were grim and mechanical. As the employees raised their hands, Dillinger stepped through a swinging door and began sweeping piles of cash off the counters into sacks. Van Meter gathered the tellers and a few employees into a tight group. "Don't kill me," one of them begged Van Meter.

"You be quiet, and I won't," he replied.

Neither Dillinger nor Van Meter noticed that a teller, France Hillyard, slipped out a door. She ran to find the police chief, Frank Culp. As Culp ran towards the bank, he came up with a plan: if he could get up into the mezzanine, he could take the high ground and drive the robbers away. But the plan was a bust the second he entered the bank. Bursting into the lobby, he found that the mezzanine elevator was on the second floor – he was trapped in the lobby with the bandits and was a sitting target. Van Meter spun around when he entered and fired his machine gun. A single bullet ripped into Culp's chest and punctured his lung. He staggered backward into the jewelry store, calling out for help.

When Tommy Carroll heard gunfire in the bank, he jumped out of the getaway car and began firing wildly into the air and up and down the street. His bullets shattered windows, ricocheted off the brick buildings, and sent citizens scrambling for cover. Two men, both slow and unlucky, were hit in the leg and the foot.

Inside the bank, Dillinger hurried to clear the remaining cash off the counters. The bank president later estimated that he got away with $17,000. "It's too hot out there," Van Meter called to him as he finished his task. "Let's go through the drugstore."

They grabbed two employees, a man and a woman, and shoved them through the drugstore and out to the street. The two were pushed onto the running boards of the car as it roared off down Tifflin Street. Through the window, Van Meter kept a tight grip on the woman's hand. The man had to fend for himself. The sped west of town, stopping once to toss roofing nails on the road behind them. A short distance away from Fostoria, they let the hostages go.

At the same time that the bank was being robbed, Van Meter's old friend, Audrey Russ, was having a crisis of conscience, likely brought on by the fear that Dillinger might return to his home and his house would end up filled with bullet holes like Little Bohemia. He approached his boss at the Western Gas Construction Company, told him everything, and asked him what he should do. His boss had once met the Bureau's resident agent in South Bend, W.J. Devereaux, and gave Russ his contact information.

On the day of the Fostoria robbery, Russ telephoned Devereaux and, without giving his name, described in general terms what had happened. Devereaux, after hanging up the phone, immediately called Chicago, briefed Purvis, and asked if he should follow up on the information.

For the moment, Purvis told him to do nothing – an order that he would soon regret.

At that moment, though, Purvis had good reason to not want to go riding off into another situation like the one that had just occurred in Wisconsin. It had taken two weeks for the simmering frustrations of Little Bohemia to finally come to a boil within the ranks of the Bureau. The general public and the press had taken Hoover and the Bureau to task for the disaster in the north woods, blaming them for the death of the innocent men and Dillinger's escape. But the public could be ignored; the new problems were coming from within the ranks of the Bureau. This was the first time in the agency's short history that internal squabbling had taken place.

The problems were coming from an unlikely source – the St. Paul SAC Werner Hanni. Hanni had clearly not appreciated having his office commandeered by Inspector Rorer and Hugh Clegg, and his irritation turned to outrage in the days after the ill-fated raid. The final straw had been his encounter on a dark country road with the fleeing Baby Face Nelson, which had left him badly shaken. Hanni's anger came to light when Clegg, sorting through papers on a desk, found a memo from Hanni that he had never seen. It had been written, addressed, but apparently never sent to Hoover.

In the memo, Hanni stated that there had been no good reason why Dillinger and the rest of the gang had gotten away. The raid had been fully staged with a lack of organization, knowledge, and good judgment. No preparation appeared to have been made, he wrote, in spite of the fact that a map had been drawn and furnished to the agents before they went to Little Bohemia.

Hanni had a bad word for almost everyone. He criticized Inspector Rorer for failing to help lift Carter Baum's dead body, because Rorer had a "kink in his back." He also complained about events that had nothing to do with Little Bohemia, criticizing Clegg, although not by name, for hindering the earlier pursuit of Dillinger by pestering his men with questions about Eddie Green's death. He claimed that they would have caught Dillinger sooner, he wrote to Hoover, if "those in charge of these investigations had undertaken leadership instead of questioning the agents, keeping them from working, to determine whether or not the shooting of Green was justified."

When Hanni's complaints came to light, everyone wrote sharply worded memos of their own, disagreeing with him. As Hoover studied these memos, he received far more worrisome news. The Justice Department prosecutor, Joe Kennan, told him he had heard a reliable story that the agents at Little Bohemia had mutinied against Purvis and Clegg, and actually locked them in a shed while Dillinger got away. Hoover pressed Keenan for the source of the story, and Keenan named a former agent named Thomas Cullen. Agents interviewed Cullen and he admitted that he was the source.

Hoover handed the whole mess over to Harold "Pop" Nathan and directed him to "make a very thorough and vigorous inquiry." It should come as no surprise that Nathan's report, released three weeks later, defended the Bureau's actions and discredited Hanni. Hanni's allegations "would appear to indicate a disordered and possibly hysterical state of mind," Nathan wrote and termed them "manifestly absurd." Hanni was quietly transferred out of St. Paul and ended up in Omaha.

After that, any agent who thought about criticizing the Bureau kept it to himself.

All over the country, newspapers were screaming about Dillinger. Little Bohemia was still in the headlines and editorials demanded that he be caught. Dillinger was all anyone wanted to write about, or talk about in local diners and coffee shops. Was he dead, was he alive, where would he go next?

Dillinger was on everyone's mind, but Dillinger was nowhere to be found.

After Little Bohemia, Dillinger knew that there was no place safe for him to hide, at least for a time. After he and Van Meter spent a few nights in a leaky shack outside East Chicago, Baby Face Nelson showed up to lend a hand.

During Dillinger's time in Aurora and in Indiana and Ohio, Nelson was staying in a cottage in Wauconda, Illinois, northwest of Chicago. Nelson had steered mostly clear of Chicago. As Dillinger found out when he was seeking help for Hamilton from underworld physicians, most criminals with Outfit connections had been told to stay clear of Dillinger, Nelson, and other bank robbers. Nelson, specifically, had been threatened by Frank Nitti, who was running the Outfit after Al Capone was sent to prison, to stop using syndicate connections for help. The bank robbers were bringing too much heat to the city and attracting too much attention from law enforcement.

Unlike Dillinger, though, Nelson had other Chicago contacts since he had grown up in the city. After showing up at Louis Cernocky's bar after his flight from Little Bohemia, Nelson reached out to a veteran fence named Jimmy Murray, who owned a Chicago roadhouse called the Rain-Bo Inn. Years later, the FBI would establish that Murray had handled stolen bonds for the Dillinger-Nelson gang, but in the spring of 1934, he gave Nelson a safe place to lie low. He owned a cottage in Wauconda and Nelson stayed there during most of the month of May. He also eventually reunited there with Tommy Carroll and his friend from out west, John Paul Chase.

On Monday, May 7, four days after the Fostoria robbery, Nelson arranged to purchase a red panel truck, a Ford Model A, which was the kind that grocery stores used for deliveries. It had an enclosed rear, windows in the back, and a sliding door on the side. Dillinger intended to use the truck as a portable hideout and placed a mattress in the back where they could sleep. He and Van Meter spent the next few days on the move, driving the truck along Indiana back roads while they planned what to do next.

Late on the night of Wednesday, May 9, running low on food, Dillinger and Van Meter returned to Audrey Russ's house in Fort Wayne. Had Purvis pursued the tip that he had been given a week earlier, Bureau agents might have been at the house to greet them. As it was, Russ climbed out of bed and let Dillinger inside while his wife prepared a meal. Both Dillinger and Van Meter looked exhausted. They were wearing denim overalls, work shirts, and battered caps. They looked the part of tired, working men, down on their luck. Neither man said much and they left soon after they ate.

The next morning, Russ went to his boss again. Together, they telephoned the Bureau, this time revealing Russ's name, and told of Dillinger's second visit. It was the Bureau's best lead since Little Bohemia. Even though he was short on men, Purvis decided to post three agents at the Russ home. When Dillinger decided to come back, they'd be ready, he thought.

And then Purvis failed to post the description of the red panel truck that Russ had given him. It was still business as usual at the Bureau.

On Thursday, May 10, Dillinger made a short visit to see his cousin, Fred Hancock, at the Dillinger filling station in Indianapolis. Fred was waiting on a customer around 3:45 when he noticed a stranger standing by a kerosene drum in one corner of the lot. He didn't recognize the man, who was unshaven and wore overalls, a sleeveless jacket, and rimless eyeglasses. When the customer left, the stranger walked over to the station window and tapped on the glass. Fred looked the man in the eyes and was startled to see that it was Dillinger.

In a parked car across the street, a Bureau agent named Whitson saw the stranger, too.

Dillinger handed Fred a package and they spoke together in low tones for only a few minutes. In the package were four smaller packages containing $1,200 in small bills: $300 for his father, $300 for Fred's mother, Audrey, and $100 each for Fred and Hubert Dillinger. He also told Fred to pass a message to his father. If anything should happen to him, he should give some of the money to Billie. Then Dillinger quickly walked away.

In his Bureau car, Agent Whitson watched as the stranger crossed LaSalle Street and walked toward Washington Street. Glimpsing the cleft in the man's chin, he decided to follow him. The man walked quickly, reaching the corner of Washington Street about 30 yards ahead of Whitson, and then he disappeared. Whitson jogged up to the intersection and turned the corner, but he was gone. The agent walked up and down the street, peering into parked cars and checking doorways, but saw nothing.

After a bit, he walked back to his car and wrote up the incident in his notebook, and then forgot all about it. The man looked like a bum, he thought, he was probably just looking for a handout.

While Dillinger and Van Meter were road tripping all over Indiana in their grocery truck, Melvin Purvis was feeling even greater pressure in Chicago. Dillinger's legend was growing, much to the dismay of the Bureau. By the middle of May, there had been no confirmed sighting of him since Little Bohemia three weeks before, but most American newspapers were carrying daily stories of the manhunt. In Chicago, the papers printed stories two and three times a day.

It seemed that every Dillinger sighting, no matter how nonsensical, was the basis of a new article. A *Chicago Tribune* story noted: "Mr. Dillinger was seen yesterday looking over the new spring gloves in a State Street store in Chicago; negotiating for a twelve-cylinder car in Springfield, Illinois; buying a half dozen sassy cravats in Omaha, Nebraska; bargaining for a suburban bungalow in his hometown of Mooresville, Indiana, and shaking hands with old friends; drinking a glass of soda water in a drugstore in Charleston, South Carolina; and strolling down Broadway swinging a Malacca cane in New York. He also bought a fishing-rod in a sporting goods store in Montreal and gave a dinner at a hotel in the Yucatan, Mexico. But, anyhow, Mr. Dillinger seems to have kept very carefully out of London, Berlin, Rome, Moscow, and Vienna. Or at least if he did go to those places yesterday, he was traveling incognito."

The press treated the manhunt like a rollicking adventure story and *Time* magazine portrayed it as a board game set in a Midwestern place called "Dillingerland," with the game starting at the Crown Point Jail. The tone of this and other articles suggested that Dillinger was a harmless comic character, being pursued by the Bureau version of the Keystone Cops. Dillinger was the "underdog" and this portrayal, especially after readers ate up the widely published photos and interviews at Crown Point, struck a chord in a country where so many felt slighted by the government. In Chicago and New York, moviegoers applauded when Dillinger's face appeared in the newsreels. *Detective* magazine polled theater owners and found Dillinger was drawing more applause than President Roosevelt and Charles Lindbergh.

As his fame grew, Dillinger was dragged into political debate. In Washington, Attorney General Homer Cummings used Dillinger's name to urge passage of a half-dozen anticrime measures, including one that made it a federal crime to kill a federal agent, a law that Hoover had been trying to get passed for years. The measures passed even as Republican senators continued to criticize the Bureau, which technically makes Dillinger the best thing that could have ever happened to Hoover's agency.

Even President Roosevelt got involved. Without mentioning Dillinger by name, Roosevelt urged radio listeners to cooperate with the authorities to wipe out the gangster culture. Will Rogers wryly wrote, "Looks like if the Democrats don't get Dillinger, they may lose this fall's election."

Every day brought more Dillinger sightings, almost all of them ridiculous. On May 4, after Louis Piquett made a joke to a reporter, there was a flurry of articles that Dillinger was on his way to England, causing Canadian, British, and American authorities to search dozens of ships in vain. Every morning, Purvis's men were rushed out to check out a new sighting, only to return to the office exhausted and frustrated by evening. Two agents looked into the Fostoria robbery, but returned not believing that it was Dillinger's work. It would be another two months before it could be confirmed that it was. One of the strangest reports received was that Dillinger was orchestrating robberies by sending coded messages from a pirate radio station, like an evil genius from a pulp magazine. After receiving dozens of similar tips, agents searched for the station, but were unable to find it.

Purvis's best – or only – hope was the stakeout at the Audrey Russ home in Fort Wayne. For the agents who pulled rotating assignments there, however, it was a nightmare. The problem was that Mrs. Russ had, as one agent put it, a "mean and avaricious disposition." One agent even referred to her as "demented." At various times, Mrs. Russ accused agents of spitting on her floors, scratching her piano, and shooting out a window. The agents paid her $2.50 each day for rent until Mrs. Russ loudly demanded, and then received, $3. As Agent John T. McLaughlin wrote, "Her whole desire seemed to be to secure as much money from the agents as possible, and furnish them the least amount of food." As the days wore on with no sign of Van Meter or Dillinger, the agents began to suspect that Mrs. Russ had concocted the story of Dillinger's visits in order to lure government boarders to her home.

In Mooresville, Earl Connelly's men kept the Dillinger farm under around-the-clock surveillance, but no one really thought Dillinger would return there. In desperation, Purvis sent agents to question anyone who had ever known Dillinger, including childhood friends, William Shaw, his teenage partner from the previous summer, and even Mary Longnaker, the Dayton woman he had romanced. But no one had anything useful to offer.

Purvis's leads were all dead ends, one after another.

For two weeks, Dillinger and Van Meter remained in the red panel truck. When they needed a bath, or just got tired of the truck, they spent the night at a tourist camp. At one point, they spent several nights in a cottage right outside of Crown Point. They were still living in the truck when Dillinger got back in touch with Art O'Leary on May 19. O'Leary drove to a tavern on the edge of Chicago to meet up with them. Dillinger arrived just after nightfall.

Dillinger was deathly sick. O'Leary guessed that his temperature was at least 140 degrees. O'Leary got into the truck while they idly drove along back roads. Dillinger was driving and talking and Van Meter remained in the back, keeping an eye out the windows. Dillinger's mood was bleak. He needed a doctor but was afraid to visit anyone that he didn't know. He also asked about Billie, whose trial was under way in St. Paul. When they returned to the investigator's car, he asked O'Leary to meet him again the next night with medicine and cough syrup.

The next night, O'Leary brought him cough syrup and a pint of whiskey. Dillinger seemed better and his mood had improved. His spirits were further lifted when O'Leary gave him a note from Billie, written in her St. Paul jail cell. In it, O'Leary later recalled, she begged Dillinger not to try and rescue her. She would only be killed. She promised to do her time in prison and then meet him afterward. Dillinger appeared to be moved by the note. He handed O'Leary a letter to get back to Billie, plus $600 for Louis Piquett. They would meet again soon, he promised.

28. Complications

Much of what we know about Dillinger's days between late May and July 1934 come directly from the testimony of Louis Piquett and Art O'Leary, who provided aid and assistance for the gangster, which means that all of their testimony has to be seen as self-serving and skewed to paint themselves in the best light. In many ways, to keep themselves out of more trouble, it often paints a picture that can be seen as the "Bureau's side of the story," which, based on the less than stellar achievements of the Bureau during this point in history, has to be taken with a large grain of salt. O'Leary, in particular, kept his story in line with Bureau "facts," which is probably why he only received a suspended one-year sentence for harboring a fugitive after the dust had settled.

The peculiar slant of the story will become very apparent in the accounting of days to follow.

On May 24, Dillinger was still wandering the back roads of northwest Indiana in the red panel truck. He and Van Meter had been living in the stale, claustrophobic truck for three weeks by this time, and Dillinger couldn't take it much longer. The two men were dirty, unshaven, and smelled of sweat and grime. Dillinger wanted to disappear, O'Leary later said, and Louis Piquett had a plastic surgeon standing by who could make Dillinger's face unrecognizable. As soon as he got the word, O'Leary said, Dillinger was ready to go under the knife.

That night, a little after 11:00 p.m., two detectives from the East Chicago Police Department, Martin O'Brien and Lloyd Mulvihill, left their station house to check out a Dillinger sighting. The two had been involved in the East Chicago bank robbery that January, which Dillinger had been erroneously blamed for, and had been involved in the hunt for the bandit ever since. Barely an hour after they left the station, the two detectives were found dead in their car on a lonely road outside of town. They had both been shot multiple times in the head and neck, apparently by a machine gun.

According to O'Leary, Dillinger later told him what happened. He said that the detectives had spotted the red truck, pulled alongside, and ordered Dillinger to pull over. Van Meter had machine-gunned them from the passenger seat, chopping up the men with bullets as they sat in their car. Apparently, the killings were linked to protection money that Dillinger had paid to East Chicago police officers, namely a detective named Martin Zarkovich. Dillinger had used East Chicago as a hideout in the past and it was always believed that he paid for the privilege and that Zarkovich was his contact. This was one of the reasons why it seemed so hard to believe that Dillinger would have pulled off the January bank robbery that he had been blamed for.

To O'Leary, Dillinger suggested that O'Brien and Mulvihill were honest cops who had become suspicious about Zarkovich's relationship with Dillinger. To protect himself, Zarkovich had sent the two to find the red truck, knowing that they would be killed. Dillinger seemed to regret the murders. "Those two police should never have been bumped off," he told O'Leary. "They were just trying to do their job and there's nothing wrong with that. Their trouble was that they were getting to know too much and Zark was getting antsy. They were sent to shake down a couple of suspicious-looking characters who were driving around in a red truck. I think Van felt bad about it, too, but there was nothing else he could do, and Zark knew what was going to happen."

Whether or not, Martin Zarkovich played a direct role in the murder of the two East Chicago detectives, this was not the only role that he would play in the Dillinger saga.

No matter what happened with the murders, they convinced Dillinger that the red panel truck was no longer safe. He and Van Meter drove into Chicago that night, where they hooked back up with Nelson and Carroll. Both of them were still in the cottage in Wauconda and taking many of their meals at Cernocky's tavern in Fox River Grove – which was still not being watched by the Bureau. Nelson had spent much of the month plotting ways to free his wife, Helen, who remained in custody after the affair at Little Bohemia. He eventually ended up hiring her a lawyer.

Other than O'Leary and Piquett, Dillinger had no one that he could trust in Chicago, but Nelson did. That night, after stowing the red truck away in a secluded garage, Nelson drove Dillinger and Van Meter to the Rain-Bo Inn, where he talked his old pal Jimmy Murray into hiding them in an attic room. Murray agreed, but he soon had second thoughts. The next night, he told Nelson that the arrangement wasn't working out. Dillinger, tired of being cooped up after his confinement in the truck, had broken his promise to stay hidden and, to Murray's chagrin, had come downstairs to have dinner with the tavern's patrons. Several of them jokingly remarked about how much he looked like John Dillinger.

Everyone involved – Nelson, Murray, Piquett, and O'Leary – realized that they needed a good place for Dillinger to hide. Coincidentally, Murray and Piquett had a mutual friend named Jimmy Probasco, a seedy fellow who worked on the fringes of the underworld, fencing stolen goods, selling liquor, and even dabbling in prize fighting and a veterinary service. Probasco was hoping to buy a tavern, so he needed money, and on May 27, he got some houseguests.

Probasco's rundown frame house was located next to a Shell service station at 2509 Crawford Avenue (now Pulaski Road), on Chicago's North Side. It was a place that no one would look twice at, with peeling paint, a sickly-looking hedge out front, and a wood fence that went around the backyard, where Probasco kept two temperamental police dogs, King and Queen. According to neighbors, his favorite pastime seemed to be yelling at the dogs. The house had two stories and Probasco rented out the top floor.

Probasco knew who he was renting to. Piquett introduced Dillinger and Van Meter on the night that he brought them to the house. Probasco nervously shook

(Left) Jimmy Probasco

(Above) Probasco's house, located on Crawford Avenue on the North Side

hands and led them into the kitchen. With Piquett as a mediator, they worked out a rental of $35 a day.

O'Leary later said that Dillinger asked about the doctor and was told that he would come to the house the next night and perform the surgery. Dillinger handed over a $3,000 deposit, promising the rest after it was done.

According to Art O'Leary's account, he brought two doctors to Probasco's house on Monday night, May 28. They entered the front bedroom and looked around. Probasco had set up a small cot for the surgery. The man who was to cut on Dillinger's face was a tall, thin German named Wilhelm Loeser. The 58-year-old immigrant was a self-important type, who had studied medicine at the University of Kansas and Northwestern University. In the mid-1920s, he made his living selling illegal drugs out of his Chicago pharmacy. He was arrested and sentenced to three years at Leavenworth in 1931, but obtained parole and promptly skipped out on it, fleeing to Mexico when it looked like he might be arrested again. Piquett was his attorney.

Loeser's assistant that night was the shaky 32-year-old alcoholic, Harold Cassidy. He was Art O'Leary's cousin. He was seven years out of the University of Illinois medical school and the cash-strapped Cassidy was plagued by an ex-wife who was always pestering him for alimony. Piquett was also his lawyer. He kept an office on the North Side where he performed illegal abortions and did anything else he could to make money. As an assistant to Loeser for Dillinger's surgery, he would receive $600.

Dr. Wilhelm Loeser

Again, according to O'Leary, the surgery went badly. Dillinger agreed to a general anesthetic, as long as O'Leary agreed to stay for the operation. Loeser asked Dillinger what he had eaten that day and the bandit replied that he had eaten only a grapefruit and some toast for breakfast. It wasn't true, O'Leary said. Dillinger had, in fact, eaten a full meal just an hour before, but was anxious to get things started. While Loeser washed his hands in the bathroom, Dillinger stripped off his shirt and lay on the cot. After assembling the tools for the operation, Cassidy leaned over him, placed a towel on his face, and began dripping ether onto it.

After a minute or two, Dillinger was still semi-conscious. Frustrated, Cassidy emptied the entire can of ether onto the towel. Suddenly, Dillinger's face turned blue and he stopped breathing. Cassidy had just succeeded where hundreds of federal agents and law enforcement officials had failed – he had just killed John Dillinger.

Dillinger's food intake had caused a reaction to the ether. Loeser ran into the room and began furiously pumping Dillinger's chest. As O'Leary opened a window to vent the ether fumes, Loeser continued trying to resuscitate the dying man. Finally, after several tense minutes, Dillinger began breathing again. O'Leary and Probasco exchanged sighs of relief, having no doubt about what Van Meter would have done to them if Dillinger had actually died. No one would believe that they hadn't betrayed him.

Once Dillinger was stabilized, Loeser proceeded with the surgery. It was slow going. Dillinger vomited several times during the surgery and bled heavily, staining the cot. Loeser wiped away the vomit and the blood and kept working. He removed three facial moles and then made slits behind the outlaw's ears so that he could pull back the skin and eliminate wrinkles. With skin from the cheek incisions, he filled the cleft in Dillinger's chin. When he was finished, he sutured the wounds and bandaged them. O'Leary said that Dillinger looked like a bloody mummy when Loeser was completed.

Dillinger was groggy when he woke up. O'Leary explained that he had almost died, but Dillinger just laughed about it. "It might just as well have been now as some other time," he supposedly said. It didn't sink in just how close he had actually come to death, or so claimed the later testimony of Art O'Leary.

But how much truth was there to this story?

There are many who believe the story of Dillinger's plastic surgery to be pure fiction. Officials from the Bureau should have been among those who thought O'Leary's story was a lie, but for whatever reason, they did not. Perhaps they used plastic surgery as the reason why the man shot down at the Biograph Theater resembled Dillinger, but did not match his appearance exactly. The Bureau would always maintain that Dillinger had recent plastic surgery, but there was a major problem with this – according to the medical examiner at the morgue in Chicago, where the body of the man killed in the alley near the Biograph Theater was taken. The medical examiner was unable to detect any signs of plastic surgery on the corpse, which the Bureau claimed was John Dillinger.

Which story was true? Did Dillinger receive plastic surgery or not? Art O'Leary maintained that he did, and so did Harold Cassidy. In fact, Cassidy would later claim that he received the $600 for assisting with the surgery from Dillinger himself. Several weeks after the nearly botched operation, Dillinger allegedly met up with Cassidy at the corner of Kedzie and North Avenue. Slouched down in a car with Polly Hamilton, Dillinger handed over six crisp $100 bills and thanked him for his help. Cassidy quickly spent the cash, celebrating a few moments of a bleak and otherwise lonely existence. Loeser and Cassidy were later indicted on charges of harboring a fugitive, but both were given suspended sentences in exchange for their testimony. Cassidy never really recovered from his brush with Dillinger, though. With his medical career in shambles, Cassidy was later reduced to practicing on an Indian reservation during World War II. After the war ended, he returned to Chicago and moved in with his sister. Deeply depressed over his station in life, he committed suicide in July 1946.

The Bureau believed the testimony of Art O'Leary about the plastic surgery, but why didn't the coroner see any sign of it on the body that was brought to the morgue after the shootout at the Biograph Theater? Could someone else have been mistaken for John Dillinger?

It certainly could have happened that way, as we will soon discover.

29. Bad News for the G-Man

On September 26, 1933, the word "G-man" became synonymous for government agents, thanks to the arrest of small-time bank robber and kidnapper George "Machine Gun" Kelly, a criminal made larger by boasts of his wife, Kathryn, and J. Edgar Hoover. Kelly's claim to fame came with the 1933 kidnapping of Oklahoma oilman Charles Urschel, for which he was easily caught, which might come as a surprise considering that his capture came at the hands of agents of the Bureau.

Kelly was the first nationally-known fugitive that the Bureau ever captured, and his arrest marked a turning point in the Bureau's history. It furthered the idea that there was a group of public enemies on the loose in America, popularized the idea that the nation was at war with these criminals, and put the Bureau in the public eye for the first time. Kelly was an overrated amateur, but the Bureau turned him into a gangster celebrity – after he had been captured, of course.

The story of Kelly's arrest was one of Hoover's favorites and one that he told over and over again for decades. According to Hoover's version of events, which was backed up by numerous FBI-approved books, magazines, and B-movies, Kelly had pleaded with the arresting agents, "Don't shoot, G-men!" It was the first time that Bureau agents had heard the term, and when the arrest was publicized, it became a slang term for federal agents across the nation.

The story, however, was absolutely untrue. Kelly never used the term. In truth, it sprung from the pen of journalist Rex Collier, who wrote FBI-sponsored stories, articles, and even comic books under Hoover's watchful eye. "G-man" didn't come from the mouth of George Kelly. It came from the fertile mind of Hoover's publicity man.

Throughout the month of May, Hoover, the head "G-man," brooded on the disastrous course of his "war on crime." Little Bohemia had turned the Bureau into a colossal joke. Dillinger had vanished, along with the Barkers. There had been no sightings of Pretty Boy Floyd in months and the Kansas City Massacre remained unsolved. In Louisiana, bandits Bonnie and Clyde had been killed, but the Bureau could claim no credit for that. They had been hunted down and killed by lawman Frank Hamer, who gave an interview saying that he would hunt down Dillinger if the Bureau asked. Hoover's position on that was obvious – absolutely not.

Little Bohemia had made several things clear to Hoover. More than anything, it was obvious that his men were unprepared for gunfights. Despite months of training, his college boy lawyers were utterly lost when it came to guns and anything approaching a combat situation. Hoover was determined that the next

Two added members of the Bureau's Dillinger Squad: Charles Winstead and (right) Herman Hollis. It would be many years before the role of these men in the Dillinger hunt was revealed, thanks to Hoover taking credit for every good thing that happened – and blaming everyone else for the mistakes

time the Bureau shot it out with Dillinger, they would be ready. That meant one thing: bringing in the western agents that didn't fit the standard bill for Hoover's agents. He had ordered Pop Nathan to search the bureau offices in the Southwest for men with firearms skills. They were rough, unpolished, and had never set foot in a law school, but if he wanted to get Dillinger, these were the men he needed. In May 1934, those men began trickling into Chicago.

Among the first to arrive was Charles Winstead, the 38-year-old Texan who had been in on the hunts for Machine Gun Kelly, Bonnie and Clyde, and bank robber Harvey Bailey. Winstead arrived on May 12 from Dallas and soon renewed his acquaintance with another Texan, the one-time Ranger J.C. "Doc" White, the humorous younger brother of Tom White, Hoover's best man during the 1920s. White, at age 55, was the oldest member of the Dillinger Squad and he was a mentor to many of the younger agents.

Not all of the new men were Texans. One of the best was Herman Hollis, 31, the resident agent in Tulsa, Oklahoma, who had been chasing the Barkers for months. Hollis, known as "Ed," was one of the rare college boys who could also handle a gun. He had earned a sharpshooter's medal with the Thompson machine gun, which was not an easy task. Energetic and hard-working, he was rated as one of the Bureau's top investigators, but he was not without problems. He had been the Detroit SAC until performance reviews questioned his administrative abilities. He was also pestering Bureau officials to transfer him to California or Arizona, because his wife, Genevieve, had a "nervous condition" that doctors felt could be improved by a warmer climate. He was also a lady's man, chatty with the female staff members, and as Hugh Clegg noted in a memo, "He possibly takes an unusual amount of pride in the neatness of his attire, particularly when passing mirrors."

But Hollis was capable and good with a gun, and Hoover didn't have enough like him. In fact, when Pop Nathan drew up a roster of men who were "particularly qualified for work of a dangerous character," Hollis was one of only a handful of names on the list. Hoover had no choice but to start looking in Southwest police departments for men. From Dallas, he hired the chief of detectives, R.L. "Bob" Jones. He hired a detective from Waco named Buck Buchanan. From Oklahoma City, Hoover was able to snag two members of the department's pistol team, Jerry Campbell and Clarence Hurt. Both men would have long FBI careers. Hurt had actually put in an earlier application for the Bureau, but had been rejected. At this point, though, Hurt was good with a gun, and that was enough.

These men became the backbone of a new and improved Dillinger Squad. The new hires had been sent to Washington for training, and then sent on to Chicago. After training was finished, Clarence Hurt wrote a friend and told him that he and Jerry Campbell were the only men in the class who weren't lawyers. Of course, that was the point. The new men had to understand that capturing Dillinger was no longer the end result – killing him was. An Oklahoma City detective named D.A. "Jelly" Bryce, who was hired a short time later, wrote, "They hired me as a hired gun, no question about it; they were getting too many lawyers and accountants killed."

But bringing in gunfighters alone would not get Dillinger, Hoover knew that. The problem was leadership, or in other words, Melvin Purvis. In later years, Purvis's fall from Hoover's graces would be attributed to jealousy. Hoover couldn't stand the fact that Purvis was getting more attention than he was from the nation's press while he pursued Dillinger. While this was likely true, it wasn't the only reason. Purvis's demise lay less in his need for publicity than in his own yearlong series of blunders. Purvis let a number of cases get out of control, but none of it was as bad as the Dillinger hunt. Hoover stuck with him as long as he could, even defending his performance at Little Bohemia, but there was no denying his ineptitude when it came to tracking down Dillinger. Suspects were found, then lost. His informants were hopeless. He raided the wrong apartments. He forgot to post surveillance on important locations. And the list went on.

Hoover already had many doubts when Purvis was handed the best bait the Bureau had been given in months. On May 26, a federal judge in Wisconsin granted the Little Bohemia women – Helen Gillis, Jean Delaney, and Mickey Conforti – probation. Before being released, the three women were questioned and Purvis assigned a half-dozen men to keep an eye on them. Mickey went to her foster parents' home, while Helen and Jean went to the apartment of Nelson's sister, Juliette Fitzsimmons, on South Marshfield Avenue in Chicago.

All three women knew they were being watched, so Purvis searched for a way to make his agents less conspicuous. There was a gas station located across the street from the Fitzsimmons home, and he forced the owner to let an agent work there. On Tuesday, May 29, three days after Helen's release, Purvis called on the man, and was stunned when he mentioned that he had seen Nelson visiting his wife the day before. Nelson had circled the block four times, apparently looking for surveillance, then walked right up to the building and went inside. The agent had no excuse as to why he had not alerted anyone.

This nearly sent Hoover over the edge. He fired off an ominously-worded letter to Purvis, telling him how concerned he had become about "developments" in Chicago. He added, "I cannot continue to tolerate action of investigators that permits leads to remain uncovered, or at least improperly covered. It is imperative that you exercise the proper supervision over the handling of this case."

Purvis looked even worse that same day when a Chicago newspaper reported that Eddie Green's widow had arrived in the city and was talking with the Bureau. When a Hoover aide questioned Purvis about the leak, Purvis said that a reporter had probably "concocted it." Hoover dashed out a memo, "It's strange they should concoct the truth." Hoover had just sent a terse telegram to Purvis requesting an explanation when a number of articles the next morning quoted Purvis saying that he thought Dillinger was dead. Once again, Hoover demanded an explanation. Once again, Purvis insisted that it was all a product of reporter's imaginations. "I would not have made a statement to the effect that John Dillinger is dead because, primarily, I do not believe he is dead," Purvis replied.

The final straw for Hoover was the Helen Gillis incident, which started on May 31. The agents who were watching Helen had moved into an apartment across Marshfield Avenue from the Fitzsimmons house. Purvis had put Ed Hollis in charge and recognized that it was a tough assignment because Helen "is quite aware that she is being followed at all times," Purvis wrote to Hoover. But he assured the director that the matter was receiving "my closest attention."

Purvis decided that he needed someone who could gain Helen's trust. His choice for the assignment was a baffling one – a Michigan City parolee named, of all things, George Nelson. A convicted swindler, Nelson claimed that he knew Dillinger in prison and actually claimed that Helen's husband had "stolen" his name. Purvis agreed to pay the man $20 a day to work for him. On May 31, he sent him to the Fitzsimmons house.

From across the street, Hollis and the other agents watched George Nelson drive up. As he did, Helen and Jean Delaney came out of the house. Nelson approached the women and told them that he had been sent as a messenger from Dillinger and Helen's husband. Neither woman knew him, however, and both would later say they assumed he was a Bureau plant. Helen and Jean then walked around the corner, where Helen went into a movie theater. Nelson followed after the girls.

Rather than tail the women themselves, Hollis and the other agents decided to wait, assuming that they would return soon. When there was no sign of them after 15 minutes, the agents hurried down to the street and jogged around the corner. They found Nelson sitting in his car and, to their surprise, the ex-con recognized them and came out to talk. He said that Helen was in the theater and assured them that he had the situation under control. He didn't. Hollis and his men returned to their apartment and waited for the women to return.

When the sun rose the next morning, they were still waiting.

Helen and Jean had vanished. Purvis passed the bad news to Hoover in a telephone call on Saturday morning, June 2. Later that day, Hoover called one of his top aides, Sam Cowley, into his office. It was time to make some changes, he said. Cowley was being sent to Chicago to assume command of the Dillinger case. The aide had been riding a desk for the past year, but even though he was completely inexperienced in field work, he couldn't do any worse than Purvis.

Samuel Cowley, who took over leadership of the Chicago Bureau office from Melvin Purvis. Hoover was irritated that the newspapers continually referred to Cowley as Purvis' "assistant."

Samuel P. Cowley was everything that Melvin Purvis was not: quiet, stern, jowly, clerkish, and the epitome of the Washington bureaucrat. He came from a prominent Mormon family in Utah and his father, Mathias, was one of the church's twelve governing apostles until he was forced to resign in 1903. He had been forced out because of his devotion to polygamy, which the church had outlawed. Growing up, Sam Cowley belonged to four separate families that his father had created with four separate wives.

After graduating high school in 1916, Cowley went on his religious mission to Hawaii, where he learned to speak fluent Hawaiian. Returning home in 1920, he attended Utah Agricultural College, played on the football team, and in the summers, worked as a traveling knit goods salesman in Nebraska and the Dakotas. He wanted to be a lawyer, but Utah had no law schools in those days. He was eventually accepted at Hoover's alma mater, George Washington University, in 1925.

After finishing law school, Cowley wanted to practice law in Utah, but was unable to find a job. As a temporary position, he applied to the Bureau, telling his family that he would return west when the economy improved. He was accepted as a special agent at age 29. Over the next three years, he shuffled through offices in Detroit, Chicago, Butte, Salt Lake City, and finally, Los Angeles, where he met and married a Utah girl, Lavon Chipman. He was a solid investigator, although not overly creative, and distinguished himself mostly in clerical duties. He frequently sent suggestions to Washington about how to improve the Bureau's clerical system, which, of course, impressed Hoover. He transferred him to Washington in October 1932 and put him in charge of the new kidnapping desk.

Bland but hardworking, Cowley was in the office early every morning, stayed late at night, and worked Sundays and holidays. He wrote stacks of memos each day and was so attached to his desk that he never bothered to qualify at the Bureau's new pistol range. Vincent Hughes, Hoover's director of investigations, noticed Cowley's appetite for work and made him his assistant in late 1933. This brought Cowley into the "war on crime," and he spent hours every day on the phone with field offices, relaying their tips, leads, needs, and concerns to Hoover.

His work was so impressive that when Hughes died in January 1934, Cowley inherited his job. His workload grew, to the detriment of his family. When his wife gave birth to a second child in March, Cowley couldn't make it to the hospital. He was so busy, in fact, that he couldn't find time to name the boy. His wife joked that if he didn't come up with a name soon, she'd have him officially named "Junior." By May, as Hoover was tiring of Purvis, Cowley had emerged as Hoover's most trusted aide. Hundreds of calls from agents working the Dillinger hunt passed through his typewriter on the way to the director's desk – although that was as close as he had ever come to actually working that case – or any case, for that matter.

No announcement about Cowley's appointment to supervise Purvis was made, publicly or privately, which would lead to years of confusion over Cowley's role in the case. In the months to come, newspaper accounts usually referred to him as "Purvis's chief assistant." At least initially, Purvis was told that Cowley's assignment to Chicago was a sort of inspection tour, a chance for Hoover's main aide to get a look at the organization that Purvis had built to bring in Dillinger.

But the truth was obvious and everyone on staff knew it when Cowley arrived in Chicago. He wasted no time taking charge of things. After a morning flight from Washington on June 3, he was at the Bankers Building by noon. When he reached the Bureau offices, Purvis wasn't there, so he busied himself debriefing the agents responsible for losing Helen Gillis. It was sloppy work, and Cowley said so. When Purvis arrived, he tried to defend his men, but Cowley wasn't interested in hearing about it. There had been 14 agents on the Dillinger case, and four of them were assigned to watching Nelson's sister's home. Cowley immediately reassigned three of them. It was his first power move, and Purvis let it happen without comment. From all appearances, he accepted his demotion, but there was no warmth between the two agents. Cowley was not vindictive; he was simply doing his job. Purvis knew that, but there was a sense of betrayal and defeat about him. His secretary, Doris Rogers, would later recall, "There was a sense that Melvin had been betrayed. You could see it by the way he walked, by the way he wore his hat. A little hunched in the shoulders. We all felt under siege. The enemy was moving in. The friends we had in Washington had all turned to enemies."

Chicago office morale sagged. It wasn't just that Purvis and his men were exhausted, or that their loyalty to Washington was shaken, but the nature of their jobs had changed. Hoover was bringing in gun hands to fight a battle that, up until then, had mostly been about detective work and surveillance. Few of the agents sought a career in law enforcement. For most, the Bureau was meant to be a temporary job, an adventure, and something to do until the Depression ended and there were real jobs on the market again. They hadn't signed up to be killed. Doris Rogers stated that almost every agent in the office could have resigned if he could. "It wasn't just loyalty to Melvin," she said. "By that time, the agents were all tired, worn out. They wished they were home jerking sodas in a drugstore. They would have done anything to get out. They were being thrown into situations where they could get killed. None of them asked for that. It wouldn't get them a Medal of Honor. It would only get them dead. They knew that. This was not their goal in life."

The office was tense that Sunday as Cowley and Purvis drove to Fort Wayne to assess Purvis's second major surveillance effort, at the Audrey Russ home. It, too, had turned into a comedy of errors. The three agents had actually moved from the Russ home to a hotel that was 12 miles away because the combative Mrs. Russ was expecting houseguests and didn't want the agents underfoot. She had offered to telephone if Dillinger showed up. After an all-night debriefing, Cowley ordered the agents back to Chicago, officially ending the failed operation. He and Purvis returned to the office at 5:15 a.m.

Cowley didn't slow down. On Monday, he spent the day reviewing the rest of Purvis's work, quizzing him on his informants and getting up to speed on the Bremer kidnapping case, on which six agents were working full time. That night, he drove to Indianapolis and he met with Earl Connelly the next morning. They drove around the Mooresville area, where he had 16 agents on the ground, watching the Dillinger farmhouse and other family homes. He also had four more men in Dayton and Columbus, Ohio. Cowley was skeptical that Connelly's stakeouts would accomplish anything, but Cowley still told Hoover that he could see no changes worth making. For the first time in weeks, Hoover was pleased with the news out of the Midwest. Two days later, he telephoned Cowley in Chicago and in a memo noted, "I was of the opinion that the new situation at Chicago would work out all right, and that I had told Mr. Purvis that until we complete the Dillinger investigation I wanted Mr. Cowley to take complete charge."

While Cowley assumed command, Purvis's failures continued. Pierpont's old girlfriend, Mary Kinder, had gotten engaged, and Earl Connelly had befriended her fiancé. The young man told him that Mary expected to see Dillinger soon. That Tuesday, Purvis drove to the town of Mishawaka, where agents had trailed Mary to a shack where Pierpont's parents were opening a barbecue stand. Purvis and his men watched the place until midnight when, to their dismay, eight police cars drove up. A dozen cops rolled out of the cars, with bulletproof vests and machine guns, and demanded to know who Purvis was. Sheepishly, Purvis explained, apologizing for not notifying the local authorities that they were in the area. Afterward, he went to a telephone to break the bad news to Washington. Once again, Purvis had screwed up. His luck couldn't seem to get any worse.

Meanwhile, as Purvis was losing his grip on the Bureau's Chicago office, Dillinger was making plans at the Probasco house. Louis Piquett had dropped by

The Dillinger farm outside Mooresville

and told him that he needed cash to pay the attorneys who represented Billie at her trial in St. Paul. As expected, she had drawn a yearlong sentence at a federal women's prison. Dillinger sent O'Leary to pick up the cash that he had left with his father for just that purpose. And he had a letter that he wanted him to deliver to his father, as well.

On Wednesday, June 6, O'Leary checked into the Claypool Hotel in Indianapolis. The next morning, he found Hubert Dillinger at his filling station. When he arrived and introduced himself, Hubert nodded in the direction of Art McGinnis, the Bureau informant who had been hanging around the station for over a month. "Be careful what you say," Hubert told him.

"What's that rat doing here?" O'Leary asked.

"I want him around where I can keep an eye on him."

O'Leary told him that he had a note from Johnnie for his dad. Hubert told McGinnis that O'Leary was a cop that wanted to see his father, Hubert drove him out to the Dillinger farm outside Mooresville. John Dillinger, Sr. met them along the road and O'Leary handed him a letter:

Dad:

I got here all right and I still have some friends who won't sell me out. Would like to have stayed longer at the house. I enjoyed seeing you and the girls so much. I have been over lots of country but home always looks good to me. This sure keeps a fellow moving. I will be leaving soon and you will not need to worry any more. Tell the girls hello. Hope everybody is well.

Johnnie

Mr. Dillinger asked how Johnnie was and O'Leary assured him that he was doing fine. Dillinger walked out to his barn and he returned a few minutes later with a package wrapped in newspaper. Inside of it, O'Leary found $3,000; the money that Johnnie had given him after the Fostoria robbery.

There is, of course, no indication that Bureau agents watching the Dillinger farm noted O'Leary's visit. If they had, they might have followed him back to Jimmy Probasco's house in Chicago that night. Art McGinnis, however, had suspicions. Hoping for a reward, he called Earl Connelly, who, in turn, called Washington to report that "some private individual endeavoring to locate Dillinger has represented himself as a government officer, in contacting John Dillinger's half-brother, Hubert. Mr. Connelly states that he has an informant advising that an unknown person took Hubert away for several hours yesterday and talked to him." The Bureau never learned the person's identity, but it was obviously O'Leary.

When he returned to Chicago that night, O'Leary found Dillinger in a terrible mood. He had been listening to the radio and the news was all about Tommy Carroll.

30. Curtains for Tommy

After vanishing with Helen Gillis from the Fitzsimmons's house in Chicago, Jean Delaney met up again with Tommy Carroll, who, by this time, had reunited with Helen's husband at the cottage in Wauconda. In early June, the couple decided to take a trip through Iowa, intending to end up at the home of Jean's parents in St. Paul. After spending the night in Cedar Rapids, they were driving through the town of Waterloo, Iowa, when they had car trouble and stopped at a filling station to have the auto serviced. Afterward, around lunchtime, a Waterloo police detective, Emil Steffen, received call from the mechanic at the service station. He told him that he had just worked on a bronze Hudson and had seen a rifle and a collection of license plates under a floor mat – and the driver looked like a "tough customer."

Detective Steffen and another officer, P.E. Walker, left the station and starting driving the streets of Waterloo, looking for the car. They didn't find it after an hour of searching, and returned downtown, only to see the car parked just across the street from the station. They pulled up nearby and watched. After a bit, they saw a young man and a pretty blonde approach the car. As the detectives watched, Carroll opened the passenger door of the Hudson for Jean to climb in. Then he walked around to the driver's-side door.

The detectives quickly got out of their car. Officer Walker called to Carroll, "Hey! Just a minute there. Who are you?"

"Who are you?" Carroll snapped back.

"Police officers," Walker replied.

Carroll took a step back and reached under his coat. Thinking that he was going for a gun, Walker charged him. Just as Carroll whipped out a pistol, Walker swung his fist and punched him in the face. Carroll fell down by the curb, but in an instant, he was up with the gun in his right hand. He ran up onto the sidewalk. Detective Steffen drew his gun and fired. From a distance of about 15 feet, the bullet struck Carroll beneath the left armpit. In the car, Jean screamed.

The gun fell from Carroll's hand and clattered in the sidewalk. But Carroll continued to try and run, stumbling along and turning into an alley. Steffen quickly caught up to him, lifted his gun and fired three times. Two of the bullets hit Carroll in the back and he fell down in the alley.

Steffen ran up to him. Standing over the fallen man, he demanded to know his name.

"Tommy Carroll," he gasped, but refused to answer any more questions. He did say, however, "I've got $700 on me. Be sure the little girl gets it. She doesn't know what it's all about."

Jean was placed under arrest and Carroll was taken to the local hospital. Two agents from the Bureau office in St. Paul made it to the hospital that afternoon. The doctors said that Carroll didn't have long. The agents stood next to his bed

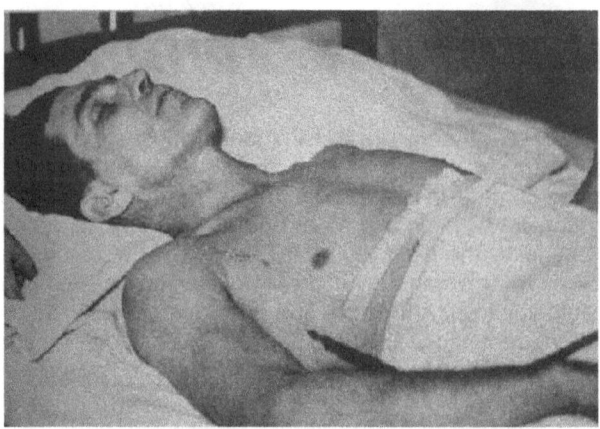

A newspaper photograph of Tommy Carroll, wounded and dying. Police questioned him until his final moments. He never talked.

and hammered him with questions for 45 minutes, but there was nothing they could learn. Tommy Carroll refused to talk – and he died that evening at 6:55 p.m.

Still hiding out at Jimmy Probasco's house, Dillinger and Van Meter had sharply different reactions to their friend's death. Van Meter swore that he would never die like that, gunned down in some dirty alley. For the rest of his career, he did his best to stay out of public view.

The same could not be said for Dillinger. On the day after Carroll's death, Friday, June 8, Dillinger decided to attend a Cubs game at Wrigley Field. Piquett went with him, and later said that he saw John Stege of the Chicago police's Dillinger Squad at the game.

But if Dillinger was worried about being spotted, he didn't show it. By all accounts, He moved about pretty freely on the city's North Side and, that weekend, he went to the movies and visited a nightclub. By Monday, June 11, he had met a pretty waitress named Polly Hamilton and spent the day with her. He accompanied Polly to the Chicago medical examiner's downtown office, where she received injections and filled out papers that were necessary for her new waitressing job.

On Wednesday morning, June 13, Van Meter decided to try and track down his girlfriend, Mickey Conforti, who he hadn't seen since he had left her behind at Little Bohemia two months before. He got up early, put on his best suit, then added his latest bit of disguise, which was a pair of pince-nez eyeglasses, attached by a long black ribbon to his vest. He took his maroon Ford sedan downtown. Reuniting with Mickey was a calculated risk, he knew. The Bureau had been watching her for weeks.

Tommy Carroll's death gave Hoover's men their first new clues in weeks. None of them came from Jean. On the morning after Carroll died, agents questioned her into the early morning hours, but she said nothing of any use to them. Even the usually persuasive Hugh Clegg could get nothing out of her. She was sentenced to a year and a day and shipped to the federal women's prison in West Virginia.

The clues they found were in Carroll's black leather Gladstone bag. Two of the dead man's shirts were still in wrappers from a laundry in Nile Center, Illinois (now Skokie). When the owner was shown a photograph of Carroll, she identified him as one of her customers. When she was shown photos of other Dillinger and Barker gang members, she identified Nelson as Carroll's friend, "Mr. Cody." He was a "nice young man," she said, who had been bringing in laundry since early May. Once, she remembered, when he arrived to pick up a load of shirts that wasn't ready yet, he snapped his fingers and remarked that he had driven 50 miles to pick it up.

They were small clues, and Cowley still had a lot to learn. His worst mistake was dropping the surveillance on Mickey Conforti. Mickey knew she was being watched, so Cowley decided it was a waste of time to keep her under surveillance when she was unlikely to contact Van Meter. Of course, he was wrong. On the night of June 14, his office received a call from Mickey's foster mother. Mickey had disappeared.

Van Meter's girlfriend, Marie "Mickey" Conforti

Cowley was angry, but only with himself. Van Meter had simply approached one of Mickey's girlfriends, sending her to Mickey's house with the message that he wanted to see her. She had quickly thrown some things into an overnight bag, met him on a corner, and disappeared. It happened two weeks to the day after Purvis had let Baby Face Nelson retrieve his wife. It was the fiasco that had led to Cowley's reassignment, and now Cowley had done the same thing.

The last known link to the Dillinger gang had just slipped out of his hands.

But Cowley kept making mistakes. The problem, obviously, was not Purvis. The majority of the Bureau's agents, which has been pointed out many times already, were tragically inexperienced. Cowley was supposed to turn around the Dillinger hunt, but he had spent his entire career sitting behind a desk, dashing off memos about the best ways to improve the Bureau's filing system.

Losing Mickey Conforti had been bad enough, but Cowley's most inexplicable oversight was his failure to put a tail on Louis Piquett. Cowley's men had investigated Piquett's background, dredging up his involvement in various stock swindles. They had interviewed his former secretary, Esther Anderson – the woman who had turned away Dillinger after the Crown Point escape – but no one thought to ask her about that day's events and she didn't volunteer anything. In May, the Bureau made an attempt at following Piquett, but gave up surveillance after only two days. Apparently, it took too many men. So, Piquett continued to roam free.

As a result, Piquett and Art O'Leary were able to continue helping Dillinger, right under the nose of the Bureau. The two visited him at Probasco's house every few days. Piquett had all kinds of schemes to cash in on Dillinger's notoriety. He offered a reporter from the *Chicago American* an interview with Dillinger for $50,000; the newspaper declined. Piquett and the paper also discussed the possibility of the *American* handling Dillinger's surrender – a plan that he didn't run past the bank robber. Instead, Dillinger wanted to write his autobiography. Piquett said that he would bring over a tape recorder so Dillinger could record his memories.

But Dillinger was more excited by the idea of a movie. He loved the movies and had been seated in countless darkened auditoriums while his face was flashed on the screen in the latest newsreel about his exploits. He was convinced that he could earn a bundle shooting films where he lectured kids about the evils of crime. Piquett proposed that they purchase cameras and recording equipment so that Dillinger could make films saying that "crime does not pay." The problem was that, at this point in his life, crime had been paying pretty well.

When he wasn't discussing pipe dreams, Dillinger spent much of his time in Probasco's living room reading newspapers. Van Meter, not much of a reader, spent hours listening to the police band on the radio, avidly relaying items he heard to Dillinger. They chuckled over the stream of bogus Dillinger sightings that the Bureau and Chicago police had to pursue. There were reports that Dillinger had been seen in Kentucky, in Wisconsin, and even in the Ozark Mountains with Pretty Boy Floyd. For the most part, Dillinger just laughed and shook his head. He only grew irritated when the radio news erroneously reported that the attorney general had issued orders that he be shot on sight.

When O'Leary stopped at the house that night, Dillinger handed him a piece of paper. On it, he had scribbled the home addresses of Melvin Purvis and Agent Harold Reinecke, who had earned Dillinger's dislike after newspapers reported that he had browbeat Billie while she was in Bureau custody. "I want you to check on these addresses and make sure they're right," Dillinger said.

O'Leary took him to Piquett. Harboring a fugitive was one thing, murder was another. Piquett confronted Dillinger the next day. "Just what are you planning to do, Johnnie?" he asked.

"They're out to kill me, aren't they? Why should I sit around and wait for it? We're going to be parked outside their houses one of these nights and get them before they get us."

Piquett shook his head. "Don't you realize what a stunt like that would mean? They'd call out the army and place the town under martial law, and hang me from a lamp post!"

Piquett won the argument, but it started a rift between the two men. It got worse when Dillinger and Van Meter, both bored from sitting around the house, playfully warned Piquett that they were planning to "rob all the banks" in his Wisconsin hometown. Piquett didn't appreciate the joke. Losing his temper, he swore that if they went forward with it, "you and I will be through." Dillinger smoothed the attorney's ruffled feathers, but was irked at how Piquett had reacted to what was obviously a joke.

Piquett was also irritated by Dillinger's forays into the streets of Chicago. He was going out almost every night now, days too. He took in another Cubs game or two, returned to the World's Fair, saw movies, ate in restaurants, and visited nightclubs. No one seemed to notice him. He had disguised his appearance by dying his hair black, growing a thin mustache, and wearing a pair of gold-rim wire eyeglasses, even though he had perfect vision. After spending weeks in the red panel truck, his confidence was growing. Van Meter, who had rented Mickey a room on the South Side, thought Dillinger was nuts for walking around so openly. He often chided him, "You're going to get it one of these days, running around so much."

The subject came up again on June 23, when Attorney General Cummings announced a new $15,000 reward for Dillinger's capture. Nelson warranted only $7,500. Dillinger joked about it to Van Meter, "Looks like my price is going up. Watch Jimmy burn when he finds out the government put a cheaper price tag on him than me. And you, Van, you don't rate at all," he grinned.

Van Meter just shook his head. "Nuts to you," he said. "You just better watch out that someone doesn't cash in on that reward."

Meanwhile, Cowley kept plugging away. He had agents on a half dozen stakeouts. He asked Washington for more men and got them. Eight agents were added to the Dillinger Squad that month, bringing the total in Chicago to 22. Even so, by Wednesday, June 27, Cowley was no closer to catching Dillinger than he had been when he took over the office.

That afternoon, he held a strategy conference at the Bankers Building. Earl Connelly drove up from Indianapolis, Hugh Clegg came down from St. Paul, and a supervisor from headquarters named Ed Tamm flew out from Washington. They debated every lead and reassessed every stakeout. In Indiana, Connelly's agents were watching a dozen places, while Connelly himself stayed in touch with Art McGinnis. Tamm argued that they should keep pressure on the Dillinger family. Clegg's agents were raiding spots all over St. Paul and Minneapolis. Earlier that day, they had their first success, arresting bartender Pat Reilly, who had been at Little Bohemia. Reilly prompted a flurry of news articles by saying that he thought Dillinger was dead. Reporters hurried to Mooresville to see Dillinger's father, who assured everyone that his son was very much alive.

Cowley's most promising stakeout – if it could really be called "promising" – was at Audrey Russ's house in Fort Wayne. The family was insisting that Van Meter could return at any time. Reversing his earlier decision, Cowley stationed four more men there around the clock. Two of them were his best marksmen, Charles Winstead and Clarence Hurt, who passed the days trying to steer clear of the antagonistic Mrs. Russ.

For the moment, Cowley was satisfied with how things were going. They had agents working half the towns between Indianapolis and Chicago. Unfortunately, though, there were none in South Bend, Indiana, where Dillinger decided to rob his last bank that Saturday.

31. The Last Ride of the Dillinger Gang

The robbery of the Merchants National Bank in South Bend, Indiana, was probably the most chaotic and confusing incident in Dillinger's career. To this day, who exactly was present that day – including Dillinger himself – remains in dispute. There are a number of mysteries that swirl around this robbery and it's unlikely that we will ever know for sure who was there, what really happened, and how much money was involved.

One of the few things known for sure is that planning for the robbery took place at a remote schoolhouse that was located in the northwest Chicago suburbs. The building, which no longer stands, was located two miles north of the intersection of State Highways 53 and 62 (now Algonquin Road), in the town of Arlington Heights. Several nights that June, Van Meter and Dillinger drove out to the school to meet with Nelson, who was usually accompanied by his own growing gang of cronies, including his pal John Chase; the rotund California hoodlum Fatso Negri; childhood friend Jack Perkins; and a Chicago mechanic that Nelson knew from his racing days, Clarey Lieder. The only person to give an account of these meetings was Negri, who offered a number of different versions of the same events, including some elaborate accounts for *Master Detective* magazine in 1941. A number of his stories were clearly the work of fiction, but some of them corresponded with FBI records, which give them at least a small amount of credibility.

As mentioned, even to this day, no one is certain exactly who took part in the South Bend robbery. Eyewitness accounts variously counted four, five, or even six bandits, but most versions put the number at five. Dillinger, Nelson, and Van Meter are confirmed participants – maybe. Jack Perkins was later tried and acquitted as part of the heist. It's possible, although unlikely, that the fourth and fifth robbers were John Chase and Fatso Negri.

One theory that has floated around for years was that the fourth and fifth bandits were Charles "Pretty Boy" Floyd and his pal, Adam Richetti, whose disappearance had been so mysterious that the Bureau had not fielded a confirmed sighting of the pair for a year. One eyewitness firmly identified Floyd as the dark-complexioned "fat man" who was with Dillinger that day. Floyd's involvement was suggested months later by Fatso Negri, who told federal agents that he overheard gang members say that they were hooking up with a "big-name southwestern outlaw." If it was Floyd, it's possible that he made contact with Dillinger through Richetti, who served time in the Indiana Reformatory in Pendleton. But most likely, the story was concocted by Negri to cover his own involvement in the robbery. As far as is known, Floyd was hiding out in Buffalo, New York, at the time. Of course,

Joseph "Fatso" Negri, one of the more "creative" storytellers about the War on Crime era.

that didn't stop the newspapers from reporting on his whereabouts. Like Dillinger, he seemed to be everywhere and nowhere at the same time. Some reporters claimed that he was dead from gunshot wounds, or dying from blood poisoning. Others claimed that he was in Hollywood, dickering with as studio who wanted to tell his life story. Or that he was in Mexico, Virginia, Arkansas, or New York. Pretty Boy was once seen on both coasts on the same day. But one place that he probably wasn't was in South Bend, Indiana, on June 30.

But whoever was with Dillinger that day, it's clear that tensions within the gang were rising. As usual, Nelson was the cause of the problems. He thought that Dillinger and Van Meter were living far too openly, and he repeatedly said so. This led to an angry confrontation at the schoolhouse one night between Nelson and Van Meter, after Nelson learned that Van Meter had reunited with Mickey Conforti. Nelson believed the girl was untrustworthy. The argument got so heated that Van Meter ended up promising Nelson that he would kill his own girlfriend if he ever got the impression that she was unreliable, or would betray the gang. Dillinger intervened and tried to cool things down.

If nothing else, the incident illustrates Nelson's renowned volatility and the lengths that Dillinger and Van Meter would go in order to pacify him. There's no suggestion that Van Meter would have ever gone through with his promise to kill Mickey. But it was in this emotional state that the gang debated its next target. According to Negri, they studied several banks in Illinois and Indiana before eventually choosing the one in South Bend. Van Meter, in disguise, had scouted it that week. On Friday night, June 29, they made final plans at a meeting at the schoolhouse, checking their guns and bulletproof vests.

They had no idea then how much they were going to need both.

The gang arrived at the Merchants Bank in South Bend around 11:30 on a hot, sunny, summer morning. They pulled up just past the intersection of Wayne and Michigan Streets in the heart of downtown. The sidewalks were busy with shoppers, trolleys rattled past on Michigan Avenue, and out in the intersection, a policeman named Howard Wagner was directing traffic. Alex Slaby, an amateur boxer, had just parked his car on Wayne Street when a brown Hudson pulled up alongside him and double-parked. Slaby saw four men get out of it. One looked

The South Bend block where the Merchants Bank was located, at 229 Michigan Street. It would be the last bank that Dillinger robbed.

familiar. He was wearing overalls, a straw boater hat, and a handkerchief over his right hand. As Slaby looked at him, trying to figure out where he knew him from, Dillinger pulled back the handkerchief and revealed a pistol, which was pointed out Slaby. "You better scram!" the bank robber said.

Slaby watched, in shock, as Dillinger and two of the others went around the corner, towards Merchants Bank. With a start, the boxer realized that the bank was just about to be robbed. He quickly got out of his car, studied the idling Hudson, and then reached in through the window for the keys, which were dangling from the ignition.

"What are you doing?" a hard voice called out. Slaby turned and saw a young blond-haired man in front of the car. A machine gun was barely hidden beneath his suit coat. It was Nelson.

"Nothing," Slaby muttered. He walked away and Nelson let him go. He was heading for a payphone to call the police.

Around the corner, Van Meter stationed himself at the bank's front door with a rifle, while Dillinger and the unidentified "fat man" entered the bank. Dillinger wasted no time with his once-familiar antics. There was no jumping rails or flirting with female tellers. Two dozen customers were in the lobby, lined up in front of the teller cages. Dillinger pulled out a machine gun and simply shouted, "This is a holdup!"

Instinctively, most of the customers raised their hands and moved out of the way, pressing toward the walls of the lobby. A bank vice president hid under his desk. A group of nine or ten people rushed into a conference room and locked the door. Ignoring them all, Dillinger pushed through a waist-high swinging door and began sweeping stacks of cash off the counters. Suddenly, another bandit – probably the "fat man" – raised his machine gun and fired a deafening volley into the lobby ceiling. Women screamed. Bits and pieces of plaster began falling all around him and the man stood there and grinned.

At the sound of gunfire, people on the sidewalks looked to see what was going on. Out in the intersection, Officer Wagner heard it, too. He started walking toward the bank, his traffic whistle dangling from one hand. Van Meter saw him coming. He raised his rifle and fired. The bullet struck Wagner in the chest. The policeman staggered backward, falling to the pavement as his hand clawed frantically at his holstered pistol. He would be dead in a half hour.

Panic broke out on the streets. People began screaming and running in every direction. A few doors down Wayne Street, a jeweler named Harry Berg ran out onto the sidewalk with a pistol in his hand. He spotted Nelson on the corner with a machine gun and he opened fire. The first bullet hit Nelson directly in the chest. He stepped backward, stunned, but his bulletproof vest had protected him from what would have been a fatal shot. He swung the machine gun around and fired a volley that sent Berg ducking back into his store. Most of his bullets slammed into a parked car, shattering the windshield and wounding the man inside of it. Another man was hit in the stomach by a ricochet. He staggered into the jewelry store and collapsed on the floor, badly wounded.

Nelson waved the gun around as people scrambled for cover. Just then, Joseph Pawlowski, a 17-year-old boy, ran across the intersection and jumped onto Nelson's back. The two grappled for a moment before Nelson managed to swing the machine gun like a club, striking Pawlowski in the temple. The teenager fell to the sidewalk, then ran off, his head streaming blood.

Alone and vulnerable in front of the bank, Van Meter ducked into the Nisley Shoes store and ordered a half-dozen customers and employees out onto the sidewalk. He lined them up in front of him as a human shield. Three traffic cops, who had heard the shots, ran up the street, and saw the group with their hands in the air. Van Meter fired between them, sending the cops looking for cover behind parked cars.

Moments later, Dillinger and the other man emerged from the bank, carrying cloth sacks that may have contained as much as $28,000. With them were three hostages, including Delos Cohen, the bank president. From the other side of the intersection, the patrolmen opened fire. Cohen fell, hit in the ankle. Another hostage, a cashier, was hit in the leg by the shots fired by the police. The cashier yelped in pain, but Dillinger shoved him forward.

As Dillinger, Van Meter, and the other man herded the hostages toward the getaway car, a furious gun battle broke out. Shielded by parked cars, the three patrolmen fired again and again, apparently not worried about the civilians that the gang had grabbed to provide them with cover. Standing next to the waiting

The scene outside the bank in South Bend in the minutes after the bullet-riddled bandits fled the scene.

Hudson, Nelson swung his machine gun in the officers' direction, firing wildly. Bullets pounded the sides of buildings, shattered store windows, and tore holes in the marquee of the State Theatre.

The bandits pushed on toward the corner, but then Van Meter went down. Dillinger turned and saw blood gushing from his head. A slug had gouged a deep furrow along the right side of his head, knocking him almost unconscious. Abandoning his hostages, he grabbed Van Meter under the arms and dragged him to the Hudson. The car was riddled with bullets and more struck it as it sped away. A half-dozen police officers claimed to have chased the car as it fled west from South Bend. Near Knox, Indiana, the car got a flat tire and when they got to Goodland, several hours after the robbery, they abandoned the bullet-ridden auto and left the area in a car likely driven by John Chase. Four farm boys saw the switch and called the police.

Van Meter was still bleeding badly when the gang returned to their rendezvous point at the old schoolhouse that afternoon. Fatso Negri said that when he arrived, Van Meter was lying on the ground, covered in blood. He wanted to get a doctor for him, but Nelson said no. Someone suggested that they kidnap a doctor and force him to help. Dillinger and Nelson got into a heated argument and eventually, Dillinger decided to take Van Meter back to Probasco's house. They could get a doctor there.

Dillinger drove his friend, who was still bleeding, back into Chicago. He arrived at Probasco's house after dark. Probasco tried to reach Hard Cassidy, but he couldn't, so he bandaged the wound as best he could. The next evening, Piquett and O'Leary came by. They found Probasco pacing around the apartment, cursing Cassidy, who had called repeatedly to come over, but who had never shown up. Luckily, he managed the first aid himself and probably saved Van Meter's life.

Van Meter was grateful, not knowing then, of course, that he would be dead in a month-and-a-half anyway.

32. "Jimmy Lawrence"

By the weekend of the South Bend robbery, Dillinger and Van Meter had already made up their minds to get out of Probasco's house. Jimmy Probasco was a quarrelsome drunk, and they were worried that he might let something slip. One night, they overheard a telephone conversation in which Probasco was arguing with someone, telling them at one point, "I don't care if you bring the cops. Go ahead and see what happens when they get here!" That was too much for Dillinger. The final straw came on Wednesday, July 4, when he and Van Meter returned to the house and found Probasco and Piquett drinking heavily. Once the two left, the bandits packed up Van Meter's car, and left for good.

That same day, July 4, Dillinger moved into an apartment at 2420 North Halsted Street in the North Side. It was only one block away from the apartment where Billie's sister lived, where he had taken refuge on the night of the Crown Point jailbreak. The other two occupants of the apartment were women, and their relationships – with Dillinger, with each other, and with an Indiana police detective – would lead to an official ending for the Dillinger story.

One of the women was Polly Hamilton, Dillinger's new girlfriend, a 26-year-old divorcee who waitressed at the S&S Café on Wilson Avenue. The other was Ana Sage, a 42-year-old Romanian immigrant whose principal means of support since immigrating to America in 1908 had been as a brothel madam.

Exactly how Dillinger came to know Hamilton and Sage remains a mystery. For decades, the accepted version of events, as passed along by Polly in a newspaper article following the execution at the Biograph Theater, was that she met Dillinger at a Chicago nightclub called the Barrel of Fun, where he introduced himself as a Chicago Board of Trade clerk named Jimmy Lawrence. However, it's much more likely that Dillinger met Polly through Ana Sage, who for years had been mixed up in the Northwest Indiana underworld, which Dillinger knew well. They had at least two mutual friends.

The whorehouse madam that would go down in history as the "Lady in Red" was born Ana Campanas in Komlos, Romania, in 1892. At 17, she married Mike Chiolek, emigrated to Chicago, had a son named Steve, and separated in 1917, when Ana was 25. Left alone with an eight-year-old son, she moved into the Romanian-immigrant community in Indiana Harbor, a lakeside collection of rundown tenements and taverns that was regarded as East Chicago's roughest neighborhood. She worked as a prostitute and a waitress, eventually ending up at the Harbor Bay Inn, where men could find prostitutes for $2 a tumble.

When her boss ended up with a six-month prison sentence for breaking state liquor laws, Ana began running the place herself. She turned out to be good at it. Standing five-feet, seven inches and a stout 165 pounds, with a thick Eastern European accent, she was an imposing presence and one not to be trifled with. She soon turned the Inn into Indiana Harbor's most infamous brothel. She kept order by playing nice with East Chicago policemen and by all accounts, her coziest

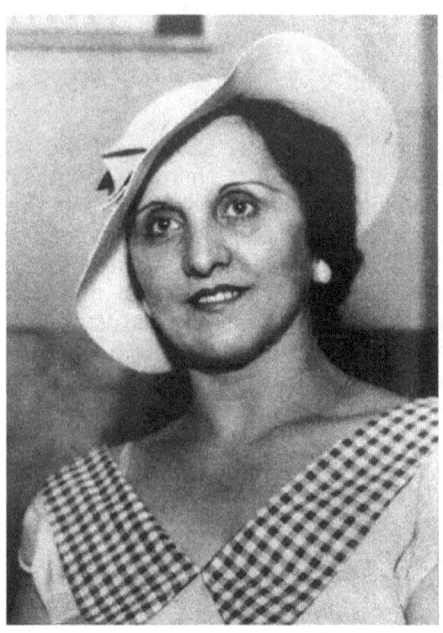

Ana Sage

benefactor was a flamboyant and corrupt detective named Martin Zarkovich – the same man that Dillinger had paid protection money to when he needed to hide out in East Chicago.

Zarkovich was something of a local legend. He cruised the streets of East Chicago in a felt fedora and suits so sharp that he earned the nickname "The Sheik." He was a loyal soldier in a police force whose primary duty was to keep the peace in East Chicago's gambling halls and sporting houses, and he was named chief of detectives in 1926. He was indicted for corruption three times in that decade and was convicted once, of violating Prohibition laws, in 1929. Half of the officials in East Chicago were convicted in that same case, so Zarkovich was soon back on the job. If anything, his conviction cemented his ties to the Lake County powers in charge. By the early 1930s, in fact, Zarkovich knew everyone who mattered in Northwest Indiana politics, and many who didn't, from William Murray, Dillinger's trial judge at Crown Point, to Piquett's investigator, Art O'Leary, who he had known for many years.

Ana came to know Zarkovich during her earliest days in East Chicago. And according to divorce papers filed by Zarkovich's wife in 1920, she apparently knew the detective a bit too well. Ana was named in her complaint, charging that she had "overly friendly" relations with her husband. Zarkovich remained Ana's protector after she opened her first brothel in neighboring Gary, Indiana, in 1921. By 1923, she was doing so well that she rented an entire hotel, the 46-room Kostur Hotel, for her business. It was a riotous place, where so many knife and gun fights took place that the police dubbed it the "Bucket of Blood."

Zarkovich's connections helped Ana weather a half-dozen prostitution arrests. She was convicted just two times, but she was pardoned by the Indiana governor both times. Her luck finally ran out in 1932 when, after yet another conviction, the new reform governor, Paul McNutt, refused her request for a pardon. The "Bucket of Blood" was closed down and Ana was referred to federal immigration authorities for deportation.

Worried and defeated, Ana fled to Chicago, where she had been commuting from since at least 1928, following her marriage to a fellow Romanian immigrant named Alexander Suciu, who changed his last name to Sage. Now Ana Sage, she had enough money saved up to buy an apartment building in Chicago's Uptown neighborhood, which may or may not have been used as a brothel. When the Sages split up in 1933, the building was sold, and Ana, after shuffling through a series of apartments, ended up in the one on North Halsted in June 1934. She was now a part-time madam with the threat of deportation hanging over her head.

One of her friends was Polly Hamilton, a girl from North Dakota who had moved to Gary in the 1920s. She married and divorced a local police officer while working for Ana in some capacity at the Kostur Hotel. Polly's place at Ana's apartment on North Halsted is unclear. Almost every account of the Dillinger story describes her as a waitress, but Bureau records refer to her as a prostitute more than once, suggesting that Ana was using her apartment as a call house and Polly was moonlighting as a prostitute. It's even possible that Dillinger met her after procuring her services. Ana later admitted to the Bureau that she let prostitutes use the spare rooms of her various apartments, and had done so as late as June 1934. Official documents suggest Polly kept a separate residence as a Chicago hotel, but from at least July 1 on, she lived with Ana Sage. Ana's unemployed son, Steve, now 23-years-old, also occupied the apartment, at least on a part-time basis.

Polly Hamilton

How did Dillinger meet Ana Sage? There is no concrete evidence of it, but most likely they were introduced by Martin Zarkovich, who knew both Ana and Dillinger's intermediary, Art O'Leary. There is a lot of evidence to say that Zarkovich knew Dillinger as well. Zarkovich would later portray himself as a gallant detective who was obsessed with bringing Dillinger to justice about the murder of his friend, Patrick O'Malley, during the East Chicago bank robbery in January – a robbery that Dillinger almost certainly did not commit.

Likely more accurate is the theory that Zarkovich was the person who had been lending aid to Dillinger in East Chicago, securing the shack where he stayed briefly in May, among other things. Dillinger hinted to O'Leary that it was Zarkovich, even calling him "Zark." And even though he never explicitly spelled it out, Dillinger made it clear to O'Leary that Zarkovich had been responsible for the May 24 murders of the two East Chicago detectives. While these links between Dillinger and Zarkovich fit well into my personal theory about what was about to happen in the Dillinger story, there is no irrefutable evidence that Zarkovich was Dillinger's contact in East Chicago, or that he arranged for him to stay at Ana

Sage's apartment. The Bureau, the one agency that could have figured out the truth, never bothered to try. The Bureau had no interest in investigating Martin Zarkovich.

What is certain is that by late June, Dillinger was spending a lot of time with Ana Sage's friend, Polly Hamilton, who would later insist, despite considerable evidence to the contrary, that she never knew that her new boyfriend was at the top of the America's Most Wanted list. We also know that it was soon after meeting Polly that Dillinger began cultivating the persona of "Jimmy Lawrence." He dyed his hair black, grew a mustache, and started wearing glasses. His recent plastic surgery had also managed to remove some – but not all – of Dillinger's distinguishing characteristics. Dillinger seemed to fall hard for Polly, the first woman to take his mind off Billie, but a lot of his activity during this period was making sure that he was seen around the North Side, not as Dillinger, but as Jimmy Lawrence.

During the end of June and into early July, their days were an endless whirl of Cubs games, amusement parks, movies, dinners, and dance clubs. It seemed that Jimmy Lawrence was always flush with cash. They took taxis everywhere. At Riverview Park, he and Polly rode the roller coaster over and over again, and he was so adept at the shooting galleries that other customers lined up to watch him. They drank and danced at the Grand Terrace and French Casino nightclubs and bought each other small gifts. On Polly's birthday, he gave her an amethyst ring. She gave him a gold ring with an inscription inside – "With all my love, Polly" – and a watch with her picture tucked in the back.

On Sunday, July 1, when Ana Sage moved into the apartment on North Halsted, Polly moved in, too. Three days later, Dillinger joined them. Ana gave him two keys, to his room and a closet, where he stowed his guns and bulletproof vest. On the day that Dillinger moved in, Polly called her boss at the S&S Café and said she had been in a car accident and wouldn't be in for several days. In fact, she took the next three weeks off, spending every hour she could with Dillinger.

At the apartment, Dillinger was a likable tenant. He told the women that he was just an Indiana farm boy and he loved to cook up his favorite farm fare, like baking-powder biscuits with chicken gravy, steak, strawberries, and frog legs. After dinner, just as he had with Billie, Dillinger cleaned up and helped with the dishes. In off hours, he played cards with Ana and her son, Steve. He and Polly sometimes went on double dates with Steve and his girlfriend, which usually meant a night at the movies. Steve thought that "Jimmy" was a swell guy.

With his new identity, Dillinger was able to relax for the first time in months. He liked the neighborhood, shopped in the stores, and had his hair trimmed at the Biograph Barber Shop. He even felt that he was safe enough to visit Chicago's detective bureau four separate times. Polly was applying for a new waitressing job, and her prospective employer required her to obtain a medical certificate. The medical examiner was in the same building as the detective bureau. There were four times when Dillinger waited for Polly outside the examiner's office on the 13th floor, while two floors below, the Chicago police kept busy looking for him.

While Dillinger was busy establishing Jimmy Lawrence's presence in the neighborhood, he remained in touch with Van Meter and O'Leary. On Tuesday night, July 10, Dillinger and Van Meter took their girlfriends on a double date to the World's Fair, wandering through the crowds along the lake. Two nights later, Dillinger met O'Leary and the two drove south, into the suburbs, where they met up with Van Meter at a barbecue stand. Dillinger talked privately with Van Meter for a half-hour and then returned to O'Leary's car. The investigator overheard part of what they said. Van Meter was complaining about Nelson and a disagreement about the disposition of some stolen bonds. Dillinger told him to forget it – they were through with Nelson anyway. It was time to move on to other things.

As they drove back to Chicago, Dillinger told O'Leary about their next job. It was to be a train robbery, proposed by Nelson's old friend Jimmy Murray, owner of the Rain-Bo Inn and the man who had planned a 1924 train robbery at Rondout, Illinois, that had netted almost $3 million – but led to the capture of the Newton brothers and others involved. Murray claimed that the current train would also be carrying millions of dollars. Dillinger and Van Meter had been scouting the train for some time and planned to pull off the heist alone. "We'll have enough to last us the rest of our lives, and right after it's over, we're lamming it out of the country," Dillinger told O'Leary.

The plan had been in the works for weeks. The robbery was the end game of a scheme that would allow Dillinger to walk away from the outlaw life for good. All of the pieces were almost together. He didn't know it yet, but the timeline for the plan would soon spin out of control, forcing him into actions that he wasn't yet prepared to take.

Dillinger spent the day on Sunday with Polly Hamilton. At one point, she and a girlfriend went bicycle riding and Dillinger spent a couple of hours watching Steve play softball. When Polly returned, she found Dillinger buying bottles of beer for both teams. He didn't seem to have a care in the world.

The next morning, though, brought unwelcome news. The newspapers were reporting that a vicious gunfight had taken place northwest of the city.

It was, not surprisingly, the work of Baby Face Nelson.

During the early morning hours of July 16, Nelson met up with his friends on a wooded side road deep on the far northwest side of the city. John Chase and Fatso Negri arrived first, followed by Jack Perkins. They parked their black Fords, turned off the headlights, and got out at the edge of the woods to talk. Helen stayed in Nelson's car, reading a magazine by flashlight.

The men were deep in conversation around 2:00 a.m. when a pair of state troopers, Fred McAllister and Gilbert Cross, passed by the entrance to the side road, heading home after being on duty all day. McAllister spotted the three darkened cars in the woods and decided they should investigate. He turned into the dirt lane, stopped, and got out of the car. Four men were standing nearby in the shadows.

"What's the trouble here?" McAllister asked.

"No trouble at all," a voice replied.

As the sound of the words faded away, they were followed by a sudden burst of gunfire, almost certainly from Nelson's machine gun. McAllister was struck in the right shoulder and fell, but most of the bullets raked across the police car, hitting Officer Cross six times. He managed to get his door open and roll out into a ditch. The two troopers were bleeding on the road as the men jumped into their cars and drove off. McAllister, after emptying his pistol at the fleeing Fords, was able to drive himself and his partner to the hospital. He and Cross both survived, in spite of Nelson's brutal efforts.

The shootings were front-page news in Chicago the next morning, and every article speculated that Dillinger was involved. Bureau agent Arthur McLawhon was sent to the Des Plaines hospital to interview the wounded troopers. He showed them photographs of Helen Gillis and Marie Conforti, but he could identify neither. The troopers were convinced that the shooting had been the work of a band of bootleggers who tended a 2,000-gallon illegal still that the officers had found inside of a barn about 250 yards from the site of the shooting. After talking to several other officers, McLawhon reported to Cowley that "they were quite positive that the Dillinger Gang were not involved in any way."

And so continued the high quality of work being done by Bureau agents.

Cowley was still working on the Dillinger case, and wasting a lot of time trying to track down Nelson, too. Agents picked up his mechanic friend, Clarey Lieder, but let him go when Lieder told them that he hadn't seen Nelson in years. The Bureau's most intriguing new lead had been uncovered on Monday, July 9. Several days earlier, the Bureau had secured an informant inside of Louis Piquett's office. The name is blacked out in FBI files, but it may have been Piquett's secretary, or his office gofer, Meyer Bogue. Whoever it was, he, or she, suggested that agents follow Piquett that day. When they did, they saw Piquett involved in a street corner argument with an unidentified man. When the two went their separate ways, agents followed the stranger to a two-story house in Oak Park. The next day, a check with the landlord revealed that the man was Wilhelm Loeser – using an alias – the surgeon who worked on Dillinger's face, although the Bureau didn't know that at the time. An agent rented an apartment next door to Loeser's building and settled in to keep an eye on him.

We will never know for sure if Homer Van Meter was right or not – was Dillinger a fool for living so openly on the North Side? The plan had been for people to get a good look at "Jimmy Lawrence," but it's unlikely that he wanted anyone to know that John Dillinger was hiding out in the neighborhood. But word had gotten out. By the third week of July, a dozen different people knew of his stays with Jimmy Probasco and Ana Sage. Dillinger began to wonder if one of them might not be tempted by the $15,000 reward to turn him in. Given the realities of the Depression, it seemed bound to happen.

During the week of July 16, Dillinger continued spending time with Polly Hamilton and he continued working on the plan for the train robbery. However, there were now hints of at least three separate conspiracies to betray him. One of them, he was aware of. In fact, he had put it into motion. But the other two were troubling, to say the least.

The first involved the surgeon, Dr. Wilhelm Loeser, who had started to worry that he might be sent back to prison if the fact that he had operated on Dillinger became public knowledge. Instead of just turning himself in, though, he sent two anonymous letters to the Bureau. His hope was that, if he was arrested, he could make a deal because he had tried to pass information to federal agents. The first letter detailed work that Piquett had paid him to do for an unrelated case. There is nothing to suggest that the Bureau acted on this tip. A second letter described the work that Loeser did on Dillinger. However, he didn't mail this second letter until Monday, July 23, so it had no effect on the Dillinger case at all, other than offer a belated account of Dillinger's plastic surgery.

It was Art O'Leary who warned Dillinger of a second, more worrisome, potential betrayal. On Tuesday, July 17, O'Leary stopped by Jimmy Probasco's house to pick up a rifle and a radio that Dillinger had left there. After swearing him to secrecy, Probasco told him that Piquett had come to him with a proposal to turn in Dillinger. Further, Probasco insisted that Piquett proposed to have O'Leary murdered – eliminating the only man who could contradict whatever tangled story they concocted for the feds.

Could the story be true? O'Leary didn't know, but he was definitely shaken when he left Probasco's house. That evening, he had a meeting arranged with Dillinger to give him the rifle and radio. He picked him up at a park that was located at Kedzie and North.

When Dillinger got into the car, he asked O'Leary if he had seen Probasco and if he had told him about Piquett. Dillinger already knew about the plot. O'Leary said that he didn't believe the story, but Dillinger argued with him.

"Don't pay any attention to Probasco," he told Dillinger. "You know he's drunk practically all the time. He doesn't know what he's talking about."

Dillinger shook his head. "Van Meter has also been warning me against him. He said he's been talking surrender too much." He paused for a moment before he continued. "Art, I want you to get out of town. Take your family and go on up to the north woods or some place."

O'Leary was now even more worried. He didn't believe that Piquett would betray Dillinger, let alone have him murdered. O'Leary was more than just the attorney's investigator; he thought they were friends. But then again, how far might Piquett go to save his own skin?

"I'm telling you to get out of town for a week," Dillinger said. "I'll get in touch with you. How soon can you go?"

"I can leave tonight, I suppose."

Dillinger nodded. "That's fine. How are you fixed for money?"

"I've got enough."

Dillinger opened his wallet and handed O'Leary $500. "That'll take care of you for a while."

And then Dillinger got out of the car, hurried across the park, and vanished from sight. That was the last time that O'Leary ever saw the bank robber. After he drove away, O'Leary went home, gathered his family, and drove to northern Wisconsin. He wouldn't return to Chicago until after he heard that Dillinger had been killed.

Dillinger now had O'Leary out of the way. Dillinger knew that Piquett had a lot to gain by betraying him. If he used Probasco as a front, Piquett could even collect the reward that had been put on the bank robber's head. He could also get himself out of hot water and perhaps dodge harboring charges that might be pressed against him after Dillinger's arrest. Dillinger's time table had now been drastically moved up. Things had to happen faster than he originally planned, so he needed O'Leary to be out of reach of the authorities. The investigator was the one civilian who had recently spent a lot of time with him and knew what Dillinger looked like.

Dillinger couldn't afford to have anyone around who could easily identify his body.

On July 20, Detective Sergeant Martin Zarkovich from East Chicago dropped in at the headquarters of the Chicago police department's Dillinger Squad and asked to see Captain John Stege. Zarkovich told Stege that he had an interesting deal for him. Zarkovich claimed that, through a long-time friend, he could deliver Dillinger to the Chicago police. There was only one catch – Dillinger had to be killed, not taken alive.

Stege refused and kicked him out of his office. "I'd even give John Dillinger a chance to surrender," he said.

Zarkovich left, but wasn't too disappointed. He knew that the Bureau would have no qualms about gunning down the man they believed was America's most wanted man.

Melvin Purvis was in his office on the nineteenth floor of the Bankers Building when a call came through around 4:00 p.m. The caller was Captain Timothy O'Neil of the East Chicago police. Purvis knew O'Neil, but not well. He told Purvis that one of his men, a detective named Martin Zarkovich, had real information for him on Dillinger's whereabouts and wanted to meet right away.

Purvis met O'Neil and Zarkovich outside of the Bankers Building less than two hours later. Together, the three men drove to the Great Northern Hotel, taking the elevator up to Cowley's room on the seventh floor. When they arrived, Zarkovich did most of the talking. He said that he had an informant, a woman that he had known for many years, whose girlfriend was dating Dillinger. The three of them were going to a movie on the North Side the next night, Sunday. The informant was prepared to tell the Bureau which theater they would be attending. The Bureau, Zarkovich said, could handle it from there. All Zarkovich wanted was the reward, he told them. He knew that the Bureau had "shoot to kill" orders out on Dillinger. Unlike Captain Stege, they had no problem with shooting him down in the street.

Cowley told them that he needed to meet the informant before he made any deals. Zarkovich told him that it had been arranged and Sage would meet with them that night. A bit later, the four men left the room and went downstairs. Outside, Purvis and Zarkovich got into one car and Cowley and O'Neil into another. With Zarkovich leading, they drove to the North Side and parked across the street from Children's Memorial Hospital on West Fullerton.

It was a sweltering night. The temperature was in the mid-nineties as Chicago was in the midst of a record-setting heat wave. Even at 9:30 p.m., the agents and cops were sweating in the two cars when Ana Sage walked up to them. She walked past, surveying the situation, and then returned to Purvis's car a minute or so later. She got in and they drove east, toward the lake, eventually parking in a secluded spot overlooking the water. Cowley remained in O'Neil's car behind them.

Ana wanted proof that Purvis was a federal agent and he showed her his badge. Satisfied, she told him that she was prepared to tell him everything she knew. She only wanted one thing in return: to stay in America. In exchange for Dillinger, she wanted the Bureau to make her deportation proceedings go away. Purvis told her that he had limited authority in such matters, but if she helped them get Dillinger, he would do everything that he could to help her.

This, of course, turned out to be a lie, but Ana said that it was enough for her. Her story for Purvis was a confusing mix of truth and lies, including her denial that Dillinger actually lived in her apartment. She claimed that he only visited there to see Polly Hamilton. The only time that he stayed there, she claimed, was after Polly's automobile accident – the one that she never had. According to Ana, who would always deny that she ever arranged to hide Dillinger, she first met him when Polly brought her to her last apartment at 2038 North Clark Street and introduced him as "Jimmy Lawrence." She said that she recognized him right away. "I told him immediately that his name might be Jimmy Lawrence, but he was John Dillinger. I made the remark in front of Polly," she said. "I called Polly into the bathroom and told her that her boyfriend was John Dillinger. I told Polly that I was going to make that man, meaning Jimmy Lawrence, admit that he was Dillinger or he could leave."

This account is not only unlikely, but based on the fact that he was living in the same house with her, patently untrue. Polly would later say that she had no idea she was dating John Dillinger. Obviously, both Ana and Polly were lying. In any event, Ana told the feds that she returned to her living room and confronted Dillinger again. He continued to deny his identity, even after she confronted him with newspaper photos.

Ana told Purvis (along with Bureau stenographers the following week) that the matter was left unresolved until the next night, when Dillinger admitted his identity to Polly. As Ana told it, Polly didn't care if he was Dillinger or not; she loved him. Ana didn't, she said. She claimed that she began trying to think of ways to alert the police, and it took her several weeks to get her courage up. Initially, she was going to tell her immigration attorney about the situation. She arranged a secret meeting, then backed out of it, unsure if she could trust him. It was then, she claimed, that she thought of Zarkovich. They spoke on the telephone, arranging to meet on Tuesday, July 17. That night, Dillinger was out of the apartment, meeting with Art O'Leary and telling him to leave town.

After the meeting with O'Leary, Dillinger disappeared and remained gone until Friday morning. Some have suggested that he was working on plans for the train robbery, but it's more likely that other planning was being done since he had now learned of Piquett's possible betrayal. Regardless, he was with Van Meter during part of that time since the two men stopped by Jimmy Murray's Rain-Bo Inn and spoke to Fatso Negri.

While Dillinger was away, Ana had telephoned Zarkovich again and asked him to visit her apartment on Thursday. According to what she told Purvis, it was only then that she told the detective that Polly was dating Dillinger, who was scheduled to return the next day. She said, "I told him I would call on Saturday and let him know definitely if John Dillinger had returned to Chicago and if he hadn't, if Polly had heard from him and knew where he was located."

Dillinger returned on Friday and spent most of the day playing cards with Polly. The next morning, he and Ana's son, Steve, took Polly and Steve's girlfriend to the beach. Soon after he left, Ana claimed, she called Zarkovich and gave him the go-ahead to contact the Bureau on her behalf.

Sitting in Purvis's car on Saturday night, Ana said that she expected to attend a movie the following evening with Polly and Dillinger. They would probably go to the Marbro Theatre on West Madison Street. As soon as she knew for certain, Ana said, she would call the Bureau and Purvis gave her his private number so it would be easy to reach him. Ana said that she would wear an orange dress to help agents spot her on the street.

There were holes in Ana's story that were large enough to drive a truck through, but if Purvis, sitting in the car next to the lake that night, had any doubts, he kept them to himself. All he wanted was Dillinger, and Ana Sage was handing him over to them on a silver platter.

It was almost, he thought, too good to be true.

33. A Night at the Movies

Sunday, July 22, was another brutally hot day in Chicago. By late morning, the temperature had reached the nineties and would eventually top out at 108. Cowley and Purvis arrived at the Bankers Building early. They telephoned most of the squad, telling them to stay in touch. A short time later, Zarkovich and O'Neil showed up, along with two other East Chicago cops. Cowley and O'Neil went over their plans for the evening. O'Neil repeatedly told Cowley he didn't think he had enough men to capture Dillinger. Cowley was planning on using 15 agents. O'Neil suggested bringing in the Chicago police, but Cowley refused. Cowley also decided against watching Ana Sage's apartment, or monitoring her in any way. Presumably, he didn't want to risk the chance of Dillinger spotting the surveillance and fleeing – or it could have just been another blunder on the part of the Bureau. As far as Cowley was concerned, this was Ana's show, and the Bureau didn't want to do anything to interfere. All they could do was wait.

Around 2:00 p.m., Cowley and Purvis began calling the men and ordered them into the office within the hour. The agents came in by ones and twos, sweat stains on their jackets. No speeches were made, no orders were given, but word spread among the men as they fanned themselves with newspapers, trying to keep cool. They had a new informant, the rumor said, and this one might be real.

The agents checked their guns and they waited for something to happen.

What we know about Dillinger's day on that Sunday comes from later accounts from Polly Hamilton and Ana Sage. Needless to say, questions exist as to the veracity of their stories, but at least portions of their accounts are likely true. Dillinger spent the day with Polly, who wasn't feeling well, playing cards at Ana's apartment. They were still playing at 5:00 p.m., when Ana began making supper. They were having fried chicken, one of Dillinger's favorites. As she began working in the kitchen, Ana said that she announced that she was out of butter. She would have to run to the store and get some. She left the apartment, went downstairs, and made her way to the payphone.

She told the Bureau that she had snuck out, but Dillinger knew she was going – and what she was doing.

Purvis took the call. Everything was going as planned, Ana told him, never mentioning that Dillinger was at her apartment at that moment. After dinner, they planned to see a movie. They would probably leave around 8:00. She promised to call when she knew something more definite. She then hung up and hurried back to the apartment. When she told the story to the Bureau agents on Monday, she forgot about her lie about the butter.

No one noticed.

At the Bankers Building, Purvis and Cowley nervously paced the office floor. And hour, then two, had passed and Sage had not called. Finally, a few minutes after 7:00, the telephone rang. It was Ana Sage, announcing that Dillinger had just arrived at her apartment. They were leaving soon, she said, but she still didn't know if they were going to the Marbro or the Biograph. She clicked off the line before he could ask any questions.

After the call, Dillinger walked out of the apartment. Neither Ana Sage or Polly Hamilton ever saw him again.

At the Bankers Building, Purvis had been startled by the call. No one had said anything about the Biograph. It was on North Lincoln Avenue, a narrow street just around the corner from Sage's apartment. Immediately, Cowley sent two agents to check out the theater. The previous night, Cowley had taken an agent and visited the Marbro, scribbling notes on entrances and exits. This new development was not good. Cowley and Purvis discussed what to do. In the end, they had no choice. Both of the theaters would have to be covered.

At 7:15, Cowley summoned the gathered agents into Purvis's office. Two dozen men were jammed into the hot room. Cowley introduced them to Zarkovich, who did all of the talking. He said that Dillinger would be attending a movie at either the Biograph or the Marbro that night. Dillinger had undergone plastic surgery, Zarkovich said, and his appearance was somewhat different than what had been printed on the wanted posters. Moles had been removed from his face and the telltale cleft in his chin was gone. His face was rounder, too, he added, although this would not have been the work of a surgeon. His hair had been dyed black and he had grown a mustache. According to their informant, he would be wearing a gray checkered suit, white shoes, and a straw hat. Without naming them, Zarkovich also described the two women who would be accompanying Dillinger. The older one, he said, was "heavily built" and she would be wearing a bright orange skirt – not a red dress, as legend would later have it.

When Zarkovich was finished describing the man they would be looking for at one of the movie theaters that night, Purvis took his place in front of the agents. He addressed the agents: "Gentlemen, you all know the character of John Dillinger. If he appears at either of the picture shows and we locate him and he effects his escape, it will be a disgrace to our Bureau. It may be that Dillinger will be at the picture show with his women companions without arms – yet, he may appear there armed and with other members of his gang. There, of course, will be an undetermined element of danger in endeavoring to apprehend Dillinger. It is the desire that he be taken alive, if possible, and without injury to any agent of the Bureau. Yet, gentlemen, this is the opportunity that we have all been awaiting, and he must be taken. Do not unnecessarily endanger your own lives, and if Dillinger offers any resistance, each man will be for himself and it will be up to each of you to do whatever you think necessary to protect yourself in taking Dillinger."

They went over the plan for what would happen if Dillinger appeared. Five men were selected to make up the group that would physically apprehend him. Purvis was to lead the group. His two best gunmen, Charles Winstead and Clarence Hurt, would assist. Two cops from East Chicago, Glen Stretch and Peter Sopsic, would complete the team. Purvis said that he would stand outside of the box office

The Biograph Theater on Lincoln Avenue

– at whichever theater Dillinger ended up at – and keep watch. When Dillinger appeared, he would give a signal by lighting a cigar. If Dillinger somehow eluded those five men, Purvis said, the other agents should do as they saw fit. He wanted all of the agents armed with pistols only. He didn't want machine guns on busy Chicago streets – Little Bohemia was still a much too recent memory.

When the meeting broke up, Purvis took Agent Ralph Brown and drove to the Biograph. Cowley stayed behind to coordinate between the two theaters. Purvis promised to check in every five minutes. Zarkovich and Agent Winstead were sent to the Marbro. Ana Sage's inability to pinpoint a theater meant that they couldn't assemble in force until after Dillinger appeared – if he appeared at all. They would have to take him after the movie ended.

Purvis and Brown arrived at the Biograph at 7:37 p.m. Brown stood by the car while Purvis walked up to the box office. The movie that night was called *Manhattan Melodrama*. It was a gangster film starring Clark Gable and William Powell. The next showing was at 8:30. Purvis returned to the car and got in next to Brown, willing himself not to scan the streets for any sign of Dillinger. He was afraid that he would be noticed if he started looking around. By 8:15, people started arriving at the theater for the next show. Every five minutes, Purvis sent Brown to a bar down the street so that he could use a pay phone and check in with Cowley.

If Sage had done as she promised, and left her apartment by 8:00, Dillinger would appear at any moment. Minutes ticked past, but there was no sign of Dillinger. Across town at the Marbro, Winstead and Zarkovich stood uneasily in front of the Marbro. In Washington, Hoover sat in the library of his home, fielding updates every few minutes from Cowley. Between calls, Cowley paced the office. The sweating agents who waited checked and rechecked their weapons.

Purvis began to feel that something was wrong. By 8:25, he was sure that the weekend had been wasted and was feeling stupid for trusting the East Chicago police.

Then, out of the corner of his eye, at 8:36, Purvis caught two women and a man walking past the car on the sidewalk. He realized that it was Ana Sage, a girl who had to be Polly Hamilton, and, amazingly, John Dillinger. Sage was wearing an orange skirt and a tilted white hat, just as Zarkovich said she would. Dillinger was wearing a straw boater. Ralph Brown saw the trio, too. As soon as the three passed by, he jumped out of the car and ran off to call Cowley. As he did, Dillinger walked up to the ticket booth and passed the cashier several bills. Stunned that he was finally seeing Dillinger in person, Purvis looked at him as closely as he could from the distance between them. The bank robber wore gray slacks, a crisp white shirt, and dark glasses. He wore no jacket, which meant that he had only one gun at most. And he was alone – no Nelson, no Van Meter.

As Purvis watched from the car, Dillinger took the tickets and guided the women into the theater. Inside, it was crowded, but the trip found two seats in the third row. Ana Sage took a seat alone in the back.

Outside of the theater, Purvis got out of the car, walked to the ticket booth, and purchased a ticket of his own. He shuffled his way inside with the crowd and went into the auditorium, which was jammed. The Biograph was one of the few theaters that offered air conditioning and with the hot days the city had been suffering under, everyone wanted to see a movie. Purvis thought that if he could find a seat near Dillinger, he could arrange to have him arrested during the show, when he was least expecting it. But he couldn't see more than a handful of empty seats in the theater. He couldn't even figure out where Dillinger was sitting. He would have to be satisfied to take him when he left.

Purvis went back to the car. Brown told him that Cowley's men were on the way. The two men got nervous. What if Dillinger left before the others arrived? What if he realized that something was wrong and left early? The two agents would have to try and take him alone. Purvis studied his watch. He got out and quizzed the young woman who was selling tickets. She gave him the running time of the film. With newsreels and trailers, the show would let out in just a little over two hours. If he stayed for the entire movie, Dillinger would exit the theater around 10:35 p.m.

Purvis grew more anxious as the minutes passed. He watched anxiously for the other agents who were supposed to be arriving and soon, he saw them taking their positions along Lincoln Avenue. When Cowley arrived, he and Purvis spoke in low tones, discussing the best positions for the men. They placed the two East Chicago cops, Stretch and Sopsic, on the sidewalk north of the theater entrance.

When Charles Winstead arrived from the Marbro, he and Clarence Hurt, took positions on the south side, the direction that Dillinger would likely take if he was returning to Ana Sage's apartment. Cowley spread the other men in pairs up and down the street. The Biograph had two side exits and one in the rear. The side exists opened into an alley that could be used as a shortcut to the apartment. Cowley placed four men in the alley.

By 9:30, everyone was in place. Standing in the doorway next to the box office with Agents Winstead and Hurt, Purvis nervously chewed his cigar. He was keyed up and thirsty, but he refused to leave the spot to get a drink of water. He had already been in and out of the theater several times, but he wanted to try and keep moving. He realized that when he stood in one place, his knees would tremble. Finally, 10:00 p.m. came and went, and no one left the theater.

Tensions rose as the end of the movie neared. All along the street, agents and East Chicago officers paced back and forth, or leaned in doorways, trying to look inconspicuous. It didn't work. Someone called the police – the real Chicago police, who had no idea that the operation was taking place.

Suddenly, at 10:20 p.m., two sedans pulled into the alley next to the theater. Several men jumped out, guns in their hands. One of the men had a sawed-off shotgun. "Police!" he yelled. "Put up your hands!"

One of the agents, E.J. Conroy, flipped out his badge. Each of the other Bureau men did the same. "Federal agents!" Conroy blurted out as he faced the muzzle of several guns. He then went on to explain that they were on a stakeout. When the police officers asked who they were after, Control refused to say. One of the officers explained that they were responding to a report of suspicious men hanging around the theater, and asked if there was anything they could do to help. Conroy said no and asked the cops to leave. Grudgingly, they got back into their squad car and drove off.

More time passed. It was now 10:30 and the movie would be letting out any moment. Just then, another car drove up in front of the theater and two men got out. One of them crossed the street and approached Agents Jerry Campbell, while the other went over to the East Chicago officers, Stretch and Sopsic. The new arrivals were Chicago detectives, also responding to the call, which had come from the manager, about mysterious men lurking around the theater. Campbell and the East Chicago men tried to brush them off, but they were suspicious about the way they were acting and insisted on lingering.

The two detectives were still asking questions five minutes later when the first people began leaving the Biograph. Purvis tensed as the crowd on the sidewalk began to grow. Leaving Hurt and Winstead in the doorway, he moved to the box office, into the path of the patrons as they left the theater. The cigar in his mouth was shaking as badly as his hands were. More people came out, swirling around him under the theater's brightly-lit marquee. Purvis saw scores of women and children – and he tried to stay calm.

Then at 10:40 p.m., he saw the two women: Polly Hamilton and Ana Sage in her bright orange skirt. Dillinger was between them. Polly was holding onto his left arm. Ana was pushing through the people on his right. Purvis tried as hard as he could to act unconcerned. Dillinger was barely five feet away from him. With one step, he could reach out and grab his arm. Purvis looked at him and for a brief moment, their eyes met, but Dillinger looked away, apparently unaware of who Purvis was.

As Dillinger walked past him, Purvis raised a shaking hand to the matchbook he held and tried to strike a match. The cigar wobbled between his clenched jaws. He struck the match once, twice, but it refused to light. His hand was shaking too badly. Dillinger stepped to Purvis's left, going around him, guiding the women south in the direction they had come from earlier. In the doorway, further down the sidewalk, Agents Hurt and Winstead saw Purvis try and give the signal. Hurt whispered to his partner, "That's Dillinger, with the straw hat and the glasses."

Directly across the street, Jerry Campbell saw Dillinger at the same time. He called out to another agent, "There they go." Both men edged down the sidewalk, moving parallel to Dillinger on the other side of Lincoln Avenue.

Even with all of the agents stationed outside of the Biograph that night, only a handful reacted to Purvis's signal. According to Bureau memos, only a half-dozen of them saw it. He was too far away, surrounded by too many people, and he never actually got the cigar to light. Cowley, standing further down the block never saw it, nor did the two East Chicago cops, standing barely 20 feet to his north. Purvis watched, amazed, as they continued talking with the curious Chicago detectives. Across the street, though, Martin Zarkovich saw the target walk out of the Biograph. He began walking toward his own men, hoping to prod them into action without drawing too much attention.

Purvis was unsure of what to do next. He took a step or two to follow Dillinger. Then he took out a second match and, after getting this one to light, applied it to the cigar. He hoped that he could draw the attention of more agents. He couldn't tell if Winstead, Hurt, or anyone else knew what was happening. Fear gripped his chest – was Dillinger going to get away again? In frustration, he mouthed the words, "Damn it! Come on!"

Ten feet down the sidewalk, Dillinger and the two women were slowly moving along in a knot of six or seven other people. As the congestion loosened and Dillinger increased his stride, Purvis walked after them. As he did, Dillinger and the women passed the doorway where Winstead and Hurt were standing. When the trio walked past, Hurt stepped out of the doorway and began following behind them. Agent Ed Hollis, who stood on the curb next to the Bureau car, was right beside him. Dillinger glanced to the right, at Hollis. Winstead took a step forward. Dillinger half-turned and looked at Winstead.

Something was wrong. Standing across the street, a rookie agent named Jack Welles noticed that Dillinger "appeared to realize he was trapped; there was a tense look on his face." For years afterward, the agents would remember the next few seconds as if they happened in slow motion. Turning a little, Dillinger appeared to lean forward into a crouch. At the same time, he slid a hand into his pants pocket, where he carried a .38 revolver. Behind him, Winstead pulled out his .45 and Hurt and Hollis also drew their guns.

Dillinger suddenly broke away from the women. He knew there was an alley ahead of him and that it was his last, best chance for escape. As he ran, he collided with a woman outside of the alley and was spun part of the way around. He grabbed at the woman and then shoved her away. He broke for the mouth of the alley. But he never really had a chance. No one yelled "halt" or "stop" or identified themselves as federal agents. It happened very quickly. As the man running away from them reached for his pocket, Winstead fired his .45 at him three times. The sudden retort of the gun stunned the huge number of bystanders on the street. Hurt fired twice, Hollis just once. Four bullets struck Dillinger. Two grazed him and a third stuck in his side. But the fourth bullet hit him in the back of the neck, smashing his spine, severing his spinal cord, tearing through his brain, and exiting through his right eye.

Dillinger only managed another step or two before he fell face first to the pavement at the entrance of the alley. A lens in his eyeglasses shattered and the brim of his straw hat snapped in two. Winstead was the first to reach him. Purvis hustled up and took the pistol from the fallen man's hand. The rookie, Jack Welles, ran up in time to see Dillinger's lips moving. One of his agents leaned down and heard the man on the ground try to speak. "He mumbled some words I couldn't understand," he later said. "That was the end."

It was later recalled that a long moment of silence seemed to follow the shooting and then chaos broke out. Women ran screaming. As the dead man's blood spilled out onto the pavement, automobiles and streetcars came to a halt on Lincoln Avenue. Passengers, followed by nearby pedestrians, poured into the street, all pushing for a closer look. Within moments, people were shouting the name "Dillinger!"

Above the clamor, the screams of two women could be heard. The first, Etta Natalsky, was the woman that Dillinger had bumped into. A stray bullet had passed through the fleshy part of her thigh. The second injured woman was Theresa Paulus, a housemaid who had been leaving the Biograph with a friend when a bullet had clipped her in the hip. Neither woman was seriously injured.

A circle began to form around the body in the alley. Men craned their necks to get a glimpse. A dozen federal agents ran up, urging the crowd to move back, but not before many of the bystanders dipped their handkerchiefs in the blood, claiming a macabre souvenir of the night.

Two of the agents crossed the alley and ducked into a Chinese Restaurant to place a phone call and announce that Dillinger was dead. They officially informed the local cops that the Department of Justice had "made an arrest" outside of the Biograph Theater.

Back outside, several of the agents hovered over the body as others tried to keep back the surging crowd. Agent Grier Woltz, who had been stationed next to Dillinger, later reported that Dillinger was "still kicking and moving around" on the pavement. He estimated that he lived about three minutes after the shooting and before taking one last shuttering breath before he died. No one did anything to try and help him. This report was denied by official Bureau statements.

Meanwhile, Polly Hamilton and Ana Sage melted away in the crowd.

The Biograph in the hours after the shooting as crowds began to gather in the street

An ambulance was called. Two cars of police officers rolled up, responding to a call of shots being fired, and their occupants helped to push back the crowds. Attendants arrived and lifted the body into an ambulance. Five Bureau agents climbed in with three Chicago cops and the body was taken to the Alexian Brothers Hospital at 1200 Belden Avenue. Dr. Walter Prusaig turned them away at the door. "This man is dead," he stated after placing a stethoscope to on his chest.

Finally, a Chicago police detective ordered the body to be taken to the Cook County Morgue on Polk Street. A mob scene greeted them when they arrived and curiosity-seekers were allowed to file past the body all night long for one last look at Dillinger.

Or whoever the dead man was.

When word of the shooting was heard on the radio, hundreds of Chicagoans flocked to the Biograph. Crowds milled about at the alley entrance until nearly dawn, even though there was nothing to see but a shrinking pool of blood. It had vanished as the number of gruesome souvenirs grew larger.

Crowds began to gather around the bloodstains in the alley. Reports of Dillinger's exploits had been part of the people's daily lives. They wanted to be there for his death.

In Washington, reporters confronted Hoover as he hurried into his office. He could have bragged, but did not, telling them that he planned to continue the hunt for Nelson and Van Meter. He told them, "This does not mean the end of the Dillinger case. Anyone who ever gave any of the Dillinger mob any aid, comfort, or assistance will be vigorously prosecuted."

The next morning, the shooting was front-page news around the world, dominating headlines in New York, London, Moscow, and Berlin. The papers in Europe played up the fact that Dillinger was given no warning before he was shot in the back. American papers, though, focused largely on Purvis, who posed for photographers while he read congratulatory telegrams and gave interviews. The caption under his picture in the *Chicago Daily Times* read "He Got His Man." *Time* printed a photo of Purvis shaking hands with Attorney General Homer Cummings captioned, "Melvin Purvis and Friend." While Sam Cowley, who was still being identified as 'Purvis's chief assistant," shunned the press, Purvis gave scores of interviews. His ego was out of control. To some, he identified the as-yet-unnamed Ana Sage as "my informant" and embellished the story of lighting his cigar. He didn't mention that it took two tries. Instead, he told the reporter, "There was no response from my men. I'll confess I was under strain and extremely uncomfortable when Dillinger saw my signal and gave me a dirty look. Once I spotted him I knew him at once, because of those killer eyes of his."

Hoover was not happy. This was not how he wanted his agents to behave, as Purvis would soon discover. There was still a lot of work to be done, in fact, and Cowley kept Purvis out of most of it. Monday night, while Cowley was dealing with a number of pressing issues, Purvis was sent to the train station to pose for photographs with Homer Cummings. The following evening, he flew to Washington, where he posed for more photos with Hoover. Cowley apologized to the director; he was too busy to go. Hoover publicly announced that Purvis and Cowley were going to be given raises. For the moment, Purvis appeared to be back in Hoover's good graces, but it wouldn't last.

The attention lavished on Purvis didn't sit well with the East Chicago police either. Zarkovich gave several interviews, trying hard to direct credit toward himself. Like Purvis, he wildly embellished his story, telling reporters that he had seen Dillinger attending movies at the Biograph several times. He also claimed that the East Chicago police had Van Meter and Nelson under surveillance. It was no use, though. The press had dunned Purvis "the man who got Dillinger," and nothing the East Chicago police said changed anyone's minds. And perhaps it was just as well – Zarkovich had a number of secrets that he couldn't afford to have anyone find out.

While Purvis was busy basking in glory, Cowley was cleaning up the mess. On Monday, after testifying at the coroner's inquest – where he refused to release the names of the agents who shot Dillinger – he was forced to deal with Ana Sage, who told him that she was convinced that Dillinger's gang was going to hunt her down. She and Polly Hamilton had fled the scene moments after Dillinger was shot. Two days later, a boy swimming in Lake Michigan found a machine gun, a pistol, and a bulletproof vest in shallow water off a pier near Lincoln Park. They were Dillinger's; the machine gun was identified as one of the guns stolen from the Warsaw, Indiana, police department. It was never proven, but the Chicago police told reporters they suspected that Sage had run home after the shooting and cleared it of Dillinger's things, tossing the guns and vest into the lake. Afterward, Polly hid out at a girlfriend's house and Ana locked herself in the apartment.

By Monday afternoon, rumors began to spread about the mysterious "lady in red" who had betrayed Dillinger. Purvis and Zarkovich refused to comment, but enough of the conspiracy managed to leak out anyway. On Monday evening, the banner headline of the *Chicago Daily Times* read, "Dillinger Doomed by Girl in Red." At her apartment, Ana panicked. This was not what she had in mind when she went along with the plot that was cooked up between Dillinger and Zarkovich. The detective tried to calm her. Finally, Zarkovich drove her to the Bankers Building, where Cowley found her "most hysterical." In tears, she begged him to hide her away somewhere. Cowley said he would do whatever she wanted, then sent her home. The next morning, he talked with Hoover about the situation. The director wanted her to be held somewhere, out of reach of reporters.

Cowley called Ana and asked her to meet him at the Stevens Hotel. He instructed her to go home, pack her things, leave town, and let him know where she was going. Ana returned to the apartment and was tossing clothes into a suitcase when the doorbell rang. Through the peephole, she could see men outside. Frightened, she called Purvis, who promised to send an agent over. The men turned out to be Chicago police detectives. Against Purvis's wishes, they took Ana in for questioning.

At the Sheffield precinct house, Captain Thomas Duffy fired questions at Ana for several hours. For unknown reasons, he allowed a group of reporters to listen in. Ana proved to be a skilled liar, denying just about everything. Again and again, she insisted that she had been leaving the movie theater when federal agents came out of nowhere and killed her girlfriend's date.

When Cowley learned that Ana was in custody, he went to the precinct house. Both Cowley and Ana acted as if they didn't know one another. Cowley asked Duffy if he was filing charges against her. Duffy said that he only wanted to question her. Cowley left, telling Duffy to notify him when he was finished. Later, Cowley told Hoover that he felt the police captain had detailed Sage at the urging of friends who were reporters, who were hoping to get her story.

That evening, when the late editions of the city newspapers identified Ana as the "lady in red," Cowley telephoned the precinct and found that Ana was still there. Duffy said that he intended to hold her until the next day, but before he rang off the line, Cowley informed him that he was not. Cowley then telephoned the Chicago police commissioner, persuaded him to release Ana into Bureau custody, and then sent two agents to remove her from the precinct house. Reporters followed them as they drove Ana to the Bankers Building, where they shouted questions at Cowley. He firmly denied that Ana was responsible for betraying Dillinger.

Behind closed doors, Cowley told Ana to call Polly Hamilton. The Bureau had been unable to locate her. By 2:00 a.m., though, both women were safely hidden away on the nineteenth floor. They were questioned all night, but managed to keep their stories straight. Polly continued to deny that she knew "Jimmy Lawrence" was Dillinger. Even though this story flatly contradicted what Ana was telling him, Cowley accepted her story. She was telling the truth, he told Hoover, who trusted Cowley's opinion.

The Bureau decided to get the two women out of Chicago. On Wednesday morning, three days after the shooting at the Biograph, Cowley had a pair of agents drive Ana back to her apartment. When they arrived, they found that the apartment had been invaded by a throng of local reporters. They had been ushered inside by very helpful Chicago police officers. After Ana packed a suitcase, cursing at reporters as she did so, agents drove her and Polly to Detroit. They spent the next several days in a hotel.

While Cowley dealt with the women, his men began rounding up those who had helped Dillinger. The first person arrested was Wilhelm Loeser. Once the Bureau confirmed that Dillinger had received plastic surgery, Cowley had no doubt about who had performed it. Agents arrived at Loeser's house on Tuesday morning. When no one answered the bell, they broke down a side door and rushed inside. As they charged up the stairs, they heard a man's voice call out. A moment later, Loeser, shirtless, appeared at the top of the steps. He was taken to the Bankers Building, where he told them everything.

Charles Winstead led the raid on Jimmy Probasco's house the next evening. By midnight, Probasco was locked in a conference room on the nineteenth floor. When his house was searched, agents found what they later described as a "suicide note." Cowley ordered Probasco watched all that night. At 9:00 a.m. on Thursday, rookie agent Max Chaffetz took Probasco to be fingerprinted, then brought him back to the conference room. A few minutes later, Chaffetz returned to find the room empty. A chair was propped beneath the window and Chaffetz hurried over to the window and looked down. There, in the alley nineteen stories below, lay the battered and bloody remains of Jimmy Probasco. He had apparently jumped to his death.

Probasco's death led to rumors that he had been pushed from the window, or had perhaps fallen while being dangled outside by interrogating agents. A chagrined Cowley recommended to Hoover that both he and Chaffetz be suspended for two weeks. Hoover chose to suspend only Chaffetz. In the wake of accusations that had been made by Boss McLaughlin, who had passed the Bremer ransom money, claiming that he had been dangled from a nineteenth-floor window, both Cowley and Hoover were concerned about bad publicity. For the most part, the Chicago press ignored the story.

Louis Piquett, Art O'Leary, and Harold Cassidy were all rounded up in the following weeks. By that point, Cowley was involved in the pursuit of Nelson, Van Meter, the Barkers, and Pretty Boy Floyd.

The Dillinger case, though, was not quite closed.

To those historians who believe the demise of John Dillinger was a straightforward killing of a wanted bank robber, the story of Dillinger's betrayal by Ana Sage and Polly Hamilton made little sense. But, in chapters to come, as what this author believes is the story of what really happened starts to unspool, their "betrayal" will not be as surprising.

But the secret that they hid almost didn't last past 1934.

As the two women told contradictory stories, it seemed a matter of time before someone questioned their various versions of events. On Friday, July 27, Matt Leach was the man who started asking the questions. Leach came to the Bankers Building and met with Cowley behind closed doors. There was already tension between the Bureau and the Indiana State Police, and things were much worse after the meeting.

Leach told Cowley that he had an informant who said that Martin Zarkovich had sheltered Dillinger in East Chicago for at least two months, that Zarkovich had arranged the May 24 murders of two East Chicago detectives to cover this up, and that he had conspired to have the Bureau kill Dillinger so that he could steal Dillinger's money. Leach said that a "serious investigation" was needed, and he suggested that it be carried out by the Bureau. Cowley was skeptical. He said that the Bureau was investigating the possibility that Ana Sage had harbored Dillinger, but noted that since Zarkovich had participated in the killing, there was no way that a court would convict him of harboring a fugitive. If Zarkovich had arranged to have the two detectives murdered, that was a state crime, he said. The Bureau had no jurisdiction.

When Leach left, very unhappy, Cowley telephoned Hoover. After the call, Hoover wrote in a memo, "Mr. Cowley stated he believes this is a frame-up. I stated I am of the same opinion; that I believe they are jealous because they didn't get him themselves." In other words, Leach's suspicions – which were dangerously close to the truth – were nothing more than sour grapes.

The Bureau had no intention of investigating Polly and Ana, much less Zarkovich. The trio had become the Bureau's de facto allies, and Hoover accepted the fact that anything that reflected badly on them, reflected badly on the Bureau. If any mistakes had been made, Hoover couldn't afford to have them made public. In the weeks that followed, agents took a single signed statement from Ana and nothing at all from Polly or Zarkovich.

Two agents did interview Polly in Detroit on August 2, and from her evasive answers, they came to believe that she was hiding something. The agents wrote to Cowley afterward: "It may clearly be seen that her information is very sketchy, and is in direct conflict with information furnished by Mrs. Anna [sic] Sage. In this regard, it is the conviction of both agents that no information will be developed that Dillinger ever resided at the residence of Mrs. Sage, as she has cautioned Polly against furnishing any information concerning this matter, and she, Mrs. Sage, is very careful that no opportunity is had to question Polly out of her presence."

That was the last time that Polly was questioned by the Bureau. Cowley and Hoover called them off and the matter was entirely dropped. Polly and Ana were released after their stay in Detroit. Polly vanished, hiding out with her parents in South Dakota. Ana fled to Los Angeles, where, in October, Cowley visited her and handed over $5,000 of the Dillinger reward money.

Instead of delving further into the conspiracy alleged by Matt Leach, the Bureau began asking questions about Leach himself. Earl Connelly nosed around Indianapolis, hoping to dig up dirt on him, and in August, notified Cowley that Leach had been paying "considerable attention" to a lady – who was not his wife – who was staying at the Spinks Arms Hotel.

Leach refused to be intimidated. He told reporters, "We want to get to the bottom of this whole mess." But he never would.

On July 25, 1934, the man identified as John Dillinger was buried during a thunderstorm at the Crown Hill Cemetery in Indianapolis. Dillinger's father had brought the body back from Chicago, the hearse trailed by a long line of cars that were packed with reporters. A crowd of 5,000 people pressed against the stone fence near the gravesite. John Dillinger, Sr. stood solemnly as the coffin was lowered into the ground. There was no way to tell if the water that streamed down his face was from his tears, or simply the rain that fell from the sky. Later that day, he returned to his empty farmhouse and the reporters went home.

The Dillinger gravestone at Crown Hill Cemetery

And John Dillinger vanished into the American past. The body that was mouldering under the ground at Crown Hill Cemetery became part of a mystery that has continued for more than eight decades.

34. The End of the Line

On Sunday night, July 22, Homer Van Meter and girlfriend Mickey Conforti fled Chicago. They drove to St. Paul, where they hoped to hide out with Harry Sawyer at the Green Lantern tavern or his partner, Jack Peifer, at the Hollyhocks Club. But Sawyer had disappeared back in the spring, and Peifer wanted nothing to do with the Bureau agents who were chasing Van Meter. In desperation, Van Meter rented a room at a tourist camp outside of the town of Walker, Minnesota. At night, he drove into St. Paul, trying to find someone who could offer him a safer place.

For the next month, the couple moved from one motor lodge to another in the woods north of St. Paul. The Bureau suspected they might be in the area, but could find no one with hard information. Cowley wrote to Hoover that most of the underworld characters in the area had apparently left town. Telephones had been disconnected and hideouts emptied out. Gangsters had disappeared, afraid of being pulled in for questioning.

Just who finally gave Van Meter up will never be known. According to a story an informant told to FBI agents about five years later, it was probably Jack Peifer. On Thursday morning, August 23, Van Meter apparently visited the Hollyhocks, where he met Peifer, who may or may not have been holding several thousand dollars for him. He was also holding money for Fred Barker and Alvin Karpis. The informant later claimed that Peifer waited until Van Meter left before he telephoned his old friend Tom Brown, a corrupt detective who had worked with the Barkers during the Bremer kidnapping. Brown was suspected of criminal activities and probably figured that bringing in a notorious bank robber would help his image.

At 5:00 p.m., a car dropped Van Meter off at a car dealership near downtown St. Paul. He was nicely dressed and was apparently expecting to meet someone. When he walked out of the dealership's front doors a few minutes later, he was confronted by Tom Brown, Police Chief Frank Cullen, two detectives, and four guns. "Stick 'em up!" one of the officers yelled.

Van Meter pulled a pistol from the waistband of his pants and sprinted across University Avenue, firing two shots over his shoulder. The straw boater hat that he had been wearing flew back off his head, but he caught it, clutching it in his hand as he ran. Brown and the other officers fired several shots in his direction and then, noticing a woman in their line of fire, ran after him. Van Meter skipped across the street, dodging oncoming cars, ran down Marion Street, and then ducked left into an alley.

It was a dead end.

Van Meter stopped and turned to find the officers behind him. Before he could even raise his weapon – or surrender – they opened fire. The first blast from Brown's sawed-off shotgun knocked Van Meter two feet into the air, slamming his body into the brick wall of a garage. He struggled to stand, but the four men continued to fire, riddling his body with more than 50 bullets. Homer Van Meter,

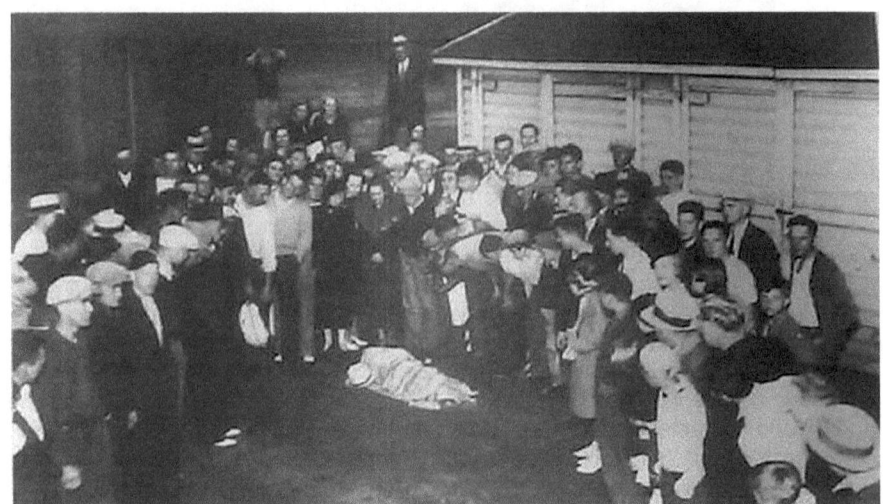

Homer Van Meter's body, surrounded by a crowd, in the alley where he was gunned down.

who had told Dillinger that he didn't want to die in some dirty alley, did exactly that.

When the news reached Washington an hour later, Hoover was enraged. He immediately telephoned the St. Paul office and chastised them over the fact that Homer Van Meter was killed in St. Paul and his agents knew nothing about it. Of course, no one mentioned the obvious to him: the local police were excluding the Bureau just as it had famously excluded the Chicago police from the takedown of Dillinger. Hoover was hungry for fame and credit – in just the same way that Melvin Purvis was.

Mickey Conforti was arrested a few days later. She told the Bureau that Van Meter had been carrying $6,000 at the time of his death. The St. Paul police only reported finding $923. If Tom Brown took Van Meter's $5,077, there was an eerie symmetry at work. When Alvin Karpis and the Barkers read of Brown's involvement in the shooting the next day, they decided to keep his $5,000 share of the Bremer kidnapping ransom.

The next day, Homer Van Meter's body was taken to his hometown of Fort Wayne, Indiana. There was no one waiting for him to arrive, save for a handful of reporters and the local undertaker. Van Meter had also lacked the charisma of his pal, John Dillinger, and his funeral didn't draw the same kind of crowds. Only his immediate family and a large contingent of police were on hand for his funeral. His brother, Harry, who was seriously ill with diabetes, could not attend, and his sister, Helen, had no interest in going. He was laid to rest on August 28, at the Lindenwood Cemetery in Fort Wayne.

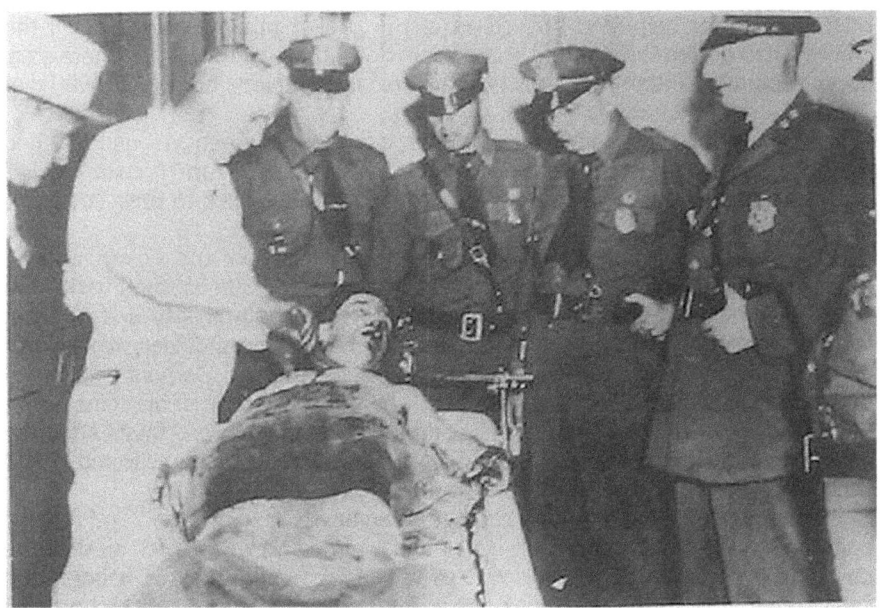

Homer Van Meter's body, placed on display for reporters by the St. Paul police.

A few more of Dillinger's old friends fared as poorly as Homer Van Meter did.

On September 22, 1934 -- possibly thinking that if Dillinger could do it, they could too – Harry Pierpont and Charles Makley attempted to escape from the death house at the Ohio State Penitentiary using fake guns. The bogus pistols looked real from a distance. Made up of soap, toothpaste tubes, and paperclips, and covered with black shoe polish, they had taken several careful weeks to create. Somehow, the guards who checked their cells each day failed to discover them.

At 10:30 a.m., a guard named Stagle carried breakfast to Pierpont's cell. The bank robber was lying on his cot and claimed to be ill. As Slagle turned to leave the cell, Pierpont jumped up, slugged the guard, and demanded his keys. Drawing his "gun," Pierpont backed Slagle into a corner. When the guard refused to hand over the keys, Pierpont slugged him again and took them. Makley drew his "gun" at the same time and threatened a guard named Pharr, who was stationed outside of Makley's cell. Using Slagle's keys, Pierpont freed Makley, Russell Clark, and six other prisoners on death row.

Pierpont, Makley, and Clark broke apart a wooden table and then, using the two guards as shields, Pierpont and Makley rushed down the main corridor to the locked steel door leading to a special guard room between death row and cell block L. They banged on it with pieces from the table. When guard J.T. Jones looked through the peephole in the door and saw what was happening, he grabbed a rifle, shouted for help, and pushed an alarm to alert other guards. Even if the convicts had gotten through the guard room door, there were still four more steel doors separating them from the outside. This was definitely not the Crown Point Jail.

When the alarm sounded through the prison, an emergency squad grabbed their riot guns and raced toward death row. As Warden Preston Thomas shouted orders, guards in the prison yard began forcing inmates back to their cells. City police were summoned and surrounded the prison.

When the prison's riot squad arrived at the cellblock door and a guard opened it, Makley pointed his fake weapon at them and ordered them to stand back. Two squad members opened fire with their riot guns and both Makley and Pierpont went down with the first volley. Shot in the spine, head, and shoulder, Makley died an hour later in the prison hospital. A bullet passed through Pierpont's abdomen and lodged in his kidney. Bullets also struck him near the base of his spine, in his back, and another shot creased his scalp. None of them were fatal. After the shootings, the other death row convicts were herded back to their cells and locked up again.

The next day, Pierpont, who had not eaten anything in two days and refused painkillers while being treated for his wounds, turned down food for most of the day. Prison physician Dr. George W. Kell said, "I ordered a bowl of noodle soup sent to him after I left, but I don't know if he ate it or not. He told me he didn't want any food." Later on, he finally took some milk and toast. Doctors thought his condition was not serious, although he was running a slight fever and had lost some of the feeling in his legs. He was able to stand, though, and he took short walks back and forth across his cell.

At an inquest, Pierpont and Clark were both questioned. Pierpont stated that Clark had no part in the plans and should not be punished. He had no idea there was an escape plan until Pierpont unlocked his cell door. The question remains whether or not Pierpont and Makley truly believed they would escape, or whether they simply wanted to go out in a blaze of gunfire. Both men had boasted that they would not die in the electric chair. Makley's claim turned out to be correct. The same could not be said for "Handsome Harry" Pierpont.

Silent and sullen, he awaited his appointment with death. He was given magazines, but he refused to read them. On October 6, Warden Thomas doubled the guard force and even assigned a personal guard for the recuperating bandit. He had officers check the license plates of all out-of-state cars spotted anywhere near the prison.

When Pierpont's parents visited him on Saturday, October 13, he told them not to make any more attempts to obtain intercession from Governor White. "I want to die," he told them.

On Tuesday, Pierpont put in a request for a quiet funeral, made a public gesture of acceptance of his Catholic faith, and asked the prison chaplain to administer the Last Sacraments. Mary Kinder tried to visit him that same day, but the warden denied her request. Pierpont wrote a letter to his attorney, Jessie Levy, during his last hours, thanking her for the efforts she had made on his behalf.

During his last supper, he picked at his chicken dinner, and then pushed the plate aside. He had no appetite. Despite what he had asked of them, his parents put in a last, eleventh-hour plea to Governor White, but their request was denied. "I see no justifiable reason to extend clemency," he said.

Pierpont's sudden, and seemingly unscheduled, execution on October 17 was ordered by Warden Thomas to prevent any attempt by the remnants of the Dillinger gang to free him. But, by that time, there was no one left who could save him. Pierpont knelt and read a prayer just a few minutes before the guards took him on his last walk to the death chamber. On his way, he passed the cell of Russell Clark, but the warden refused to let the two meet, even for a handshake. Pierpont limped on down the corridor, kissed a crucifix, and handed it to his priest.

There was a slight, sardonic smile on Pierpont's face when he seated himself in the electric chair. The switch was flipped and he was pronounced dead at 12:14 a.m.

His body was taken to a small house that adjoined a filling station and tourist camp operated by his parents on Highway 31, eight miles south of South Bend, Indiana. Family and friends were allowed to view the body, and a private service was held on October 20. After it was over, Pierpont's body was taken to Holy Cross Cemetery in Indianapolis and he was buried in the family plot, next to his sister, Fern.

Mary Kinder wept.

The death of Homer Van Meter marked a turning point for the Bureau. The Dillinger gang was finished. As far as Hoover was concerned, the "War on Crime" was almost over. They just needed to clean up the mess now. More than once, he had publicly stated that there was no place left for the "rats" to hide, and in a way, he was right. One of the benefits of the Dillinger publicity craze was the attention given to other public enemies – their mugshots were now being splashed on the front pages of newspapers from coast to coast.

Hoover had the utmost confidence in Sam Cowley. On September 6, he formalized Cowley's position as the Bureau's wartime general, handing him unrestricted power to hunt down Nelson, Pretty Boy Floyd, Alvin Karpis, and the Barkers. He could go anywhere, assume command of any office, take any agent that he needed to get the job done. Hoover expected the "mopping up" effort to last no more than 45 days.

Cowley's new status came at the expense of Melvin Purvis. Since the Dillinger shooting, Purvis had fallen deeper and deeper into Hoover's disfavor. Twice, Hoover had fired off terse letters when he was unable to reach Purvis by telephone. For the most part, Purvis had been removed from all investigative work. He spent most of his days filling out personnel reports, interviewing job applicants, going to lunch, and shining his shoes.

In October, though, Purvis was in Cincinnati, hunting for the kidnapper of a Kentucky woman. It wasn't glamorous work, but it was better than doing paperwork, and it got him out of the office. He happened to be in just the right place in time when word arrived that Pretty Boy Floyd was in Ohio, being hunted

Oklahoma bandit Charles "Pretty Boy" Floyd ended up in the national spotlight after Dillinger was taken out of play by the Bureau.

down by local authorities. Purvis was in his hotel room when he received the call about Floyd. He telephoned Washington and spoke to Hoover. The relationship between the two men had gone from cool to downright frigid. In one bizarre letter from the previous month, Hoover had harassed Purvis for refusing to speak clearly over the telephone. Hoover wrote, "I have had the phone checked here, and found that our phone is technically satisfactory. It might also be desirable for you to speak in a little louder tone of voice." On October 2, Hoover sent Purvis a telegram berating him for failing to report a man who had visited the Chicago office with a tip on the 1932 Lindbergh kidnapping. In it, Hoover stated, "I am instructing Mr. Cowley to take personal charge of this matter so that it will be given the proper attention."

But on this morning, Hoover gave his grudging permission for Purvis to charter a plane and supervise the manhunt for Floyd, who remained the Bureau's prime suspect in the Kansas City Massacre case – a thorn in Hoover's side because it wouldn't go away and it remained unsolved.

On October 20, Charles "Pretty Boy" Floyd and his pal, Adam Richetti, had left Buffalo, New York, where they had been hiding out, with the long-suffering girlfriends, sisters Juanita and Beulah Baird. In the dark, they crossed Pennsylvania and made it into Ohio, then turned south. Richetti had relatives in Dillonvale, across from Wheeling, West Virginia, and they were heading there. Floyd drove past Youngstown and, at around 3:00 a.m., reached the Ohio River at East Liverpool. He turned onto Highway 7, a two-lane blacktop that ran along the western edge of Ohio. It was raining and just before the city limits of Wellsville, four miles below East Liverpool, Floyd lost control of the car on the wet pavement and skidded into a telephone pole.

There was steam coming from under the hood when Floyd got out to inspect the damage. The little Oklahoma outlaw knew cars, and this didn't look good. Irked, he managed to get the car back onto the road, but knew he wouldn't get far without repairs. He told the Baird sisters to drive into Wellsville and find a mechanic. He and Richetti couldn't afford to be seen. The girls coaxed the car south on the road and soon disappeared from sight.

Floyd and Richetti took some blankets and their guns and hiked up onto a wooded hill to wait for the girls to return. From this position, Floyd could see up and down Highway 7 and across some railroad tracks to the river below. A few dozen yards behind them, at the top of the hill, sat a row of darkened houses. Feeling relatively safe, they gathered some leaves and branches and started a small fire to stay warm.

Hours passed as they waited. At dawn, lights flickered on in the houses above them. By 8:00, there was still no sign of the sisters. Around 10:00, a man named Joe Fryman came out of one of the houses to check on his vegetable garden. He was standing near the highway with his son-in-law when he saw someone on the hill below. They decided to take a look and halfway down the hill, found Floyd and Richetti sitting on their blankets. At first, they thought they were tramps, but their expensive suits suggested otherwise. Floyd greeted them and explained that he and his friend had been out taking pictures with their girls, but had gotten lost. They were waiting for them to return.

Suspicious, Fryman went home and spoke to a neighbor, Lon Israel, who agreed that the story sounded fishy. Israel hiked to a nearby store and telephoned the chief of Wellsville's two-man police force, John H. Fultz. That Thursday, a bank had been robbed in Tiltonsville, an hour's drive south, and it occurred to Fultz that the two strangers might be connected to that crime. Before leaving, he deputized two men, William Erwin and Grover Potts, and asked them to come along. A few minutes later, the three arrived on the hilltop. None of them wore a uniform. Only Fultz had a gun, a .38 revolver. Israel offered to show them where the strangers were camped and led the group down a muddy path.

As they went down the hill and rounded a clump of bushes, Floyd suddenly appeared in front of them. "What do you want?" he demanded, but before they could reply, he pulled out a pistol and leveled it at Fultz. "Stick 'em up!" he said.

Fultz tried to pass himself off as a worker on his way to the nearby brickyard and he refused to raise his hands. When Floyd insisted, he continued to argue. He even took a few steps closer to Floyd. "Don't come another inch, fellow, or I'll pump you," the outlaw warned.

"You wouldn't shoot a working man," Fultz said, but Floyd stepped forward and shoved the muzzle of the gun into the chief's stomach. Fultz brazenly pushed past him, followed by Lon Israel and the two deputies. Floyd let them walk by, then descended the path after them, his gun still aimed at Fultz. "Don't run or I will shoot you," he threatened the men.

Fultz assured him that no one was going to run. The brave – and perhaps foolhardy – lawman led the men down the dirt path. They continued to bicker and then Fultz came upon Richetti, who was still lying on his blanket. "Hello, buddy, how are you?" Fultz cheerily asked. "You seem to be taking it pretty easy."

"Yeah," Richetti warily replied.

Floyd had had enough by this time. "Don't let him kid you – shoot him! He's an officer!"

Richetti dutifully whipped out his .45, aimed it at Fultz, and pulled the trigger. The gun misfired. Fultz pulled his own pistol, turned back toward Floyd, and snarled, "You big yellow son of a bitch!" He fired at Floyd, missing, then turned and fired at Richetti. In the confusion, the other men – all unarmed – scattered into the woods. Fultz stopped to reload his gun and by the time he was finished, Floyd was nowhere to be seen. Fultz spotted Richetti running off into the woods and he ran after him.

Richetti raced through the trees, leapt a fence, and made for the back of a house. Fultz reached its yard just as Richetti slammed into the back door. Fultz fired once, the bullet striking the house about two feet away from Richetti's shoulder.

"I give up!" Richetti shouted, raising his hands.

While Fultz handcuffed Richetti, Floyd stepped out of the trees and removed a machine gun from where it had been hidden under their blankets. Meanwhile, Lon Israel and the two deputies hurried up the hill and retrieved shotguns from Israel's house. The three men had just walked back out into Israel's yard when, to their left, they saw Floyd emerge from the trees. Floyd spun in their direction and fired a burst from the machine gun, then it jammed. One bullet struck Potts in the shoulder and he fell. Erwin got off one blast from his shotgun before he went looking for cover. Floyd sprawled into a ditch, then got up and ran across the hilltop and into the trees on the far side. He tossed the useless machine gun into the weeds as he ran.

The woods Floyd entered were a rugged area on the northern reaches of Appalachia. West of the river, the land was broken by steep, rocky hills, the hollows were cut by shallow brown creeks, and the hillsides were littered with tar-paper shacks and a scattering of trash. On the far side of the hill, an auto mechanic named Theodore Peterson and his brother, William, were standing outside of their garage talking to a teenager named George McMillen. He had stopped by to buy a vacuum tank for his Model T Ford. McMillen was startled when he looked up to see a man in a mud-streaked blue suit come scrambling down the hillside.

Floyd walked over to them and asked if he could pay any of them $5 to drive him to Youngstown. When they asked him why, he explained that he had been out hunting and his car had broken down.

"What part broke?" one of the Petersons asked. "Maybe we can fix it."

"The front axle," Floyd answered. He put his foot on the axle of McMillen's Ford to show where the break had occurred. He went on, "I've got to get to Youngstown. I've got business to attend to up there. I'll give you $10." He pulled a wad of one-dollar bills from his pocket to show that he had the cash.

Ted Peterson finally agreed to drive him. He and Floyd got into the car and Peterson was backing out of the yard when his mother stuck her head out of the house and asked where he was going. Peterson shouted back that he was taking the man in his car to Youngstown. But his mother objected. He couldn't get to Youngstown and then get back across the river by 1:00 p.m. It was 12:40, and Peterson was due at another man's house in 20 minutes.

"Sorry, buddy," Peterson said.

"That's all right," Floyd replied. He turned to the teenager, George McMillen, and offered him the $10 to take him. McMillen quickly agreed and he shoved the bills into his pocket. Once they were in the car, Floyd told the young man to stick to back roads.

"I suppose you know who I am," Floyd said after they had driven for a few minutes.

"Don't believe I do."

"My name's Floyd. Pretty Boy Floyd."

McMillen looked at him and shrugged. He had no idea who his passenger was.

Floyd seemed a little offended. "The radios are flashing it all over the country, the papers are full of it."

McMillen shrugged again. "I don't know anything about it. I'm just back from Cannon's Mill and haven't been reading the papers except the funnies or to look through the paper for a job."

Five more minutes down the road, McMillen's car stalled. Above the road was a set of greenhouses owned by a florist, James H. Baum. He sold his flowers at a shop in Wellsville; his biggest customer was the local funeral home. He and a friend were stacking lumber when Floyd and McMillen walked up his driveway. Floyd motioned toward the stalled Ford. "How about some gas? I'll pay for it."

"I haven't any gas," Baum replied.

Floyd suggested taking some gas out of Baum's Nash sedan, but the florist said that he didn't have a way to drain it. Floyd then asked him to take them to a filling station, and Baum agreed. Climbing into the Nash, Floyd pulled out his gun. "Now, Dad, I want you to do just what I say," he told Baum.

He directed Baum to drive them north toward Youngstown, keeping to the back roads. They bumped along rough, muddy tracks for nearly two hours, eventually reaching the highway a few miles north from where they started. Just as they gained speed, they spotted a roadblock. Two deputies had placed a railroad car across the road. A long line of automobiles was waiting to pass.

At the roadblock, Deputies George Hayes and Charley Patterson watched the Nash stop and turn around. Needless to say, it looked suspicious. Hayes called out to Patterson and they hopped in their car and tried to give chase, but were slowed down by the tangle of parked cars.

Ahead of them, in the Nash, Floyd peered out the back window. When he saw the patrol car try and give chase, he told Baum to step on it. The mouth of a hilly dirt road – with so many dips and rises that the locals called it "Roller Coaster Road" – opened to the left and Floyd told Baum to turn onto it. The Nash roared down the narrow lane and sped east into the woods north of East Liverpool. The deputies gave chase. A half mile down Roller Coaster Road, they began honking their horn. At that point, James Baum had reached his limit and stopped the car. The deputies slammed to a stop about 50 yards behind the Nash. From the backseat, Floyd opened fire. His shot blew out the back window of the Nash, and shattered the windshield of the patrol car. The deputies were searching for cover as Floyd hustled out of the car and ran into the woods.

By nightfall, the county was in an uproar. Volunteers, mostly farmers who were armed to the teeth, flooded into Wellsville and milled around the jail. Inside, Chief Fultz tried to question Adam Richetti. Locked in a cell, Richetti gave his name as "Richard Zamboni." He said that his fleeing partner was a gambler from Toledo. Inexplicably, George McMillen never told anyone that the "gambler" had identified himself to him as Pretty Boy Floyd.

On Sunday morning, the manhunt for the missing "gambler" continued. An overnight rain had wiped out any footprints that Floyd had left behind. He had disappeared into the wildest area of the county, a maze of wooded hillsides that lined Little Beaver Creek. Around 1:00 p.m., Ray B. Long, the sheriff of Steubenville, Ohio, arrived in Wellsville to join the posse. When he entered the jail, he immediately recognized Richetti from a wanted poster. "That's Adam Richetti," he told Fultz. "He's wanted in the Kansas City Massacre." When the sheriff recognized him, Richetti admitted who he was.

Sheriff Long said that they had to call the Bureau. Fultz objected, though. He was enjoying his moment in the spotlight and he apparently didn't want to share it. Long called anyway. The switchboard at the Bureau's Cincinnati office forwarded the message to the senior agent in the area, which is how Purvis ended up taking the call.

By 2:00 p.m., he and his men were on a plane. At the Wellsville jail, Purvis immediately butted heads with Chief Fultz. It was now almost dark and the volunteers had dispersed, heading home for supper. There had been no sightings of Floyd for more than 24 hours. Purvis said that he wanted the entire area cordoned off. Fultz said that it couldn't be done. To make matters worse, Fultz refused to release Richetti to the Bureau. He had a strong case against him for assault. Purvis telephoned Hoover and reported that the situation was "impossible to control."

Purvis left the jail and drove to East Liverpool. He set up his command post at the Travelers Hotel. By 3:00 a.m., nearly 20 agents from Pittsburgh, Cleveland, and Cincinnati had assembled in his room. Purvis split them into five squads of three and four men and decided to send two squads to raid the homes of Richetti's relatives at Dillonvale, an hour to the south. The other three squads were sent to patrol Highway 7 and the network of adjoining roads north of East Liverpool. For some reason, Floyd was believed to be wounded, so other agents were kept busy checking hospitals, doctor's offices, and taxi companies. More than 200 police and sheriff's deputies, arriving from all over the state. Manned roadblocks up and down the Ohio River Valley.

Around 1:00 p.m. on Monday, after two days with no sightings of Floyd, a reliable report came in. Three of Purvis's men were checking farms north of East Liverpool when they were flagged down by a constable, who told them that Floyd had been seen on a farm north of Little Beaver Creek. A farmer's wife had fed him a sandwich and let him wash up. The news was relayed to Purvis. Hoover telephoned just as he was leaving his room. He told Purvis to leave at once. If Floyd was going to be captured, Hoover wanted to be sure that it was by the Bureau.

Purvis met up with his men on a dirt road seven miles north of East Liverpool. He was willing to bet that Floyd was heading north, trying to get to Youngstown. They split into two groups and began searching farmhouses and barns. In one

The Conkle Farm, near East Liverpool, Ohio

barn, Purvis was rooting around in the hayloft when he heard a noise below. He quickly drew his gun. He heard footsteps coming up the ladder and aimed his .45, ready to fire – and felt ridiculous when one of his own men came up the ladder.

Around 3:00, as they cruised dirt roads, watching the nearby fields, Purvis and his men met a car driven by the East Liverpool police chief and three of his men. They decided to join forces.

Meanwhile, Floyd had just emerged from the woods north of Little Beaver Creek. His shirt was soaked with sweat and his pants were streaked with mud and covered in thistles and pine needles. He had covered eight miles of ground since fleeing from the sheriff's deputies. All he wanted was some food and a ride out of Ohio. As he stumbled along, he came across an isolated farmhouse.

Ellen Conkle, a widow who worked her farm with the help of in-laws, was cleaning her smokehouse when Floyd knocked on her door. "I'm lost and I want something to eat," Floyd said. "Can you help me out with some food? I'll pay you."

Mrs. Conkle had no idea who Pretty Boy Floyd was, and she knew nothing about the manhunt.

Floyd apologized for how he looked. "I was hunting squirrels with my brother last night and I got lost. The more directions I got, the more confused I became. I don't know where I am now."

Mrs. Conkle knew that no one hunted squirrels at night, certainly not in a business suit and black oxfords, and said so. A sheepish look crossed the outlaw's face. "To be honest, I've been drinking. I guess I got lost."

Ellen Conkle, who has made a mark in history as a simple woman kindly helping a stranger, was not a fool. In fact, she was frightened. As she told investigators a few days later, she was afraid of what might happen if she denied the man food, so she agreed to make him something, hoping that it would hurry him on his way. She asked him what he wanted to eat and Floyd replied, "Meat. All I've been eating is apples, and some ginger cookies. I'm hungry for meat."

While lawmen and Bureau agents were scouring the hills and woods for him, Floyd sat down in a rocker on the back porch and read the Sunday edition of the local newspaper. Mrs. Conkle went out to her smokehouse, fetched some ribs, and went into the kitchen. A short time later, she returned with a heaping plate of ribs, fresh bread, and pudding. Floyd devoured all of it, except for the pudding, then accepted the widow's offer of coffee and a slice of pumpkin pie. He pronounced the meal "fit for a king."

Floyd asked for a ride to Youngstown and while Mrs. Conkle said she couldn't take him, her brother-in-law, Stewart Dyke, might do it. He and his wife were currently out in the fields picking corn. She would ask him when they returned. Floyd climbed into Dyke's Model A and waited. The keys were in the ignition, but he didn't steal the car.

Around 4:00 p.m. Dyke and his wife walked up to the house and Floyd asked for a ride to Youngstown. He offered to pay for it, but Dyke said he was too tired. He did agree to take him to Clarkson, though, where he could catch a bus that would take him the rest of the way.

Floyd agreed. He also borrowed a powder puff from Mrs. Dyke and began to apply make-up to his face, perhaps as a half-hearted attempt to disguise himself. As the car backed out of the yard, he waved goodbye to Mrs. Conkle.

And then Stewart Dyke saw two cars coming toward them on the road.

The cars eased around a wide curve and rolled up a short hill to the Conkle farm. It was the last place on Sprucevale Road. In the first car was an East Liverpool policeman named Glenn "Curly" Montgomery. He spotted Floyd first. "Stop!" he hollered. "That's him!"

Floyd spotted the lawmen just before they spotted him. He ducked down and pulled out his pistol. He ordered Dyke to drive behind the corn crib, a 15-foot-wide raised wooden shed used to store corn. As the car slid to a stop, Dyke reached over and unlocked the door. "Get out, you son of a bitch!" he yelled at Floyd and the outlaw scrambled out of the car and ducked behind the corn crib.

Officer Montgomery was the first man out of the East Liverpool patrol car as it coasted to a stop in the Conkle's yard. Purvis's car stopped right behind it, and the four agents jumped out. The cops pointed to the corn crib and called out that Floyd was hiding there. All of them drew their guns. The corn crib was only about a foot off the ground and they could see Floyd as he scurried from one side to the other, unsure of what to do.

Purvis shouted at him. "Floyd, come to the road! If you don't, we will shoot!"

It's likely that, by this time, Floyd had read about how the lawmen had handled the "arrests" of Dillinger and Homer Van Meter. They were going to shoot anyway; he must have thought. It was worth a chance to make a run for it. He left the shelter of the corn crib and darted across open ground toward the Conkle's garage.

Shouts from Purvis and others, ordering him to stop, rang out across the yard. Floyd kept running. Behind the garage, he raced into an open field. At the far end of the field, maybe 200 feet away, was a thick stand of woods. If he could make it there, he might escape. Floyd began to run, zigzagging across the wide open area.

"Let him have it!" Purvis cried.

Gunshots rang out. The Bureau men had pistols, shotguns, and a machine gun. Their bullets splintered Mrs. Conkle's apple tree and leaves and tree branches began raining down into the yard. Floyd kept running, though, looking once over his shoulder. More shots rang out, accompanied by the thumping beat of the machine gun. Bullets flew. Some officers fired from where they stood, others ran after Floyd out into the field. He was getting away. Then, as he neared the crest of a small rise, Floyd's right arm flew up and he fell forward, landing hard in the grass.

Three of the East Liverpool policemen were the first to reach him. As they came crashing up to him, Floyd swung his arm around to defend himself, his .45 ready to fire. Officer Chester Smith grabbed Floyd's wrist and wrenched the gun from his hand as the second officer fell on top of Floyd and pinned him to the ground. Floyd pulled a second pistol from the waistband of his pants, but the third officer, Herman Roth, took it away from him and tossed it on the ground. Later, Purvis would claim that he kicked the pistol out of Floyd's hand, but the best he could have managed was moving it further away from Floyd with his foot.

The officers demanded that Floyd lay still. He was fighting like a wildcat. The East Liverpool chief, Hugh McDermott, ran up. "How bad are you hurt?" he asked the outlaw.

Floyd coughed out, "I'm done for. You've hit me twice." A .45 slug had hit him below the left shoulder blade and lodged in his chest. Another bullet had struck his right side and come to rest beneath his heart. His lungs, ribs, and heart had all been damaged. The Bureau –with help again from the local police – had once more gunned down a fleeing outlaw from behind.

"What's your name?" Officer Montgomery asked. By then, Purvis and the other Bureau men had arrived on the scene.

Floyd insisted that his name was "Murphy," and he asked about his partner, "Eddie," the alias that had been used by Adam Richetti. The cops told him that they didn't know where Richetti was. "Oh, hell," coughed Floyd.

"Your name's Floyd," Purvis said.

Floyd just stared at him.

"Is your name not Pretty Boy Floyd?" Purvis asked.

Floyd's mouth turned into a twisted smile. "Yeah, I'm Floyd."

Purvis needed to call Washington, and for a doctor. There was no telephone at the Conkle farm, so Purvis and a second agent drove to a store in Clarkson. When Purvis left, Agent Sam McKee hunched down next to Floyd and began questioning him. He asked if Floyd had been involved with the Kansas City Massacre at Union Station.

"To hell with Union Station," Floyd said.

"You're dying," McKee stated.

"I know, I'm through."

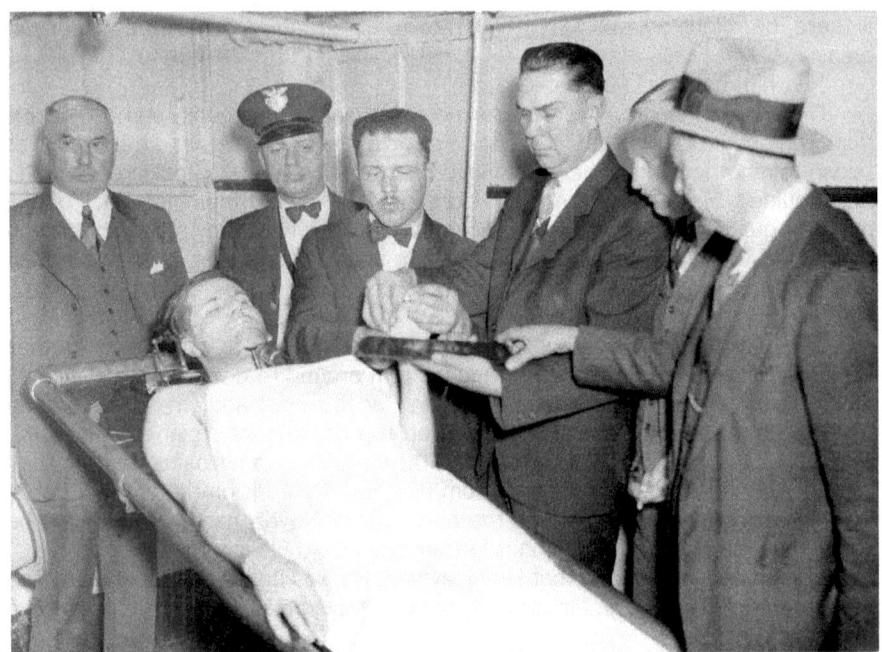

Pretty Boy Floyd on the funeral home slab, surrounded by local officials, who posed for news photographs

"Then do the decent thing and tell me what you know about the massacre at Union Station."

Floyd said nothing to him.

"Is it not true that you, Adam Richetti, and Verne Miller did the shooting at Union Station?"

Floyd just glared at him. "I ain't telling you nothing, you son of a bitch." A moment later, Floyd lapsed into a state of semi-consciousness and McKee gave up. The young outlaw drifted in and out and he seemed to be near death.

"Who tipped you I was here?" he asked in a lucid moment. Several times, he tried to get up but the East Liverpool cops held him down. He was fading quickly. "Fuck you," he said at one point and then at 4:25 p.m., he said, "I'm going."

And Pretty Boy Floyd died in a field outside of East Liverpool, Ohio.

Floyd's body was taken to the Sturgis Funeral Home in Wellsville, which was soon mobbed by reporters and curiosity-seekers. Much to Hoover's irritation, more reporters were drawn to Melvin Purvis than to the body of the slain bandit. He was surrounded by newsmen when he showed up at the funeral home, where Hoover was finally able to reach him, about an hour after the shooting. Hoover wrote in a memo, "Purvis advised me that he had his picture taken, that he had been receiving inquiries from newspapers, whereupon I instructed him to tell the newspapers statements would have to come through Washington."

But, of course, Purvis would be unable to help himself.

All evening, even as friends and reporters telephoned their congratulations, Hoover was unable to think of anything but Purvis. Around 9:00 p.m., Purvis and Sam Cowley, who had gone to Ohio from Chicago, called Hoover to report that they expected to take custody of Richetti within the hour. When Purvis stepped away from the phone, Hoover told Cowley that he wanted Purvis out of Wellsville immediately. Purvis was "to leave tonight and the curtain pulled down on publicity there." He feared that if he remained in town, "there will be a lot of motion pictures and the like."

But Purvis, being Purvis, loved the spotlight. After three months of being chained to his desk, he was once again a star, and when reporters asked him what happened, he was happy to tell them. The next morning's newspapers portrayed "the man who got Dillinger" as the hero who had now brought down a second major public enemy. The *Chicago Tribune* painted a lurid picture: "A normally mild-mannered southerner, who 'sees red' when dealing with criminals, Purvis today became the most dangerous nemesis of the desperado."

In Washington, Hoover steamed. He was the attention lavished on the Bureau – *his* Bureau – not on Melvin Purvis. If there was any one man who was responsible for bringing down Floyd and Dillinger, he felt, it was Sam Cowley, whom the newspapers continued to portray as Purvis's subordinate. Two nights later, a headquarters supervisor reached Purvis at his home in Chicago and told him to stay away from the office. In fact, he was to tell no one that he was even in the city. Purvis, who had been lauded during a trip to Washington after Dillinger was brought down, asked if he was to come east and he was told there was no reason for him to do so. Any relationship that had remained between Purvis and Hoover was now damaged beyond repair.

With Dillinger and Floyd now both off the public enemies list, Sam Cowley focused his attentions on Baby Face Nelson. His files were thick with new intelligence. Cowley felt that the manhunts for Dillinger and Floyd had been resolved by dumb luck, with the Bureau taking advantage of an opportunistic snitch and a car accident. Cowley was determined that the capture of Nelson would be different. The Nelson files were indicative of the progress being made by Bureau agents, finally rising above the bungled investigation of the Kansas City Massacre and the Purvis-era embarrassment of Little Bohemia.

Under Cowley's direction, agents had rounded up almost every contact from Nelson's early days, interviewing old partners and staking out the homes of his and Helen's siblings. Several family members had quietly cooperated with the Bureau, including Nelson Fitzsimmons, whose wife had taken in Nelson's son, Ronald.

Cowley's best hope of finding Nelson was a girlfriend of John Chase's, Sally Backman, who had spent time on the road with Chase, Nelson, and Helen, and who had a mutual dislike for Nelson. Sally had been arrested in San Francisco –

and she was talking. Her best lead was a vague story she told of visiting a town in Wisconsin where Nelson said that he planned to spend the winter. Agents spent days poring over maps with her, trying to identify the town, but it was no use. No matter how hard she tried, Sally could not remember the name of the town.

On October 23, Cowley had the young woman flown to Chicago in hopes that a tour of Northern Illinois might jog her memory. Charles Winstead and two agents drove her. They headed northwest out of Chicago, inspecting the towns of Crystal Lake, Harvard, and Woodstock, then crossed into Wisconsin to drive around Delavan and Walworth. At Elkhorn, Sally thought she recognized a tavern, but when Winstead took her inside, there was a lunch counter where she had remembered a bar.

Winstead, realizing that the "tour" could take forever, dropped by to see a deputy sheriff that he knew in Elkhorn. Winstead described the town that Sally remembered – it had an inn, two small lakes, and an iron bridge. He also described a man named "Eddie" that she recalled meeting. Without hesitation, the deputy identified the resort town of Lake Geneva, where a local character named Eddie Duffy ran errands for the Lake Como Inn.

The Lake Como Inn in Lake Geneva

They drove to Lake Geneva and it all came back to Sally. She recognized the town, pointed out a tavern where she had eaten breakfast, and then led Winstead to a lakeside cabin where she had met the man named Eddie. As luck would have it, she also spotted Eddie Duffy on the street an hour later, and knew it was the man she had met before.

Winstead returned to Lake Geneva on November 2 and confronted Duffy. He became "very nervous" and claimed that he knew nothing about Nelson. He admitted that he knew John Chase, but only as a guest at the Lake Como Inn. He insisted that the agents talk to the inn's owner, Hobart Hermanson. Duffy was just an errand boy, in charge of driving a beer truck.

On Sunday night, Cowley met with Hermanson in his Chicago office. Confronted with the possibility of an indictment for harboring Nelson, Hermanson admitted everything, confirming Nelson's visit to the inn as well as his plans to return to Lake Geneva for the winter. The next day, Cowley, along with Winstead and Agents Ed Hollis, drove to Lake Geneva to inspect the resort. Hermanson volunteered to let them stay in a nearby cottage, but Cowley chose the inn itself.

By the end of the week, Winstead and two agents were camped out in a second-floor bedroom.

If Nelson came back to Lake Geneva for the winter, they would be waiting for him.

After the news had spread about Dillinger on July 22, Nelson, Helen, and John Chase had fled Illinois and went to California. Over that summer, Nelson and Chase made several trips back and forth to the Midwest and, on one occasion, they were stopped for speeding in a small town. They paid the $5 fine at the local police station and were released. The automobile, which contained machine guns, rifles, and ammunition, was never searched.

By late fall, Nelson was in Nevada and Chase was in New York City. They met up again in Chicago in late November and on Monday, November 26, Nelson and Chase drove into the city. They left Helen on a street corner on the North Side. She said that she wanted to see a movie, but instead, she wandered into their old neighborhood. She walked past the homes of her siblings and her parents, hoping to see someone that she knew. She would have never knocked on their doors. She only wanted to peer into the windows of the people she loved.

While Helen wandered familiar streets, Nelson and Chase stole a new black Ford V-8 from a dealership. Afterward, they met with Fatso Negri and Clarey Lieder outside the city. Nelson wanted to put a new gang together, perhaps joining up with Alvin Karpis and the Barkers, if he could find them.

Later that evening, he picked up Helen on the North Side. They slept in the car that night and the next day, Tuesday, he had people to see in Wisconsin, after which he planned to return to Chicago and meet up with Jimmy Murray, who was still talking about the train robbery that he had pitched to Dillinger.

Around 2:00 p.m. on November 27, Agent Charles Winstead was in the upstairs bedroom of the Hermanson inn, just as he had been for the past three weeks. Cars came and went from the place all day, many of them stopping to check into the cottages that were nearby. Agent Jim Metcalfe was in the kitchen. They had sent a rookie agent named Colin McRae into town to pick up some groceries.

Winstead was looking out the window and saw a big Ford V-8 coming up the road. He hollered downstairs to Metcalfe to get ready, there was a car coming. Metcalfe wasn't concerned since, on most days, at least a dozen cars visited the house. He looked out the window. The car was coated with dust. It looked like the Hermansons' Ford. They had left on a trip the previous Saturday, and he assumed they were returning. He called up to Winstead and told him that it was okay; it was the Hermanson car.

Metcalfe walked out onto the porch to see if Mrs. Hermanson needed help unloading the car. The sun was shining on the windshield and neither Metcalfe nor Winstead could see inside. Squinting, Metcalfe later said that he could just make out a woman sitting in the front seat. She looked young. She was wearing a dark coat with a fur collar.

The driver of the car called out, asking if Hermanson was home.

"No, he isn't here," Metcalfe replied.

"Well, is Eddie here?"

Metcalfe said that he wasn't. He had gone into town to do some shopping, he told the driver.

The man in the car gave a friendly wave, thanked him, and started backing out to the road. Upstairs, Winstead grabbed his rifle and, though he couldn't see the man's face, aimed it at the driver's head. As the Ford drove away, he caught a glimpse of the driver. He was wearing sunglasses and a flat cap. "Who was that?" Winstead yelled down to Metcalfe.

Metcalfe didn't realize it until the car had driven out of sight. "That was Baby Face Nelson," he said.

He ran for the telephone.

In the Ford, Nelson pressed down on the accelerator. That had been a "G-man," he told Chase and Helen. They had been caught with their pants down. He had just driven into an ambush, but he was not unprepared. He had his .38 on his lap, and he had been prepared to shoot Metcalfe on the spot. Now on alert, he drove into Lake Geneva, hoping to find Eddie Duffy. Instead, Nelson was spotted by Agent McRae, who was returning to the Lake Como Inn with groceries. He quickly jotted down Nelson's license plate number.

Nelson nervously drove through town and then turned south. He had a feeling that trouble was coming. When he made it to the highway, he turned southeast toward the Chicago suburbs. If he could make it back to the city, they could disappear.

Cowley took a frantic telephone call from Lake Geneva at 2:45. Most of his men were out of the office, but Cowley called in two agents and told them to head for Wisconsin at once, watching for Nelson's car. He then took a call from Agent Bill Ryan, who had been manning a telephone tap with a rookie agent named Tom McDade. Cowley told the two of them to also head for Lake Geneva right away.

But Cowley knew that if the driver that had been spotted really was Nelson, then four men might not be enough. He grabbed Ed Hollis and the two of them would also head north. On his way out, he passed Purvis's office. He told him that Nelson had just left Lake Geneva.

"Let's get going," Purvis said, getting up from his desk.

"It won't be necessary," Cowley said. "Hollis and I are just going to cruise around and see if we can spot their car on the highway. When we get set, I'll phone you."

Purvis offered to call Washington, but Cowley told him not to bother since the information was so vague. Purvis called anyway, briefing one of Hoover's aides.

A half hour later, the first team of agents, Ryan and McDade, encountered Nelson's car near Fox River Grove, Illinois. McDade had been driving their Ford coupe as they passed through town, and Ryan told him to pull over so they could check Louis Cernocky's tavern. There was no sign of Nelson or his car, so they pulled out, headed back toward Wisconsin. Just as they were leaving Fox River Grove, a black Ford raced past, heading toward Chicago. Both agents spotted the plate – it was Nelson!

"Turn around!" Ryan yelled. He craned his neck to look at the passing Ford and spotted two men and a woman in the car. McDade eased into the median and completed a u-turn to follow the Ford.

Nelson spotted the move and slowed down. "What the hell is this?" he asked Chase, who was in the backseat with a powerful Browning Automatic Rifle in his lap. He also turned into the median and completed a u-turn of his own, pulling into the northbound lane.

As the two vehicles passed one another a second time, Nelson spun the wheel and, instead of running, started pursuing the Bureau agents. McDade wanted to stay ahead of them, but Ryan ordered him to slow down so that he could get a good look at them. He had his automatic gripped tightly in his hand. Nelson stayed a few hundred yards behind the Bureau car, going about 40 miles an hour. Both drivers closely watched the other car. Then, without warning, Nelson slammed his foot on the accelerator, and the big Ford shot forward. As he revved the engine, he grabbed Helen's shoulder and pushed her down to the floor of the car. A moment later, he was in the lane next to the Bureau car. He honked his horn. "Pull over!" Nelson shouted. McDade and Ryan glanced over and saw Chase pointing the automatic rifle at them. Ryan shouted at McDade to drive faster and McDade ducked and hit the gas pedal. The Bureau car surged ahead.

"Let 'em have it!" Nelson cried, but Chase hesitated; he didn't know who was in the car.

Agent Ryan didn't hesitate. He aimed his pistol at Nelson's car and opened fire, squeezing off shot after shot, the shells ejecting into McDade's face. Nelson, holding a pistol in one hand and steering with the other, fired back. Windows on both cars exploded. Glass flew everywhere and metal popped as bullets plowed into it. Chase still didn't fire.

"What the hell are you gonna do, just sit there?" Nelson screamed at him. "Can't you see they're shooting at us?"

As the Bureau car pulled ahead of them, Chase began firing the automatic rifle, but the heavy slugs missed the car. Ryan and McDade pulled ahead. Nelson couldn't catch up. The bullets fired by the feds had hit the engine and they were losing speed.

Meanwhile, McDade struggled to keep control of the racing car, which was now traveling at more than 75 miles per hour. They were rapidly overtaking a slow-moving milk truck, lumbering along in the lane ahead of them. As Ryan's automatic emptied, he reached for a second pistol and realized that Nelson's car had backed off. He told McDade, who had not had time to worry about the gangsters behind them. He swerved into the opposite lane to miss the milk truck and was horrified to see a westbound car hurtling towards them. He pushed the car ahead and managed to pass the truck, and swerve back into the right lane, narrowly avoiding a fatal collision.

Ryan continued to watch through the ragged glass of the back window as he saw Nelson maneuver around the milk truck, and then slow down to widen the gap between them. Suddenly, McDade missed a sharp turn in the road and their car bounced into a field and came to a stop. Both agents jumped out, guns in hand, and took cover behind the vehicle. However, Nelson's sedan never appeared.

Ryan and McDade were not aware that within moments of pulling away from Nelson, two more Bureau agents had joined the chase, once again turning Nelson into the one being pursued. At some point between the towns of Fox River Grove and Barrington, Sam Cowley and Herman Hollis encountered the high-speed gun battle that was taking place. Wondering why it was going in the wrong direction with the wrong car in pursuit, they turned around to try and catch up with Nelson from behind.

Nelson tried to pick up speed, but it was no use; his engine was failing. Cowley and Hollis got closer. Through the smoke that was churning from the damaged engine, Nelson saw that they were entering the northwest side of Barrington. The Bureau car continued to gain on them and then pulled alongside. Nelson had to make a desperate move. Ahead, along the north side of the highway, were three gas stations – a Standard, a Shell, and a Sinclair. On the opposite side of the highway, surrounded by a mostly open field, was a gravel road leading to Barrington's North Side Park. About 400 yards ahead, houses began to appear on both sides of the road. Thinking fast, Nelson suddenly swerved into the park entrance and hit the brakes, causing the Ford to slide to a stop. Hollis slammed on his brakes but the Bureau vehicle slid past the entrance in a long, shaking slide.

Nelson ordered the others out of the vehicle and lunged out of the driver's side door. He hurried around to the back of the car as Chase and Helen tumbled out of the passenger's door. He yelled at his wife to run, instructing her to get into the nearby field and lay flat on the ground. Helen sprinted through the tall grass between the road and the park's football field, dropping to her stomach as gunfire erupted.

The first shots came from Chase, who was crouched down at the front of the Ford. Steam from the damaged radiator slightly concealed his position and he used the distraction to open up on the two agents on the road. Seconds later, Nelson, standing at the rear of the sedan with a machine gun, also opened fire.

Hollis and Cowley's Hudson had screeched to a halt in the middle of the highway, about 120 feet away. Bullets tore into the vehicle as Cowley jumped out of the passenger side and took cover behind the vehicle. Hollis, shotgun in hand, scrambled out of the same door and hid behind the front bumper. For the next three minutes, a furious battle raged as bullets slammed into the two cars, kicked up clouds of dust, and bounced off the pavement of the road.

Cowley held a machine gun in his hands. A desk man for his entire career, the pudgy Mormon was the last man that Hoover would have wanted facing off against Nelson. Neither Cowley nor Hollis wore a bulletproof vest. Cowley complained that they were too heavy. Nor had Cowley ever bothered to qualify on the pistol range;

he was just too busy. In spite of that, Cowley was blazing away with the machine gun at Nelson, who returned fire.

Hidden in the weeds about 20 yards away from the Ford, Helen raised her head for one quick look as the shooting continued. She later said, "I saw Les jump and grab his side. I knew then that was the end."

At least six of Cowley's bullets struck Nelson in the stomach and chest, shredding his insides. He was jolted by the slugs, but, with adrenaline coursing through his body, he somehow continued firing at Cowley. Doubled over and clasping his side, he then ran to the running board of the car and exchanged weapons with Chase, firing the other bandit's gun as Chase reloaded his own. No words were spoken, according to Chase, who later swore that he didn't know his friend had been wounded.

With a fresh drum in Nelson's machine gun, he attempted to fire through the Ford's side window. Between shots, Chase heard him complain about his weapon jamming and he threw it aside. Nelson picked up a rifle from the backseat and moved to the rear of the vehicle. Chase assumed that he was going back to his original position, but soon discovered that Nelson had walked out into the open and was advancing on the Bureau agents and their Hudson.

Nelson charged at them, almost manically, firing at them and sweeping his weapon back and forth. Cowley suddenly abandoned his position and darted left to the south side of the highway, where he stumbled into the ditch. Rising to his knees, he attempted to shoot at Nelson, but his machine gun refused to fire. Nelson sent several slugs in his direction and Cowley was hit twice in the midsection. He sagged to the pavement, rolling into a ditch next to the car. A bulletproof vest likely would have stopped both rounds.

A second later, Hollis leaned out and fired his shotgun. The impact from the heavy weapon knocked the legs out from under Nelson. He fell to the ground, but managed get back up and kept on coming toward the agent. Nelson fired at Hollis, turned to fire several more shots at the downed Cowley, and then hammered the front of the Hudson.

As Nelson came closer, Hollis turned and tried to run. He ran toward a telephone pole on the north side of the road, located between the Standard and Shell stations. As he ran, he fired backward at Nelson, but then his gun jammed. As he neared the telephone pole, he dropped the shotgun and drew an automatic from inside his coat. Before he could fire, Nelson's next barrage of bullets caught him. Nelson kept coming at the agent, firing again and again as Hollis slumped against the wooden pole, which was now chewed up by stray bullets. He cried out, and then fell facedown onto the edge of the highway. One of the bullets from Nelson's gun struck Hollis in the center of the forehead.

Nelson staggered toward Hollis, badly wounded. Nelson stood over the agent for a moment, his weapon poised to fire more shots into the man on the ground, but then he lowered it, apparently satisfied that Hollis was dead. He limped across the road toward the agent's Hudson, dragging his left leg behind him and spattering blood on the pavement. He climbed behind the wheel of the car and pulled up behind the disabled Ford. He shouted for Helen and Chase gathered up

Bystanders point to the bullet holes in the cars involved in what became known as the "Battle of Barrington."

their weapons and trotted over to where Nelson was parked in the car. When he saw Chase, Nelson groaned, "Drop everything and get me to a priest."

Chase told him to wait a minute while he grabbed their cases from the other car, but Nelson told him to forget all of it. He tried to crawl over the passenger side, leaving a trail of gore on the seat. He told Chase, "You'll have to drive, I'm hit pretty hard."

Helen came running out of the field and climbed into the car. Chase hit the accelerator, pointing the vehicle back west toward Fox River Grove. Helen sat in back, next to her wounded husband, cradling his head in her arms. Nelson looked up at her, his eyes blurry and filled with pain. "I'm done for," he gasped.

The first witness to reach the bloody, steaming scene was William P. Gallagher, an Illinois State patrolman who happened to be selling tickets for an American Legion benefit at the nearby Shell filling station. Hearing the shots, Gallagher had taken a rifle from the station owner and fired at Nelson's fleeing car. As it drove away, the patrolman and another onlooker, who had stopped his own car when he encountered the battle, ran across the highway to Hollis. He was laying facedown next to the telephone pole – the back of his head had been blown off. Gallagher tried to speak to him. Hollis, who would be dead in a matter of minutes, managed only a gasp.

Gallagher hurried over to Cowley, who lay in the ditch with his feet on the pavement, and blood covering the right side of his face. There appeared to be a gunshot wound next to his eye. "Don't shoot... government officer," he groaned in a whisper. Gallagher crouched down next to him.

"Was Hollis hurt?" he asked quietly.

Gallagher nodded.

"Look after him first," Cowley said. He told Gallagher to call the Chicago office and report what had occurred. He also asked the patrolman to try and reach his wife and tell her that he had been called out of town and wouldn't make it home for supper.

By this time, traffic was backing up along the highway and a crowd was starting to form around the horrific scene. Gallagher flagged down a car and loaded Hollis inside, directing the driver to Barrington Central Hospital. Hollis died on the way. Gallagher had lifted a rosary from the agent's pocket and called a priest. As Hollis was dying in the back of a stranger's car, his wife, Genevieve, and their young son were waiting in the lobby of the Bankers Building. They had taken a moment from a downtown shopping trip to surprise him at the end of his workday. An agent had to break the tragic news to her.

While this was happening, Agents Ryan and McDade were still lying in a field further down Highway 12. They knew nothing of what had occurred. At 4:15, Ryan went to a payphone and called the office to report the running battle on the highway that they had participated in. Five minutes later, Purvis was on the phone with Hoover when the police chief in the nearby town of Stamford called with the news that Hollis was dead and Cowley had been shot.

Purvis left immediately for the hospital in Elgin, where Cowley had been taken. He arrived just as Cowley was being taken into surgery. Cowley asked a doctor whether he was going to die. Then he saw Purvis standing nearby. Whatever tension remained between the two men vanished. "Hello, Melvin, I'm glad you're here," Cowley whispered.

Purvis gripped the other man's hand. "Rest quiet and you will be all right," he said.

"Do you have any doubt about that?"

"No," Purvis assured him.

"I emptied my gun at them," Cowley said.

"Who were they?"

"Nelson and Chase."

Chase drove as fast as he could along the unfamiliar road with no idea of where to go. Nelson was slumped against the passenger door, drawing deep breaths, while Helen wept and continued to hold his sagging body. Nelson did the best he could to direct his friend to safety. Three miles west of Barrington, he told him to turn right on Kelsey Road, then right again on Route 22. Heading east again, they passed two miles north of Barrington, heading toward Lake Zurich. When not in town, Chase kept the gas pedal mashed to the floor and within a half hour, they reached Highland Park. Nelson was fading fast, but he instructed Chase to head south on Skokie Road. Entering Wilmette, they drove to 1155 Mohawk Road, a home that belonged to the sister of a Father Phillip Coughlan, a Catholic priest who had grown up on Chicago's West Side and who had close ties to a number of underworld figures, including Nelson.

Late in the afternoon, the family maid notified Father Coughlan that there was a young woman knocking on the back-door window, asking to see him. The priest went to the kitchen and found Helen Gillis in the doorway. She urgently told him that her husband had been shot and needed his help. Coughlan grabbed his coat and hat and followed her. Chase had pulled into the garage and helped Nelson get out, hoping to bring his wounded friend into the house. Nelson muttered a faint greeting when the priest arrived. He was leaning against the back of the car, his face white and bloodless. He had been shot 17 times.

Helen begged the priest to bring Nelson inside, but Coughlan refused because it was his sister's house. Instead, he offered to lead them to a safe location. Helen asked that they all go in the same car, but again, the priest refused. The bullet-riddled Hudson could not remain in his sister's garage. Coughlan helped to ease Nelson into the passenger seat of the Hudson. Once the bandit was situated, the priest noticed a warm stickiness on his right hand. He looked down to see it was covered with blood.

Father Coughlan got into his Ford coupe and backed out into the street. With the Hudson following, he turned north on Ashland Avenue, then west on Skokie Road. Two blocks later, he noticed the Hudson do a quick u-turn and speed off in the opposite direction. He turned around and tried to catch up with them, but he lost the vehicle in traffic near Lake Street. He later confessed that he was relieved, but also saddened. He realized that Nelson must have thought he was leading them into a trap.

Coughlan was right. Even in his weakened state, Nelson was suspicious about the way that the priest was acting, mistaking his confusion about where to safely hide the injured outlaw for possible betrayal. As they drove, he instructed Chase to lose him, and they drove off with an alternate destination in mind. Nelson feebly told Chase where and when to turn, traveling south and keeping mostly to residential streets as they left Wilmette and entered Winnetka, then Niles Center (which is now Skokie). At one point, Nelson appeared to pass out and Chase turned into an alley to wait for him to wake up. A minute or so later, Nelson regained consciousness and urged his friend to keep driving.

When Father Coughlan lost sight of the Hudson, he drove back to his sister's house and called the Bureau office at 6:15. Agents were at his home within the hour.

On Hoover's orders, agents raided all of Nelson's gangland contacts that night, including Louis Cernocky's roadhouse, Clarey Lieder's garage and home, Jimmy Murray's house and the Rain-Bo Inn, the home of Nelson's sister on South Marshfield Avenue, and the cottage in Wauconda where Nelson had been hiding out back in May. There was no sign of Nelson.

As the raids were going on, Cowley was wheeled out of surgery. Doctors said that his condition was serious, but he had a chance to pull through if infection didn't set in. Or at least that's what Hoover told Cowley's brother, Joe. Privately, he told an aide that the surgeons gave the agent a 1-in-25 chance of making it through the night.

Not surprisingly, as Cowley lay dying, Hoover was preoccupied with publicity. It was Purvis – again. He had remained at the hospital and had actually given an interview to a *Chicago American* reporter as they watched over an unconscious Cowley in a hospital bed, his wife, Lavon, and her two little boys next to her. "If it's the last thing I do, I'll get Baby Face Nelson – dead or alive," Purvis had dramatically whispered. "Nelson ought to know he hasn't a chance at eventual escape. We aren't particular whether we get him alive or dead."

Hoover was beside himself. He tried to find anyone to rid him of Purvis. His deputies, Hugh Clegg and Pop Nathan, were delivering speeches in Pittsburgh and Tucson, respectively, and Hoover ordered both of them to Chicago. He wanted Purvis out of the hospital and away from the reporters. He even told them to "impress upon Mr. Purvis the necessity of staying away from the office and from any public places." When Clegg suggested that Purvis work in a back room at the Chicago office, Hoover refused even that. Within days, news leaked to the papers that Purvis "is incapacitated by overwork and is on sick leave. Insiders do not expect him to return to the command of the Chicago office."

Cowley's conditioned worsened during the night. In the early morning hours, an agent overheard a doctor say that he wouldn't last until dawn. Purvis, against orders, returned to the hospital. He was there when Cowley died at 2:17 a.m. on November 28. His wife collapsed in tears. Doctors gave her a sedative.

On Sixteenth Street, back in Wilmette, Nelson told Chase to slow down. Pointing to a narrow alley that ran behind Walnut Street, he told him to make the turn. Chase drove down the alley to a red two-car garage at the rear of a light gray stucco cottage that faced Walnut Street. The address of the cottage was 1627 Walnut Street. Chase pulled into the garage and asked Nelson who lived there. Nelson mumbled, "Friends."

Chase went to the front door and knocked and a tall, dark-complexioned man in his late 30's answered. Chase told him that someone outside needed him and the man accompanied him back to the garage. When the man saw Nelson in the car, Chase knew that he instantly recognized him. The two men, with Helen following, carried Nelson into the house. They entered through a side door and passed through the kitchen. Along the way, Chase glimpsed an older man and a young woman who appeared frightened at the sight of the bloody and wounded bandit. They went into a small bedroom, where they placed Nelson on a large iron bed. The other man walked out, leaving Chase and Helen to take care of Nelson. Helen later recounted, "All three of us knew Les was dying, but there was nothing we could do."

They did their best to make him comfortable and stop the bleeding. Helen was given scissors and other supplies and she cut the bloody clothing from her husband's body. She stuffed cotton into the bullet hole in his stomach and the gaping exit wound in his back, and then covered both wounds by wrapping him with long strips of cloth that were torn from a bed sheet. Helen cleaned his buckshot-spattered legs, and then covered him with a blanket when he told her that he was cold.

Nelson sighed. He felt better, he told his wife and friends, the pain was gone and now he just felt numb all over. Helen held onto his hand and waited for the end to come.

About an hour after Nelson, Helen, and Chase had arrived at the house on Walnut Street, the man who had helped carry the bank robber inside came and told Chase that he needed to move the damaged government vehicle. Chase agreed, but Nelson begged him not to leave. Minutes later, the man came back again and reiterated that the car had to be moved. Nelson again appealed to his friend to stay and Chase promised to stay, but noticing that Nelson was slipping in and out of consciousness, he made the decision to slip away for a few minutes. Before long, Chase quietly left the bedside, exited through the side door, and drove away. He later insisted that he had planned to return after he ditched the car, but being unfamiliar with the area, he soon became lost. Attempting to head south into Chicago, he ended up going north and found himself back in Winnetka. When the Hudson ran out of gas, he abandoned it near some railroad tracks. This forced him to make another decision. Knowing there was nothing he could do to help his friend, he realized that he needed to try and get away. Chase caught a train to Chicago and disappeared.

Helen was left alone with her dying husband. Shortly after Chase departed, Nelson seemed to realize that he had little time left. He asked her to say goodbye to their family and when he began to talk about their children, he cried a little bit. Finally, he gasped out his final words, "It's getting dark, Helen. I can't see you anymore."

Lester Gillis's eyes glazed over and his breathing became shallow and raspy, and then stopped altogether. The infamous "Baby Face Nelson" was dead.

Rain fell on the Walnut Street cottage until the early morning hours. Helen Gillis sat with her husband's corpse for hours, and then the man who had helped them came into the room and told her that the body needed to be moved. Helen wanted to take her husband to an undertaker's, but she knew it was impossible. The man told her that he would find a place where the body could be left. He promised to call an undertaker later on.

After wrapping the body in an imitation Indian blanket, Helen and the man carried it outside and placed it in the backseat of an Oldsmobile that was parked in the driveway. She climbed in next to her husband, cradling him in her arms as the man drove. They drove deeper into Niles Center and at the southwest corner of Niles (now Conrad) and Long Avenues, they reached St. Paul's Cemetery. The driver pulled over to the curb and they wrestled the body from the car. Nelson's naked, bloody corpse was placed on the grass. Helen tucked the blanket around him, hoping that he would be comfortable because Lester "always hated the cold."

A few blocks away, just south of Howard Avenue, Helen dropped Nelson's bloodstained clothing out the window. The drive continued south until they reached Chicago's North Side. The man asked her if this was a suitable spot for her to be let out and she said that it was, even though she had no idea where she was or where she should go. Before she stepped out of the car, she gave the driver the name of a mortician who had handled the funerals of her mother and her sister. He promised to call and notify the undertaker where to find Nelson's body and then drove away.

Helen wandered the unfamiliar streets for over an hour. Finally, around 5:00 a.m., she hailed a cab and slipped into the warm backseat. The driver asked her where she wanted to go and she just told him to drive on.

At 6:45 a.m. the bullet-riddled Hudson was discovered by a Winnetka milkman, who notified a local patrolman. Federal agents arrived at the scene within an hour and found bullet holes and plenty of blood.

At 7:30 a.m., Philip Sadowski, the owner of a funeral home on North Hermitage Avenue, received a telephone call from a man with a "rough voice" who informed him that the body of a man named Gillis was lying in a graveyard in Niles Center, a block away from Harms Road. Sadowski told him that he was unable to retrieve the body. He was in the midst of preparing for a funeral and besides, he added, morticians don't recover bodies, he would have to notify the coroner to do that. The man on the other end of the line told him to notify anyone he wanted to, but that he wanted him to handle the arrangements.

Sadowski reported the anonymous call to the Chicago Coroner's Office and was advised to contact the Niles Center Police. Acting on the undertaker's information, Captain Axel Stolberg and a patrolman went out to the area to look around. Sadowski, however, had failed to mention the name of cemetery and the body was not found. The pair returned to the police station, only to hear about a call that had just come in from someone who found bloody clothing near where the officers had just been searching.

News of the discovery was passed on to federal agents who had spent the morning searching Winnetka. Four agents arrived to help Captain Stolberg search the area again. It was almost noon when FBI agent Sam McKee signaled that he had found the remains of Baby Face Nelson.

Nelson's body lay in the grass, with his head resting on the curb. He was naked, except for the cloth strips that had been wrapped about his waist and he was drenched with blood. His right arm was across his chest and his left hand was frozen into a claw just above the wound in his stomach. His feet were crossed and the agents realized that he had been dead for a while because rigor mortis had set in. The body was picked up, carried to a car, and then driven to the mortuary for an official identification. Fingerprints confirmed that the dead man was Lester Gillis, a.k.a. Baby Face Nelson.

The body was photographed and examined. By mid-afternoon, news of Nelson's death was sweeping the city. The body was transported to the Cook County Morgue and placed on a slab for public display. More than 2,000 morbid curiosity-seekers filed past the dead bank robber during the hours that followed.

The bloodiest day in the Bureau's brief history was followed by two somber funerals. Herman "Ed" Hollis was buried in his hometown of Des Moines, Iowa,

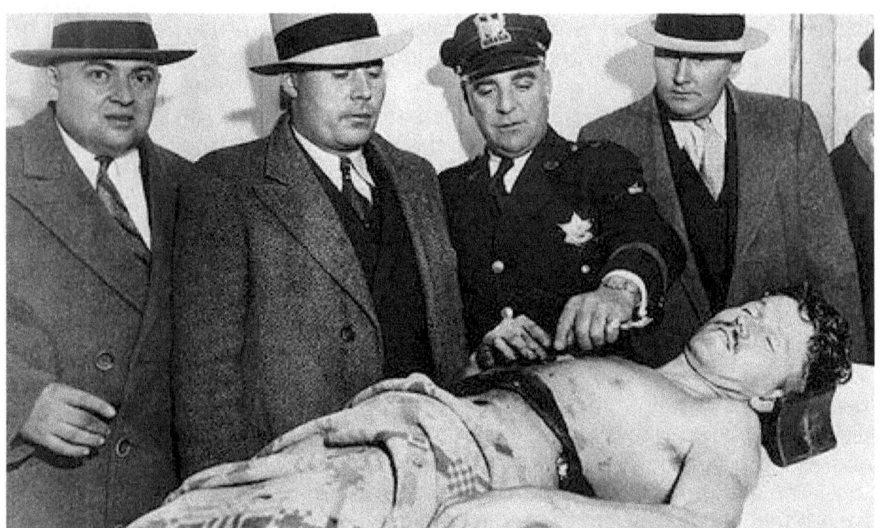

Nelson's body was placed on display at the Cook County Morgue. Thousands filed past to get one last look at the outlaw.

and Sam Cowley, in Salt Lake City. Cowley's body lay in state beneath the capitol rotunda while thousands filed past in silence.

Pop Nathan gave Cowley's eulogy, calling him a "martyred hero." He went on to say, "We of the division are very proud of him. As generations of new agents come into our service they will be told of the life and death of Sam Cowley. He will become a tradition. He will have attained his earthly immortality."

Nathan was true to his word. For decades to come, Hoover pointed to Cowley as the ultimate FBI man, quiet, hardworking, and dedicated. He remains the most senior agent ever killed in the line of duty.

But for all his "earthly immortality," he never achieved the same fame as John Dillinger.

Once Nelson was confirmed dead, the massive manhunt for the killers of Agents Cowley and Hollis shifted to his two companions at what became known as the "Battle of Barrington" – John Chase and Helen Gillis.

With little cash and no car, Chase had checked into the Garfield Arms, a downtown hotel, and hid out in his room, only venturing out a couple of times to buy newspapers. Chase soon devised a clever way to get out of the city by answering a newspaper ad looking for drivers to deliver automobiles to the west coast. Using the name Elmer Rockwood, he applied and was accepted. He received a paycheck for driving a Studebaker to Seattle, and when he arrived there, he disappeared once again.

The search for Helen got the most publicity. When Hoover ordered his agents to "find the woman and give her no quarter," the press interpreted this to mean that Helen was to be shot on sight. Some stories even suggested that she had replaced her husband as "Public Enemy Number One." Even worse, a United Press story labeled Helen as "the Tiger Woman" and portrayed her as a "ruthless gun moll of the Bonnie Parker type, leading her cohorts in bank raids and battles with officers of the law." She was the brains of the gang, they claimed, pushing her husband into a life of crime. The account also claimed that during the gunfight in Barrington, Helen had been loading guns for Nelson and Chase.

Of course, nothing could be further from the truth, but even the Bureau started to believe the newspapers. One agent was quoted as saying, "I'd hate to shoot a woman but I'm not following Cowley and Hollis because of ideas over a woman like that." Hugh Clegg echoed the sentiments when reporters asked him what the government's procedures were in apprehending Helen. He told the newsmen, "From now on, mercy goes by the boards."

On Thanksgiving morning, November 29, Helen Gillis – America's most wanted "outlaw" and the so-called "Tiger Woman – resumed wandering around the streets of Chicago. She had spent most of the night sleeping in the doorway of an abandoned building. She eventually wandered into her old neighborhood, where she watched her father, from a safe distance, as he left for work with a small crowd of people around him. The ones that were not reporters were Bureau agents, waiting for Helen to show up. Asked if he had a statement for his daughter, Vincent Warwick made a plea that was published the following day: "Come home. Surrender and give up alive or you'll be mowed down by machine guns. Remember your babies."

Helen moved on and spent the rest of the day around Humboldt Park. She considered calling her sister-in-law, Julie, but was certain that her telephone was tapped. As evening approached, she dreaded the idea of spending another night on the streets. Near Lafayette School, she stopped a young girl and paid her a dollar to deliver a note to Julie's apartment.

At that moment, Julie's husband, Bob Fitzsimmons was on the phone, as he had been most of the day. This time, he was speaking with Agent McKee, who had called to ask about the time and place of Nelson's funeral. According to Helen's wishes, the body had been turned over to Sadowski's funeral home, but no arrangements had been set. McKee urged Fitzsimmons to try and get Helen to turn herself in. Bob agreed to do his best to get the family to contact her. If they were successful, he asked that agents take her into custody in a quiet manner, avoiding publicity if possible.

Just minutes after Fitzsimmons hung up, the girl arrived with Helen's note. Bob and Julie immediately left the house and when they were certain they were not being followed, they went to the school and found Helen sitting in the dark on the front steps. For the next hour, they drove around as Helen tearfully told them of everything that had taken place. She said that she would have surrendered sooner but she was afraid that she might be shot. She added that she was hopeful that a deal could be arranged with the Bureau that would allow her to attend Nelson's funeral.

At 10:25 p.m., Fitzsimmons called the Bureau and was put in touch with Agent Virgil Peterson. He passed on the wish that Helen wanted to surrender, but also asked if she could be allowed to attend her husband's funeral. Peterson was in no mood to bargain. He told Bob that no promises could be made and demanded that Helen immediately turn herself in. It would be in her best interests, he emphasized, if she surrendered. After Helen agreed, Fitzsimmons told him that they would meet agents at the southwest corner of Jackson Boulevard and Halsted Street.

A short time later, Helen was taken into custody. The press was not notified of the arrangement. At the Bankers Building, Helen was surrounded by six agents and hurried into the building through a rear entrance. After checking to be sure that no newsmen were present, she was taken to the nineteenth floor, led along a little-used passage that cut through a storage room, and placed in the main office.

For the next five days, Helen's presence in the building was kept secret while she was being interrogated by the Bureau. Hoover stressed that she must be made to talk and that Earl Connelly, who had stepped into the role of head of the Chicago office after Cowley's death, should question her constantly so that she would be unable to sleep. But Connelly was not cruel. In fact, Helen later stated that he was very nice and treated her quite well.

Helen did talk, however. She reluctantly shared an abundance of information while carefully avoiding the mention of any crucial names. Many of Nelson's associates were merely "friends of Les's," whose names she claimed to not know or could not recall. Their companion at Barrington, Helen said, was "a fellow named George."

Helen spoke of her entire history with Nelson, but agents were most interested in the gangster's final hours. They were determined to know where he had gone to die and who had helped him in his final hours.

Helen was evasive at first, insisting that Les had been conscious and had directed "George" during the entire trip. Nelson guided him to a house that she had never been to before, but she described it when pressed for details. Finally, she was taken in a car and forced to lead them, block-by-block, then turn-by-turn, to Wilmette and eventually to Walnut Street. The bungalow she took them to was just as she had described it in the Bureau office.

An immediate and rather extensive investigation was started. With the cooperation of neighbors, agents began an around-the-clock surveillance of the cottage at 1627 Walnut Street. Over the next several weeks, the agents noted the coming and going of the occupants and their visitors. They spoke to neighbors, checked license numbers, consulted public records, and even got the local postman involved. According to what they learned, the occupants of the house were Raymond J. Henderson, an unemployed truck driver who was currently receiving relief checks; his wife, Marie; a son, age 14; and a daughter, age 12. The Hendersons had a questionable reputation with the local police – but this was not the most interesting discovery the agents made.

According to the postman, several different individuals used the mailing address of the house and, from time to time, actually lived there. The part-time residents included Guy McDonald, a known hood and one-time business associate of Jimmy Murray. McDonald often vanished and then returned to the house and, lately, he had been back around again. He was often seen at the house and neighborhood gossip claimed that Mrs. Henderson was heard bragging about the fact that she was sleeping with McDonald.

The Hendersons and their houseguests were eventually brought in and questioned, and all of them adamantly denied knowing Nelson and swore that he had not come to their house on the day of his death, or at any other time. And there, the Bureau's probe into the house at 1627 Walnut Street unexpectedly ended. The fact that no arrests were made and no charges filed was likely because of lack of evidence. But this hardly explains the abrupt closing of the case, especially since Hoover's direct orders to the agents in Chicago were to uncover the identities of everyone involved and have them prosecuted.

Today, the circumstances surrounding Nelson's death, and exactly who was present, remain an intriguing and unsolved mystery. Few details were reported in the usually obsessive press and the Bureau never publicly revealed where Nelson died or charged those who offered him shelter. Bureau files still remain strangely silent concerning the investigation that took place.

The only clue in this seemingly odd decision not to prosecute was found in a document that was filed four years later, in 1937. It contained a statement from a neighbor, who told agents that the woman still living in the house said it belonged to someone closely connected to the FBI, probably as an informant, who had also been supplying Nelson with inside information about the movements of law enforcement officials. Nelson, the neighbor said, had decided the Walnut Street house would be the last place that federal agents would think to look for him – hiding with one of their own.

Although the amount of information offered in the report is limited, it does allow speculation that the Bureau, upon discovering where Nelson died, decided to let the matter go rather than reveal that he had spent his last hours in the care of someone connected with the agency. Public disclosure of this would have proven embarrassing and so the whole thing was covered up. Who the informant may have been remains unknown to this day. The person's identity, and his or her relationship with the Bureau, was concealed by blotting out the name on the existing records.

No further information ever appeared and either the investigating agents never wanted to solve the mystery of Nelson's death – or they already knew what happened.

On December 4, word finally leaked to the press that Helen Gillis had been in federal custody since Thanksgiving night. No details were given about her surrender, only that she had been "cooperating" under questioning. The Bureau wanted to hold her longer for further interrogation, but once word got out, they were forced to proceed with the only legal recourse that was available.

On December 6, Helen was delivered to the Dane County Jail in Madison, Wisconsin, where she was taken after the raid on Little Bohemia. The next morning, she was brought to the judge's chambers and he asked her why she had violated her probation. She could only tell him, "I knew Les didn't have long to live, and I wanted to be with him as long as I could."

More than 150 spectators jammed the courtroom for her hearing. Looking small and frail, Helen admitted that she had violated her probation. Her probation was revoked and she was taken immediately to serve her sentence of a year and a day at the Women's Correctional Farm at Milan, Michigan.

In December, the authorities were still looking for John Chase. On December 26, he hitchhiked to Mount Shasta and visited a fish hatchery where he had worked five years before. He told a foreman that he was broke and borrowed a few dollars. That same foreman called the police after Chase left and said that the fugitive had stated that he was staying at the Park Hotel. When Police Chief Al Roberts and a deputy sheriff arrived at the hotel, they discovered their suspect had just left. A few blocks away, they spotted Chase walking along the street and quietly arrested him.

Chase was turned over to federal agents, who took him to San Francisco for several days of questioning. He admitted that he had been Nelson's friend and had traveled with him for nearly a year, but he denied taking part in any bank robberies or gun fights – except for the Battle of Barrington, in which he insisted he had only fired in self-defense and had not been responsible for the murder of either of the federal agents.

Chase was taken by train to Chicago on New Year's Eve, where he was the first person to be tried under the law that made it a federal crime to murder a federal agent in the performance of his duties. Chase's trial began on March 18, 1935. One week later, the jury found him guilty of murdering Sam Cowley, but recommended leniency. He was sentenced to life imprisonment on Alcatraz.

Chase was a model prisoner on "The Rock," well-liked by other inmates and the staff. During his time there, the only hint of trouble occurred in 1937 when prison officials suspected him of conspiring with two inmates who attempted to escape. As it turned out, the inmates had befriended Chase to take advantage of his knowledge of the Bay area. Chase was happy to give them information, but he never planned to take part in the escape.

Over the years, he developed a passion for painting and was regarded by many as an accomplished artist. He also became close friends with the prison chaplain, who obtained painting materials for Chase by selling some of his work in San Francisco.

In 1955, Chase became eligible for parole and the chaplain became his strongest advocate, insisting that Chase was a changed man who could be a useful part of society. Hoover heard of the chaplain's campaign on Chase's behalf and immediately started to work against him, ensuring that Chase remained on Alcatraz. At the bottom of a memo, he wrote, "Watch closely and endeavor to thwart efforts of this priest who should be attending to his own business instead of trying to turn loose on society such mad dogs."

Two years later, Hoover was stunned to learn that one of his former agents had supported Chase's parole. Tom McDade, one of the men who had been shot at by Chase on the Northwest Highway, wrote the Alcatraz chaplain saying that he had no objection to Chase's release. Hoover branded McDade, who was already retired, a traitor to the Bureau.

In September 1954, Chase was transferred to Leavenworth, and seven months later, received his first parole hearing. He discovered that federal prosecutors, prodded by Hoover, were ready to indict him for the murder of Ed Hollis if he were set free. Hoover had used FBI agents to track down a dozen witnesses against Chase, including a feeble Father Coughlan, who was living out his final days in a retirement home in Jasper, Indiana. Chase filed a petition in federal court charging that the government had intentionally withheld the 22-year-old murder charge in order to block his application for parole at this time. A judge ruled to dismiss the indictment, stating that the idea of prosecuting a man on a charge that had been gathering dust for two decades "shocks the imagination and the conscience."

In spite of the federal judge's statements, Hoover continued to write letters and make calls to the parole board in protest. Finally, on October 31, 1966, Chase was released. He moved to Palo Alto, California, where he lived a quiet life, working as a custodian and performing odd jobs until his death in October 1973 from colon cancer.

Despite being a model prisoner while behind bars, Helen Gillis served almost the entire year of her sentence. On December 6, 1935, federal agents escorted her to San Francisco, where she was arraigned on charges of harboring her late husband, and placed in a cell to await trial.

Assistant U.S. Attorney R.B. McMillan, who was supposed to prosecute Helen, wrote a letter to the attorney general stating that the 22-year-old widow was clearly no threat to society and appeared so pathetic that further prosecution seemed pointless. Hoover received a copy of the letter and was, of course, enraged. He insisted that the wife of Baby Face Nelson belonged in prison.

Helen appeared in court on December 13. The young woman who had married Lester Gillis seven years earlier, and who had been the constant companion of Baby Face Nelson, quietly pleaded guilty and applied for probation. Her attorney stated that she was only guilty of being a faithful wife to a misguided husband, adding that she had been punished enough. Prosecutor McMillan (likely to Hoover's chagrin) added his recommendation to her plea for probation, citing her record of excellent behavior over her past year in federal custody. Finally, the judge declared, "I believe you've been punished enough. I want you to lead a good life and be a good mother to your children."

Helen was ordered to serve one year's probation and finally, she was free.

She gave very few interviews in the years that followed, but on one occasion, she summed up her life with Nelson. "I loved Les. When you love a guy, you love him. That's all there is to it. If I had my life to live over again, I'd do just as I did. I'd stick to my husband any time, any place, no matter what he did."

Helen grieved, and then she got on with her life. In 1937, she returned to Chicago with her children and spent the next 50 years staying away from publicity. Her children married and moved away, Ronald to LaFox, Illinois, and Darlene to southern Wisconsin. Helen visited them frequently and in her last years, she lived with Ronald. She never remarried.

In late June 1987, she suffered a cerebral hemorrhage, and died one week later, on July 3, in a hospital in St. Charles. Her last wish was to be buried next to her husband in the Gillis family plot at St. Joseph's Cemetery in River Grove.

All that was left now were Alvin Karpis and the Barkers. They were the final remnants of the public enemies and the last survivors of Hoover's "war on crime."

While Karpis was skating all over the country, and even to Cuba, staying one step ahead of the Bureau, the Barkers bounced to Cleveland, where they met up with Karpis for a brief time to discuss a job. Dock Barker was back in Chicago in early January 1935.

Earl Connelly had received a tip and Bureau agents began staking out two apartment buildings on Pine Grove Avenue. By January 8, they had been watching them for a week. The night before, "Mr. Esser," the man they suspected was Dock Barker, had returned to the nearby Surf Lane Apartments. Two couples lived in the other apartment next door. The agents suspected that one of them was Barker's pal, Russell Gibson. The other man, tall and thin, they had not been able to identify. An hour earlier, they had spotted one of the women taking her little dog into the alley. A little after that, they had seen the thin man on the back porch in his bathrobe.

Connelly himself was at the stakeout that night. He studied the area and saw that the apartment had a single rear entrance, up a flight of wooden steps from the backyard. Below the stairs was a four-foot fence that fronted the alley. Along the walls of the surrounding apartment building and garages, he could station at least 20 agents. He was satisfied, and if all four occupants were inside the apartment at nightfall, they would raid the building. After that, they would hit the Surf Lane address.

Agents began gathering around 6:30 p.m. It was a mild January night and agents were lingering at spots all around the building. Connelly had left orders for everyone to remain in place unless the man they believed was Dock Barker attempted to leave.

Jerry Campbell, the marksman that Hoover had hired away from the Oklahoma City Police Department, was sitting in a car outside of Surf Lane with a rookie agent named Alexander Muzzey when they saw Dock Barker and a woman emerge from the apartment's courtyard and start walking toward them. Campbell reacted immediately. Tucking his machine gun under his overcoat, he stepped from the car. Muzzey got out, too. As the couple strolled onto the sidewalk and turned west, the agents fell in behind them, several paces behind.

Muzzey asked if they were going to take them and Campbell replied that they were.

They walked a little further down the street. Barker glanced back over his shoulder, but the woman kept walking. When Barker turned around once again, Campbell took out his machine gun. Muzzey removed the pistol from his holster. They could see other agents starting to move toward them, including several who were ahead of the couple on the street. At Campbell's signal, Muzzey called out, "Stick 'em up! Federal agents!" At the same time, three agents in front of the couple also drew their guns.

Barker froze. He began to raise his hands, then wheeled around and stepped between two parked cars into the street. He had barely started to run when he slipped on a patch of ice, pitched forward, and fell face down in the muddy show that clogged the gutter. The agents were on him within seconds. Jerry Campbell pulled Barker to his feet while another agent locked the handcuffs into place. A couple of the other agents took the woman into custody.

One of the agents asked Barker his name. "You know who I am," he laughed.

As they began to haul Barker toward their cars, he sighed. "This is a hell of a time to be caught without a gun," he sighed.

Barker had been taken without incident, but the agents were still watching the occupants of the other apartment. They believed one of the men could be Barker's friend, Gibson, but they suspected the other was Alvin Karpis. The people in the apartment had not been seen since Barker had been arrested. Finally, around 11:00 p.m., agents saw a man stroll down the back alley. He disappeared behind the building and then a moment later, the kitchen light clicked on. At the same time, agents saw the tall man and the two women walk up the front sidewalk and into the apartment building's lobby.

Connelly, stationed with 10 agents next door, walked out of the building. He walked over to a waiting car and told the four men inside to go around to the back alley and reinforce the agents already there. He then took a moment to arrange other men in front of the building. When he was satisfied, he took three agents into the lobby. There was no doorman. The apartment was up a flight of stairs and down a hallway. Standing in the lobby, Connelly pressed the apartment's call button.

"Hello?" a woman's voice answered.

"Is Mr. Bolton in?" Connelly asked. It was the name on the car registration that belonged to one of the suspects. The woman paused, and then said that "Bolton" would be back at the end of the week. Connelly then identified himself as an agent of the U.S. Department of Justice. He added, "The building is completely surrounded. All of you come downstairs, one at a time, with your hands up, and no one will get hurt."

Connelly looked over at Agents Sam McKee and Ralph Brown, who were holding machine guns at the foot of the stairs. Another agent drew his service revolver. There was no response from the woman upstairs. Connelly pressed the call button again and gave them another warning. Again, there was no response. The agents exchanged glances. A minute ticked by, then two.

Finally, Connelly leaned on the button one last time. "All persons occupying the apartment come down immediately. Do not attempt to escape through the rear. The apartment building is completely surrounded, and anyone attempting to escape will be killed."

In a matter of seconds, a woman shouted down the stairs. "We're coming down!" she cried. Her name was Clara Gibson and she was married to Russell Gibson, a friend of Dock Barker. She walked down the stairs to the lobby, carrying a little brown dog. Behind her was another woman, the wife of a man named Willie Harrison. Connelly ordered both women to lie down on the lobby floor.

A few moments later, the tall, thin man that had been observed by agents walked down the stairs with his hands in the air. It was not Alvin Karpis. His name was Byron Bolton and he has his own underworld pedigree in Chicago, even having been rumored to have had a hand in the St. Valentine's Day Massacre

Byron Bolton, who freely talked to the feds and spilled details on everything from Barker gang operations to the St. Valentine's Day Massacre

in 1929. But Bolton was most infamously known as the sidekick of "Shotgun George" Ziegler, whose real name was Samuel Goetz. He was a bootlegger and bank robber who later became associated with Karpis and the Barkers. He was involved in several bank jobs, as well as the Bremer kidnapping. Ziegler was shot outside a Cicero restaurant, the Minerva, on March 20, 1934, and he later died from his wounds. Alvin Karpis believed that Outfit boss Frank Nitti had ordered Ziegler's murder. The Barkers, along with Dillinger, Nelson, and others, had been warned about keeping the "heat" out of Chicago and Ziegler had paid the price.

Bolton was also ordered to lay down on the lobby floor and Connelly asked the trio if there was anyone else in the apartment. Clara Gibson told him that her husband was still upstairs. Just moments after she said this, gunshots rang out behind the building. "Oh no," she wailed, "They've shot my husband!"

While Connelly and the others were accepting surrenders in the lobby, the dozen agents arrayed behind the apartment were crouching in the darkness. Closest to the backdoor was Doc White and Agent Al Barber. Rookie agent Jack Welles was peeking out from behind a garage on the far side of the alley. He was about 40 feet from the kitchen window. At 11:30, he heard a woman's voice, apparently talking to someone in the lobby.

As the woman spoke, Welles saw a second woman look out between the kitchen blinds. He carefully aimed his service revolver at her head. The woman disappeared. A second later, a man attempted to open the window. Welles now put the man's head in his sights. He gave up after a few tries, then moved to a second window, beside the back door. He tried to raise it and failed. The kitchen light went off, plunging the back porch into darkness. The agents continued to watch. There was the sound of a door closing, and then came what one of the agents later called "soft noises" on the back stairs. In the darkness, Agents White and Barber saw the outline of a man carefully descending the steps. When he reached the bottom, White saw the rifle in his hands.

"Stop!" White yelled at him.

The man raised the gun and fired. The bullet slammed into the fence in front of the two agents and ricocheted into a brick wall. White fired, six shots in all, and the man in the shadows also fired several times. Agent Barber raised his gas gun and fired a shell into the apartment window. Tear gas hissed inside. The agents heard what sounded like a body thumping onto the pavement. A second later, another group of agents that were

Barker gang member, Russell Gibson

running along the side of the building saw a man in silhouette, staggering into an adjacent vacant lot. "Halt!" someone shouted.

The man turned and fell down. Agent John T. McLaughlin was the first to reach him. He was bleeding heavily from gunshot wounds to his head and chest. He was wearing a bulletproof vest, but not a good one. At least one bullet had torn right through it. "Are you Alvin Karpis?" McLaughlin asked the fallen man.

"No," the bleeding man mumbled, shaking his head. "Russell Gibson."

Moments later, agents stormed the now-empty apartment. Gibson was loaded into a Bureau car and taken to the American Hospital on Irving Park Boulevard. Emergency room doctors summoned a surgeon. A bullet had entered Gibson's back and blown out through his stomach. Another Bureau fugitive shot in the back. Gibson didn't have long.

Two agents hammered the dying man with questions. Did he know the Barkers? Karpis? Gibson weakly shook his head. A helpful doctor told him that he was on the verge of death and that he should answer the agent's questions.

Just before he died at 1:40 a.m., Gibson whispered his last words: "Tell you nothing."

After his arrest, Dock Barker was hauled away to the Bankers Building. Several newspapers complained that the Bureau had failed to tell them about the raids, but Hoover and Connelly were unconcerned. The papers had carried news of the shoot-out at Pine Grove Avenue, but none of them had learned that Dock Barker had been captured. This gave Connelly's men an opportunity to possibly get Barker to divulge the rest of the gang's whereabouts before the others learned that he was in custody. Connelly suspected that his capture wouldn't stay a secret long, however. The agents went to work on him, but Barker wasn't talking that night.

By the next morning, he had still said nothing. As the hours wore on, Hoover grew convinced that the Chicago agents weren't working hard enough. One of his top men, Ed Tamm, told Connelly to use "vigorous physical efforts" to break Barker. Just what those efforts were, the FBI never disclosed, but we can imagine. In later years, one agent, Ray Suran, reportedly bragged that he had broken two telephone books over Barker's head. But whatever they did, Barker still wouldn't talk.

Byron Bolton was no Dock Barker. Connelly's men initially had no idea how much Bolton knew, dismissing him as a "minor member of the gang." On Friday morning, though, after spending two days in custody, Bolton suggested otherwise. If the Bureau would let him go, he would tell them everything: who committed the Bremer kidnapping, what happened to the money, and best of all, where Fred Barker and Alvin Karpis were hiding.

Connelly sat down with Bolton and made the proposal that policemen have been making throughout history – he could make no promises, but if Bolton gave them information that helped the Bureau, it would be taken into account by the prosecuting attorney.

Bolton talked and to Connelly's amazement, he had a lot of information. Bolton laid out every detail of the Bremer kidnapping, naming all of the participants, and identifying the house in Bensenville where Bremer had been kept, which the Bureau had been searching for to no avail. Most importantly, Bolton said that Fred Barker and Alvin Karpis were staying at a lake house in central Florida. He had visited in December, but wasn't sure how to get there. He said that it was south of Ocala. He couldn't remember the name of the lake. But he recalled that it was locally famous as the home of a gigantic alligator named "Big Joe."

Soon after getting this information from Bolton, agents who were searching Dock Barker's apartment found a map that pointed out the location of the lake house. Why it took three days to discover Barker's map to the Florida hideout is a mystery. It wasn't the first (or last) time that agents overlooked an important item during a search, a phenomenon that never failed to enrage Hoover. When the map was given to Connelly, it had a ring drawn around the area of Lake Weir, located 12 miles south of Ocala.

Connelly could see that there were dozens of houses around the lake, as well as several smaller lakes nearby. They had to quickly narrow down the search area. It was only a matter of time before reporters figured out that they had Dock Barker, and when they made it to the newspapers, the Barkers would run.

On Saturday, January 12, Connelly and three agents boarded a 1:00 p.m. charter flight that got them to Jacksonville, Florida, by nightfall. They were met by 10 more agents, bringing trunk loads of machine guns and rifles, who had taken an overnight train. Everyone gathered at the Marion Hotel in Ocala, trying to keep a low profile. The area south of Ocala was sparsely populated with small towns where strangers would be easily noticed. He knew the Barkers were in the area. The arrival of 15 men in dark suits was going to attract attention.

Connelly sent agents around to look for any sign of the Barkers, while also trying to track down the lake with the alligator "Big Joe." He sent Jerry Campbell and Bob Jones east to check out Lake Bryant. Connelly and another agent went to look at Lake Weir and Lake Bower. Neither group came up with anything and both felt they had been noticed in the small communities. Connelly came to the conclusion that they needed local help. On Monday morning, he contacted a deputy sheriff name Milton Dunning and described the story about the alligator. Dunning said that it sounded like Lake Warburg. But when he called a friend on the lake, he found out that Lake Warburg's "Big Joe" had died in 1925. Connelly decided to give up on the alligator angle – every lake in central Florida seemed to have a "Big" something-or-other.

The more that he examined Dock Barker's map, the more convinced he became that the gang must be hiding on Lake Weird. It was at the center of the ring that Dock had drawn. The only problem was that the lake was six miles long and four miles wide and there were dozens of houses and cottages on its shores. The Barker house was a needle in a very large haystack.

In Washington, Hoover was spending a lot of time pacing his office. In Chicago, rumors were already flying that Dock Barker had been arrested. They had days, maybe hours, before the newspaper broke the story. On Tuesday morning, as Connelly's men were checking out Lake Weir, a reporter from the *Chicago American* called the Bankers Building. The call was passed on to Agent Mickey Ladd. The reporter wanted to know where Barker was being held, but Ladd denied they had him in custody. But the reporter wouldn't give up. He called several more times that morning and finally, Ladd called Washington. If they kept Barker in Chicago, Ladd warned, the story was going to get out. Hoover ordered Barker moved to the Detroit office. Ladd promised to move him at nightfall.

As Chicago was working to dodge the inquisitive reporter, Agent Bob Jones climbed into a motorboat with the deputy sheriff, Milton Dunning, and cruised along the shoreline of Lake Weir. We can only assume the two men were out of uniform. While they were inspecting lakeside cottages, Connelly took a chance and spoke to the postmaster in the village of Ocklawaha, on the north side of the lake. He couldn't identify photographs of either Fred Barker or Alvin Karpis. But when Connelly asked if any strangers had moved into the area, he mentioned a Mr. Blackburn, who was renting a nice lakefront house with a dock. He received several out-of-town newspapers. The postmaster suggested they approach Mr. Blackburn's neighbor, a man named Frank Barber, who had once worked as a guard at Leavenworth. Connelly drove to Barber's house and immediately received the confirmation they needed. Barber immediately identified a photo of Fred Barker as his new neighbor, Mr. Blackburn.

Connelly studied the Blackburn house through the trees. It was on the south side of Route 41, the area's main road, and as he drove slowly past at 11:00 a.m., he caught a glimpse of a small man and an older woman in the yard. It was Fred Barker and his mother, Kate Barker. Fred had brought her to Florida with him after she begged not to be left alone any longer. She had been spending all of her time alone in a Chicago apartment, mostly spending each day putting together

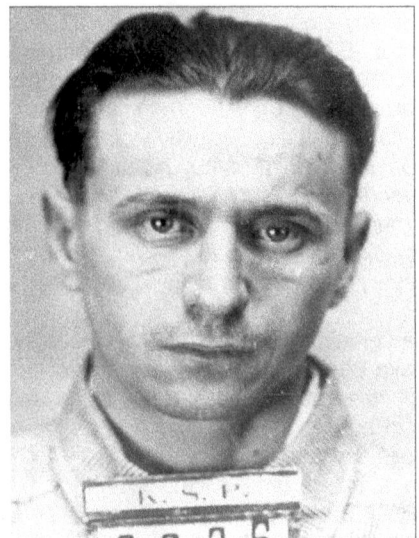

Fred Barker and his mother, Arizona Donnie "Kate" Barker, who would become widely known as "Ma Barker" after her death. In the days that followed her slaying, Hoover turned her into a monster

crossword puzzles. Legend has it that Arizona Donnie "Kate" Barker was the one who actually ran the Barker gang. She groomed her sons to be lawbreakers and managed their criminal careers, planning their crimes for more than a decade. There's no doubt that she knew her sons were criminals, which made it necessary for her to be moved or sometimes left behind when avoiding the law, but she never did any more than that. She befriended their various girlfriends – if she approved of them – and often made them meals, but she was involved in their crimes. Alvis Karpis once characterized her as an ignorant hillbilly who traveled with her sons because they were her family. Gang member Harvey Bailey once said, "The old woman couldn't plan breakfast. When we'd sit down to plan a bank job, she'd go in the other room and listen to Amos 'n' Andy or hillbilly music on the radio." The idea of "Ma" Barker as a cunning and ruthless gang leader was comical.

So, where did her infamous reputation come from? It was created after a single bullet blew her head apart.

Returning to Ocala, Connelly called and briefed Washington. The situation at Lake Weir looked ideal. The house was about 100 yards back from the road, and maybe a dozen yards from the lake. There were no natural obstructions around it, only what appeared to be a guesthouse, a garage, and some chicken coops. Those buildings could be used as cover. Connelly was determined not to have another Little Bohemia on his hands. In the wake of the battle, Hoover made sure of it.

Later that day, he sat down with his men, drew detailed maps of the area around the cottage, and outlined each man's position in the raiding party. Weapons were checked and double-checked, and then in the dark, early morning hours, they left for Ocklawaha.

It was still dark when the Bureau cars came to a stop and turned off their headlights along Highway 41. Fifteen agents got out of the cars and gathered under the surrounding oak trees, which were draped in curtains of Spanish moss. They could just make out the outlines of darkened houses and outbuildings. There was no movement and no lights. There was nothing that made them think that anyone knew they were coming.

The Barker house, a two-story, white clapboard cottage with green trim, was a short distance from the road. It faced south, towards the lake. There was a screened-in porch looking out toward the water, a long dock to a boathouse, and two grassy drives on either side of the house. Connelly positioned cars at the end of each driveway. At 5:30 a.m., he began moving men into place, surrounding the house. Connelly took five men and crept down the west side of the property, passing through some orange trees as they took shelter behind a small guest house, which was just about 30 steps from the front porch. He was so close that he could have underhanded a ball and hit it.

A group of Hoover's most experienced gunmen – Charles Winstead, Jerry Campbell, and two others – took positions behind the stone wall at the roadside, covering the back of the house. Two more agents hurried down the east side of the yard, hunching down behind the home of former Leavenworth guard, Fred Barber. Two more agents remained on the highway, ready to block any traffic that came along.

The sun was supposed to rise around 7:00 and Connelly wanted to wait until daylight before they made their move. In the meantime, they waited. Finally, as the first rays of the sun appeared over Lake Weir, Connelly walked out from behind the guest house and took two steps toward the front porch. He shouted, "Fred Barker, come out! We are Department of Justice agents, and we have the house surrounded!"

He was met with silence. Connelly repeated the command. If they came out with their hands raised, no one would get hurt, he called out.

Connelly stood motionless in the yard. No sound came from the house. Minutes passed. Another agent, on the other side of the house, shouted for the Barkers to come out and surrender. A few men thought they saw motion behind the window screens, but they couldn't be sure. Undoubtedly, they pictured Barker, Alvin Karpis, and perhaps other gang members, armed with machine guns, waiting inside. But there was no sound except the lake water, lapping against the wooden dock. In the small orange grove, there was a scraping sound as Agent Bob Jones laid his rifle across a concrete block. He was sighted in at one of the windows.

After perhaps 15 minutes had passed, Connelly shouted again: "Fred Barker, come out with your hands up! We have the house surrounded!" Once again, there was only silence from the cottage. Connelly looked over at Doc White, the gunman who had shot Russell Gibson. White was standing behind an oak tree to his left.

Five more minutes passed with still no sign, no movement from the house. Back in the trees, some of the agents wondered if the Barkers had already fled. Their car, a black Buick, was still parked in the garage next to the house, but that meant nothing. Connelly motioned to two agents, Alexander Muzzey and Tom McDade, to fire tear gas guns. Both men raised the guns and fired, but the gas projectiles missed the windows, thudding against the side of the house and falling to the ground. They were hissing in the grass, filling the yard with smoke. There had to have been one of the agents that immediately thought of the Little Bohemia debacle.

Connelly shouted once again: "Fred Barker! Kate Barker! Come out with your hands in the air!"

Hiding behind an oak to Connelly's side, Doc White thought he heard a woman's voice inside of the house. "What are you going to do?" it asked. There was no answer that he could hear, but in a moment, he later stated, he clearly heard the same voice say, "All right, go ahead!"

Connelly said that he heard the voice, too. He looked at White. They later said that they interpreted this to mean that the Barkers were coming out of the house to surrender. Connelly called out, "Come ahead, Fred! You come out first!"

Just then, a machine gun fired from a second-story window. Bullets tore up the grass and sand around where Connelly was hiding and ripped through the orange trees, causing small green leaves to rain down on the agents crouched beneath them. Connelly ducked behind the guest house as Doc White opened up with a .351 rifle, its booming thud echoing across the lake. The morning stillness was shattered by the gunfire. All around the yard, agents also opened fire on the house. Bullets punched holes into the white clapboard, tore chunks from the green trim, and shattered windows. The curtains danced and jerked as bullets ripped them apart.

White crouched behind an oak tree as bullets struck all around him. He was pinned down. Seeing his predicament, Connelly raced around the guest house, emerging on the far side, closer to the front porch. He raised his shotgun and fired, hoping to draw the attention of the shooter in the house away from White. It worked. The machine gunner shifted positions and bullets began to clatter against the side of the guest house. Connelly took cover again, and so did White. Three agents nearby retreated into the trees.

For the next five minutes, the gun battle raged. The shooter – or shooters-- inside the house seemed to have an endless supply of ammunition. Shots seemed to be coming from all directions, from the bedroom windows at the north and south, and from the front door. And then, as suddenly as it began, the shooting stopped. Perhaps the gang needed to conserve their bullets after all. Connelly peered at the upstairs windows. He wanted more gas canisters. He sent an agent back to the car to retrieve them and ordered a second tear gas attack. Again the canisters were fired, and again, they missed. This time they were blocked by the window screens and fell to the ground. Gas began drifting pointlessly into the woods.

Bureau agents outside the house where Fred and Kate Barker were hiding on Lake Weir in Florida

By this time, Connelly noticed a commotion had started somewhere behind him, in the trees down along the lake. Within minutes of the first shots, many of Ocklawaha's residents began peering out their windows and coming out into their yards, trying to figure out what was going on. By 8:00, crowds of people were milling out onto the highway, blocked from coming closer by the two agents left to mind traffic. The more curious of them, largely teenage boys, crept into the woods, where they could make out the figures of Bureau agents, firing at the house. A young man named Harry Scott would recall the incident decades later. "The agents were firing all over the place because Fred was running all around from room to room," he said. "They must have thought they had the whole gang inside."

And yes, a 16-year-old boy figured out that Fred Barker was the only gang member inside of the house, long before more than 15 Bureau agents came to realize that fact.

Across the grassy driveway to the east of the Barker house, Mrs. A.F. Westberry was asleep when the shooting began. Bullets ripped through the thin wooden walls of her frame house, striking the headboard of her bed. In a panic, she crawled to the window and saw men in dark suits shooting at her neighbor's house. She had no idea who they were. Terrified, she grabbed her daughter's hand and jumped out a window. On the ground, the two women began running.

About 50 yards away, Agent Ralph Brown saw the women start running across the grass. He had no idea who they were since the Bureau could not be bothered to check out the surrounding houses before launching a full-out assault on the Barker house. He yelled at them, "Stop! Halt! Federal officers!" but the two women kept running. He opened fire above their heads, stopping only when they reached another house.

The rest of the country, including Hoover, learned about the battle in progress from an Associated Press reporter in Ocala, who received a call from a local hotel wondering what all of the shooting was about. On a hunch, the reporter called the Bureau's Jacksonville office at 10:45, and the SAC there, Rudolph Alt, passed news of the assault to Washington. Hoover, worried that Connelly might run out of bullets, immediately told Alt to charter a plane to take extra ammunition to Ocklawaha.

Meanwhile, intermittent gunfire continued at the Barker house over the course of the next hour. When shots seemed to come from one window, agents fired at it. They were never able to get any tear gas canisters inside. Finally, around 10:00, the shots slowed down. By 10:30, the house had fallen silent. Connelly watched the windows. There was no way to know if the gang had run out of bullets, or if they were waiting to ambush the agents when they approached the house.

In the silent gloom, Connelly turned to see a pair of agents bringing up Willie Woodbury, the home's 25-year-old caretaker. Woodbury and his wife had been asleep in the guest house when the first shots rang out – the Bureau agents, of course, had not checked first to see if anyone was inside – and they had crawled under their bed as bullets flew through their windows. Connelly looked at the quiet house and asked Woodbury if he would be willing to check inside. Woodbury looked terrified. Connelly assured him that the Barkers wouldn't shoot him, although how he could possibly know this remains a mystery. If they were alive, Connelly said, maybe he could talk them into giving up. He implied, of course, how heroic his efforts would make him. Woodbury reluctantly agreed to try.

The caretaker cautiously climbed the front steps and pulled on the handle of the screen door. It was locked. That was enough for him. He scrambled down the stairs and returned to where Connelly was hiding. "That door's shut," he said. Water was streaming from his eyes; the tear gas was starting to get to him. But someone handed him a pocketknife. "Go back and cut the screen and kick it down," Connelly said.

Unbelievably, while the Bureau agents hid, Woodbury went back to the door. He sliced open the screen, shoved the door open, and, while pressing a handkerchief to his face to keep out the drifting tear gas, he crossed the porch to the front door. Inside, the house was silent. There were beer bottles sitting around the dining room. He called out, "It's okay, Ma, it's me! They're making me do this!" But there was no answer.

He saw blood on the stairs. Woodbury crept up the steps to the second floor. Each step caused the wooden floor to creak. It seemed loud in the silence. Upstairs, there were four bedrooms. He walked to the door of the southeast bedroom, where Kate slept. It was empty. The door to the southwest bedroom, where Fred usually stayed, was slightly open. He walked over to it and pushed it open.

Bureau agents hid while caretaker Willie Woodbury entered the Barker house alone after the gunfight. In one bedroom, he found a bloody scene of carnage and death.

Outside, Connelly and his men anxiously waited. There was a minute of silence, perhaps two, and then Woodbury's face appeared at an upstairs window. Tears from the gas were streaming down his red, blotchy face. "They're both up here!" he shouted.

"What are they doing?" Connelly asked.

"They're all dead!"

Connelly led a group of agents into the house. They found Kate Barker dead on the bedroom floor, a single bullet hole in her forehead. Fred lay next to her. He had been shot 14 times. It was impossible to know how long they had been dead.

There was no sign that anyone else lived in the house. But a search uncovered an assortment of hotel bills, business cards, and receipts from a hotel in Miami where Alvin Karpis was believed to have stayed in November. Several receipts were made out to "Mr. D. Wagner," an alias that Karpis was known to use. Connelly was sure that Karpis was in Miami. He ordered Ralph Brown and three other agents to catch the first available flight to Miami. As it turned out, Karpis was still there, but they narrowly missed him. As agents flooded into the city, he was already fleeing north on the Dixie Highway. He managed to stay one step ahead of the Bureau for more than a year.

Local legend around Ocklawaha states that the ghost of Kate Barker still lingers at the once bullet-riddled house on the shores of Lake Weir. Not only have curiosity-seekers heard an old woman's cries of desperation inside of the house,

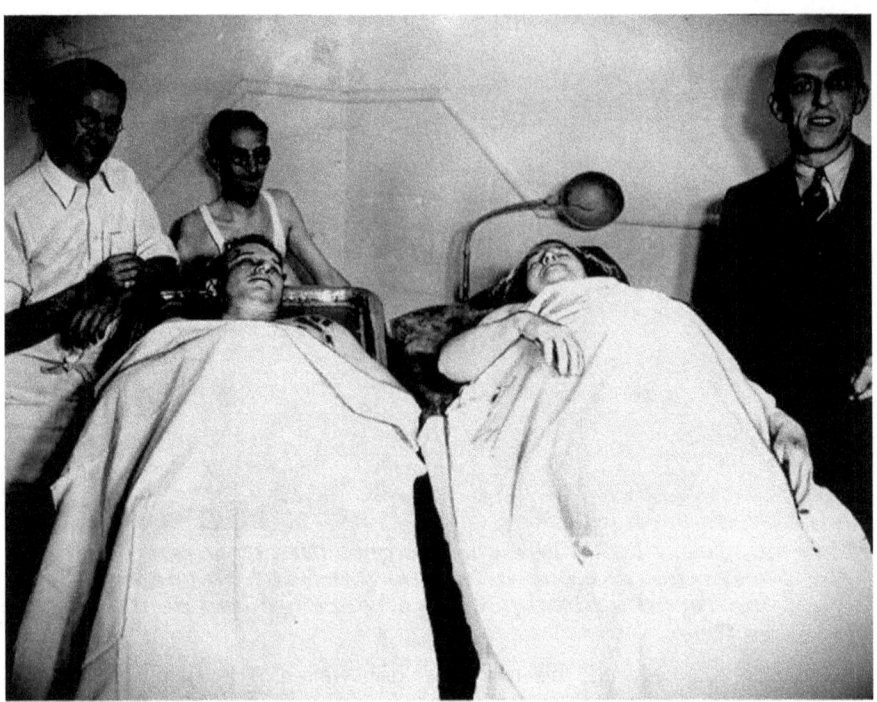

The bodies of Fred and Kate Barker, on display after death

but locals claim they have actually seen her face peering out the windows, perhaps frantically watching for federal agents who ended her life, and that of her son, on that January day. Those who saw her fearful face behind the glass initially believed that someone living in inside the house, perhaps it was a tourist or a macabre souvenir-seeker. Once they realized that no one came to door, though, they realized that the woman was an otherworldly resident of the house – one that was unable to leave as she relived that morning in 1935 over and over again.

And, of course, that is not the only tale told of Kate Barker after her death, but in truth, it's the tale that is the easiest to believe.

When J. Edgar Hoover held a press conference in Washington on the afternoon of the Barker gun battle, he found himself with a predicament. There was little chance that the Bureau would be criticized for killing Fred Barker. He was a bank robber and a cold-blooded killer, who had fired on federal agents with a machine gun. But Kate Barker was another matter entirely. Hoover had to explain to the nation's press just why his men had slaughtered an elderly woman with no criminal record. But, Hoover being Hoover, decided not to wait for that question to be asked. He decided to go on the offensive, taking advantage of the fact that the Barker-Karpis gang was the least known of America's public enemies.

As reporters listened and hurriedly took notes, Hoover announced that Ma Barker, who none of the newspapers or their readers had ever heard of, was the "brains" of the gang. He said that she had been found dead with a machine gun in her hand, which was completely untrue. To give credence to the idea that the elderly woman had been an active participant in the gun fight, Hoover described a dramatic scene in which Earl Connelly approached the house and talked with Ma, who slammed the door shut in his face and yelled to Fred, "Let 'em have it!" Needless to say, none of the agents' reports after the battle made mention of this incident, and Connelly never even got close to the house. He sent the caretaker inside in his place.

Unfortunately, there was no one left alive to dispute Hoover's fabricated story. Never mind that there was no indication whatsoever in the Bureau's files that said Ma Barker had ever fired a gun, robbed a bank, or done anything more criminal than live off her sons' criminal gains. According to Hoover, Kate was a "criminal mastermind," who planned the gang's robberies and raids. Never mind that, according to those who actually knew her, "she couldn't plan breakfast." Reporters loved it and ran with the story.

But as well as Hoover concocted his tale, the stories of Ma Barker did not immediately produce anything like the public fascination people had with John Dillinger. It took time for reporters to embellish the myth that Hoover created. Six weeks after death, the first notion of Ma Barker's criminal genius was explored in great details in a multi-part story that was distributed by King Features Syndicate. The Bureau, of course, cooperated with the piece, which was headlined "Ma Barker: Deadly Spider Woman." The story included such dramatic sections as, "The withered fingers of spidery, crafty Ma Barker, like satanic tentacles, controlled the skeins on which dangled the fate of desperadoes whose activities hit the headlines on an average of once a week."

Hoover was quoted as saying, "In many ways, they were the smartest outlaws we've encountered. And Ma was the mind behind the operations. She was so smart that we never got anything on her – although we knew plenty. We had to kill her to catch up with her."

For the rest of his life, Hoover never changed his tune. In fact, "Ma Barker" became one of his favorite stories. He even made her "criminal genius" the centerpiece of his 1938 book, *Persons in Hiding*, which was chock-full of ridiculously concocted scenes inside the Barker gang. Hoover's demonization of Ma Barker, as he had done with Hellen Gillis and other so-called "molls," went beyond the need to defend the facts of her death. It fit neatly into themes he had been airing in interviews since the 1920s. The root causes of crime, he stated, were not poverty and economic disparity. Crime was the result of the deterioration of family values, of parents who failed to teach their children the difference between right and wrong. In time, Ma Barker – or rather the imaginary character that he created with her name – became Hoover's favorite symbol of what was wrong with American families. It was far more than Kate Barker had ever been in life.

But it proves a very important point. If Hoover would lie about Kate Barker, then he would lie about anything, including something that would damage the credibility of the Bureau more than just shooting an old lady to death.

After the killing of the Barkers, Alvin Karpis and pal, Harry Campbell, fled to Atlantic City. They were cornered by police at the Dan-Mor Hotel on January 20, 1935, but managed to shoot their way out and escape. Their girlfriends, Dolores Delaney and Wynona Burdette, were captured and sentenced to five years in prison for harboring fugitives. Dolores gave birth to a son while in prison, named him Raymond Alvin Karpis, and gave him to Karpis' parents in Chicago to take care of.

Karpis stayed on the run, landing in Ohio, but soon became bored and went looking for another big score. His friend, Fred Hunter, suggested a mail train that ferried bags of cash from the Cleveland Federal Reserve to Youngstown to fill the payroll needs of the eastern Ohio steel mills. Karpis had never robbed a train and he got excited about the idea. They decided to hit the train at Garrettsville, north of Youngstown. The gang would include Karpis, Hunter, Harry Campbell, Sam Coker, an aging bank robber named Ben Grayson, and a 21-year-old kid from Oklahoma named Milton Lett.

Preparations went smoothly until October 19, 1935, when Lett and Clayton Hall bought a getaway car at an Akron Ford dealership. Their roll of cash caught too much attention. Later that day, Akron detectives arrested them as "suspicious persons." They were released on bail, and Karpis decided not to let the arrest derail his plans. As it turned out, he should have.

Two weeks later, on November 7, they were ready. At 2:00 p.m., Karpis, driving a new Plymouth sedan, turned into the station lot at Garrettsville. There were about 60 people milling about on the platform. The men took their positions and at 2:13, the train appeared down the line and then came to a stop just where Karpis knew it would. Walking to the mail car, Karpis and Grayson climbed into the cab. The mail door opened and Karpis pulled out a machine gun, startling the two clerks. Before he could say anything, the clerks disappeared back inside. Just then, he was distracted by a commotion in the parking lot. Fred Hunter had been positioned there to keep anyone from leaving and he was now chasing two men, taking his attention off a couple who were starting their car.

Karpis hopped down from the mail car, stalked to the automobile, and pulled open the door. The terrified driver froze as Karpis reached in, ripped the keys out of the ignition, and tossed them across the lot. In a moment, he was back in the mail car. The clerks were nowhere to be found. He tossed an unlit stick of dynamite into the car and called out that he was going to count to five, and then he was going to throw in another stick. That one would be lit. A moment later, the two clerks appeared with their hands in the air.

Karpis, machine gun in hand, demanded the payroll bag for Warren, Ohio. A clerk lifted one padlocked bag and handed it to him. When he asked for the Youngstown bag, the clerk said it wasn't on the train. Karpis aimed his gun at the man's chest. Just then, Harry Campbell climbed into the car. "Look out, Harry," he said, "I'm gonna shoot this guy."

The clerk, on the verge of tears, produced a ledger to prove the Youngstown payroll really wasn't on that train. Irate, Karpis told him to grab several bags of registered mail instead. Then he forced the clerks to load them all in the trunk of the waiting Plymouth. It was all over in five minutes.

The getaway went smoothly. They slipped away to the town of Port Clinton, on Lake Erie, and emptied the money bags. Karpis was disappointed. They had only gotten away with $34,000. He had expected five times that much. The next morning, they flew to Hot Springs, Arkansas, which was still a safe hideout from underworld figures. Karpis picked up his new girlfriend, Grace Goldstein, and they, along with Hunter and his girl, drove to Texas. They drove along the Gulf Coast, relaxing, fishing, and sunbathing. After three weeks, they returned to Hot Springs and moved from apartment to apartment, never staying in the same place for long.

In January 1936, Karpis decided it was safe to find a more permanent place and rented a lake house. He passed the days fishing and he and Grace went out drinking and dancing at night. Fred Hunter was gone most of the time, driving through Florida and Texas with his girlfriend. In March, Karpis moved again, renting a farmhouse south of Hot Springs.

For the Bureau, the manhunt for Karpis is one of the least flattering chapters in the "war on crime." There was an air of lethargy and anticlimax about it from the start. None of the agents could get very excited about risking their lives in one last battle of a war that already seemed to have been won. And it showed.

After ten months of work, following tips from Boston to Havana to Los Angeles, the Bureau – which had now been re-named the FBI – had no serious leads about his whereabouts. The Bureau had no jurisdiction over the Garrettsville robbery, so they never investigated it. But Garrettsville brought another entity into the hunt for the last of the public enemies – the federal postal inspectors. Their dogged pursuit of Karpis quickly overshadowed the FBI's search. Working from Youngstown, they had managed to connect Karpis and Campbell to the Garrettsville robbery in just 24 hours. Eyewitnesses quickly identified their photos.

Keeping things strictly within the postal inspector's team, the lead investigator, Sylvester J. Hettrick, reached out to the Kansas State Highway Patrol, which already had a detective named Joe Anderson pursuing rumors that Karpis was involved in several robberies in Kansas. Anderson was the kind of investigator that the FBI needed, and didn't have. Within weeks, working his contacts in the Tulsa underworld, he had identified Sam Coker as one of the men involved in the Garrettsville robbery. Coker had left town days before the mail robbery, stupidly telling friends that he was headed east to rob a train.

At first, Anderson and the postal inspectors had freely cooperated with the FBI, passing on tips about Coker and others. When Earl Connelly heard the rumor that Karpis had robbed the Garrettsville train, he asked the Cleveland office to investigate. The agents simply chatted up the inspectors, who happily shared their leads – leads that the FBI largely ignored.

Through December and into January, the postal inspectors' investigation gathered steam. They traced the car used in the robbery to Akron, where a salesman identified Milton Lett as its purchaser. They soon identified Clayton Hall, and then Fred Hunter. Connelly ignored it all. He had already discounted rumors of Lett's involvement in the crime because the FBI had already interviewed him and considered him a confidential informant. From all appearances, it really just looked like the FBI couldn't bring itself to believe that a rival agency had mounted a more thorough investigation than its own. Despite the progress that the postal service investigators were making, Connelly dismissed them.

Instead, the Bureau, trying an old tactic that never worked out well for them, began surveilling the Karpis and Campbell families. In Chicago, agents had the Karpis family apartment thoroughly bugged and even hired a Lithuanian man to translate conversations between Karpis's parents, which mostly boiled down to which side of the family could be blamed for his life of crime.

In Tulsa, they kept watch on Karpis's friend, Burrhead Keady, even as rumors were flying that postal inspectors were getting ready to arrest him – which they did. The FBI learned about the arrest in the newspaper. When agents demanded to know if the story was true, senior inspector Sylvester Hettrick denied it. Arguments broke out between Hettrick's men and the Cleveland FBI office. The inspectors, irritated by the adoring publicity lavished on the Bureau, had finally stopped sharing leads with Hoover's men. Agents were ordered to ignore the postal inspectors and concentrate on breaking the case on their own.

Unfortunately, though, the same leads that the postal inspectors were using to make arrests were coming into the Bureau, but Hoover's men didn't bother to follow up on them. Joe Rich, a heroin addict who had robbed an Ohio payroll with Karpis, ended up in jail and tried to swap information for his freedom. FBI agents who debriefed him didn't believe his "fanciful story," even though it was true. They also failed to show any interest in Clayton Hall, even though tips from three different sources linked him to Karpis. They didn't follow up on his involvement with the Garrettsville robbery until six weeks after they received the first tip. They watched his house for a few hours, and then left.

In Chicago, Connelly wearily looked over the investigation and knew they were getting nowhere. The only ones making progress were the postal inspectors. As irritable as it made him to admit it, he knew that he needed them. But he couldn't come out an ask because the two groups were now openly hostile to one another. Somehow, Connelly had to force their hand. Looking through reports, he came upon one from the Cleveland office about the short surveillance of Clayton Hall's house. There were rumors that the inspectors had been seen with Hall.

On Wednesday, March 25, Connelly telephoned the Cleveland SAC and told him to find Hall. An agent named E.J. Wynn drove to Youngstown and found him at home. Hall admitted to knowing Fred Hunter for years. He identified a photo of Karpis as Hunter's friend, "Ed King." He admitted that he had seen them both as recently as January. It was the best lead that the FBI had turned up in more than a year. Agent Wynn gave Hall $5 and told him to come to the Cleveland FBI office the next day at 1:00 p.m.

Connelly rushed to Cleveland for the meeting. Not surprisingly, Hall didn't show up. When he hadn't come in by nightfall, Connelly drove to Youngstown to look for him. His wife said that he had left that morning, and she thought he was going to the FBI. Thinking that Hall was trying to avoid them, Connelly sent two agents to watch his house the next morning. A few minutes after they had parked, a Ford drove past them. One of the two men inside could be seen jotting down their license plate number. They were postal inspectors; the agents were sure of it. Irritated, they drove to the Youngstown post office and parked outside. From an upstairs window, the inspectors saw them.

A short time later, the phone rang in the Cleveland office. Sylvester Hettrick was on the line and he wanted a meeting. Agent Wynn drove to the Youngstown post office and found himself in a room with eight angry postal inspectors and two members of the Ohio Highway Patrol. Hettrick announced that they had arrested Clayton Hall, who after being threatened with prosecution, had agreed to give up Karpis. But he would only talk if there was an FBI agent in the room.

The next day, Connelly sat down in the Cleveland office with one of the inspectors, who reluctantly agreed to let him talk to Hall. Just before noon, Connelly called Pop Nathan in Washington with the news. Nathan was unimpressed. His lack of interest was attributable to the embarrassing fact that the Bureau was piggy-backing on work done by the postal inspectors. Hoover definitely did not want this in the newspapers.

Connelly went to Youngstown the following morning and spent several hours with Hall. When he was finished, he called Washington and said that the frightened man had given them everything, including the location of a house south of Hot Springs where Karpis was living. Connelly was arranging a charter flight to Arkansas – and he was forced to take some of the postal inspectors along with him.

Connelly's group didn't arrive in Little Rock until 4:35 p.m. on Sunday, March 30. A reporter caught wind of their arrival and a story appeared the next morning under a headline stating they were in Arkansas on a "mysterious mission." Hoover went ballistic over the leak and ordered an investigation. In the meantime, reporters were told that agents were gathering in Arkansas for a conference. But this was bad news for the planned raid. Connelly knew they only had hours before the news broke that the FBI was in the state. They hurried to Hot Springs and soon found the house that Hall told them about. Night had fallen and lights were blazing in the house. Someone was home.

Connelly got 14 men together for the raid, including Clarence Hurt, one of the men who had been at the Biograph Theater; Rufus Coulter, who had traded gunshots with Homer Van Meter in St. Paul; and Loyde Kingman, who had once gotten close enough to Karpis that he had inadvertently shared an elevator ride with him. Kingman, especially, had an ax to grind. In the predawn darkness, they crept into position around the house. In Washington, Hoover waited by the phone. He wanted Karpis, and, just as important, he wanted the FBI to get credit for taking him, not the postal inspectors. He told Connelly to "spare no expense" to insure he got the news first so that he could make the announcement. In Little Rock, agents phoned Washington every 15 minutes, just to say they had no news.

By 8:00 a.m., Connelly was ready to move in. The house was quiet; they would take Karpis by surprise. Connelly called for him to come out with his hands up. There was no answer. With a wave of his hand, Connelly signaled for tear gas guns. This time, they didn't miss. The canisters shattered the windows and crashed into the house. Waves of gas began seeping out of the shattered panes. Connelly called again for Karpis to surrendered. He called once more, but there was no answer.

When the FBI finally stormed the house, it was empty.

Karpis and Hunter had left Hot Springs four days earlier, after they had learned about the presence of postal inspectors in town. Stupidly, one of the inspectors had approached a taxi driver who was sweet on Fred Hunter's girlfriend, Connie Morris. The man had gotten drunk and told Connie that agents were going to arrest her. Connie told Grace Goldstein, who told Karpis. They were packed up and gone within minutes. Weeks later, the FBI would learn that the lights they had seen on in the house the night before the raid were turned on by Grace, who was also packing to leave.

Karpis and Hunter drove west into Texas. They went fishing for a few days and read about the raid in newspapers. They went on to Biloxi and a week later, to New Orleans, where Karpis rented an apartment on St. Charles Avenue. Hunter and Connie Morris moved into a place on Canal Street.

Not surprisingly, the FBI stayed one step behind. Connie was naïve enough to mail a letter to her mother from Corpus Christi. Agents were on the Texas coast soon after, but Karpis was long gone. Connelly, meanwhile, had Grace Goldstein picked up. Connelly, unaware of how well she knew Karpis, though, released her and he returned to Ohio. He didn't think she was important enough to keep under surveillance. They soon found out this was a mistake.

Karpis was gone, but agents stayed in Hot Springs. Everyone they contacted pointed them toward Grace Goldstein, who they had just released. But Grace had now disappeared, which triggered a frantic scramble to find her. Where Grace was, locals assured them, Karpis would be also.

In Washington, Hoover was having troubles of his own. On the day that Grace had vanished, Hoover went into a Senate hearing to seek a doubling of the FBI's budget. He was expecting problems. All of the hoopla over the "war on crime" – the press stories, the movies, the radio shows – was creating a backlash against the Bureau, especially among supporters of other law enforcement entities. The budget's subcommittee chairman, a Tennessee senator named Kenneth McKellar, was an old enemy of Hoover's, dating back to an incident when Hoover refused to hire a pair of Tennessee men that the senator had recommended. When McKellar complained, Hoover promptly fired three other Tennessee agents, simply out of spite.

Hoover came into the hearing with an array of statistics, charts, and graphs with which to make his case. He pointed out that the FBI had all but eliminated kidnapping as a national threat. When he was finished, McKellar began his attack, first asking about money spent for advertising, which the FBI did not do, Hoover assured him. McKellar asked if the Bureau appeared in any moving pictures. Hoover said it did not. A number of "G-Men" films had appeared but Hoover only objected to them because he wanted the Bureau, not Hollywood, to produce them and reap the profits. McKellar noted that such films damaged the credibility of the FBI, and he was just getting started. He pressed Hoover whether any writers or publicists were on the FBI payroll (answer: there were) and another senator asked why the Bureau didn't cooperate more with local police. Hoover insisted that it did, when they weren't corrupt.

"It seems to me that your department is running wild, Mr. Hoover," McKellar said. "I just think that, Mr. Hoover, with all the money in your hands you are just extravagant."

"Will you let me make a statement?" Hoover asked.

McKellar smirked. "I think that is a statement."

They quibbled over how many cases the FBI had solved and then the questions turned to other things. "How many people have been killed by your department since you have been allowed to use guns?" McKellar asked.

"I think there have been eight desperadoes killed by our agents and we have had four agents in our service killed by them."

"In other words, the net effect of turning guns over to your department has been the killing for four desperadoes and four G-men."

Now clearly seeking to embarrass Hoover, McKellar questioned his qualifications to run the Bureau. Hoover pointed out that he had been with the Department of Justice for 19 years.

"I mean crime school," McKellar said.

"I learned first-hand," Hoover replied.

"Did you ever make an arrest?"

"No sir, I have made investigations."

"How many arrests have you made and who were they?"

Hoover mentioned several cases that he handled as a Justice Department prosecutor, but McKellar waved this away, pressing him again. "Did you make the arrests?"

Hoover stammered. "The arrests were made... made by officers under my supervision."

McKellar now barked at him. "I'm talking about actual arrests. You ever arrest them, actually?"

When Hoover left the hearing, his face was flaming red. He stormed into his office as angry as he had ever been in his life. It was galling that after everything the Bureau had achieved, he was still subject to petty politics. He got on the telephone to Earl Connelly and gave him a very pointed and straightforward command: find Alvin Karpis. He wanted him arrested and when he was, Hoover would do it himself.

By the time that FBI agents realized that Grace Goldstein was missing, she was strolling through Audubon Park in New Orleans at the side of Alvin Karpis. He had rolled right into Hot Springs, under the nose of Bureau agents, and picked her up himself. After reuniting with Fred Hunter and Connie Morris, they took a vacation, stopping in Biloxi before heading to Florida. They later returned to New Orleans and Karpis ferried Grace back to Hot Springs. The FBI was waiting for her.

By now, the town was filled with agents and postal inspectors, who were mostly tripping over each other trying to wring information out of anyone they could. When Grace returned on April 25, they used Clayton Hall to spring a trap on her and trick her into revealing where Karpis was. She had no idea that he was now an informant for the Bureau. Hall soon had big news to report: She and Karpis were renting an apartment in New Orleans, he said. But he had forgotten to get the address of the apartment.

Connelly needed that address. He left Ohio that afternoon, after ordering agents to get Hall back in touch with Grace that night. Hall talked to Grace, but he still couldn't get the address out of her. Connelly couldn't wait. He was already on a train to New Orleans. They would have to find Karpis themselves.

Everyone realized that they were close. In Washington, Hoover was already busy lining up a national audience for his moment in the spotlight. On Monday morning, April 27, when Connelly arrived in New Orleans, Hoover met with officials at the NBC radio network. NBC was proposing two separate programs on Karpis's capture, both of which would highlight the director's first-hand involvement.

Of course, there was still one very large problem: the FBI had no idea where in New Orleans Karpis was hiding. Connelly decided to use Grace Goldstein. Agents arrested her in Hot Springs on Monday afternoon. She was whisked away to Little Rock for intense questioning, but Grace refused to talk. She told them that she wasn't going to become known as the next Ana Sage. But the FBI had leverage by using her family. Agents had tracked her siblings to their homes in Texas. They made it clear that if she didn't talk, they would indict all of them for harboring Karpis. The threat worked. The next day, Grace agreed to a deal. If the FBI promised not to arrest her family, she would have over Karpis's address – but only to Connelly himself.

That night, agents took her to Jackson, Mississippi, and checked her into a motel. Connelly drove up from New Orleans and questioned her for three hours, finally giving up at 3:00 a.m. It turned out that she didn't know Karpis's address, but she knew Fred Hunter's, where she and Karpis had eaten most of their meals. By dawn, agents had Hunter's apartment under surveillance. It was right on Canal Street, on a busy corner with Jefferson Davis Parkway. Two of the Bureau's most reliable gunmen, Clarence Hurt and Jerry Campbell, flew in to join the raiding party.

Now all they needed was Hoover. A charter flight was arranged through Trans World Airlines and Hoover, along with his personal aide, Clyde Tolson, arrived at 9:30 p.m. They checked into the Roosevelt Hotel and Hoover told Connelly there would be no raid until morning. Connelly had two men in a vacant house across

A rather ridiculous "action" shot of Hoover, cooked up by the Bureau's publicity machine. There was nothing that Hoover wanted more than to look like he had first-hand experience in the field – but if he ever fired that machine gun, it was only at paper targets.

the street from the apartment building. So far, there had been no sign of either Hunter or Karpis.

By the next morning, Friday, May 1, there had been no change. In his hotel room, Hoover paced. Then at 9:45 a.m., from his position in the vacant house, a rookie agent named Raymond Tollett spotted a red Essex Terraplane pull up in front of the apartment building. A man got out – it was Alvin Karpis. He entered the building, and then emerged with another man. Both got into cars. When they drove off, Tollett ran to a nearby drugstore and telephoned Connelly.

While missing from the city, Karpis had been in Mississippi, scouting a couple of possible jobs, a construction company payroll and a train robbery in the town of Iuka. He had just returned to New Orleans that morning, dropping his things off at his St. Charles Avenue place before swinging by to pick up Hunter. They drove to a deserted road near Lake Pontchartrain, where Karpis transferred his guns to Hunter's car. Then they dropped off Karpis's car at a garage to be serviced. While they waited, the cruised around the city. Hunter told him that he was nervous. He had seen strangers around his building. At one point, he thought he saw a maroon couple following him. Karpis was now worried, too. They drove back to Hunter's apartment.

In the vacant house across the street, Connelly watched them drive up. Leaving two men behind to watch things, he quickly drove downtown to the FBI office, where Hoover was waiting. Connelly gathered the raiding party and ran through the plan. He had 14 men. Two would stay in the vacant house. Two groups would guard the rear of Hunter's building. When they were certain that both

Hunter and Karpis were still inside the apartment, the raiding party itself – Connelly, Hoover, Dwight Brantley, Clarence Hurt, and Buck Buchanan – would go in the front door.

At 4:30, while the FBI was still making plans, Connie Morris asked Hunter and Karpis to go to the grocery store and buy some strawberries to have with dinner. The two men exchanged glances. As Karpis waited by the door with a machine gun, Hunter walked outside, taking a look around. Everything seemed fine. Karpis put down the gun and followed him out. At the grocery store, Karpis waited in the car. He watched as a DeSoto sedan pulled behind him. Hunter came out a minute later and told him that he had seen the DeSoto the day before. It was fine. Karpis laughed; they were imagining things. They had to calm down.

They returned to the apartment. It was a warm and humid day and in the kitchen, Connie had changed into shorts and a white halter top. Karpis tried to relax, but he was too keyed up. He walked down to the drugstore – the same one the FBI agents were making calls from – and bought a pack of cigarettes and a *Reader's Digest*. As he walked back to the apartment, he studied every man he saw on the street. He willed himself to relax, and this time, he did. His car was supposed to be ready around 5:00, and a few minutes after, he stood up and announced that it was time to pick it up. It was too hot to wear a jacket, so he slid his pistol under a sofa cushion for safekeeping.

As Karpis was getting ready to leave, the five-man raiding party was waiting in two parked cars across the intersection of Canal and Jefferson Davis. Connelly and Clarence Hurt were in the front car, and Hoover and the others were behind them. A few minutes after 5:00, the two cars pulled away from the curb and began to cross the intersection. Their plan was to park beyond the building and return on foot. Just then, Karpis and Hunter walked out onto the sidewalk and started toward their waiting Plymouth. Karpis slid behind the wheel, rolled down the window, and then leaned over to unlock the passenger door for Hunter.

Connelly saw them and reacted immediately. He swerved the car in front of the Plymouth and slammed on the brakes to block it in. In the second car, Hoover saw a boy on a bicycle veer between him and Karpis. The boy was just moving past when Connelly and Hurt leapt from their car with guns drawn.

What happened next has been in dispute for the last eight or nine decades.

According to Hoover's version of events, which he recounted numerous times in articles and books in the years that followed, he jumped from the second car and rushed to the driver's side door while Connelly charged the passenger door. Before Karpis could reach for a rifle in the backseat, Hoover said that he grabbed Karpis by the collar. Hoover told a reporter what happened next: "Stammering, stuttering, shaking as though he had palsy, the man upon whom was bestowed the title of public enemy number one folded up like the yellow rat he is."

Karpis offered no resistance, raising his hands as he stepped out of the car.

"Put the cuffs on him, boys," Hoover said.

Most likely, after everything that has come before in this book, the reader will have some doubts about the veracity of this story, especially the quotes from Hoover, which sound like badly written dialog from a gangster movie. The next day, Hoover's publicity machine was already churning out tall tales, including that Connie Morris was in the car when Karpis was arrested. "We nabbed the three after they had entered the car," he told a reporter from the Associated Press. And that was just for starters.

There was another version of the story, told by Alvin Karpis. According to his account, Hoover was nowhere to be seen when he was arrested. He didn't reach for a rifle in the backseat, because the coupe didn't have a backseat. An agent from the blocking car, apparently Connelly, jumped out and aimed a gun at him. He yelled, "All right, Karpis! Just keep your hands on the steering wheel!" It was only after Karpis surrendered that one of the agents yelled, "Chief, we got him!" It was then, Karpis said, that Hoover emerged from behind the apartment building and helped make the arrest.

FBI files, unsurprisingly, suggest that Hoover's version is closer to the truth. Connelly's report on the arrest, and an aide's memo detailing a conversation with Hoover the next morning, make it clear that Hoover was in the raiding party, not behind the apartment building. But neither of these sources – nor any report that was filed that day – says anything about Hoover approaching Karpis's car, let alone grabbing him by the collar. That part of the story is as fanciful as Ma Barker's "criminal genius" or, as we will soon see, the actual eye color of John Dillinger.

In the end, what really happened made little difference. The next day's front-page headline read: "Karpis Captured in New Orleans by Hoover Himself." Of course, the investigations of the postal inspectors, which truly led to the discovery of where Karpis was hiding, was never publicized.

However it all happened, Karpis and Hunter gave up with no resistance. Within minutes a crowd started to form and people began hanging out of apartment windows, trying to see what the commotion was all about. None of the agents had a pair of handcuffs with them, so one took off his tie and wrapped it around Karpis's wrists. Karpis was placed in a Bureau car and they started toward the FBI office downtown. Clarence Hurt was driving, and he got lost. "Does anyone know where the Post Office building is?" he asked at one point.

"I can tell you," Karpis replied.

"How do you know where it is?" asked Clyde Tolson, who was in the backseat with Hoover.

"We were thinking of robbing it," he replied with a grin.

The killing of Fred and Ma Barker, and the subsequent capture of Alvin Karpis, marked the end of the three-year "war on crime." Aside from a few critics, the Karpis arrest cemented the FBI as America's preeminent national police force, the Bureau of Hoover's dreams, and a department whose unchallenged resources would make Hoover a power in American government for the next four decades. It also put Hoover in the role of a national hero, celebrated in newsreels, movies, and comic books. It was Hoover who now stood in the spotlight, not the all-but-forgotten Homer Cummings, and certainly not the dozens of anonymous Bureau agents who had risked, or in some case given their lives in pursuit of John Dillinger, Pretty Boy Floyd, Baby Face Nelson, the Barkers, and Alvin Karpis.

And it was certainly not Melvin Purvis, whose glory had continued to shine in the months after the Barkers had been killed. His tenuous position inside the Bureau had been lost on the general public and a magazine poll that winter named Purvis as the seventh-most-respected man in the country. In time, though, as Hoover buried him in a deeper and deeper out of the public eye, Purvis's popularity faded. He resigned from the FBI in 1935 so that he could write about his exploits and take advantage of the other opportunities that his fame as "the man who got Dillinger" brought to him. He published a book called *American Agent* in 1936, and began hosting a radio show for children called "Junior G-Men." He also became a newspaper publisher and radio station owner in South Carolina; was briefly engaged to Janice "Toots" Jarratt, a famous New York model; became a JAG (Judge Advocate General) colonel during World War II; and hunted Nazi war criminals for the War Crimes Office in Europe.

Hoover never forgave Purvis for his hubris in the wake of the Dillinger and Floyd cases. He repeatedly frustrated his chances to return to the public eye, blocking his chance for a federal judgeship in 1952. Hoover, in fact, did everything he could to destroy the legacy of his former protégé – Purvis's name does not appear even one time in the Bureau's 1956 authorized history, *The FBI Story*.

On February 29, 1960, Purvis was found dead in his study, a single bullet wound to his head. The gun in his hand had been given to him by fellow agents when he retired from the Bureau. Some called it suicide, others said it was an accident. Hoover made no comment at all. He sent no note of condolence. His widow, Rosanne, wrote to Hoover: "We are honored that you ignored Melvin's death. Your jealousy hurt him very much but until the end, I think he loved you."

Few of the other Bureau agents who fought the "war on crime" received any public credit for their work either. A number of them enjoyed long careers in the FBI before retiring in the 1960s and 1970s. Others left the Bureau as soon as they could after the Depression ended, joining hometown law firms or becoming corporate executives. The last surviving member of the Dillinger Squad, rookie agent Tom McDade, died in 1996.

Bill Rorer, the man who exchanged gunfire with the Dillinger gang at Little Bohemia, left the FBI in 1937. He was the CEO of a Georgia dairy until he passed away in 1967. Charles Winstead, who was on the street that night in front of the Biograph, retired from the FBI in 1943. He died at age 82 in 1973. His partner, Clarence Hurt, retired in 1955 and was a sheriff in his native Oklahoma for several years. He died in 1975. Jerry Campbell, who captured Dock Barker, died in Palo Alto, California, in 1991.

Hugh Clegg, the assistant director who helped create the disaster at Little Bohemia, founded the FBI Academy in 1935. After his retirement, he served as the special assistant to the chancellor at the University of Mississippi, where he was a pivotal figure in the school's acceptance of its first black student, James Meredith. Earl Connelly remained a top administrator at the FBI for two decades after the "war on crime" came to an end. He retired in 1956 and died one year later. Pop Nathan, often called the "grand old man of the FBI," retired in 1945. He died in 1963.

Many of those captured by the FBI during the "war on crime" years became the earliest inmates at Alcatraz prison, which opened in January 1935. When Alvin Karpis arrived there, he joked that it was like "old home week." On his first day, he renewed acquaintances with Machine Gun Kelly, Harvey Bailey, Dock Barker, Harry Sawyer, and Volney Davis. He would later come to know Nelson's partner, John Chase, and, of course, Al Capone, whose eminence in the criminal world predated his own.

Alvin Karpis spent 33 years behind bars. After Alcatraz was closed down by Attorney General Robert F. Kennedy, he was sent to McNeil Island in Washington, from where he was paroled in January 1969. He was immediately deported to Canada. It's likely that Hoover had a hand in that. He authored two ghostwritten books, including an autobiography, before moving to Spain in the early 1970s. He died on August 26, 1979, after an apparent accidental overdose of pills.

Others involved in the "war on crime" era met a multitude of fates. On February 6, 1935, Karpis's future fellow Alcatraz resident, Volney Davis, was arrested in St. Louis and packed onto a charter flight to Chicago. When the plane stopped to refuel in Yorktown, Illinois, Davis joined two Bureau agents drinking beer in a local bar. When one agent went to make a phone call, Davis smashed the other agent in the face with a beer mug, jumped out a window, and disappeared. The same day, Davis's girlfriend, Edna Murray, and another gang member, were arrested after a running shoot-out in Kansas. Davis wasn't recaptured until June 1, in Chicago. It was the last arrest that Melvin Purvis ever made.

Dock Barker was shot and killed attempting to escape from Alcatraz in January 1939. Ma Barker's last living son, Lloyd, who never joined the Barker gang but was pursued by Hoover anyway, was released from Leavenworth in 1947. He was shot to death by his wife in their Denver home two years later.

John Chase was captured in California in December 1934, and was flown back to Chicago, where he went on trial for murdering Sam Cowley on March 18, 1935. He was the first criminal to be tried under the new law that made it a federal crime to kill a Bureau agent in the performance of his duties. Chase was found guilty one week later and sentenced to life imprisonment at Alcatraz. He became eligible for parole in October 1955, when a district judge dismissed the indictment, charging him with the murder of Agent Hollis because he had never been tried for the crime. He was released from prison on October 31, 1966, and died seven years later.

The side players in the Dillinger story lived lives that usually seemed to end in obscurity. After the night at the Biograph Theater, John Dillinger, Sr. was offered

Members of the Dillinger family toured the country with traveling carnivals and sideshows, appearing in "Crimes Does Not Pay" performances for a number of years

$10,000 for the corpse of his famous son. He declined. This was at a time when carnival sideshows traveled the country with such macabre displays as the "death car" of Bonnie and Clyde and the electric chair that claimed the life of killer Ruth Snyder. Dillinger's pickled corpse would have been just par for the course. Dillinger's father was determined that his son would not fall victim to body snatchers. He had the burial plot at Crown Hill Cemetery filled with concrete and scrap metal and to combat souvenir hunters. He didn't place a stone on the grave for two years. This only slowed down the destruction, though, and it was soon chipped away to nothing. The marker that rests on the grave today is the fourth replacement.

Mr. Dillinger did eventually accept invitations to lecture in stage shows, in traveling carnivals, sideshows and even at Little Bohemia, where the industrious Emil Wanetka established a "Terror Gang Museum. After his death in 1943, Dillinger was buried next to his son's gravesite.

Things did not go well for the infamous "Lady in Red," Ana Sage. She received $5,000 of the Dillinger reward money, but the FBI couldn't stop her from being deported. It's unknown if anyone even tried. Back in Romania, the authorities refused to let her perform for a vaudeville company when she announced she wanted to tell the "true story" of the Dillinger gang. She opened a restaurant and night club, but when criminals tried to extort money from her, she fled. Desperate, she changed her name and even tried to have plastic surgery to alter her appearance. Her face was so badly disfigured after the surgery that she entered a private sanitarium for many years.

Her life ended in April 1947, in Romania. She died from liver cancer.

Martin Zarkovich remained the chief of detectives in the East Chicago Police Department and later became the police chief from 1947 to 1952. His career was unaffected by whatever connections he had to the Dillinger case. After his retirement, he worked as a probation officer until his death in October 1969, at the age of 71. Whatever secrets he harbored about John Dillinger, he took them with him to the grave.

Polly Hamilton, the other person who shared Dillinger's greatest secret, went into hiding after the incident at the Biograph. She rarely spoke of her brief time with Dillinger and was never charged with anything after his death. She lived a normal and quiet life, under assumed names, mostly working as a waitress. She later married William Black, a Chicago salesman, and died as Edythe Black in February 1969.

After Billie Frechette, whose life might have been very different if she had not been arrested, finished her prison sentence in 1936. She then toured with John Dillinger, Sr. in a "crime does not pay" carnival show, talking about her famous boyfriend to rapt audiences. When interest faded, Billie vanished into obscurity. She married a Wisconsin man name Arthur Tic, bore him children, and died of cancer in January 1969, just one month before Polly Hamilton.

Beryl Hovius, Dillinger's only wife, lived the longest out of all of Dillinger's women. She died of a stroke on November 30, 1993, in Mooresville, Indiana, just a mile from the Dillinger farm. She was 87 when she died.

After Opal Long finished her prison sentence, she slipped into obscurity and died in Chicago in 1969. Her sister, Pat Cherrington, was released from the prison farm at Milan, Michigan, in July 1936. She also toured on the carnival circuit for a time, then worked as a waitress, tavern hostess, and dice girl on North Clark Street in Chicago. She retained her ties to the underworld and in 1938, she and two men were accused of trying to hustle a pool player out of $9,000. For the rest of her life, she lived a poor existence in rooming houses. Harry Copeland sent her love letters from prison, saying that he thought he would be out by November 1949. An employee found her dead in her room at the Burton Hotel on May 3, 1949. She only had $2.16 to her name. Harry Copeland did get out of prison on November 24. He died on December 7, 1963, when he was run over by a car.

Mary Kinder also used her notoriety to perform in a carnival sideshow and traveling wax museum called "Scott Younger's Exhibit of Outlawry." She lived until 1981, when she died from a combination of pulmonary edema, heart disease, emphysema, and acute respiratory failure.

John Hamilton's sister, Anna Steve, was indicted for harboring two fugitives in June 1934. She and her son, Charles Campbell, went to trial in 1935. Anna was found guilty and sentenced to four months in prison, but Charles was found not guilty.

Helen Gillis returned to Chicago after her release from the federal prison farm in Milan, Michigan. Working under the name Helen Nelson, she spent the rest of her life avoiding any kind of recognition. She lived out her years working in a Chicago factory and raising the couple's children. Helen died in 1987, and was buried next to her husband.

Russell Clark remained at the Ohio State Penitentiary after the attempted breakout and execution of Pierpont and Makley. He was one of the ring leaders of a strike by nearly 1,000 convicts in April 1935, which led to a lengthy stay in solitary confinement. In 1940, he and three other convicts made an escape attempt – used a fake gun they had carved out of wood. It didn't work.

Clark eventually faded into obscurity. Friends and family members died, and even federal agents stopped coming to question him as the "war on crime" became a thing of the past. He spent more than 34 years in the penitentiary. He first came up for parole in April 1954, but his request was denied. He was finally released in September 1968, after doctors learned that he had lung cancer and estimated he had less than six months to live. He was taken in by his sister, Dorothy Pierce, in Hazel Park, Michigan, where he died on December 24, 1968.

Ed Shouse, the gang member that Dillinger had kicked out of the group, was released from prison on September 9, 1946. His fortunes rapidly declined and he was arrested in Spokane, Washington, on a vagrancy charge in 1952. He was arrested for not paying for a meal in Minneapolis in 1955. Four years later, in Chicago, he was dead.

Harold Cassidy, the doctor who assisted with Dillinger's plastic surgery, committed suicide in 1946. Dr. Wilhelm Loeser later settled in Oklahoma, where he died around 1956. Dillinger's lawyer, Louis Piquett, was convicted of harboring Homer Van Meter. He was disbarred, ordered to pay a $10,000 fine, and was sent to Leavenworth for two years. He became a bartender after his release, stayed out of trouble, and lived quietly with his wife. He was pardoned by President Harry S. Truman in 1951, despite opposition from Hoover. He died of a heart attack at age 71 on December 12, 1951. Art O'Leary was able to avoid any prison time in return for testimony that put Piquett behind bars. He is believed to have died in Dubuque, Iowa, around 1970.

Matt Leach, the cop who would have "tried to pin the Lincoln assassination" on Dillinger lost his job with the Indiana State Police in 1937, largely due to his lack of cooperation with the Bureau. He wrote a book about the Dillinger case, but it was never published. Leach and his wife died together on June 14, 1955, in an accident on the Pennsylvania Turnpike.

One oddity: In 1936, two high-ranking Secret Service officials, Joseph E. Murphy and Grady Boatwright, tried to look into Eddie Green's death to see if there was any merit to the claims that he had been murdered in cold blood by the Bureau. But Hoover was tipped off to the investigation. Attorney General Cummings filed a complaint with Secretary of the Treasury Henry Morgenthau, and the two Secret Service officials were transferred to other positions. Hoover kept a .45 bullet that was taken out of Green's body for many years in his personal collection.

Of course, Eddie Green was just one of the "public enemies" that was shot in the back, executed in cold blood, or shot down while running away.

For the rest of his life, J. Edgar Hoover remained obsessed with the era of the "war on crime." As the FBI sank into controversies over its handling of civil rights and other cases, Hoover's fascination with Dillinger and the other bandits of the era only grew. FBI Assistant Director William Sullivan once said, "Hoover had a thing about Dillinger. If he were alive today and you went to see him, he'd tell you about Dillinger. The older he got, the more he talked about John Dillinger... He would talk on and on about this stuff. Hooved died in his sleep on May 1, 1972, and his Dillinger obsession continued literally until the day he died.

One has to wonder if he always wondered if the truth might someday come out. As he grew older, I believe that he came to fear it.

35. Dillinger: Dead or Alive?

When the body of the man believed to be John Dillinger arrived at the Cook County Morgue, it was greeted by mobs of people, and yet the scene at the Biograph Theater remained chaotic. Spectators swarmed Lincoln Avenue outside of the theater, blocking traffic and milling about in confusion. The "extra" edition of the newspapers were soon hitting the streets. "John Dillinger died tonight as he lived, in a hail of lead and swelter of blood," one of them reported. "He died with a smile on his lips and a woman on each arm."

Tradition holds that passersby ran to the scene and dipped their handkerchiefs in the blood of the fallen legend, taking away a macabre souvenir. But it was not just at the Biograph. "I'll give him $1,000 for his shirt!" a man reportedly called out at the Bankers Building the next morning, trying to buy the shirt off Melvin Purvis's back because it allegedly was spotted with the gangster's blood. On Lincoln Avenue, some tried to pry bullet fragments from a wooden light pole at the alley where he was shot. Some of the stray bullets were said to have damaged the pole, but souvenir-seekers made the pole so unsteady that it had to be replaced by city workers soon after the shooting. The Biograph itself became famous – and infamous – in the days, weeks, and years to come. A nearby tavern placed a sign in its window that falsely claimed "Dillinger had his last drink here."

All of this is part of the lore of the Dillinger shooting. But underneath all of the stories, official accounts given by men like Purvis, who later claimed that he called out, "Stick 'em up, Johnnie, we have you surrounded," even though he clearly didn't do so before the agents at the scene shot the fleeing man in the back, and the eyewitness accounts that tell a number of different versions of what happened that night, there is a lingering mystery.

It began in the moments after the shooting. Around 10:45 p.m., a Chicago police wagon was called to serve as an ambulance and soon arrived at the Biograph Theater. It approached from the back of the theater, backing down the alley. The dead man was still lying in a pool of blood at the alleyway's entrance. Several men lifted the corpse onto a stretcher and then placed it on the wagon's floor. The wagon drove off with five unidentified agents and three Chicago police officers inside. The wagon went first to the Alexian Brothers Hospital where, on the front lawn, the fallen man was pronounced dead. Then it went straight to the morgue, arriving there around 11:15 p.m.

There were a few items that should have been with the dead man, but they had been taken by Bureau agents at the scene. One item was the dead man's straw hat. Another was the gun that was allegedly taken off Dillinger that was later

Even on the morning after the shooting, people were still gathering at the alley entrance near the Biograph to see the spot where Dillinger was allegedly gunned down.

placed on display at the FBI museum in Washington. It was a .38 Colt automatic, bearing the serial number of 119702. When this weapon was later traced through the records of Colt's Patent Fire Arms Manufacturing Company, it was discovered that it was sold for the first time to the L.H. Kurz Company of Des Moines, Iowa, on December 19, 1934 -- five months after the death of the man claimed to be Dillinger. While this is certainly strange, it's not unexplainable. It's possible that someone kept the real gun found on the body that night as a souvenir, replacing the weapon with a lookalike. Or perhaps the genuine gun was simply misplaced.

What is more disturbing is the problem with the pair of glasses that the man was wearing to the theater that night. The glasses were also taken by Bureau agents before the body was taken to the morgue, so there is no mystery about what happened to them. It is the nature of the glasses themselves that has

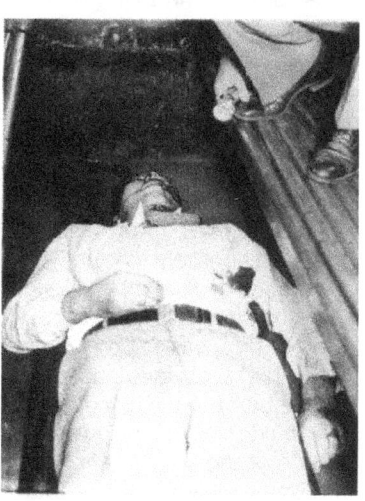

The dead man was placed inside the police wagon that served as an ambulance.

never been explained. Melvin Purvis later claimed that the glasses Dillinger wore that night were dark, but this was not the case. The glasses had rather expensive gold rims and, although the lenses were shattered by the man's fall, they were regular prescription glasses. In 1934, sunglasses were cheap and sold in drug stores. They did not come fitted with expensive rims and they were not available with eye prescriptions. The glasses worn by the dead man that night were corrective lenses. The dead man had poor vision, and yet John Dillinger's eyesight was perfect. So, who did the glasses belong to? Or perhaps the better question is, who was wearing the corrective glasses that night?

And this was just the beginning.

In the wake of the shootout at the Biograph, eyewitness accounts (and even official records, as you are about to see) have given support to the theory that the dead man in the alley that night might not have been Dillinger. Rumors have persisted that another man was killed in his place, set up by Martin Zarkovich so that Dillinger could escape. Many mainstream historians have called this theory "revisionist nonsense," but it's impossible to ignore some of the strange *facts* that have come to light. Over the years, I have started to seriously consider the idea that Dillinger escaped death in 1934, and have even developed my own theory about how this was all pulled off, a little of which has been hinted at already in this volume.

First, let's look at some of the incidents that seem suspicious about the behavior of "John Dillinger" that night at the Biograph, and then we'll delve into some of the undeniable problems with the pathology examination that occurred that night, and the autopsy that took place the following morning.

It is hard not to call attention to how the man believed to be Dillinger acted that night at the theater. During the film, Bureau agents, including Melvin Purvis, entered the theater auditorium several times and walking down the aisles, insuring that their target was still in his seat. It seems hard to believe that Dillinger would not have noticed this careless surveillance. It's true that Dillinger had made himself very visible on the North Side for the past few weeks (more about that soon), but it seems very likely that he would have noticed the Bureau men as they canvassed the theater that night. Dillinger had eluded capture for months since the Crown Point breakout, largely because of the carelessness of poorly-trained Bureau agents. This was another example of that and yet Dillinger supposedly did not notice these obvious and clumsy attempts to check up on him. It's difficult to believe that the movie could have been that riveting.

In addition, it's also very odd that Dillinger would not recognize Melvin Purvis outside of the theater after the movie was over. Purvis ridiculously stepped right in Dillinger's path, fumbled with his cigar, and did practically everything but shout that he was there to arrest him. But "Dillinger" never noticed. By this time, Dillinger should have recognized Purvis since his face had been plastered on the front pages of newspapers across the country, especially in Chicago, and Dillinger was an avid reader of the current papers. He loved to read about his own exploits, as well as false reports about what he was up to. It seems hard to believe that he would not be familiar with the men who were after him – especially since we know he was familiar with Matt Leach of the Indiana State Police – especially Purvis, who was in every paper, especially after the Little Bohemia fiasco.

And yes, when "Dillinger" walked out of the theater, he looked directly at Purvis, even met his eye for a moment, without a flicker of recognition, and kept on walking. Was it because the man in the straw hat didn't know who Melvin Purvis was, even though John Dillinger would have recognized him and realized he was walking into a trap?

Of course, this is all just speculation. It's asking questions about things that seem odd, or out of place, but all of it can be explained away by simply saying that Dillinger had an "off" night, or he had just become so convinced of his own invincibility that he didn't need to watch out for the law. Homer Van Meter had accused Dillinger of living too openly, and of acting like a fool. Was he right about that, or did Dillinger have a longer end game in mind with his costumes and his false identity?

For now, let's look at what the medical records had to say about the body that was brought to the Cook County Morgue on July 22, 1934.

The Evidence

On the night of July 22, the body publicly acknowledged as that of John Dillinger was first examined at the morgue by Dr. Charles D. Parker, who was assistant to the coroner's pathologist, Dr. J.J. Kearns. Parker had also been involved in other famous Chicago crimes, including conducting an examination of young Bobby Franks, who was murdered by Nathan Leopold and Richard Loeb in 1924, and the 1929 slayings of seven men during the St. Valentine's Day Massacre.

Dr. Parker arrived at the morgue at a few minutes after 11:00 and had to make his way through more than 2,000 sweat-soaked people who were milling about outside, shouting and calling out that Dillinger had been killed. He managed to get into the receiving room in the morgue basement. There were only a few people in the room. The body had not yet arrived. Everyone present was wearing civilian clothes, but Parker believed that they were Bureau agents and Chicago detectives.

Parker was not only there to do his job, but he also had an ulterior motive: to try and get an exclusive for his pal, Tony Steger, at the *Chicago Tribune*. He was going to try and prevent rival newspaper photographers and reporters from getting into the morgue to get the story.

Without any actual authority, the young doctor took charge of the situation. He hustled a receiving cart with wheels up to the entrance door and waited. As would later be seen in photographs, he was wearing a white shirt, short tie, and a straw boater pushed back on his head. He rolled up his sleeves, adjusted his glasses, and waited with the silent men for the body of the bandit to arrive. A few seconds later, the receiving door flew open, and uniformed policemen brought in the body. It was placed on Parker's cart, and he wheeled it back to the center of the room under the lights.

As Parker went to work on the corpse, he noticed that its white shirt was stained with blood. The dead man was wearing neatly pressed gray pants – there were blood spots in the crotch and the tip of the right front pocket – white oxfords, black socks, and a gray tie. Slowly, he removed the clothes and when they were off, he began washing blood from the body. Exploding flashes from *Tribune*

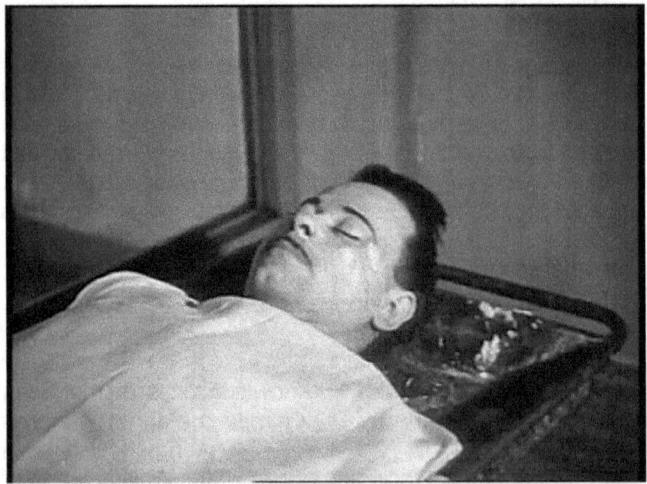

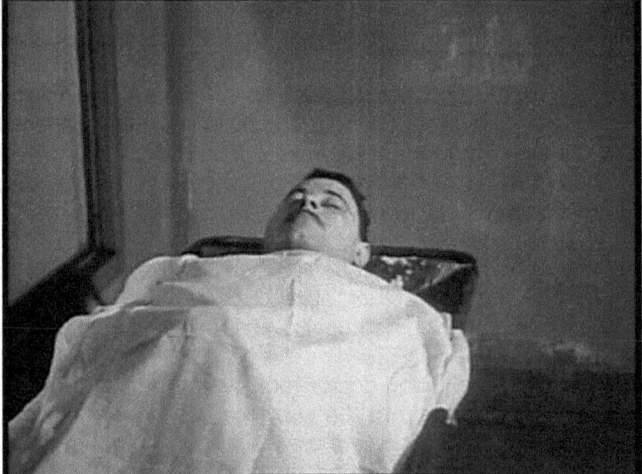

Two different views of the body in the morgue, which was never officially identified nor fingerprinted on the night of July 22, despite later claims by the Bureau.

cameras were now bathing the morgue room in brilliant light. Parker washed the body, especially the face, over and over again.

According to Parker's account, no one had yet come into the morgue to identify the body or take fingerprints. Parker noticed that the fingerprints of the corpse were scarred, but this was a common practice in those days, for many criminals — although not John Dillinger. Dock and Fred Barker had attempted to have their fingerprints removed by Dr. Wilhelm Loeser, the same man who had performed Dillinger's plastic surgery, but the operation had failed. Homer Van Meter also attempted it, using a hydrochloric acid solution, but it hadn't worked for him either.

Everyone who was present in the morgue — attendants, newsmen, unidentified lawmen — all crowded around Parker for a better look at the corpse. Parker later said, "Everybody sort of identified him." He spoke up, "That's him, that's Dillinger." No one asked questions.

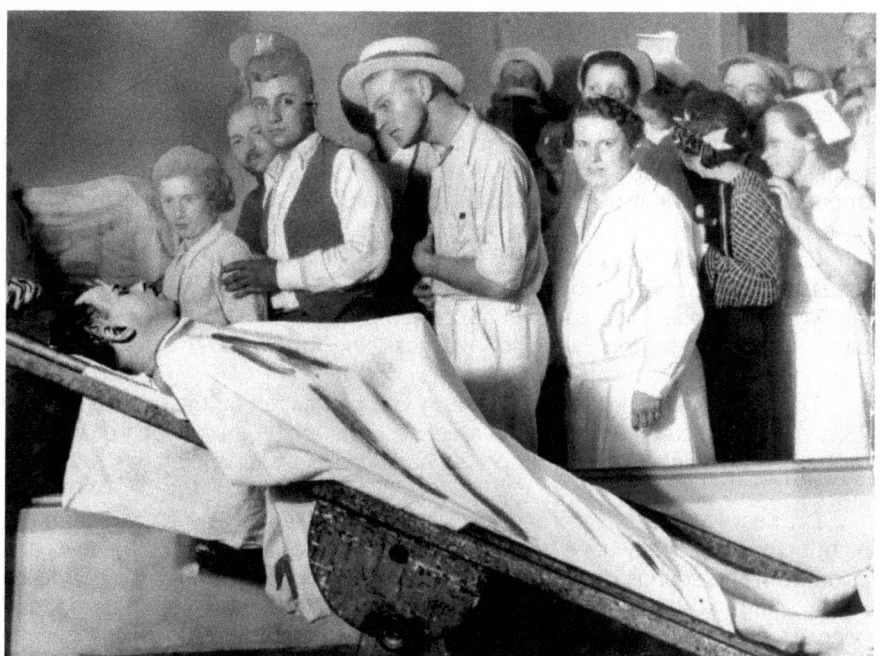

After the initial examination of the body, Coroner Frank Walsh allowed what he called the "morbids" waiting outside to view the body. Over the course of the next few hours, thousands of people walked past to stare at the corpse.

Parker stayed with the body for about an hour. It was after midnight before he left the morgue. In spite of this, the fingerprints that were allegedly taken from the corpse, which eventually appeared on a Chicago Police Department identification card (even though they should have been on a Bureau card, since it was strictly a Bureau case) were dated July 22, 1934. However, this is impossible since Parker was present at the morgue during the last hour of July 22 and no one ever came to take the prints. This seems to be a glaring mistake and does throw some doubt on their authenticity. But that's just the beginning of the problems with the fingerprints, as we will soon discover.

Before Parker left, he washed the face again, wiping it down over and over again to remove the blood that was welling up from several head wounds. He was careful to note the color of the dead man's moustache, hair, and eyebrows. Dillinger had brown hair and the Bureau later claimed that he had dyed his hair black as a disguise. That much is true; Dillinger had dyed his hair as part of the new identity that he had adopted to blend in on the North Side. But according to Dr. Parker, none of the color came out of the dead man's hair. It was "as dark when we left as when we got there," he said.

The dead man had black hair. It had never been dyed.

Parker labored for an hour over the dead man. He was nearly exhausted by the oppressive heat in the room. Finally, he left with the newsmen and the lawmen. The crowd outside of the morgue had been growing steadily, and all of them were restless for a peek at the dead man. A 19-year-old girl squatted down to look through the basement window. Dozens of others pressed against her for a look. "I see him!" the girl squealed in delight.

Coroner Frank Walsh thought it prudent to allow the "morbids," the couple of thousand people milling around outside, a chance to file in for a last look at the famous bank robber. The doors were opened to the public and they began to file past, whispering, staring, laughing, and gossiping for hours. The dead man had been placed on a tilted cart, for better viewing.

The autopsy was still to take place. It was conducted on the morning of July 23, by Dr. J.J. Kearns and it would reveal some startling information of its own, far beyond anything revealed during the preliminary examination.

Dr. Kearns went to work the next morning in silence. The crowds from the night before had finally gone home. The doors had been closed to the public, and aside from the sounds of routine activity in the building, the morgue had fallen silent. A tag had been tied around the dead man's toe. Even though he had not been fingerprinted or officially identified, it read: "#116 July, John Dillinger, by Dist. 37, 7-22-34," meaning that it was the 116th body to be registered at the morgue during the month of July, and it had been delivered there by the Sheffield Avenue police district.

Dr. Kearns began to work on the body, and this was where the problems began. Some of the issues were minor, like the fact that Dillinger's age was listed as 32-years-old, even though he had turned only 31 just one month before the Biograph slaying. There was also the dead man's weight of 160 pounds. If this was accurate, it was heavier than Dillinger had ever been in his life. When he had been weighed at Crown Point in March, he was listed as 153 pounds. It seems unlikely that he would have gained seven pounds after four months, spent largely on the run, but it's possible. There was also his height of five-foot-seven, which some say would have been inaccurate because Dillinger would have expanded beyond his normal height in the hot and humid weather conditions in Chicago at the time. Dr. Kearns was so meticulous that he would not have made an error like this, it has been pointed out. But again, these were minor discrepancies, easily explained, but others were not.

In fact, some of these discrepancies make it impossible for the body on the table to have been that of John Dillinger.

It began with the scars, or rather, the lack of them. During the exam, Dr. Kearns made no mention of Dillinger's telltale scars, as listed on the Bureau's order no. 1217: "A half-inch scar on the back of the left hand and a scar running on an angle up from the middle of the upper lip to the left nostril." He also did not find a bullet-wound scar in the corpse's right shoulder, which was impossible since

Dillinger had been shot during the First National Bank robbery in Mason City, Iowa, just five months before the Biograph shooting.

And then there were the facial scars, which were not recognized as being the result of plastic surgery, even though plastic surgery was exactly how the Bureau explained away the missing scars, cleft chin, and other marks on the corpse in the morgue. The Bureau would come to accept all of the claims made by Dr. Loeser about his "skill" with the knife, even though during the trial of Louis Piquett, it was shown that Loeser was basically a butcher who possessed only the basic skills of plastic surgery. The Bureau only saw that the corpse had facial scars and since Dillinger was rumored at that point to have undergone cosmetic surgery, then the corpse had to be Dillinger.

But the Bureau's reasoning was based on a number of mistaken notions and outright fallacies. First, it was assumed that the human face could be altered through plastic surgery so that it would give the appearance of a totally different person. This was not true in 1934, and today, it takes multiple surgeries to achieve such a thing. Dillinger had one, short surgery, that made minor alterations. And yet, the Bureau later used plastic surgery as the reason why Dillinger's father, brother, sister, and others failed to identify his corpse.

Second, the Bureau implied that the reason that certain scars that were known to be on Dillinger and were not on the corpse were because they had been removed by surgery. But again, plastic surgery cannot totally remove a scar. Scars could, in 1934, be minimized through a series of operations but could not be totally removed. For example, if Dr. Loeser had tried to remove the scar on Dillinger's upper lip a few weeks before the shooting, it still would have been marked by a reddish area. In fact, in those days, a removed scar could remain in a reddened state for up to two years. As mentioned, Dr. Kearns made no mention of this scar on Dillinger's face.

Everyone who saw the corpse noted how much "fuller" Dillinger's face was, even though this was the opposite of what Dr. Loeser claimed that he did to the bandit's face. He claimed that he had pulled back the skin of Dillinger's face to change his appearance. There was also no mention of Dillinger having his nose changed, and yet, oddly, Melvin Purvis, on examining the corpse outside the Biograph, admitted that the corpse's nose was different from that of Dillinger. In fact, he felt compelled to remark that the nose was "a neat piece of plastic surgery." Bur Dr. Kearns mentioned no evidence of scarring or grafting on the nose of the dead man. His nose had not been changed.

As the autopsy continued, and the body was opened up, Kearns examined the dead man's heart. He discovered: "Rheumatic mitral verrucous endocarditis... The mitral leaflets were thickened, the commissures partly obliterated. The corda tendinae and papillary muscles were thickened. There were pin-point to pin-head-sized, semi-firm warty vegetations of the auricular surface of the free margins of the mitral leaflets. The intima of the aorta and coronary arteries contained a few atheromatous plaques." In other words, in laymen's terms, the dead man had a rheumatic heart condition that had chronically developed since childhood. He also had arteriosclerosis, a thickening and hardening of the walls of the arteries.

But, John Dillinger never had rheumatic fever as a child, or as an adult. Dillinger's naval service records said that his heart was in perfect condition. He could not have played baseball, joined the Navy, or carried out many of his athletic bank robberies with the sort of heart condition that the dead man had.

And then there is the famous tooth – or rather the one that John Dillinger did not have. In dozens of photographs that were taken of Dillinger during that period, he is clearly missing his top right incisor. And yet, the body on the table at the morgue had the tooth.

But there was still one other thing that Dr. Kearns noted on the autopsy report, and it's the one thing that truly makes it impossible for the corpse on the table to have been John Dillinger. During the exam, Kearns leaned over the face and carefully opened the eyelids. He stared into the dead man's eyes. It was noted in the report: "Size of pupils, dilated. Color of iris, brown."

Brown? According the U.S. Navy records, John Dillinger's eyes were blue. According to the Bureau's identification for wanted posters, they were gray. According to Billie Frechette, they were bluish-gray. But they were certainly never brown. So, who was the brown-eyed man on the slab in the morgue? As far as Kearns and the rest of the world knew, the man was John Dillinger. No one bothered to check the records and find the discrepancies, at least not then anyway.

There was still the issue with the mysterious fingerprints. According to Dr. Parker, the dead man's fingerprints had been scarred, but not obliterated, so they should have been identifiable. Medical experts who have studied photographs of the fingerprints report that the fingerprints were hardly disturbed, and attempts that were made to disfigure them were not done professionally.

Newspaper reports almost immediately stated that the body was matched to Dillinger by way of a fingerprint card, but this was not the case. No one came into the morgue while Dr. Parker was there, so any fingerprinting of the corpse was done at a later time.

The Bureau never officially released the name of the man who allegedly took the dead man's prints and matched them to Dillinger's. He remains unknown to this day. The signature at the bottom of the print card is illegible, and it cannot be attributed to either Bureau Agents Richmond or Chaffetz, both of whom, at one time or another, were reported to be the ones who took the prints for the Bureau.

Interestingly, during the 1935 trial of Louis Piquett, Dillinger's attorney, the fingerprint expert who testified about the alleged prints was none other than Deputy Sheriff Ernest Blunk of Lake County, Indiana – the same man widely believed to have aided Dillinger in his escape from the Crown Point jail. He was even indicted for his role in it. Blunk, a friend of Martin Zarkovich, was appointed to his position by Zarkovich's friend, Judge William Murray. At the trial, this so-called fingerprint authority – the only one used by the government prosecution – claimed that Dillinger's and the dead man's fingerprints were the same.

When interviewed years later, former Agents Virgil Peterson and Walter Devereux, both of whom were with the Bureau during the Biograph shooting, reported that they could not recall who it was that took the prints, vaguely stating that they thought "some little guy came in from the east coast to take the prints."

Neither could recall the man's name. It seems far-fetched to believe that the Bureau flew in some expert from Washington to take the prints when there were 50 or so agents in Chicago at the time, and any one of them could have taken the dead man's fingerprints. It became apparent, both from the record of the prints and the statements of the Bureau, that no agent ever actually took the prints. And honestly, this should come as no great surprise based on the many mistakes that were being made by agents in the Chicago office at the time.

We do know that the only record that exists of Dillinger's prints from *after* the shooting were taken on a Chicago Police Department card, so this rules out the idea that the Bureau ever took them. Since the Biograph stakeout was an exclusive Bureau operation – and no Chicago officers were used – makes it very strange that the Chicago police would have *definitive* prints. Dillinger was never arrested by the Chicago police and could not have obtained his prints prior to the shooting. Even though the Bureau insisted that they had fingerprinted the corpse, this seems to be impossible, which has led many to believe that the prints that identified Dillinger as the dead man were planted after the fact.

The evidence for this is compelling. Not only are the prints on a Chicago PD fingerprint card, not on a Bureau card, but the date is incorrect. The card states that the fingerprints were taken on July 22, 1934, but according to Dr. Charles Parker, the dead man was not fingerprinted while he was present. He was there into the early morning hours of July 23. Also, the person who filled out the card was unsure of the Bureau's official title. He wrote, "Dept. of Fe," then crossed part of it out and wrote, "Justice Print." The Bureau, even the Chicago police, would not have made that kind of error. If it had been a genuine Department of Justice print, the Bureau would have used the official system of classification as it appeared on the Bureau's Order no. 1217, and all other Bureau fingerprint records relating to the Dillinger gang, which were totally disregarded. Still, there are the prints that were upheld by the Bureau as its own and exclusively offered as its evidence of identification – a card that is not even dated correctly.

To make it even worse, the shooting was even given the wrong address. On the card it states, "Shot and killed by Gov. Men, 2424 Lincoln Avenue July 22, 1934." Oddly, no Bureau agents of the time referred to themselves as "government men" or "G-men." That was underworld slang and soon, the stuff of movies and comic books. But ignoring that, no Chicago cop (and this was a Chicago PD fingerprint card) would put down the wrong address for the shooting. The Biograph was located at 2433 North Lincoln, on the east side of the street. The fingerprint card places the body at 2424 North Lincoln, which is the west side of the street. Only someone other than a law enforcement officer would place the body across the street from the actual site of death.

Silly mistakes? Coincidence? Perhaps. But the reader can certainly see how the fingerprint card, which appeared in the files after a long absence has added fuel to the fire about a conspiracy to cover up the fact that the Bureau killed the wrong man. Of course, there is no proof that the card – riddled with mistakes – was actually "planted" in the files, and it's this small doubt that mainstream historians used to dismiss the possibility that someone other than Dillinger died that night. But accepting the card as legitimate is one thing, but what about ignoring the absence of scars, the color of the dead man's eyes, and his heart condition?

It seems hard to believe that people refuse to even consider the idea that the Bureau got the wrong man that night, but they do. Even when faced with this evidence, they laugh and say that it couldn't have happened the way that myself, and others, suggest. But, wait, because there is more to come.

The Family

Except for a crowd of curiosity-seekers that gathered at the rear of the building, waiting around the exit used by funeral homes, the morgue was nearly deserted when Ray McReady, owner of the McReady Funeral Home, located at 4506 North Sheridan Road, arrived for the dead man. How and why McReady came to handle the embalming of the dead man remains a mystery. If he had any connection to the underworld in Chicago, to Martin Zarkovich, Dillinger or Dillinger's family, it has never been found. McReady was a secretive man and he never spoke of the service that he provided. But there is one very strange thing about the embalming. According to McReady's files, the date that was recorded for Dillinger's death was July 14, 1934 – eight days before the actual shooting. This oddity has never been explained either.

The funeral home was located about nine miles away from the morgue, at Polk and Wood Streets. This seemed strange since it was the usual custom of the time to turn bodies over to funeral homes in the vicinity of the morgue after they had been processed. Some maintain that moving the body to McReady's was done to dissuade the crowds of gawkers from further mobbing the body. But there was no secret to the move. The newspapers published the fact that McReady would handle the body, and thousands showed up there.

When McReady arrived to pick up the body, he was delayed by Coroner Walsh, who wanted to give the crowds another look at the corpse. He ordered the doors opened again to the public. Again, several thousand people were ushered past for another look at the now-famous body. While this was taking place, Walsh continued making out the Coroner's Certificate of Death – No. 20810. At the line reading "matter of injury?" Walsh wrote: "Deceased shot by unidentified Department of Justice officials." He then added that cause of death was "justifiable homicide."

Soon after, Dillinger's father, John Dillinger, Sr., and Dillinger's half-brother, Hubert, arrived from Mooresville, with their own hometown mortician, E.F. Harvey. Everett Moore, from the *Mooresville Times* newspaper, came with them.

When Mr. Dillinger looked at the corpse, he leaned on Hubert's arm. He made no positive identification. He stared at the body and then said to the reporters who were present, "I think he got a raw deal from the start. I don't believe it was right to kill him the way they did." Hubert looked carefully at the body, but he did not speak.

The body being removed from the morgue, bound for McReady's Funeral Home, in a wicker basket

The body was then taken to McReady's in a wicker casket. A newsman that was perched on a second-story ledge of the morgue building cranked a camera, capturing it all for a movie newsreel. When shown, the shorty clip did not draw the same kind of applause that had followed Dillinger's appearances in newsreels earlier in the year.

The Dillingers traveled to the McReady Funeral Home and while the body was being embalmed, they waited upstairs in McReady's office. Soon after they arrived, they found several Bureau agents waiting for them. They demanded to know where Van Meter and Nelson were hiding, where John Hamilton was, had they been contacted by any members of Dillinger's gang, what had happened to the thousands of dollars taken from banks that remained unaccounted for, and more.

Mr. Dillinger steadied himself against McReady's desk. "Gentlemen," he said to the agents," I really don't know the answers to any of your questions."

The Bureau men stormed out of the office, but were soon replaced by reporters, who began badgering the elderly farmer with questions of their own. Hubert, who had remained silent during the Bureau agents' questions, suddenly became upset and shouted at the press men. "You god-damned vultures, get out of here!" he yelled.

But Mr. Dillinger calmed him down. He had been dealing with the press for the last year, after his son had started appearing on the front pages of papers across the country. "This is the first trip that I've made to Chicago since the Columbian Exposition in 1893," he told them.

"What about your son, Mr. Dillinger?" one of them asked.

"They shot him down in cold blood," the old man shook his head. "He was surrounded by 15 men and that ain't fair. I'd rather have him shot than captured, though, and John would rather have had it that way."

That night, the Dillingers were taken to a nearby hotel to rest. The next morning, Mr. Dillinger saw the corpse again and stated, "He is changed considerably." He made no further statements about the body.

E.F. Harvey, the mortician from Mooresville, told Mr. Dillinger that the brain, along with other vital organs, had been removed from the body for study by a pathologist from the University of Chicago. This was done without the permission of the family, and to make it worse, the brain was never replaced.

When the embalming process was finished, the body was loaded into Harvey's hearse. The Dillinger's got inside and they began the journey back to Mooresville. All along Route 41 into Indiana, crowds gathered to watch the hearse pass by them. Chicago police cars, with lights and sirens, had escorted the vehicle to the Indiana border. When it finally stopped at the Harvey Funeral Home, Mr. Dillinger shakily climbed out. He had spent the entire trip sitting next to the corpse.

The next day, the *Mooresville Times* reported: "Dillinger comes home for the last time. Men stood with heads uncovered, and women spoke in hushed tones – a tribute to Dillinger's father, John W. Dillinger, who, throughout the many months his son has terrorized the nation, has held the respect of the community."

The corpse, draped with a brocaded blanket, was placed on a cot in the small funeral parlor. Harvey explained, "John's face isn't just right, but we're going to straighten it up." An expert mortician from Indianapolis had been hired to come and patch up the dead man's face, which was marred with abrasions from the fall to the pavement.

Soon, the show started all over again as Harvey opened the doors to over 5,000 people who had assembled to view the body. Almost the entire town of Mooresville, and many from the surrounding area, filed past the corpse on the cot. When they saw the body, many people who had known John Dillinger recoiled in disbelief, stating matter-of-factly that the body at the funeral home was *not* Johnnie. Some assumed it was a joke, or a hoax, or some sort of publicity stunt. "If that's Johnnie Dillinger, I'll eat my hat," one man said. Another told his wife, "Mother, I think the wrong man has been killed."

Of all of the people who came to see the body, though, one of them should have been able to recognize the dead man instantly as John Dillinger: his beloved sister, Audrey, who had raised him as a boy and who remained devoted to him even as he became the most wanted man in America. She entered the funeral parlor silently and stared at the body for a very long time. Then she slowly began

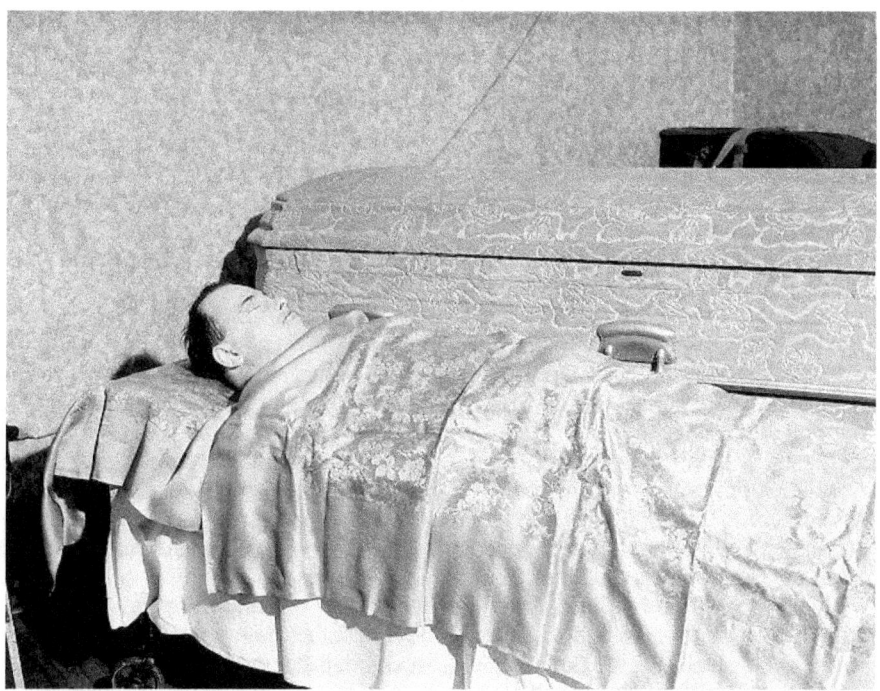

The body on display at the Harvey Funeral in Mooresville, where people who had known Dillinger his entire life could take one last look at him. Scores of them refused to believe that the body was that of John Dillinger.

to shake her head back and forth. She did not recognize the man's face. In fact, she told Harvey that she was not convinced the dead man was her brother.

Oddly, it was Harvey, the man who had helped McReady embalm the body and who had ample time to note all of its various scars, who created a method of identification for Audrey. He told her to look for a scar John had allegedly received in childhood from a barbed-wire fence. This was Audrey's sole method of identification. She looked at a scar he pointed out on the back of the man's left thigh. Finally, she said," There is no question in my mind, Mr. Harvey. Bury him." And she left the room.

Audrey's "identification," which was not hers, but Mr. Harvey's, was far from positive, but it was all the public would ever get from the Dillinger family.

But which scar was it? According to pathologist J.J. Kearns, there were three scars on the left leg of the corpse: one appeared to be a healed bullet wound; another was the shape of a half-moon, on the calf; and the third was on the thigh and was 10 centimeters in length. Just what scar was Audrey referring to when she made the identification? According to Billie Frechette, the body could not have been identified by a scar on the left thigh – because Dillinger didn't have one. She would have noticed a scar that was four inches long on her lover's leg. Dillinger didn't have one.

Using some of his son's clothing for sizes, Mr. Dillinger sent away to a clothier in Indianapolis for the dead man's burial suit. The body was exhibited at Harvey's Funeral Home in a white shirt with a starched collar, gray tie with white dots, black patent leather shoes, and a gray herringbone suit. Yet, even though the suit was the exact size of the clothing in Dillinger's wardrobe, the sleeves of the new suit came well down past the wrists of the corpse. In other words, the body in Dillinger's suit was not Dillinger.

Late during the evening of July 25, the body was taken to Maywood, a suburb of Indianapolis, where it was placed in Audrey's home. The next day, it was taken to Crown Hill Cemetery, located in the city's north side. Crown Hill is, ironically, one of the most distinguished burial grounds in the region. It holds the remains of prominent Indiana writers Booth Tarkington and James Whitcomb Riley, former President Benjamin Harrison, three vice-presidents, and two Indiana governors. When word leaked that Dillinger would be buried among these men, many local citizens balked at the cemetery becoming the resting place of a notorious bank robber, but the family could not be stopped. The plot had already been paid for.

On the afternoon of July 26, five cars with flags fluttering were waved through the cemetery gates by a guard. Any cars that did not contain family members were turned away. More than 5,000 people pressed against the tall iron fence near the grave, watching the service in the summer rain.

When the short service ended, the family went back to the car, and they left the cemetery. Some of the policemen who were standing guard for a time took away the flowers and the funeral wreaths that were left at the grave.

Two days later, Mr. Dillinger returned to the cemetery. The casket in which the dead man had been interred, a common wooden coffin with rose-colored cloth over it, was unearthed and then concrete with scrap iron mixed in it was poured over it. The grave was partially closed, and then four large slabs of concrete, reinforced with chicken wire, were placed in staggered gradations above the casket. There would be no way to then remove the coffin from the ground. It would keep away grave robbers, curiosity-seekers – and law enforcement officials who might become curious.

We may never know who exactly is buried under the earth in Crown Hill Cemetery. No one will ever be able to discover who that man truly was. The only one who really knew was John Dillinger – wherever he ended up.

So, who paid for Dillinger's elaborate burial and concrete entombment?

It was said that before the Biograph shooting, Dillinger had visited his father and left a sum of money with him with which to pay off his funeral. He told his father that he planned to get away so that he would "not have to worry about his son anymore," which was similar to what he had earlier written to him in a note that was delivered by Art O'Leary. Dillinger's sister, Audrey, it was said, was well aware of the fact that her brother was alive (as were other members of the family).

In the late 1930s, a federal agent who was passing through Mooresville, Indiana reported that a substantial number of citizens remained convinced that Dillinger had somehow slipped out of the hands of the FBI and had escaped. He also learned that the bank robber's family had received a letter from someone claiming to be Dillinger --- and that it contained enough private information that they were convinced it was genuine.

The agent was unable to learn any details about the letter but it seemed to be common knowledge around town that the Dillingers believed "Johnnie" was alive. Those who had doubts were asked the simple question of how John Dillinger, Sr., a farmer with little money, had managed to pay for his son's elaborate burial, which involved encasing his casket in concrete. Wouldn't this have been very expensive? And well beyond his means?

Some claimed that Dillinger had been killed with thousands of dollars in his pocket and that the money went to his father. This was not the case. The man shot down at the Biograph Theater had the clothing on his back, and not much else. The official record stated that Dillinger was carrying $7.70 in his pocket ---- hardly enough to pay for a funeral.

There were plenty of stories floating around about what happened to Dillinger *after* he died. In 2001, I interviewed a man named Norm Alder. His father, Norman John Alder, had grown up in Loda, Illinois, a small town in Iroquois County, which is south of Chicago and along the Indiana state line. According to the elder Mr. Alder, he had met John Dillinger when he was a small boy in the early 1930s.

When he was eight or nine, Norman would hang around the local tavern in Loda with several friends. The Maddox family owned the tavern and the neighborhood kids often did odd jobs like emptying boxes, sweeping the porch, and taking out the trash to earn a little money that could be spent on soda and candy. One day, a new customer showed up in town and claimed to be a farm hand, even though he certainly didn't dress like one. He became friendly with the local boys, and when they got to know him, he introduced himself as "John." He often gave the kids money for candy and played cards with them. One day, he asked if they wanted to play blackjack and most of the boys were excited and agreed, although Norman was embarrassed because he didn't know how to play. Realizing the boy's awkwardness, John took him aside and taught him how the game was played. On many days that followed, John and Norman would sit by themselves and play blackjack.

Then one day, John suddenly disappeared. The kids were disappointed that their friend never told them goodbye, Norman especially. Not long after, though, he was in the Loda post office and happened to see a picture of John on the wall -- it was a wanted poster, naming his friend as John Dillinger. Norman later told his son that he knew that it was his friend John without any doubt, even though the John in the picture was missing his mustache. "Dad soon learned that Dillinger was often in the area," Norm Alder told me, "and that he even had a girlfriend outside of town. Dad's uncle, Earl Alder, ran a service station not far away and he claimed that Dillinger often stopped in for gas."

A few weeks passed and Norman heard the sudden, sad news that his friend John was shot to death by police in Chicago. Notorious bank robber or not, the stranger had been a good friend to the young boy and he was devastated by the news.

A few years later, when Norman was a teenager, he traveled with his parents to visit relatives in Mooresville, Indiana, outside of Indianapolis. His father and his uncle decided to stop in the local barbershop for a haircut, so Norman waited outside for them on a bench in front of the shop. An old man with white hair and a beard was also sitting on the bench and they struck up a conversation. Norman finally got around to asking the man, since this was Dillinger's hometown, if he knew John Dillinger.

"You bet I knew him," the old man replied. "I knew him when he was only this tall." He indicated the height of a small child.

"Then I guess you know that he was shot and killed in Chicago," Norman replied.

"No, he wasn't," the old man told him. "I was at the funeral. It looked a lot like him, but it wasn't him."

"Really? Then where is he?" Norman asked in astonishment.

The old man gave him a shrewd answer before getting up and walking away. "He's on a chicken farm in Wisconsin and that's where he's gonna stay!"

Norm Alder finished his story. "Many years passed and my dad often wondered about this. He even went into law enforcement himself, serving as police chief for two cities, and he wondered if the cops in Chicago might really have goofed when they thought they had gotten Dillinger. I enjoyed your account on the Dillinger mystery and hope that now I have gotten a chance to help you tell the whole thing."

The Letters

If the man in Crown Hill Cemetery really isn't Dillinger, there is still no way of knowing where the real Dillinger ended up. Over the years, his sister, Audrey, received many letters from men claiming to be her brother. Officially, she dismissed them all as cranks and crack-pots, but one man came forward in 1959 who was not so easy to dismiss.

The man, who claimed to be Dillinger, actually wrote two letters, one in 1959 and one in 1963. The first one arrived at the *Indianapolis Star* newspaper on July 8, 1959. It read:

Dear Sir:
On the 22nd of July the 28th anniversary of the slaying of John Dillinger at the Biograph Theatre in Chicago; please put my picture in your paper, with a write up if you wish.

I have always had a keen sense of impending danger, therefore I knew they were setting a trap for me.

James Lawrence, an employee of the Chicago Board of Trade said, "To prove I was superstitious he would take my place and say he was Dillinger. I warned him it meant death.

Although the body was identified as mine, the face and finger prints did not match.

To prove these facts am sending a photo of John Dillinger as he appears today.

Yours sincerely,
John H. Dillinger

The photo enclosed showed an elderly man who looked – eerily – like an older version of John Dillinger. Was it real? Editors from the newspaper turned the letter over to a state official for a cursory examination of the handwriting, but it was dismissed. It didn't look enough like Dillinger's handwriting, they said. There was no comment about the photograph.

The reader should keep in mind that, at this time, there was little information available about Dillinger. The man had not written because he was inspired by a wave of public interest in the outlaw. There had been a movie made, more than a dozen years before, but there were no current books or magazines that would have spurred a crank to pen such a letter. However, over the course of the next three years, two books did appear about Dillinger, written by authors Robert Cromie and John Toland. This might have inspired the same man to write again.

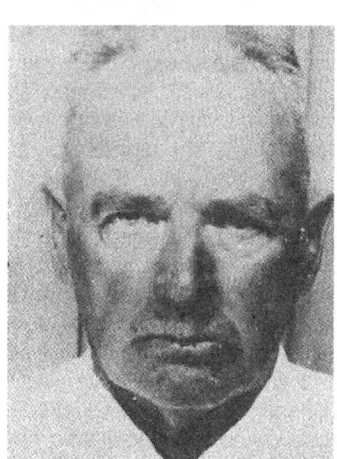

The photo that was enclosed with the letter, purporting to be Dillinger later in life.

In the second letter, postmarked Hollywood, California, the man revealed, as a way of proving that the wrong man was killed, a fact that no one had ever made mention of – that the man shot at the Biograph had "brown eyes." Because Dr. Kearns's autopsy report was not made public until crime writer Jay Robert Nash tracked it down in 1969, no one knew that the man shot down at the Biograph had brown eyes. Dillinger's eyes were bluish-gray. When the 1963 letter was written, there was only one man (assuming the FBI was still in the dark about the case) who would absolutely know this fact: John Dillinger.

But why would a man who escaped his own death to live out a peaceful existence write two letters to announce to the public that he was still alive? To explain that, we only need to look back at the character of John Dillinger.

He was a man who reveled in beating the law. After escaping from the Crown Point Jail, he wrote a letter to his sister telling her how he had used the wooden gun to fool the guards into letting him out: "Haha, pulling that off was worth ten years of my life!" He had a massive ego, a devilish sense of humor, and the need to be in the spotlight. Dillinger created a persona, flirting with bank tellers, jumping over railings, and making sure that the common man knew, "We only want the banks money." Dillinger wrote and called his pursuers, from Matt Leach to Frank Reynolds, from the Chicago Police Dillinger Squad. He taunted them and laughed at them, and at the World's Fair convinced a police officer to snap his photo.

Dillinger loved his notoriety and pored over the newspapers to see just what they claimed he had been up to. He created a mythology. He was kind to female hostages, even dropping one woman off at her home when he happened to be along the getaway route. He stopped Homer Van Meter and Baby Face Nelson from killing innocent people during bank jobs.

And he would be just the sort of man who, looking back on the empty years that followed his so-called death, might hunger for one more moment of fame, one more big risk, and one more mockery of the lawmen who claimed that he was dead. It was the ultimate taunt.

But why, then, if Dillinger wanted people to know he was alive (even though he did not offer his address in the letters or on the envelopes), wouldn't he surrender to the police or to the newspapers? Believe it or not, the answer is not a complicated one. Even though the statute of limitations might have run out on the bank robberies he committed, there was still the indictment for the murder of the East Chicago detective that he supposedly committed. In addition, Dillinger's return might have implicated others who were involved in the plot to fake his death and who were still alive. But finally, I think it was vanity more than anything. Dillinger cared how he looked, how he dressed, and the image that he portrayed. How would a Dillinger who had been in hiding all those years have compared to the bold, aggressive, and daring young man that he had once been? Would he still be the same man that once struck terror in the hearts of people all over the country?

The answer to that is no. He sent two letters and he disappeared again, perhaps enjoying the fact that he had communicated with the world once more as John Dillinger, the infamous bank robber. In 1959 and 1963, the world refused to believe that he was still alive. But years later, after the facts that he passed along were finally corroborated with an autopsy report that had not been seen in 35 years...?

Perhaps John Dillinger had the last laugh after all.

The "Other Man"

If the man who died at the Biograph Theater wasn't John Dillinger, then who was he? Those who have questioned the death of Dillinger in 1934 (myself included) believe that the dead man was a look-alike for Dillinger, who, I believe, was purposely set up by Dillinger, Martin Zarkovich, Ana Sage, and Polly Hamilton to die in the bank robber's place. Through Zarkovich, Dillinger had arranged for the "trap" at the Biograph to be sprung and he spent several weeks laying the groundwork for the event to take place. And it almost didn't happen the way he planned, because his timetable was moved up because of a possible betrayal by Louis Piquett and Jimmy Probasco.

But perhaps we should start at the beginning of this plot.

Finding a look-alike for John Dillinger was not as difficult as most would believe. In fact, "looking like Dillinger" became a serious problem for a number of men in late 1933 and the first half of 1934. On May 8, 1934, Ralph Alsman was arrested for the fifth time in St. Paul, Minnesota, because he looked so much like John Dillinger. Alsman had grown up in Brookville, Indiana, but apart from a face that gave him an almost identical resemblance to Dillinger, they had nothing in common aside from their home state. Police officers in St. Paul refused to believe that he was not the famous outlaw until they took him to the station and fingerprinted him. At that point, they had to let him go.

Looking like John Dillinger was a big problem for a lot of men in the Midwest during the frenzy that surrounded the hunt for the bandit

And Alsman was not the only one with this problem. On June 19, 1934, a man named Fred Weber was arrested by six police officers in the lobby of Chicago's Uptown Theater. They threw him on the ground and threatened to "blow his brains out" if he moved.

On July 15, 1934, G. Clay Baker, the Kansas Commissioner of Workmen's Compensation Claims, got off a plane in Columbus, Ohio, and was almost immediately surrounded by a group of police officers. They were convinced that he was John Dillinger and were acting on a tip from an Indianapolis woman who had made a "positive" identification the night before, when Baker had stayed the night in her rooming house.

On the night of the Biograph shooting, July 22, another man narrowly missed being shot to death because he looked exactly like Dillinger. Frank Slattery, a detective from the Sheffield Avenue station, had been checking out the Biograph after getting calls from the management about "suspicious characters" outside who turned out to be Bureau agents and East Chicago cops.

Moments after the shooting, Slattery reported that a Bureau agent approached him and told him that he was lucky to be alive. When he asked what he meant, the agent jerked a thumb toward the dead man sprawled in the alley. "When we got the signal, you were close to Dillinger. You looked just like him and I was about to shoot you when the other fellows let loose and killed the right man."

But, of course, the "right man" wasn't Dillinger at all. He looked like him, though – but then so did Ralph Alsman, Fred Weber, G. Clay Baker, Frank Slattery, and scores of other men. Three months prior to the shooting, Dillinger had been "positively" identified all over the country. Finding a look-alike wasn't all that hard to do, although I believe that Dillinger didn't have to look for the man who died in his place. He inadvertently dropped into his lap, thanks to Billie Frechette.

When Billie was arrested by Bureau agents on April 9, 1934, she was picked up at a tavern on North State Street in Chicago. Dillinger had been waiting for her across the street. But of more interest than the arrest was the photograph that she was carrying in her purse at the time. The photograph, which Dillinger had seen, showed a young man of the same general size and build of Dillinger. He had dark hair

The photograph of the black-haired man with the ring that was found in Billie's purse when she was arrested. It was man she already knew, living on Chicago's North Side, when she met Dillinger.

and a mustache and under his coat, the belt from a shoulder holster could be seen. The man was obviously a hoodlum, the kind of man that Billie was attracted to.

Another interesting aspect to the photo is that the man is wearing a large ring on his left hand. The ring is in the exact location as a ring that was on the hand of the dead man at the Biograph Theater. While it can be seen in photographs of the corpse, the ring mysteriously disappeared inside of the police wagon during the ride to the morgue. I don't believe that was a case of anything other than a

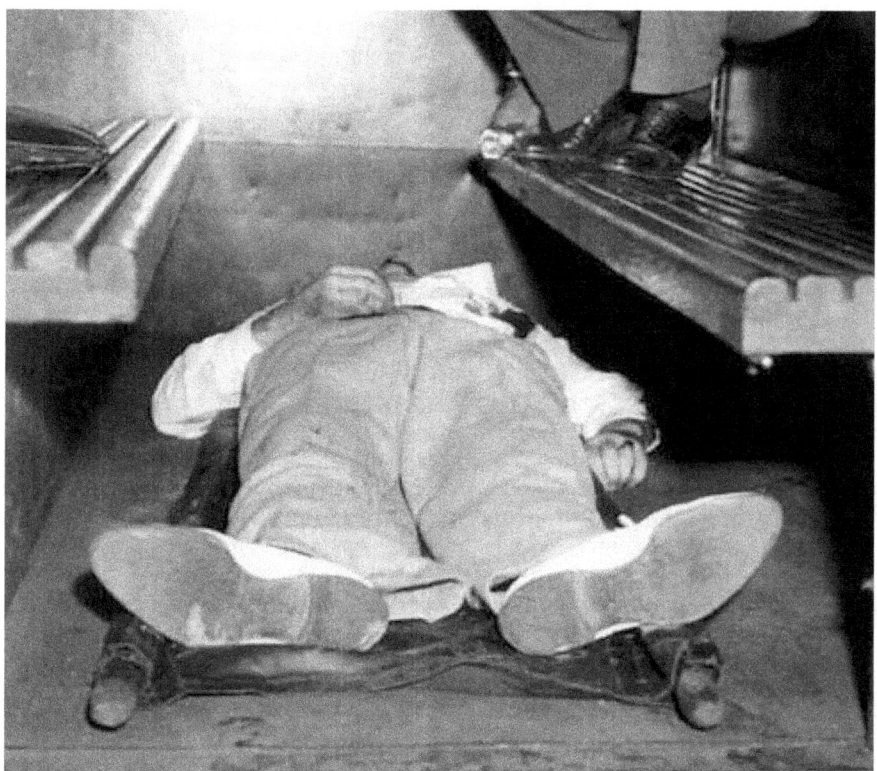

What appears to be the same ring, worn in the photo with Billie, can be seen on the body that was loaded into the police wagon at the Biograph Theater.

cop or agent who wanted a souvenir of the night, but it does make it even more difficult to establish the man's real identity.

Who was this man?

The most likely suspect for the man in the photograph – and the man killed in Dillinger's place – was a North Side man named Jimmy Lawrence. On the night of the Biograph shooting, Lawrence disappeared. He was a small-time criminal who had moved to Chicago from Wisconsin in 1930. He had moved in the neighborhood around Lincoln Avenue during the same time that Dillinger had been in prison in Michigan City, Indiana. Lawrence had an apartment at 3967 Pine Grove Avenue, but did most of his living in the Lincoln-Fullerton area, about two miles south of that. He was quiet, wore expensive clothes and gold-rimmed glasses, and he liked to go to the movies. If asked, he usually gave his place of employment as the Chicago Board of Trade. It seemed plausible since he always had money to spend freely. Few talked about Jimmy Lawrence, other than to occasionally mention his almost uncanny resemblance to John Dillinger.

Does this sound familiar?

It should, even down to the name. While staying at Jimmy Probasco's house, and after taking up residence at Ana Sage's apartment, John Dillinger dyed his hair black and grew a mustache, started wearing glasses that he didn't need, claimed that he worked for the Board of Trade, and adopted the name "Jimmy Lawrence" to fit his new identity. It seems very possible that his frequent appearances all over the North Side – what Homer Van Meter called his "foolish, open living" – was to convince people that he was the real Jimmy Lawrence. Dillinger planned this so that when he was "murdered" by the police or by Bureau agents, "Dillinger" would be dead and he could simply disappear.

I believe that Dillinger's plan to walk away from his life of crime had been in the works for some time. He and Van Meter had hoped to rob the train that Jimmy Murray had told them about and have enough money to disappear in Mexico. Even without it, Dillinger had collected a considerable amount of money from his final bank robberies and always had extra cash to give to his father, his sister, and even Art O'Leary when he needed O'Leary to get out of town. As hinted at earlier, I believe that Dillinger's timetable was moved up when he learned that Louis Piquett was talking of betraying him. He sent O'Leary up to Wisconsin, knowing that if he was called upon by the authorities, O'Leary could identify the real Dillinger, and put the last pieces in place for his own disappearance.

Dillinger's willing accomplice in all of this was, not surprisingly, Martin Zarkovich, the corrupt East Chicago detective who had been paid to protect Dillinger in the spring of 1934. It's almost certain that Zarkovich is the one who arranged for Dillinger to meet, and subsequently move in with, Ana Sage, whose operation he had protected for years and likely had a long-term affair with. Polly Hamilton became embroiled in the scheme when Dillinger began dating her, making sure that she also knew the real Jimmy Lawrence, who would not be surprised when she asked him to accompany her to the Biograph on the night of July 22.

Zarkovich seemed to be mixed up everywhere in the plot to kill Dillinger. He was on Lincoln Avenue that night, he showed up at the morgue after the shooting (he is seen in photographs taken that night) and, of course, he had insisted to both the Chicago Police Department and the Bureau that Dillinger must be killed, not captured. It wouldn't work if Jimmy Lawrence was arrested. The Bureau would soon learn that he was the wrong man. If he was shot down, there would be no one to answer the questions that would undoubtedly be asked. Zarkovich did his job. Lawrence was killed, Dillinger walked away, and Polly Hamilton settled down to a quiet life. Only Ana Sage ended up with a bad deal. After leaving Chicago, she received a portion of the Dillinger reward and seemed to be doing well until she was deported. Either the Bureau really couldn't help her stay in the country, or someone pulled strings to make sure she was kicked out. If she talked after that, who would believe her?

And that brings us to the big question: did the Bureau know that they got the wrong man?

The answer to that is complicated. At first, I believe the Bureau officials, namely J. Edgar Hoover, honestly believed that Dillinger had been shot to death at the Biograph Theater. I'm not quite as certain about Melvin Purvis.

For starters, Purvis was still stinging from the debacle at Little Bohemia and from the arrival of Sam Cowley in the Chicago office. Hoover had already lost faith in him, following one blunder after another in the hunt for Dillinger. If the director found out that Purvis had killed the wrong man at the Biograph, he would have been drummed out of the Bureau as a national disgrace. The whole thing nearly spun out of control after the shooting, but Purvis was quick enough, or desperate enough, when rolling over the body and seeing that the man he allowed to be executed only looked like Dillinger, to immediately come up with the plastic surgery story. An immediate admission of what happened would have ruined Purvis, but it might also have taken Hoover down with him.

It's possible that, immediately after the Biograph shooting, Purvis discovered his error and the fact that he had been duped. Only hours after the Biograph shooting, communication between Purvis in Chicago and Hoover in Washington all but ceased. Hoover was unable to get a response from Purvis as to the details about what had occurred, although those details most certainly became known to Hoover weeks later, if not sooner, and they compromised Hoover, who had been receiving acclaim for bringing down the most wanted criminal in the country. Hoover's "war on crime" was almost over after Dillinger – so what if it was learned that they had the wrong man? This would have expanded the cover-up to Hoover, and it was at this time that the director undoubtedly decided to force Purvis out of the Bureau. His enthusiasms had already cooled toward him, but this was the final straw.

The Biograph affair had followed Little Bohemia by only three months, and if it were made public that Purvis had *again* killed the wrong man, it would have destroyed his career and enemies of the Bureau would have made sure that he ended up in prison. And he might have taken Hoover along with him. Purvis was, of course, powerless to stop the autopsy from being performed on the dead man, but he likely did prevent the autopsy report from being inserted into Cook County Files. It would not be discovered until 1969, when author Jay Robert Nash began researching the shooting and the possibility that Dillinger had survived the night at the Biograph.

Purvis was apparently not counting on Dr. Kearns keeping another copy of the autopsy. It's also likely that he didn't count on Kearns presenting the very damning evidence about the dead man in the file. It should be noted that Dr. Kearns was assisted in the autopsy by a second doctor, who checked Kearns's findings on the spot and those findings were then double-checked by a medical stenographer. The autopsy was performed in front of 20-30 medical students, interns, and other medical officials. The pathologists knew how important the autopsy was and no room was left for error. No mistakes were made about scars, heart conditions, or eye color – everything was recorded just as they saw it. Dr.

Kearns, who had handled every important autopsy in Chicago dealing with major crimes, from Bobby Franks to the victims of the St. Valentine's Day Massacre, examined the man slain at the Biograph more closely than with any other case that he had worked on. He also kept a second, personal copy of the autopsy report, which makes some wonder if perhaps Kearns knew that there was something off about the case. Was he aware at the time of the many differences in physical characteristics between John Dillinger and the man on his table? If he was, he never spoke about, but he did keep a second copy of the autopsy report, which was not his common practice.

Purvis's fall from Hoover's grace had already begun that summer, but his rapid descent came in the wake of the Dillinger shooting. The plunge could have easily resulted after Hoover discovered how the limelight-seeking agent had been fooled and how Purvis took part in a cover-up to hide his error. Purvis finally left the Bureau in 1935, giving no official reason for his resignation. Hoover was doing everything he could at that time to enhance the image of the Bureau and if it became known that John Dillinger had slipped through the agency's fingers, Hoover's plans for an expansion of the Bureau would have been destroyed. He had no choice but to keep Purvis's secret, although, after 1935, Hoover never publicly mentioned Purvis's name again.

Hoover kept the secret, and it wasn't hard. Purvis was gone and could never speak of what he had done. Sam Cowley had been killed during the gun battle with Baby Face Nelson. Cowley had nothing to do with those who set up the wrong man. He didn't arrange anything with Martin Zarkovich, and he never met Ana Sage. He had remained in his own car. All of that had been Purvis's responsibility. Cowley didn't even set up the stakeout at the Biograph; that had also been Purvis.

It's possible that the fiasco at the Biograph haunted Purvis to the grave. He was killed, and most say he committed suicide, in 1960. It is possible that the same man who sent letters to the Indianapolis newspaper in 1959 and 1963 also sent one to Melvin Purvis? There has been some suggestion that this was the case.

Of course, all of this is speculation, stories based on stories, based on second- and third-hand accounts of what happened in Chicago in 1934. In this way, we make attempts to explain the evidence that was left behind in the wake of the shooting at the Biograph. If it wasn't Dillinger, then it had to be someone else. Was it Jimmy Lawrence, or was it someone else altogether?

Whoever it was, he resembled Dillinger but his fingerprints didn't match, he wasn't the same size, he wore eyeglasses, he didn't have the same scars that Dillinger did, he had a heart condition and most of all, he had brown eyes. A man was dead, but it certainly didn't seem to be John Dillinger.

Legend into Myth
So, if the man who died at the Biograph wasn't John Dillinger, then what happened to the real Dillinger?

That's a question that many of those with an interest in what happened that night have been pondering for years. And, like the question of who was killed in Dillinger's place and who knew about it, it enters the realm of speculation and, in some cases, tall tales.

There have been literally thousands of stories told over the years. Hundreds of letters have been written, telephone calls have been made, and off-hand comments have been reported. There are the mediums, the crackpots, the cranks, and the armchair detectives who often have interesting theories, but have little practical information to share. There are the sad people who claimed Dillinger was their father, brother, or long-lost uncle. There were those who called in the middle of the night and spoke in hushed tones about secret information about Dillinger. Many of them promised solid evidence, but it never arrived.

When Jay Robert Nash was on Dillinger's trail, he hoped for a call or letter from the man who sent the 1959 and 1963 missives. He never contacted him, but he did receive a couple of telephone calls from the Los Angeles area. They were from men who said they were Dillinger. They spoke briefly, offering that conclusive proof was coming, but it never arrived.

One man wrote to him from Waco, Texas, claiming to be a former FBI agent, and said that Dillinger was practically his next-door neighbor. The writer not only turned out to be wrong, he was also mentally disturbed. Another contact told him that the Dillinger cover-up was a plot hatched by the military, and someday, he promised, it would all come out. Another writer claimed he was in Kentucky, another in Virginia, many claimed California, and one insisted that he had stayed in Chicago after the shooting. Who would look for him there?

Nash spoke to many people who were sure that Dillinger was their father and he later wrote that these letters, in particular, were sad and depressing. The letter writers were children who had grown into adults, men and women without fathers, who had no connection to Dillinger, who, of course, had no children by 1934. Yet many of them persisted with the story. One woman said that she had been living with her mother and father in Chicago and then moved to Kentucky after the Biograph shooting, when her father disappeared. Dillinger was her name and her father was *the* bank robber. She had been six-years-old when he had vanished. Could Nash find him? He would be living under an assumed name as he had when she was a child living with him in Chicago.

One elderly woman contacted him to say that she had been operating a walk-down poolroom in the alley just south of the Biograph for years prior to the shooting. Because of the heat of that night, she said she was "trying to get some air," sitting on the ledge of the stairs that led down to the poolroom. She was looking down the alley, toward Lincoln Avenue, and saw a crowd walking past as the show at the theater let out around 10:30 p.m. Suddenly, she witnessed a young man being pushed into the alley by a "large man, this fellow Zarkovich, I learned later." Then she said that she watched as he lay face-first in the alley. "There seemed to be another man shooting at the fellow on the ground, from the other side of the alley, but I could not be sure. I ducked back into the poolroom and slammed the door then, and fast." A short time later, she gathered the courage to go outside and down the alley to see the dead man being lifted onto the floor of a police wagon. "I looked at him good," she said. "I knew this fellow. We called him Jimmy. He had been hanging around my poolroom for about three years, from about the fall of 1931." At the time the woman claimed that the Biograph victim started hanging around her poolroom, Dillinger was in prison.

Nash asked the woman why she had not gone to the police about what she had seen. "I did," she replied, "but the Chicago cops told me – you say something like that, lady, and you'll get a hole in your head. So, I kept my mouth shut." He asked her for her name and address, but she wouldn't give it to him. "I don't want a hole in my head," she told him. Nash checked to see if there had ever been a poolroom located off the alley next to the Biograph and learned that it had been there, but the building had been torn down decades before.

Stories like that one, Nash later wrote, robbed him of sleep for years.

But there were other stories that were more concrete and had actual names and places attached to them, including a story that would have a great impact on Nash's own theory about Dillinger's disappearance. A man named Donald J. Thompson of Middleton, Michigan, wrote to say that he was absolutely positive that he had met Dillinger and another man in June 1934, near La Crosse, Wisconsin, when Thompson was hitchhiking toward Duluth, Minnesota.

After getting a ride from North Chicago to a spot about halfway across Wisconsin, Thompson was picked up by two young men in a Ford. During the ride, Thompson became sure that he recognized Dillinger as one of the two men. He had seen his photograph in the newspapers and knew that he was no one to fool with. Dillinger never asked if he recognized him, but they did make small talk. After a while, they reached a small town along the rural highway. Dillinger said to him: "If you'd like a job I could set you up here for a week in a second floor room across from the bank. You could keep track of when it opened and closed and what the bosses look like." Thompson wasn't very enthusiastic about the idea and Dillinger dropped the subject after three or four minutes.

While in town, Thompson was treated to a chicken dinner by a "plump woman of about 35" that Dillinger and his friend referred to as "Bea." While this doesn't fit the description of any known female companions of Dillinger gang, his contacts were widespread, especially in rural areas of the Midwest, and this could have been one of the many way-stations Dillinger had developed. The road they were traveling on, which paralleled the Minnesota border, was a route that Dillinger was known to use when traveling back and forth to St. Paul.

Following the dinner, Thompson parted company with the two men. He had some apprehension about leaving, especially after Dillinger suggested that he travel on with them. He was afraid that he might be taken into the woods and left there. But Thompson didn't want to continue on. He told Dillinger that he needed to get to Duluth and the gangster ended up wishing him a good trip. The woman known to him as "Bea" was leaving for a short trip to see someone and she ended up leaving Thompson on Route 35, where he hitched another ride to Duluth.

Days later, the young man thought of the reward that had been offered for Dillinger but dismissed the idea of going to the authorities. He wrote the whole thing off as a youthful adventure, but always remembered it and eventually told the tale to Nash.

The question was, though – what was Dillinger doing on that road in June 1934, a road that led to St. Paul, where he had almost been captured months earlier, and a town that was by then crawling with Bureau agents who were looking for him? Nash began to believe that Dillinger was not headed toward St. Paul, but was checking a route that led beyond it to the North Woods region of the Midwest. This was the "northern route," an escape route that he would take after arrangements had been made in Chicago for his very public death.

Nash believed that the man who was with him on the road was unknown to the authorities at the time, but would be vital to Dillinger's escape plan. He was a man who knew the area in ways that Dillinger did not and he was able to show him a northern route across the country, leading west. The man had already robbed banks on the West Coast and he knew where to take Dillinger after his "death" and how to get him to safety. According to Nash, this was James Henry "Blackie" Audett.

Audett, who died in Chicago in 1979, was a bank robber, contemporary of Dillinger, and Nash believed, one of the few people who knew about Dillinger faking his death from the start. He was there, before the shots were fired outside the Biograph, standing on the street, waiting, an assigned witness from the underworld who knew the identity of the man who was to be murdered in place of Dillinger. He knew all of the details: how it had been arranged, who was paid, who wasn't, and even where Jimmy Lawrence and Polly Hamilton were sitting in the theater when they watched the movie.

James "Blackie" Audett was born outside of Calgary, Canada, in 1902. His father was a stern farmer and Audett ran away from home at an early age. He began working for the railroads in Washington state and there he earned his nickname of "Blackie," because of his thick, dark hair and eyebrows.

In late 1916, Audett was taken by some railroad men to the red light district in Spokane, where he got drunk, ended up in a brothel, and woke up to find himself in the Canadian Army recruiting office the next morning. He had lied about his age and enlisted in the military to serve in World War I. Sent to France, he served with distinction and won several medals for bravery. After being seriously wounded, he was taken to England to convalesce. Doctors gave him repeated injections of morphine to dull his pain and he became addicted to the drug.

After being released from the service, Audett returned to Washington, where he committed several small robberies to support his drug habit. In time, he weaned himself off the drug and returned to railroad work, laboring in Portland, Oregon, for the Union Pacific. In 1920, he married a childhood sweetheart, Patty Siefert, and bought a house using profits from robberies that he committed. He attempted to live an honest life, though, until late 1920, when the son of a local banker, drunk behind the wheel, smashed into his wife's car and killed Patty and the couple's two young children.

Crazed with grief, Audett earned his first prison sentence, a seven-year stretch, after he assaulted the driver of the car, who had been given a suspended sentence for manslaughter. After news reporters exposed the unfairness of the two sentences, Audett's time was reduced to just six weeks.

Audett became involved in bootlegging and went to work for the most successful liquor smugglers in Oregon: Irv Wilks, Joe Parsell, and Albert Moore, who owned a string of sandwich shops that fronted for speakeasies. Since he knew the Canadian border so well, Audett and a friend from the Army, Albert Nolan, began running cases of Canadian whiskey into the United States. After a variety of adventures, he was arrested in 1926, but managed to escape from the McNeil Island Federal Penitentiary where he had been locked up.

He then moved to Denver and went to work for Jake Fleagle, one of America's first celebrated bank robbers. Audett was involved in several bank robberies before being captured in McCook, Nebraska. In jail, he was locked up with Earl Thayer, another early bank robber, who helped him escape from McCook. Thayer headed for Mexico and Audett went to Chicago, where he began robbing banks and cracking safes with Al Sutton. Audett claimed that, in 1927, they robbed a bank outside of Chicago that caused so much "heat" that Al Capone himself told the pair to leave town. Audett then went to France, but after getting mixed up in illegal activities, he was deported. He was arrested when he returned to the United States and sent to the federal penitentiary at Leavenworth to serve out the rest of his McNeil Island sentence.

At Leavenworth, Audett's cellmate was Frank Nash, the unlucky gangster who was killed during the Kansas City Massacre. Through Nash, Audett became connected to Kansas City's most powerful underworld figure, Tom Pendergast, who used his influence to get Audett released from prison. In 1930, he began working for Pendergast in Kansas City, rigging elections, destroying ballot boxes, voting as a repeater, distributing slot machines, and more. He learned to cook in prison and with this experience, became the head chef in one of the syndicate hotels in Kansas City.

During the course of many hours of interviews, Audett claimed to be a bagman to important politicians, had robbed at least 120 banks, and was a close friend of John Dillinger. They had reportedly robbed a number of banks together in the late spring and early summer of 1934, or so Audett claimed. In all fairness, it should also be mentioned that Audett also claimed, at one point, to have witnessed the Kansas City Massacre, even though he was in jail at the time. So, it's possible that many of his stories were "tall tales," to use the term generously.

According to Audett, a "foolproof" plan was designed in June 1934 by Louis Piquett, Dillinger's attorney, to fake the famous bank robber's death. Audett insisted that he did not know all the details, but he did know everyone who was involved. Audett's part of the plot was to get Dillinger out of the city, and out of the Midwest, after the shooting took place.

On the night of the shooting, Dillinger was hiding in Aurora, and the two of them escaped from Illinois in the hours that followed. Audett claimed that they had taken the "northern route," to Wisconsin, Minnesota, and then straight west.

Dillinger's only regret, he said, was that he had to leave Billie Frechette behind. She was in jail at the time for harboring Dillinger. Audett claimed that he left Dillinger at an Indian Reservation out west, where he later settled down and married a local woman.

Before the shooting, Dillinger had visited his father and told him that he planned to get away so that he wouldn't have to worry about him anymore. Dillinger's sister, Audrey, along with other members of the family, Audett said, was well aware of the fact that her brother was alive. She corresponded with Audett for many years.

After leaving Dillinger at the Indian Reservation, Audett was apprehended for his own crimes and sent to serve time on Alcatraz. He was the last prisoner to leave "The Rock" in 1962. Audett claimed that he saw Dillinger on the West Coast several times before he was arrested again for a Seattle bank robbery and sent to prison in 1974. Audett died of a stroke in 1979 and until the day he died, he claimed that Dillinger was still alive. He refused to say where Dillinger was living in the 1970s.

Truth or fiction? Was Blackie Audett just an old man who was spinning tales to get attention in his last years? Many writers have referred to him as a "notorious liar," and, admittedly, many of this tales have proven to be untrue.

But, in the end, does the testimony of Blackie Audett really matter? Even if we disregard his tale, we are still left with a disturbing amount of evidence that suggests that Dillinger was not the man who was killed outside the Biograph Theater. Did Dillinger survive? Did he escape out west to live out his last years in peace?

Believe it or not, it's possible. These are not just wild theories concocted by revisionist historians and conspiracy theorists – the evidence actually exists. It's written in black and white and it's impossible to dispute.

We have to ask ourselves, though, does it matter? After all of these years, Dillinger – if he did survive his encounter with the Bureau at the Biograph – has undoubtedly passed away. He faded into history and out of the record books forever.

Epilogue

They call it "Dillinger's Alley." It's that narrow passage that crosses the sidewalk near the Biograph Theater today and cuts through the alleyway to the part of the neighborhood where Ana Sage's apartment used to be. There's not much to see here these days. It's a nondescript, paved alley that cuts between buildings that were not even standing in 1934. There are no signs in windows that say that "Dillinger drank here," no drug stores, barber shops, or hat stores. Next to the alley now is a Mexican restaurant that has been there for years. The Biograph Theater no longer shows movies. It's a live playhouse now, home to the Victory Gardens Theater, although a restoration a few years ago restored it to the glory days of the 1930s.

There is no sign or historical plaque that marks the significance of the alley, where the Bureau claimed that John Dillinger was killed, but tourists, tour guides, and neighborhood people all understand the significance of the spot.

And many of them tell stories of the ghost.

The stories were said to have started in the 1930s, not long after the fatal shooting that occurred there, but it was not widely reported until the 1970s. It is in the alley where the man who died seems to have left a lasting impression. People who passed by the theater began to tell stories of seeing a hazy figure running down the alley near the Biograph. The figure only managed a few steps, fell to the ground, and then vanished. Along with the sighting of this strange apparition were reports of cold spots, icy chills, unexplainable cool breezes, and odd feelings of fear and uneasiness. Local business owners noticed that people didn't use the alley as a shortcut to Halsted Street. Many of them didn't realize they were avoiding the alley until it was pointed out to them – and the stories became public.

It's been called "Dillinger's Alley," but is the phantom who haunts this alley really John Dillinger, playing out the last second of his life, over and over again?

But what if Dillinger got away? Despite official denials and the derision of mainstream crime historians, the evidence exists to say that another man died in his place. There are many unanswered questions that remain about the shooting at the Biograph, including, eerily, the identity of the ghost who has been linked to the alley. It seems to be re-enacting the final moments of the man who died there in July 1934.

Is it John Dillinger, or could this specter be the ill-fated Jimmy Lawrence, doomed to repeatedly run for his life after being betrayed by people he had no idea that he couldn't trust?

We may never know the truth, but if you find yourself in this alley someday, be sure to spare a thought for the man who was gunned down there. Misunderstood farm boy, notorious bank robber, cold-blooded killer, or unlucky sap who got tricked into giving up his life, we'll never know for sure who the man really was, but he remains an essential part of the fabric of American crime in the 1930s – and maybe, just maybe, he was the man who got away.

Bibliography

Burrough, Bryan – *Public Enemies*; 2014
Congdon, Don – *The 30's: A Time to Remember*; 1962
Cook, Fred J. – *The FBI Nobody Knows*; 1964
Corey, Herbert – *Farewell, Mr. Gangster!*; 1936
Cromie, Robert and Joseph Pinkston – *Dillinger: A Short and Violent Life*; 1962
David, Ruth E. – *Inventing the Public Enemy*; 1996
Friedman, Lawrence M. – *Crime and Punishment in American History*; 1993
Gentry, Curt J. – *J. Edgar Hoover: The Man and the Secrets*; 1991
Girardin, Russell G. with William Helmer – *Dillinger: The Untold Story*; 1994
Gorn, Elliott J. – *Dillinger's Wild Ride*; 2009
Goulart, Ron – *Line Up Tough Guys*; 1966
Helmer, William with Rick Mattix – *Public Enemies: America's Criminal Past, 1919-1940*; 2007
Hollatz, Tom – *Gangster Holidays: Lore and Legend of the Bad Guys*; 1989
Karpis, Alvin with Bill Trent – *The Alvin Karpis Story*; 1971
King, Jeffrey S. – *Life and Death of Pretty Boy Floyd*; 1998
----------------- - *Rise and Fall of the Dillinger Gang*; 2005
Louderback, Lew – *Bad Ones: Gangsters of the '30's and their Molls*; 1968
Maccabee, Paul – *John Dillinger Slept Here: Crook's Tour of Crime & Corruption in St. Paul*; 1995
Matera, Dary – *John Dillinger*; 2004
Merle, Clayton – *Union Station Massacre*; 1975
Nash, Jay Robert – *Dillinger: Dead or Alive*; 1970
--------------------- -- *Dillinger Dossier*; 1983
Nickel, Steven and William J. Helmer – *Baby Face Nelson*; 2002
Potter, Claire Bond – *War on Crime*; 1998
Poulsen, Ellen – *Don't Call Us Molls: Women of the John Dillinger Gang*; 2002
Purvis, Melvin – *American Agent*; 1936
Sullivan, William with Bill Brown – *The Bureau: My Thirty Years in Hoover's FBI*; 1979
Summers, Anthony – *Official and Confidential: Secret Life of J. Edgar Hoover*; 1993
Swierczynski, Duane – *This Here's a Stick-up: Big Bad Book of American Bank Robbery*; 2002
Taylor, Troy – *Haunted Chicago*; 2003
Toland, John – *Dillinger Days*; 1963
Unger, Robert – *Union Station Massacre: The Original Sin of Hoover's FBI*; 1997
Urschel, Joe – *The Year of Fear*; 2015
Wallis, Michael – *Pretty Boy: Life and Times of Charles Arthur Floyd*; 1992
Watkins, T.H. – *The Great Depression: America in the 1930s*; 1993
Weir, William – *Written with Lead*; 1992
Whitehead, Don – *The FBI Story*; 1956

Personal Interviews and Correspondence

Magazines and Newspapers
Argosy
Auburn Evening Star (Indiana)
Bluffton Evening News-Banner (Indiana)
Chicago American (Illinois)
Chicago Daily Times (Illinois)
Chicago Herald (Illinois)
Chicago Herald and Examiner (Illinois)
Chicago Reader
Chicago Tribune (Illinois)
Cleveland Press (Ohio)
Dayton Daily News (Ohio)
Dayton Herald (Ohio)
Fort Wayne Journal Gazette (Indiana)
Fort Wayne News-Sentinel (Indiana)
Fostoria Review Times (Ohio)
Gary Post-Tribune (Indiana)
Greencastle Banner (Indiana)
Hammond Times (Indiana)
Indianapolis News (Indiana)
Indianapolis Times (Indiana)
Joliet Evening Herald (Illinois)
Mason City Globe Gazette (Iowa)
Michiana
Muncie Evening Press (Indiana)
Sandusky Register (Ohio)
South Bend Tribune (Indiana)
Startling Detective Adventures
State Trooper Magazine
True

Special Thanks to:

April Slaughter: Cover Design and Artwork
Lois Taylor: Editing and Proofreading
Lisa Taylor Horton and Lux
Haven and Helayna Taylor
Rene Kruse
Rachael Horath
Elyse and Thomas Reihner
Bethany Horath
Jay Robert Nash
Ken and Sunny Berg
Jennifer Engelbrecht
Eric Quamme
Tom and Michelle Bonadurer

And to all of my friends and family who have tolerated my fascination with the eventual fate of John Dillinger for so many years. You've all heard me telling the story over and over again (likely rolling your eyes) but thanks for putting up with it for so long! This book was a real labor of love, which I have no idea if anyone will read. But if you have gotten this far, I hope you've enjoyed reading it as much as I've enjoyed writing it. Thanks!

ABOUT THE AUTHOR

Troy Taylor is the author of nearly 120 books about ghosts, crime, and the unexplained in America. He is also the founder of American Hauntings, ghost tours, books, events and excursions across America. He was born and raised in the Midwest and currently divides his time between Illinois and the far-flung reaches of America.

www.ingramcontent.com/pod-product-compliance
Lightning Source LLC
Chambersburg PA
CBHW070959160426
43193CB00012B/1835